Business Disclosure: Government's Need to Know

REGULATION OF AMERICAN
BUSINESS AND INDUSTRY SERIES

Goldschmid: Business Disclosure: Government's Need to Know

Edwards: Issues in Financial Regulation

Business Disclosure: Government's Need to Know

edited by

HARVEY J. GOLDSCHMID
Professor, Columbia University School of Law

Columbia University Center for Law and Economic Studies

McGRAW-HILL BOOK COMPANY
New York St. Louis San Francisco Auckland Bogotá Düsseldorf
Johannesburg London Madrid Mexico Montreal New Delhi
Panama Paris São Paulo Singapore Sydney Tokyo Toronto

Library of Congress Cataloging in Publication Data

Main entry under title:

Business disclosure—government's need to know.

(Regulation of American business and industry series)
Papers and dialogues from a conference held at
Airlie House, Nov. 5–6, 1976 and sponsored by the Center for Law and Economic Studies of Columbia University.
Includes bibliographical references and index.
1. Financial statements—United States—Congresses.
2. Disclosure of information (Securities law)—United States—Congresses. 3. Business records—United States—Congresses. I. Goldschmid, Harvey J.
II. Columbia University. Center for Law and Economic Studies. III. Series.

KF1446.A75B87 353.008'2 78-11911
ISBN 0-07-023670-4

1234567890 DODO 7865432109

The editors for this book were Ellen M. Poler and Virginia Fechtmann Blair, the designer was Elliot Epstein, and the production supervisor was Thomas G. Kowalczyk. It was set in Palatino by University Graphics, Incorporated

It was printed and bound by R. R. Donnelly

Contents

Preface

In September 1975, the Faculty of Law of Columbia University established the Center for Law and Economic Studies. The Center's basic mandate was to develop interdisciplinary research and teaching programs in order to shed new light on the "fundamental economic and legal problems of the modern industrial society."

This volume is one of the early, important fruits of the Center's new interdisciplinary effort. Information issues are at the heart of many of the nation's most significant law-economics debates.

The segment reporting issues, for example, cut across a number of agency boundaries (e.g., FTC, SEC, Department of Defense, FEA, and Bureau of the Census), and, in terms of the litigation they have inspired, are the information equivalent of World War I in the trenches or of the current IBM monopolization case. "Uniform reporting dealing with corporate ownership" and "the information required for indicative (noncompulsory) national planning" present "inflow" of information to government issues in all their complexity. Is the information available at tolerable cost, and, more basically, what is the likelihood that government will use it well?

"Government mandated business disclosure addressed to consumers" focuses on "outflow" problems. On the most fundamental level, I suppose, we come down to a debate as to whether, when government mandates disclosure, any reasonable consumer cares. The "confidentiality claims" chapter pits Justice Brandeis' aphorism about "sunlight is the best disinfectant" against his equally wise advocacy of the "right to be left alone."

Mark Twain once wrote that there were three kinds of lies—"lies, damn lies and statistics." At approximately the same time, Oliver Wendell Holmes was writing:

For the rational study of law the black-letter man may be the man of the present, but the man of the future is the man of statistics and the master of economics.[1]

The all too complex worlds of segment reporting, indicative national planning, and the other subjects discussed herein demonstrate, to my mind, that both Twain and Holmes were partially right. We must deal wisely with information questions in a modern industrial society. But doing so will not be easy, and, in general, the members of the bench and bar are not well prepared.

This volume provides both an excellent introduction for the uninitiated—and a sophisticated compendium for the cognoscenti—to the intricate, at times excruciatingly complex, information questions with which we must grapple. A first-rate group of scholars has both illuminated fundamental issues and ploughed much new ground.

The volume grew out of a conference sponsored by the Center and held at Airlie House, in Virginia, on November 5 and 6, 1976. It has a number of distinctive features. First, it contains specially commissioned research (pursuant to a detailed syllabus provided to each scholar) by leading authorities in the various information fields. Second, the scholars were encouraged to exchange drafts and, where differences of view appeared, the conference format allowed for direct oral confrontation. In the light of such confrontations, papers were revised, and in several instances, responses were preserved by means of the "commentaries" contained herein. Most of the papers were completed for publication in early 1977 and have not been further updated.

Third, the "dialogues" to be found in each of the major chapters represent a significant interdisciplinary success. In attendance at Airlie House were many of the nation's leading thinkers on informational issues. Approximately one hundred lawyers, law professors, economists, judges, and government policymakers took part in what at times were heated debates.[2] Questions often produced answers which significantly clarified, modified, or added to a scholar's point of view. I selected excerpts from the conference proceedings and condensed them to provide what I believe is a most valuable pedagogical and policymaking resource. While, for the sake of readability, connectives have been added and many words deleted (all without ellipses or other warnings to the reader), the substance of discussions has been preserved.

At this time, I would like to express my gratitude to some of those who made this volume possible. My first debt is to Betty Bock, John C.

1. Oliver Wendell Holmes, "The Path of the Common Law," *Harvard Law Review*, vol. 10, 1897, p. 469.

2. Appendix 1 gives biographical information on principal researchers, chairmen, and the editor; Appendix 2 identifies conference participants.

Burton, David T. Hulett, Frederic M. Scherer, Howard Siers, and Irene Till, who formed a special steering committee for the Center's "information project" and provided me with invaluable advice. My second—and even larger—debt is to Ellen Haven, the Center's Associate Director from its beginning through July 1977, and to Eloise M. Coiner, her successor in the job. Ellen and Eloise prepared the manuscript for publication, and performed associated tasks, with great skill and truly appreciated good cheer. Joan S. Fine, the Center's Research Secretary, and Helen S. Scott, my student research assistant, also worked on the manuscript with wonderful dedication. Two law students from Columbia, Suzanne McSorley and Stephen C. Sherrill, performed onerous, but necessary, footnoting chores with admirable care.

Also, Ellen M. Poler, Senior Editor of Legal Publications at McGraw-Hill, and her colleagues were invariably patient, helpful, and in sum, an editor's delight. I am, of course, very much in their debt.

Finally, a word about the Center's eight corporate founders.[3] We could not, of course, have gone forward on this volume without them. In general, their willingness to contribute to the Center—a new venture dedicated to unbiased, high quality, interdisciplinary scholarship—represents the highest form of business statesmanship. I take delight in acknowledging their indispensable contribution.

HARVEY J. GOLDSCHMID

---

3. Amoco Foundation, Inc., Bell System, Exxon Corporation, Citibank, General Electric Foundation, IBM Corporation, Kraftco Corporation, and Xerox Corporation.

CHAPTER ONE

The Segmental Reporting Debate

EDITOR'S NOTE

Today, at what appears to be an accelerating pace, reformers are challenging the size and power of large modern corporations. Questions are raised about their efficiency, social responsibility, and accountability. A basic response of the corporate community is to point to the traditional corporate goal of long-term profitability and the discipline imposed (regarding both efficiency and accountability) by competitive markets.

Paradoxically, particularly in an age of increasingly powerful electronic methods to process and retrieve information, the data base for judging the performance of large corporations may be growing steadily less reliable.

The 1960s saw a conglomerate merger wave which seems to be gathering force again as this book goes to press. A general diversification trend has led many old-line, single-product corporations into a wide array of new activities. These diversified firms often report only composite profit figures for what are, in effect, multiple separate businesses. As Professor William K. Jones, who chaired the dialogue on segmented reporting, put it:

> To whom are these organizations accountable? The answer typically is that they are accountable to the public through the functioning of competitive markets. Then comes the question, "Is this really true?" Do the markets run the corporations or do the corporations run the markets?

Segmented financial reporting is the method proposed for monitoring corporate performance. (The Federal Trade Commission's program is called *line of business,* but parallel programs exist at the Securities and Exchange Commission, Federal Energy Administration, and other federal agencies.) It requires the reporting of information which will allow users (e.g., investors, market researchers, antitrust enforcers, regulators, or scholars) to judge the profitability of particular—more or less narrowly defined—subdivisions of a corporation.

Professor Scherer, pointing to the information loss caused by diversification and the overall difficulty of determining what is happening in many important markets, sees many significant benefits to be derived from segmented reporting.

Professor Benston, on the other hand, after carefully examining the FTC's program, claims that "serious and perhaps fatal measurement problems," disparities between accounting numbers and economic values, and the "conceptual impossibility" of dealing adequately with common cost allocations mean that only negligible (or negative) benefits can be expected.

The disagreement between Scherer and Benston is basic. If Scherer is correct, government policymaking in areas as diverse as antitrust and taxation and private decision making about where and how to invest will be meaningfully enhanced. We will have a sophisticated tool for judging present-day corporate performance. If Benston is correct, we will have engaged in one more costly governmental program, one that will afford misleading economic signals and will ultimately be paid for, in large measure, by unwary consumers.

SEGMENTAL FINANCIAL REPORTING: NEEDS AND TRADE-OFFS

Frederic M. Scherer, *Professor of Economics, Northwestern University*

What role should the federal government play to foster segmental financial reporting by large industrial corporations? This question has stirred the fires of controversy in Washington out of all proportion to its arcane substance. Much of the fury has been directed toward the Federal Trade Commission's line of business (LB) reporting program, which well over one hundred companies have resisted in suits before federal district courts in the Southern District of New York, in Delaware, and in the District of Columbia. However, there have also been parallel programs of varying scope and complexity by the Securities and Exchange Commission (SEC), the Federal Energy Administration (FEA), and the Department of Defense. Private sector initiatives are evident too, for example, by the Financial Accounting Standards Board (FASB) and the Strategic Planning Institute (a consortium of private companies). In this paper I review the background and rationale for this flurry of activity and analyze some issues and trade-offs critical to determining what kind (or kinds) of segmental reporting might best meet the needs of potential data users, both governmental and private. The analysis is more personal than one might expect in a scholarly work, for I spent the better part of two years attempting to make segmental financial reporting a reality at the FTC. Forewarned, the reader can apply appropriate discount factors to the personal value judgments I shall attempt to point out as such. The facts, I believe, are precisely that.

By segmental financial reporting, I mean the reporting of information with which the user can judge the profitability of particular, more or less narrowly defined, subdivisions of a corporation. The junction of the words *profitability* and *subdivisions* is crucial. Most corporations have been publishing information on the profitability of their consolidated operations since the 1930s, if not earlier, but the disclosure of subdivisional profitability is a relatively new phenomenon. Likewise, manufacturers have been reporting to the Bureau of the Census finely segmented information on a variant of sales, materials costs, and labor costs since at least 1880, but those data do not always track company financial accounts closely, and they are not complete enough to permit full-fledged profitability analyses. What is new, then, is the attempt to obtain profitability data by subdivisions of industrial corporations.

There appear to be two main reasons why a call for segmental financial performance information has materialized on so many fronts during the past decade. For one, the spread of increasingly powerful electronic data processing methods has made it possible to store, recall, and analyze business financial information in previously unthinkable ways. The chairman of Gould, Inc., for example, can sit in his boardroom, tap a few code letters into a keyboard, and have displayed almost instantaneously information on 75 financial control variables for any of his company's divisions or product lines.[1]

There is more to the story, however, than supply merely creating its own demand. There has also been a sharp increase in the demand for segmental financial performance information as corporations have diversified to encompass an increasingly wide array of business activities. Diversification is, of course, not new. In the late eighteenth century, Matthew Boulton's factory at Birmingham, England, made buttons, Sheffield plates, copying machines, and sword hilts; it also minted coins and manufactured steam engine components. General Electric and Du Pont were already significantly diversified by the 1920s. Using internal census data on 111 large corporations, Professor Gort found that 31 percent of the sample firms' payrolls in 1947 originated outside their four-digit industry of primary specialization, and the number of four-digit industries in which those firms operated increased by 30 percent between 1947 and 1954.[2] Although data of comparable quality on more recent developments are not yet available, it seems clear that the pace of diversification accelerated during the massive, predominantly conglomerate merger wave of the 1960s.[3] One consequence of this continuing and increasing diversification has been

---

1. See "Corporate 'War Rooms' Plug into the Computer," *Business Week*, Aug. 23, 1976, p. 65.

2. Michael Gort, *Diversification and Integration in American Industry*, Princeton, N.J., Princeton University Press, 1962, pp. 60–61.

3. See Richard P. Rumelt, *Strategy, Structure and Economic Performance*, Harvard Graduate School of Business Administration, Division of Research, Boston, 1974, pp. 47–77; Federal Trade Commission Staff Report, *Economic Report on Corporate Mergers*, Washington, 1969, pp. 219-225; and (for data extending only up to 1965) Charles H. Berry, "Corporate Growth and Diversification," *Journal of Law and Economics*, vol. 14, no. 2, Oct. 1971, pp. 371–383.

"information loss"[4]—i.e., the disappearance of financial performance information on specialist companies that once played a prominent role in particular industries but whose activities were consolidated following merger into the accounts of much more diverse corporations. It has become more and more difficult if not impossible to learn how those once-independent entities are faring, and more generally, it has become much harder to determine what is happening in many important industries whose principal members belong to conglomerate enterprises.[5] Concern over these accumulating information deficiencies reached the action point in the late 1960s, triggering a series of governmental and private segmental financial reporting initiatives.

WHAT NEEDS ARE SERVED?

Essential details on those programs will emerge when we analyze the problems and trade-offs faced in segmental reporting. First, however, it is useful to explore the demand side of the matter further. Specifically, what kinds of information needs might be served?

It is natural for me to begin with those categories closest to my own professional experience. Most of my working life has been spent as a student of industrial organization. Although hundreds have toiled in this vineyard for many decades, it is fair to say that what we know is outweighed by what we know we should know, but don't. One of the most important questions in our field is how and why such performance indicators as profitability are related to the structure of markets. As the conference preceding this one demonstrated in March 1974, our ignorance concerning these relationships is vast.[6] There is disagreement over whether profitability rises with increasing market concentration—i.e., as the combined market share of, say, the four leading sellers increases. And assuming (with the weight of the present evidence) that such a positive relationship does exist, there is disagreement over what it means: does it reflect the exercise of monopoly power in pricing by

---

4. The phrase was first used, I believe, in the Federal Trade Commission Staff Report, *Conglomerate Merger Performance: An Empirical Analysis of Nine Corporations*, Washington, 1972, chap. V (hereinafter cited as FTC, 1972).

5. For example, the financial analysis of my own 12-industry study had to be truncated at 1967 because after that year conglomerate mergers made it "increasingly difficult to get useable profits data for many companies, especially in the brewing, cigarette, paint, bottle, and battery industries." Even before 1967, financial data were unavailable for most of the leading refrigerator and antifriction bearing manufacturers. See F. M. Scherer, Alan Beckenstein, Erich Kaufer, and R. D. Murphy, *The Economics of Multi-Plant Operation: An International Comparisons Study*, Cambridge, Mass., Harvard, 1975, pp. 343–354.

6. Compare the papers by Harold Demsetz and Leonard Weiss in Harvey J. Goldschmid, H. Michael Mann, and J. Fred Weston (eds.), *Industrial Concentration: The New Learning*, Boston, Little, Brown, 1974, pp. 162–233.

firms in concentrated industries or the differential realization by the leaders in such industries of scale economies in production, physical distribution, sales and service representation, advertising, and technical research? These are not idle questions of interest only to scholars seeking full employment in the academy. They lie at the heart of important antitrust policy questions. Should the United States maintain a virtual per se rule against concentration-increasing mergers? Should section 2 of the Sherman Act be strengthened to permit more frequent and extensive fragmentation of concentrated industries? Should resources used to enforce section 1 of the Sherman Act be allocated more liberally to relatively concentrated or unconcentrated industries? The answers depend critically upon whether the "concentration leads to monopolistic pricing" or the "concentration yields scale economies" hypothesis is more nearly correct. Yet at present we cannot fill these knowledge gaps and develop a systematic understanding of structure-performance links because the available data permit no clear, reliable matching of structure measures (compiled on a disaggregated basis) with highly consolidated financial performance indexes.

Professor Benston and I have debated this point privately, and I am sure it represents one of our areas of most profound disagreement. As I understand him, he believes my hope for achieving deeper understanding of structure-performance relationships through the analysis of segmental reports is in vain because accounting data tell little about the true state of the industrial world and because economists lack the conceptual apparatus for conducting decisive tests of alternative structure-performance hypotheses. I disagree with both contentions.

I concede that it is more difficult to defend accounting data than to attack them. On such disputes, the analogy of an unmerciful God is apt: "Ye have sinned; depart from Me therefore into the everlasting fires." Accounting data *are* imperfect indicators of economic reality, and anyone who uses them for economic analysis sins. Their use can be defended, however, on three main grounds, stated in ascending order of importance. First, they are not so bad that intelligent decision makers inside and outside corporate offices find them unsuitable for use. To the contrary, most analysts consider them highly useful, and although nearly everyone agrees that improvements can and should be made, it is recognized that one must get on with one's business using the best information available. And that, for better or for worse, is typically accounting data. Second, many of the problems in accounting data are common to most if not all companies, and so the valid use of such data for interenterprise comparisons is not precluded even though, say, profits are measured poorly relative to some absolute standard such as the ideal of ascertaining a "true" economic rate of return. For the analysis of structure-performance relationships, serious problems intrude only if intercompany differences in accounting bases or conventions are systematically associated with the structural variables. Otherwise, such differences only introduce what communications engineers call "noise." There is, in my opinion, no reason to believe that such noise need drown out the true underlying signals or relationships. Third, the problems in accounting data are well understood, and the kinds and magnitudes of bias those problems cause can be predicted and measured. The intelligent analyst, therefore, should not simply throw up his hands in despair, but should find ways of detecting systematic biases in his data and filtering them out. I am convinced that such an approach is feasible if a rich but not oppressively detailed set of data on such variables as accounting conventions, capital structure vintage, and the like can be combined with raw financial performance data.[7]

On the question of testable structure-performance models, this is not the forum for presenting a detailed econometric specification. Also, I believe truth emerges best under pluralism, with a variety of plausible alternative specifications being tested. Still, the basic outline of how one would use segmental performance data to test structure-performance relationships is simple. First, one would analyze cross-sectional relationships for a given year or span of years. One would want *inter*

---

7. In his discussion of accounting numbers and economic values (pp. 91–94), Professor Benston expresses skepticism over the feasibility of this approach. His analysis, however, is in my opinion flawed by omissions and errors.

For example, at p. 100, he cites an interview with Dr. William Long, the FTC's line of business program manager, as evidence that advertising and R&D capitalization procedures had not been specified or tested with actual or simulated data. This is true with respect to the LB program. The work cited was done in conjunction with the FTC's cereal industry litigation, which was handled by a separate organizational entity, with the explicit expectation that the computer programs would subsequently be turned over to the LB group.

He also analyzes at length (pp. 101–102) the dummy-variable technique I used in an earlier study, citing my mention of it in a letter to the General Accounting Office as "the only reference to a specific procedure that I could find." His quotation of my reference is incomplete and therefore misleading. Immediately following the quoted material, I continued in my letter of August 6, 1975:

> It must be recognized however that the analysis in *The Economics of Multi-Plant Operation* is extremely crude compared to what we will be able to do with the Line of Business data. For one thing, I was limited to a maximum of 71 nation-industry observations, whereas the Line of Business survey will provide roughly 4,000 separate observations. . . . Second, in analyzing the effect of international productivity differences I was limited to using a zero-one "dummy" variable discriminating between employment-based plant size observations which had and had not been appropriately adjusted. The Line of Business correction factor data will be incomparably richer, measuring *inter alia* the *proportions* [emphasis in original] of individual lines' inventories valued on diverse bases, the proportions of plant assets in diverse age classes, etc. . . .

It was the zero-one character of the correction variables in my multiplant operation analysis that gave rise to the prediction errors Professor Benston criticizes. With the FTC's LB data base, no such limitation is encountered. Also, in observing that different specifications of my productivity-adjustment model gave varying magnitude estimates, he fails to note that I had developed criteria for judging which specifications were more appropriate. See Scherer et al., op. cit., pp. 116–117.

alia to learn the separate influences of concentration (which is likely to reflect collective pricing power) as distinguished from individual firm market share (which, some other things held equal, is more apt to reflect scale-economy influences). To make this distinction, data much richer than any available thus far are needed. The scale-economy relationships would then be analyzed further by incorporating measures of plant-scale economies[8] and by investigating how such individual cost components as advertising, other marketing effort, and administrative overhead relate to company size and market share. Second, we now have some fairly solid theory on how market shares change over time as firms choose pricing policies that tend to maximize expected long-run profits, given the cost and price advantages associated with scale economies and successful product differentiation.[9] One would therefore test econometric models explaining the dynamics of market structure on the basis of such variables as historical profitability, plant size, advertising outlays, R&D expenditures, price trends, and the like. A considerable amount of innovation will have to be exercised in testing these dynamic models, because up to now no one has had the data needed to estimate more than a fragment of them. Yet I am convinced that the job can be done and that the result will be vastly improved understanding of how our industrial economy functions.

This view is evidently not confined to industrial organization scholars. A considerable number of business firms appear to be sufficiently similarly inclined that they have provided active data and financial support for the Strategic Planning Institute's research program. Specifically, some 57 companies have supplied to the Institute in Cambridge, Massachusetts, extremely detailed sales, cost, profit, market structure, and other data on 620 of their "businesses," defined as divisions, product lines, or profit centers selling a distinct set of products or services to identifiable groups of customers.[10] I have been told that the businesses are quite narrowly defined—much more narrowly than the average of 11 per company might imply, since only selected units in any given company participate. Although differences in accounting systems were said to pose problems, they have allegedly been surmounted, among other ways by having the participating businesses follow stan-

---

8. See Richard E. Caves, J. Khalilzadeh-Shirazi, and M. E. Porter, "Scale Economies in Statistical Analyses of Market Power," *Review of Economics and Statistics,* vol. 57, no. 2, May 1975, pp. 133–140.

9. See, for example, F. M. Scherer, *Industrial Market Structure and Economic Performance,* Chicago, Rand McNally, 1970, pp. 125–130 and 213–234; Darius W. Gaskins, Jr., "Optimal Pricing by Dominant Firms," Ph.D. dissertation, University of Michigan, Ann Arbor, 1970; and Richard B. Mancke, "Causes of Interfirm Profitability Differences," *Quarterly Journal of Economics,* vol. 88, no. 2, May 1974, pp. 181–193.

10. See Sidney Schoeffler, Robert D. Buzzell, and Donald F. Heany, "Impact of Strategic Planning on Profit Performance," *Harvard Business Review,* vol. 52, no. 2, March–April 1974, pp. 137–145; and Robert D. Buzzell, Bradley T. Gale, and Ralph G. M. Sultan, "Market Share: A Key to Profitability," *Harvard Business Review,* vol. 53, no. 1, Jan.–Feb. 1975, pp. 97–106.

dardized cost allocation guidelines.[11] The first published results provide impressive support *inter alia* for a conclusion that economies of scale are quite important. They are sufficiently impressive to lead me, at least, to believe that much critical rethinking of the conventional industrial organization wisdom is in order. They suffer, however, from two credibility problems. One is the restricted scope of the sample. Although an attempt has been made to have participating companies provide data on "businesses" with widely varying profitability, growth, and other characteristics, there is no way of knowing how representative of all industry the 620 businesses are. Second, an essential guarantor of integrity in research is the replication of experiments. In the social sciences, this means the ready transfer of one's data to other scholars. But access to the Strategic Planning Institute's data base is limited according to unwritten criteria interpreted by representatives of the companies supplying data. Full and free access has not been allowed, although there is reason to believe that access has at least been granted to scholars of diverse ideological persuasions proposing a variety of narrowly defined projects.[12]

I have much less experience in other branches of economics, but I suspect segmental performance data will be as valuable there as in the field of industrial organization. Thus, an important macroeconomic policy question is the relative significance of market growth and high capacity utilization as compared to cash flow and profitability in explaining industrial investment. The greater the impact of cash flow, the more feasible is business cycle mitigation through corporate income tax adjustments. I am told by my colleague Robert Eisner, who is one of the nation's leading students of investment behavior, that our understanding of such links is quite imperfect, in part because capacity utilization and production growth data are collected by industry whereas profitability data are available only at the multi-industry corporation level. Similarly, a central question in labor economics is the relative role of profitability, reflecting *inter alia* ability to pay, as distinguished from demand growth in wage determination. Again, understanding is impeded by the fact that production and wage-change data are collected according to industry categories dovetailing poorly with the available profitability information.

Although Keynes was no doubt right in his dictum that madmen in authority distill their frenzy from the work of defunct academic scribblers,[13] segmental financial performance information is likely also to be

---

11. Schoeffler et al., op. cit., p. 139; and Buzzell et al., op. cit., p. 105.

12. Confidentiality of the data is maintained not only by limiting access, but also by company submission of the data to the Strategic Planning Institute only in coded form. In particular, the supplying company's identification is deleted from the data file, and in order to disguise the data, all dollar magnitudes are multipled by a scaling factor known only to the company.

13. John Maynard Keynes, *The General Theory of Employment Interest and Money*, New York, Harcourt Brace, 1935, p. 383.

of more direct use to government authorities. My own two years as an FTC madman provided some perspective on the problem. I joined the agency convinced, and continue to be convinced, that high-powered mathematical models can never replace more broad-ranging qualitative inquiry in the antitrust case selection process. At best, segmental performance information can suggest where to concentrate the costly, time-consuming quest for qualitative facts and help focus the inquiry on the most economically meaningful questions. If we had possessed adequate segmental financial performance information, I suspect we would not have initiated our household appliance and detergent industry investigations or we would have conducted them quite differently. We might also have brought no suit to disentangle diverse SKF mergers and joint ventures in the antifriction bearing field. Where the data would have led us instead is unknowable. Since its inception the FTC has also played an important role in informing the public on the state of competition in American industry. There, I believe, the value of segmental performance information might be even greater than in enforcement decision making. Nothing I did in my two years at the Commission captured the public's interest more than the two reports we published showing, albeit with quite imperfect data, that food chain and certain processing industry profit increases could not have been responsibile for the early 1970s food price explosion.[14] A few members of Congress and consumerists were angry at us, but a widely held myth was punctured and public confidence in the private enterprise system was at least marginally strengthened through the dissemination of a closer approximation to the truth. I do not know how to measure the value of having a well-informed public, but I am convinced such a public could be one of our most precious national treasures.

My knowledge of other federal government agency programs is more meager, but it is clear that at least some programs have compelling needs for corporate segmental performance information. In its plan for collecting detailed five-year segmental profit information from 133 defense contracting companies, the Department of Defense stated its reasoning as follows:

> American defense industries are presently the center of controversy. Defense industry spokesmen constantly voice their opinions on the low profitability of defense work. Much of the blame for this is placed upon Government and Department of Defense procurement policies. Many members of Congress and the press appear to focus on the high cost of weapon systems and take the position that defense industry profits are too high and that procurement policies must be tightened. Therefore, Department of Defense procurement authorities are caught in the middle and there are no recent impartial studies or facts evident to indicate which view

14. Russell C. Parker, "Food Chain Profits," undated FTC Staff Report, 1975; and Alison Masson and Russell C. Parker, "Price and Profit Trends in Four Food Manufacturing Industries," FTC Staff Report, Washington, D. C., July 1975.

> is correct. In addition, Defense authorities know that the "defense industry" is not a homogeneous industry but is widely diverse in products, technology, size and financial strength, percentage of assets devoted to defense production and dependency upon a sub-contracting base. There also exists the uneasy feeling that the defense industry's production base is shrinking as contractors are attracted to more profitable work in the commercial sectors. . . . The focus of interest in this study is centered on those procurement policies followed by Defense which govern or impact the profitability, capital investment policies, and overall financial conditions of defense contractors.[15]

In promulgating a proposed approach to collecting extraordinarily detailed segmented annual financial information from petroleum companies, the Federal Energy Administration (FEA) stated that the data would enable it *inter alia* to determine the cost of energy development by energy type and geographic area, assess the adequacy of cash flows for investment, analyze the competitive situation in various sectors of the petroleum industry, and determine the impact of proposed regulatory and legislative policies on costs, prices, and profits.[16] In late August of 1976, when my initial research for this paper had been completed, a revised version of the plan had reportedly been on the FEA Administrator's desk for "several months" awaiting an approval that might not come because of strong industry opposition. During the period of active price controls in the early 1970s, the Cost of Living Council and related agencies implemented a comprehensive segmental quarterly financial reporting program.[17]

A staff member of the new International Trade Commission informed me that, as one of the agencies without their own reporting proposals, the Commission is virtually compelled to seek segmental profitability information under a statutory mandate that it proceed on an industry basis and take into account "the inability of a significant number of firms to operate at a reasonable level of profit."[18] And the Postal Rate Commission was reportedly unable to analyze magazine publisher claims that they could not absorb second-class mail rate increases because diversified publishers declined to break down their consolidated financial reports into magazine and nonmagazine components.

---

15. Department of Defense, Office of the Assistant Secretary of Defense (Installations and Logistics), Study Plan, "Profit '76," June 20, 1975, p. 3. The first results of the survey were presented in testimony by Deputy Secretary of Defense William Clements before the Joint Congressional Committee on Defense Production on Nov. 18, 1976.

16. Federal Energy Administration, "Petroleum Company Financial Report," Proposed Report Form, *Federal Register*, Sept. 22, 1975, p. 43612.

17. Cost of Living Council, "Phase III Regulations: Reporting Forms," *Federal Register*, May 7, 1973, pp. 11414–11426. The basis of reporting was four-digit SIC codes unless a "customary pricing unit" included more than 1 four-digit code.

18. Trade Act of 1974, 19 U.S.C. §2251(b).

Needless to say, the Securities and Exchange Commission (SEC) also has a substantial interest in segmental financial reporting. Unlike most of the other federal agencies cited here, it seeks data not for internal decision making but to serve a broad external constituency—investors and related members of the investment-banking community. In 1969, after a special SEC task force concluded that "the key to an understanding of [many of today's corporate enterprises] and [their] future prospects is a breakdown of revenues and, to the extent feasible, of profits by separate lines of business,"[19] the Commission issued regulations requiring limited segmental disclosure in new securities registration statements.[20] This requirement was extended to registered corporations' annual 10-K reports in 1970.[21]

The SEC's interest in this respect is presumably paralleled by that of the private sector's Financial Accounting Standards Board (FASB), which in late 1976 issued somewhat broader segmental reporting standards to which corporations must conform to be certified by their auditors as complying with generally accepted accounting principles. Explaining the basis for its conclusions, the FASB stated that "information relating to an enterprise's industry segments . . .is useful to analyze and understand the financial statements of the enterprise" and that such information was especially useful in evaluating the differential risks and returns of a corporation's diverse segments.[22]

Professor Benston has been a leader among scholars holding that financial disclosure requirements like those imposed by the SEC since the 1930s do little good in making the stock market work more perfectly, in large measure because they provide little or no information not already available to traders.[23] Underlying his and others' similar statistical results is the apparent ability of insiders and analysts with good insight into company operations to anticipate profit results long before they are formally reported. It is perhaps surprising, therefore, that the first analogous study of the SEC's 1970 segmental disclosure action showed that knowledge of profit breakdowns within company lines of

---

19. Quoted in the Securities and Exchange Commission Advisory Committee on Corporate Disclosure staff memorandum, "Evolution of SEC Policies and Practices Regarding Segment Reporting," Oct. 8, 1976, Attachment A, p. 13 (hereinafter cited as SEC, 1976).

20. *Federal Register*, July 23, 1969, pp. 12176–12177.

21. *Federal Register*, Nov. 3, 1970, p. 16919.

22. Financial Accounting Standards Board, *Statement of Financial Accounting Standards No. 14*, "Financial Reporting for Segments of a Business Enterprise," Dec. 1976, pp. 27–28 (hereinafter cited as FASB, 1976). In its earlier exposure draft on segmental reporting, the Board used the word "essential" rather than "useful" in an otherwise similar justification. See FASB, *Exposure Draft*, "Financial Reporting for Segments of a Business Enterprise," Sept. 30, 1975, p. 21 (hereinafter cited as FASB, 1975).

23. George J. Benston, "Required Disclosure and the Stock Market: An Evaluation of the Securities Exchange Act of 1934," *American Economic Review*, vol. 63, no. 1, March 1973, pp. 132–155.

business *did* provide information with which investors might have made more profitable stock selections. Specifically, Collins found that an earnings forecasting model using 1967–1969 segmental profit data achieved lower prediction errors for 1968 and 1969 (but not 1970) than several models using only consolidated earnings reports, and that investors using such segmental data-based predictions in conjunction with a naïve buy-sell rule could realize appreciable "abnormal returns" in the stock market.[24]

I reveal my bias as a "real sector" (as contrasted to money sector) economist in observing that such stock price prediction studies, while interesting and relevant, miss much of the point of segmental disclosure. The stock market is remarkably efficient in incorporating investors' knowledge and expectations concerning differential short-run company earnings performance. But its horizon appears much shorter than any plausible span of time—whether it be five years or twenty—that entrepreneurs must take into account in making the *real* (as opposed to stock-buying) investments underlying economic growth. Its disciplinary impact on real investment is also debatable. The total capital of U.S. manufacturing corporations grew in the 1965–1974 decade by approximately $320 billion. Of that growth, only 25 percent was financed through new securities offerings reported to the SEC, and only 3.5 percent involved new SEC-regulated common stock issues.[25] The remainder was financed by internal earnings plow back (i.e., about 56 percent of the total) subject to only the loosest stock market discipline[26] and increased borrowing from financial institutions that were presumably able to extract the information they needed before committing large sums.

It seems to me, therefore, that the main benefits of segmental financial information to investors are likely to fall in areas other than merely ensuring that stock prices on any given day are at the "right" level. For one, segmental information will permit stockholders (and even outside directors, who are often poorly informed)[27] to ascertain whether certain

---

24. Daniel W. Collins, "SEC Product-Line Reporting and Market Efficiency," *Journal of Financial Economics*, vol. 2, no. 2, June 1975, pp. 125–164.

25. Estimated from various issues of the FTC's *Quarterly Financial Report* series, making appropriate corrections for sample and accounting convention changes, and the SEC's monthly *Statistical Bulletin*. "Total capital" is defined here to be total liabilities and net worth less current liabilities.

26. See, for example, Ajit Singh, "Take-Overs, Economic Natural Selection, and the Theory of the Firm," *Economic Journal*, vol. 85, no. 33, Sept. 1975, pp. 497–515; Henry G. Grabowski and Dennis C. Mueller, "Life-Cycle Effects on Corporate Returns on Retentions," *Review of Economics and Statistics*, vol. 57, no. 4, Nov. 1975, pp. 400–409; and Robert Smiley, "Tender Offers, Transactions Costs and the Theory of the Firm," *Review of Economics and Statistics*, vol. 58, no. 1, Feb. 1976, pp. 22–32.

27. See Myles L. Mace, *Directors: Myth and Reality*, Harvard Business School, Division of Research, Boston, 1971, especially pp. 23–32, 52–61, and 103.

company activities exhibit persistent losses and to compare the performance of their company in particular lines of business with that of other firms. Armed with such evidence, they can bring well-focused pressure to bear on management for corrective action, and if need be, they may even seek to throw the offending rascals out.

By the same token, segmental financial performance information could give management competitive benchmarks against which to judge their own efficiency and strive for improvement in areas of deficiency. To me this has always seemed a most important benefit. The paint industry's principal trade association has for many years operated its own segmental reporting program under which detailed annual sales, cost, and profit data are collected from member firms' paint divisions, aggregated, and published. The 1973 edition is prefaced with the following observation: "One of the most valuable management tools provided by your Association has proven to be our Annual Operating Cost Survey."[28] It goes on to note that by aggregating the reported company data in quartiles, the report "permits accurate analysis of an individual company's operations." Likewise, a vice president of a major corporation told me that an annual ordeal in his job was being called before the company's chairman and having his division's performance compared unfavorably to the published financial reports of specialized competitors who, he insisted, had operations quite different from those of diversified companies like his own. The availability of segmental performance information from conglomerate competitors would at the least permit a fairer comparative evaluation, and it might well reveal correctable deficiencies.

Last but by no means least, segmental performance information should, I believe, be of use to market researchers and corporate decision makers contemplating investments in new lines of business. Evidence that returns in some lines are relatively high should stimulate a closer look; and further analysis (e.g., of how returns and costs vary with seller size) could provide important clues concerning the structure of costs, whether there are significant scale economies a newcomer might have difficulty achieving, and the like. To be sure, only a fool would enter a new field solely on the basis of data on other firms' financial performance. Detailed studies of technology, costs, marketing channels, and plant location must also be made. But these are costly. One undertakes them only if one has preliminary indications that attractive returns may lie at the end of the road, and having detailed data on existing sellers' costs and profits also helps ask the right questions. The end result of better information to inform competitive entry investment decisions should be higher profits for would-be entrants, lower profits

---

28. National Paint and Coatings Association, *Operating Cost Survey for the Year 1973*, Washington, June 1974, p. 1. The responsible committee includes representatives of such highly diversified companies as Union Carbide, Sherwin-Williams, Du Pont, Allied Chemical, Glidden-Durkee, and PPG Industries.

for the existing firms in capacity-short industries, and, if the economist's notion of competitive resource allocation makes any sense, a better overall use of society's scarce resources.

I do not know any way to quantify these benefits from the availability of better financial performance information. As is too often the case in economics, those benefits that can be measured most precisely—e.g., the impact of segmental performance information on the best-informed investors' stock market returns—may be among the least important. Yet I am persuaded, as one who has spent two precious years struggling to implement segmental reporting might be expected to be, that the potential benefits to business, government, and society are substantial.

THE FIRST MAJOR TRADE-OFF: SEGMENT DEFINITION

All this has proceeded on the implicit assumption that the reporting of segmental financial performance is in fact feasible and that it can be accomplished without extraordinary additional cost and effort on the part of reporting corporations. We turn now to some key questions of feasibility—notably, to the problems of segment definition, transfer pricing, and common-cost allocation and to the question of who can best implement a segmental reporting system and how that choice is influenced by data confidentiality considerations. To maintain focus within space constraints, I make no attempt to deal with accounting issues that affect all corporate financial reporting and not just segmental reporting—for example, how plant and inventory values should be reported in an inflationary era and whether uniform rules should be followed on such matters as the treatment of lease obligations, foreign exchange rate fluctuations, and "goodwill." The emphasis will be on problems unique to segmental reporting.[29]

The problem begins at the beginning—in defining the business segments on which financial reports are compiled. Along with various gradations in between, there are two polar possibilities: letting the individual corporations decide, subject to threshold materiality constraints; and prespecifying in detail the industry categories for reporting. The advantage of the first alternative is that companies will normally define their segments to conform with existing accounting records so that the costs of reporting and the need for special estimates are minimized. The main disadvantage, as we shall see, is that segments may be defined quite differently from company to company, rendering intercompany and interindustry comparisons difficult or impossible. Prespecifying reporting categories maximizes comparability, but the categories may mesh only imperfectly with companies'

---

29. Professor Benston's paper fails to make this distinction and is therefore in significant measure a criticism of *all* financial disclosure, consolidated *or* segmental. I believe it is fair to say that his views on financial disclosure generally are not widely accepted.

books of account so that special tabulations and estimates must be carried out at high cost. In short, a trade-off must be made between minimizing deviations from existing accounts and hence compliance cost versus maximizing segmental comparability.

The SEC's 1969 segmental reporting rule approaches the "let the company decide" pole with only minor "jawboned" exceptions.[30] Near but not at the opposite pole would be the Defense Department's "Profit '76" study, the FTC's LB program, and the FEA's proposed Petroleum Company Financial Reporting program. The FASB's segmental reporting standard appears to lie somewhere between the extremes, although much will depend upon how its ambiguous specifications are interpreted by companies and their auditors.

The SEC rules promulgated in 1969 and 1970 require listed corporations to include in their annual 10-K reports sales and profitability data for each line of business that accounts for 10 percent of sales, income, or losses in corporations with sales of $50 million or more, with the materiality threshold rising to 15 percent for corporations with sales of less than $50 million. Disclosure is not required for any more than 10 segments. I believe it is both accurate and fair to say that many large corporations interpreted the SEC rules in such a way as to report data of the least possible utility to outsiders. Many of their profit centers had sales below the 10 percent threshold. They could be and were grouped together with other centers so that only a blurred picture of individual operations emerged. In addition, there have evidently been numerous cases in which bona fide profit centers accounting for more than 10 percent of sales were defined into larger, less homogeneous groups so that precision of insight on individual operations was avoided. One important criterion in choosing groupings has apparently been avoiding the disclosure of losses. An FTC staff analysis of nine conglomerate corporations showed that no loss was revealed in any of the 53 segments on which the companies reported in 1971. Yet when data on the nine firms' 361 internal reporting divisions were obtained, 79 proved to be losing money. On the average, one among the firms' eight largest internal divisions showed a loss.[31]

Some indication of the problems resulting from the permissive SEC approach to segment definition is provided by an extension of data I had prepared while with the FTC.[32] We began with *Fortune's* 1,000 largest industrial corporations for the year 1974. An attempt was then made to see how diversified both the 100 largest companies and those ranking from 501 to 600 in size were. To measure diversification, one needs both a standardized criterion and data. Our criterion was the number of three-digit Standard Industrial Classification (SIC) manufac-

---

30. *Federal Register*, July 23, 1969, p. 12177.

31. FTC, 1972, N. 4 *supra*, pp. 119–122.

32. I am indebted to Lenore Leviton for her work in preparing the data.

turing and mining industries in which a company operated. The three-digit code is a moderately broad classifier; at present the SIC encompasses the entire manufacturing sector with a total of 143 three-digit categories and the mining sector with 20. We then used the best comprehensive data source available to us—the Economic Information Systems (EIS) data file—to identify the three-digit industries in which plants of the target corporations had sales of $10 million or more, as reported by EIS. The sales data are generally "outsider" estimates by EIS and are therefore subject to sometimes significant errors—more frequently than not, in the direction of overlooking sizable activities. The distribution of companies by number of three-digit categories occupied was as shown in Table 1-1. One immediate implication is that if the three-digit SIC were viewed as an acceptable level of detail for segmental reporting, the SEC's 10-category ceiling provides abundant leeway for *Fortune's* second tier of industrial corporations. But among the 100 largest, 33 operate in more than 10 categories.

To carry the analysis further for this paper, I examined the 1975 stockholder and 10-K reports for the 20 corporations on our list of 200 found to be operating in 15 or more three-digit indistries. For each of those 20, I list in Appendix A—Form 10-K and Three-Digit Industry Structures the number of categories on which profitability data were reported for 1975, a verbatim description of the categories, the number of three-digit SIC manufacturing and mining industries occupied domestically, and a (sometimes truncated) description of those industries. Three things stand out. First, as would be expected for this outlying group, the 10-K reporting categories tend, with some notable exceptions (such as Rockwell International's) to be much broader than the three-digit industry definitions. Second, many of the 10-K category names (for example, leisure time, consumer products, shelter, and energy products and services) provide at best an imprecise description of what activities are covered. Without further information, one could hardly guess that General Electric's consumer products category

TABLE 1-1

Number of three-digit industries	*Leading 100 corporations*	*Corporations 501–600*
0–3	10	64
4–6	17	24
7–10	40	7
11–15	18	0
16–20	7	0
21–25	4	0
Over 25	4	0
Total	100	95*

*Five companies were not covered in the EIS file, largely because their home base was some industrial sector other than manufacturing.

includes refrigerators, light bulbs, television receivers, hair dryers, and broadcasting station operation, among other products; or that its aerospace category spans such diverse products as jet engines, rapid-fire cannon, missile guidance systems, radars, and missile reentry systems. Third, even for companies as similar as Beatrice Foods and Borden or Westinghouse and General Electric, the categories are defined in such disparate ways that intercompany comparisons are virtually impossible.

I have deliberately chosen for analysis the reporting profiles of atypically diversified corporations. But the problems of broad, vague, and inconsistent reporting category definitions diminish only gradually until much smaller and less diversified companies are caught in the net. And even with relatively small firms, for which the segmental performance reports are often quite revealing, heterogeneity of definitions renders intercompany comparisons difficult. It is impossible to escape the conclusion that if one seeks to make interfirm comparisons or analyze performance in specific industries, the SEC-mandated segmental reporting system is of little use.

Whether the system emerging under FASB auspices will be significantly better in this respect remains to be seen. In its 1975 exposure draft, the FASB proposed that groupings should be along *industry* lines and that "the three-digit categories of the SIC will, in many cases, serve as a meaningful reference point for delineating industries."[33] In its final statement it retained the emphasis on industry segmentation but backed off from the three-digit SIC suggestion, expressing its belief that no classification system was suitable by itself for determining reporting segments.[34] Instead, it listed factors to be considered by corporate management in defining segments, including relatedness of products or services, commonality of production processes or raw materials, and similarity of marketing channels or areas.[35] The industry segmentation requirement seems to imply a break from the very broad categories used by many large corporations, but company managers and auditors are accorded much discretion for interpreting FASB's guidelines. Moreover, the FASB standard goes on to articulate SEC-like 10-percent-materiality thresholds and to suggest 10 reporting segments as "a practical limit" beyond which information may become overly detailed.[36] This virtually ensures that the most diversified corporations will report in broader categories than smaller firms and that the outside world will learn little about such absolutely large but (for the company)

---

33. FASB, 1975, N. 22 *supra*, p. 8.

34. FASB, 1976, N. 22 *supra*, p. 8. The statement observes at page 9 that "if an enterprise's existing profit centers cross industry lines, it will be necessary to disaggregate its existing profit centers into smaller groups of related products and services. . . ."

35. Ibid., pp. 47–48.

36. Ibid., pp. 10–11 and 49–50.

relatively small segments as General Electric's electric lamp and refrigerator operations, General Motor's bus and diesel locomotive production, Du Pont's paint and dynamite divisions, or Union Carbide's industry-leading dry cell business.

This result might be sad but inevitable if companies lacked the records needed to provide more detailed segmental reports. But most diversified corporations have divisional and profit center data much more richly subdivided than the categories on which they report to satisfy the SEC. Among the nine conglomerates studied by the FTC staff, none had fewer than 12 divisions on which profit data were readily available. The average number of divisions on which profit breakdowns were provided to the Commission was 40, whereas to satisfy the SEC, the companies reported 1971 profitability for 5.9 categories on the average.[37]

It was this presumed richness of profit center accounts that led the FTC, Defense Department, and FEA to believe they could successfully gravitate toward the opposite extreme of prespecifying reporting categories for their segmental reporting programs. Before considering this strategy further, however, some additional background on industrial classification systems is required.

The world is awash with alternative systems. Each major nation seems to prefer its own variant, and some nations employ multiple variants. I have on occasion made serious use of the Standard Industrial Classification (SIC) and the Tariff Schedules of the United States, the Standard International Trade Classification, the Brussels Nomenclature, the British Standard Industrial Classification, the classification system of the German Federal Statistical Office, the French Nomenclature des Activités Économiques, and the Canadian Standard Industrial Classification, among others. All have their strong points and limitations. The U.S. SIC fares well in any comparison, although it would be rash to say that it is palpably superior to all the alternatives. A considerable amount of learning and organization is required to live comfortably with any system, and so inertia discourages all but incremental deviations from the status quo once a system is adopted. For that reason, and also to maximize the linkages to other well-established data sources such as the Bureau of the Census, the SIC is the most compelling candidate for guiding segmental financial reporting in the United States unless particular industry conditions suggest specific modifications.

The SIC is structured to provide additional detail as industry descriptor digits are added. The first digit denotes the broad economic sector—e.g., manufacturing versus agriculture versus trade. In manufacturing, the first two digits delineate the broad industry group—e.g., food products (20) versus chemicals (29) versus transportation equipment (37). There are 20 two-digit manufacturing industry groups. The

---

37. FTC, 1972; N. 4, *supra* pp. 119–122.

third digit provides a finer breakdown to some 143 industry categories, many of which are illustrated in Appendix A—Form 10-K and Three-Digit Industry Structures. With a fourth digit the industry lines are drawn more narrowly—e.g., to distinguish among malt liquors (2082), malting (2083), wines and brandy (2084), other distilled liquors (2085), and soft drinks (2086) within the three-digit beverage category. There are currently 451 four-digit SIC manufacturing industries. The SIC stops at four digits, but the Bureau of Census subdivides manufacturing further into five-digit product codes (there are 1,293 of them) and some 11,500 seven-digit categories as detailed as beer sold in 16-ounce cans (code 20821 15).

Given this wide range of alternatives, the question naturally arises, what level of detail does one choose in specifying financial reporting categories? The answer almost always involves a complex trade-off between utility and feasibility. Maximum detail is usually desired, but it costs money and may aggravate accounting problems.

In its Profit '76 survey, the Department of Defense asked companies to break down their operations into 13 categories of direct interest plus one residual category. The categories were built up from the Standard Industrial Classification. Four (chemicals, rubber products, primary metals, and instruments) were at the two-digit level; three involved combinations of three-digit codes; and most of the remaining categories comprised either single four-digit industries (such as guided missiles and space vehicles) or combinations of 2 four-digit industries (e.g., aircraft plus aircraft parts). Participants were instructed to organize their responses according to profit centers, and when more than one profit center served a particular industry category, reports were requested for each such profit center separately. The reporting instructions observed that activity properly attributable to a reporting category might "account for a very small fraction of the business of a particular profit center."[38] Under these circumstances, the instructions advised, "the contractor and his CPA may agree that failure to report product type A separately or failure to report product type A at all will not materially distort the data . . . and they may accordingly combine the data for product type A with that for the other product type(s) produced by the profit center or to omit product type A altogether." No specific instructions were given for cases in which the combined reporting of multiple category activities within a single profit center would cause material distortions. I was told by the coordinating CPA firm that some such cases did arise and that they were referred to the Pentagon. A Department of Defense spokesman said that the contractors typically had the data needed to make further sales and cost breakdowns and that, after discussion, they agreed to use various allocation formulas to

---

38. Department of Defense, "Profit '76 Study: Data Collection Forms and Instructions," Oct. 14, 1975, p. 8.

split the consolidated profit center data into narrower Department of Defense categories.

The FTC's more sweeping LB category specification approach is similar in many ways to that of the Defense Department, although it reached the methodology embodied in its 1974 and subsequent reporting forms by a circuitous route. Two strands of history illustrate the trade-offs.

When an LB reporting proposal was submitted for clearance review to the Office of Management and Budget (OMB) in August 1973, it included a list of 357 manufacturing and 97 nonmanufacturing categories on which surveyed corporations were to report.[39] Some involved combinations of three-digit SIC categories, some pure three-digits, some four-digit industries singly or in combination, and some required breakdowns all the way to the seven-digit product code level. Companies were to disaggregate their operations into "business segments"—i.e., subsidiaries, divisions, departments, branches, sections, or groups—until "each lowest level business segment comes as close as possible to operating in only one of the economic markets listed in [the category list]." This approach drew intense criticism for its alleged burdensomeness, and so in December 1973 the Commission proposed a quite different approach. Companies were to report according to "establishments," or in effect, plants, unless in the normal course of business they allocated "all expenses and assets" to establishment subunits. The draft form embodying that approach was circulated to some four hundred business firms and trade organizations. I have personally analyzed the 61 written comments received. Only six suggested that the establishment approach to reporting might cause problems; however, two of those six, along with five other commentators, considered it to be an improvement. Most comments did not mention the issue. But when compliance with a truncated version of the 1973 form was ordered, a wave of motions to quash and supporting affidavits demonstrated that many companies do not in fact keep books at the plant level adequate to support accurate profitability calculations. The Commission thereupon returned to what was in effect its original approach, requiring in its 1974 LB form (and subsequent versions) that companies build up their reports from "basic components" that could be establishments, product lines, profit centers, or other organizational units—whichever struck the best balance between accuracy of reporting and the compliance burden.[40] In addition, the Commission set forth guidelines indicating the degree to which it was willing to accept within an industry category report the inclusion of activities that truly

---

39. Federal Trade Commission, *Statement of Purpose: Annual Line of Business Report Program*, Aug. 1973 (hereinafter cited as FTC, 1973).

40. Federal Trade Commission, *Supporting Statement: FTC Form LB, 1974 Survey Version*, July 1, 1975, p. 12 (hereinafter cited as FTC, 1975); and FTC *1974 Form LB*, Instructions, p. 7.

belong in some other category, but whose segregation might increase reporting cost. There was to be no more of such "contaminating" secondary product sales than existed in the company's establishments, and that magnitude was known to average between 5 and 8 percent. In no case, however, were such sales to exceed 15 percent.[41] Deviations from the criteria could be authorized through consultation with the FTC staff.

While the rules for matching company records with the FTC's reporting categories were changing, the category list changed too. From the 357 manufacturing and 97 nonmanufacturing categories proposed in August 1973, the list shrank to 219 manufacturing and 9 nonmanufacturing lines in the version actually implemented for 1973. This change reflected three main considerations. First, requiring companies to report in fewer categories implied less detailed accounting breakdowns and hence lower reporting costs. Second, many of the original categories were so narrow that they aggravated certain accounting problems. For example, the August 1973 list included seven different primary steel mill product categories, such as hot rolled sheet and strip, cold rolled sheet and strip, hot rolled bars and structurals, etc. Many of these products are made in a single integrated works with pig iron tapped from common blast furnaces and steel refined in common converters. The common-cost allocation problems would have been formidable, and to avoid them, categories were consolidated. Third, the breakdowns to five- and seven-digit product levels complicated links to census data and were opposed by other federal statistical agencies. The final 1973 category list therefore entailed, with only one exception, either single or combined three-digit or four-digit SIC codes. For 1974, the list was expanded again to 261 manufacturing and 14 nonmanufacturing categories. This expansion followed an analysis of the 1973 questionnaire returns and, for companies refusing to comply with the 1973 survey or not included in it, the less reliable EIS data file. For each category an attempt was made to determine whether participating companies were specialized in some narrower slice of the 1973 categories or covered the whole waterfront. Where strong specialization patterns emerged, it was believed that category subdivision would have no appreciable impact on compliance cost, and so the more detailed breakdown was implemented. The end product is reproduced here as Appendix B—Industry Category List for FTC Form LB (1974).

As the first attempt to develop a prespecified segmental financial reporting approach covering all manufacturing industries, the FTC

---

41. In his paper Professor Benston emphasizes the 15 percent (i.e., 85 percent specialization) rule and fails to mention the existing establishment specialization rule. Since the latter is likely to be the binding constraint in the vast majority of cases, he greatly exaggerates the "contamination" problem. It should be noted that adding "overstatements" and "understatements," as he and Dr. Bock propose, is double-counting, since what is included as contamination in one line must be an understatement of some other line's activity.

category system reflects a painstaking three-way trade-off: between securing maximum industry detail, minimizing compliance cost, and minimizing such accounting problems as the allocation of common production and marketing costs. The effort has been much criticized.[42] Criticism would no doubt be inevitable even in the absence of strong adversary interests. Any trade-off is likely to leave everyone dissatisfied in one way or another. Nevertheless, two further limitations in the FTC category system deserve explicit discussion.

In its August 1973 proposal to the OMB, the FTC stressed the formulation of categories that correspond as closely as possible to "meaningful economic markets."[43] It admitted at the outset that this goal could never be completely achieved, and in the changes made during the subsequent two years, there was perceptible movement away from a market approach and toward an industry approach. Much has been made of that change by critics. In my judgment, the criticism has been overdone. The trade-offs were sensible ones, and I consider the most recent category breakdown to be extraordinarily useful, even though far from an unattainable ideal. Furthermore, the critics have overlooked an important consideration. They have uniformly emphasized substitution on the demand side as the sole criterion of market definition. But substitution in production may also be relevant.[44] An auto manufacturer cannot substitute steel I-beams for steel strip in making rear quarter panels. But broad-line steel companies can shift readily from one such product to the other if the market signals are favorable. Many of the FTC categories that fail a demand-side substitution test miserably do rather well in terms of supply substitutability.

There remain, however, some patently bad categories. They entail for the most part "catchalls" such as "miscellaneous foods and kindred products, except coffee" or "household appliances not elsewhere classified." Any industrial classification has to have such catchalls. The alternative would be extremely detailed proliferation of categories for products whose sales are typically quite small—a poor benefit-cost trade-off. By my calculations, 29 manufacturing categories in the 1974 FTC classification which were indisputably catchalls accounted for 12 percent of total 1972 value added in manufacturing.[45] Inclusion of such catchall categories is essential to reconcile individual LB reports with company aggregate figures.

To sum up, complex trade-offs must be made in determining how

---

42. See especially Betty Bock, *Line of Business Reporting: Problems in the Formulation of a Data Program,* National Industrial Conference Board, New York, Nov. 1974, pp. 6–39 and 73–78.

43. FTC, 1973, N. 39 *supra,* p. 9.

44. FASB, 1976, N. 22 *supra,* at paragraph 100(b).

45. The categories are 20.29, 22.07, 22.12, 23.06, 23.07, 24.05, 25.06, 26.09, 27.04, 28.17, 29.03, 30.05, 30.06, 31.04, 32.03, 32.18, 33.13, 34.05, 34.21, 35.15, 35.21, 35.29, 35.36, 35.37, 36.07, 36.12, 36.28, 37.14, and 39.08.

segmental financial performance data should be categorized. The choice taken depends in significant measure upon who one's constituency is, what data uses are contemplated, and ultimately on the weight assigned the various dimensions of the trade-off. Criticism of any given solution is easy, finding the "best" or even "good" solutions difficult. In this respect, the problems of segmental reporting are little different from most other interesting economic policy problems.

THE SECOND TRADE-OFF: TRANSFER PRICING

Another tough problem in segmental reporting concerns the valuation of interline, intracompany transfers. An automobile company, for example, might make engines in one division and transfer them to other divisions for assembly or after-market distribution. There may be few direct sales on a competitive basis to outsiders, so it may be hard to tell what price might have been set at arm's length. The transfer price may be established, therefore, by bargaining or on the basis of some arbitrary rule ranging from cost to cost plus some standard markup. If it is set too high relative to a "true" (but unknowable) market price and if the engine and assembly divisions report in different categories, profits will be overstated in the engine category and understated in the assembly category. If it is set too low, the obverse will be true. The economic meaningfulness of the reported category returns is therefore impaired.

Some quantitative perspective on this problem is provided by a survey of 404 corporations' internal accounting practices. Dr. Robert Mautz found intersegment, intracompany transfers as a percentage of external sales plus internal transfers to be distributed as shown in Table 1-2.[46] A virtually identical distribution was found for companies reporting in the 1973 FTC LB survey.[47] Evidently, transfers are of substantial magnitude, and hence the pricing problem is potentially severe, in much less than a majority of all corporations. Mautz also found that of 341 companies with some internal transfers, somewhere between 130 and 180 used arm's length prices, while transfers were made at cost in at least some cases by 134 companies.[48] Again, this delimits the problem's scope, but it also shows that for a considerable number of companies a possibly serious arbitrariness problem remains.

There are various ways of coping with the problem. In its August 1973 LB reporting proposal, the FTC staff stipulated that transfers

---

46. Robert K. Mautz, *Financial Reporting by Diversified Companies,* Financial Executives Institute, New York, 1968, p. 38.

47. The similarity is so striking that it is difficult to reconcile with Professor Benston's assertion that the FTC categories are more narrowly defined than those studied (but not described) by Dr. Mautz.

48. Mautz, op. cit., pp. 36–37. The sets of companies are not necessarily mutually exclusive, since more than half of the firms used more than one transfer pricing method.

TABLE 1-2

Transfers as a percent of external plus internal sales	*Percent of all companies surveyed*
0–5	61.6
6–10	16.8
11–15	10.6
16–20	4.2
21–25	3.2
26–30	1.8
Above 30	1.8

should be accounted for "at fair market value." Following complaints that establishing market value prices would be impossible or prohibitively costly for some companies, the Commission backed off and permitted the use of existing pricing methods. With the LB program's first full-scale implementation covering companies' 1974 fiscal year, this more permissive approach was coupled with two measures designed to minimize the impact of possible distortions. First, a set of vertical integration guidelines was articulated. Certain lines of business known to have extensive interline transfers were singled out for integration into a single reporting entity, and consolidation of other intermediate stages was permitted if more than half the intermediate stage's output was used by a final stage in the same company. The one-half cutoff was set in the belief that if at least half a segment's output were sold outside, it was likely that a good approximation to arm's length prices could and would be achieved for the internally used output. Second, companies were required to disclose the percentage of transfers made at other than market prices and, when a line's transfers amounted to more than 10 percent of total line sales, to detail significant values of transfers by receiving lines. In this way, it was believed, clear distortions could be identified and aggregated report users could be warned when reported profitability figures might be distorted as a consequence of appreciable nonmarket transfers.

The SEC's approach has been to let companies work out the transfer problem in the best way they can in their choice of reporting categories. Integration of categories with material transfer amounts between themselves is explicitly authorized.[49] Despite the discretion conferred upon them, some companies include in their annual 10-K segment reports disclaimers stating that, owing to internal transfers, they are reluctant to vouch for the profit breakdowns.

The FASB's September 1975 *Exposure Draft* on segmental reporting proposed that "intersegment . . . transfers . . . shall be accounted for at

49. SEC, 1976, N. 19 *supra,* Attachment A, p. 15.

amounts that are consistent with the objective of determining as realistically as practicable the industry's segment's profit or loss. . . ."[50] In plain English this evidently meant: Use arm's length prices if you can, but if you can't, don't. A somewhat different tack was taken in the final December 1976 statement: Revenues were to be "accounted for on the basis used by the enterprise to price the intersegment sales or transfers";[51] such bases were to be disclosed;[52] and the Board made it clear that the disaggregation of vertically integrated operations was not required.[53]

The Defense Department's Profit '76 reporting instructions required that transfers at other than arm's length or market prices be integrated either forward into the buying entity or backward into the selling entity.[54] Prices, costs, assets, and employment values were all to be integrated in this way. Determining the appropriate profit margin to be shifted in such cases was probably made easier by the existence of standardized Defense Department guidelines for setting profit margins on various types of negotiated contracts.

Finally, the FEA's proposed Petroleum Company Financial Reporting System would permit firms to report transfers of crude oil and natural gas at the prices used for income taxation purposes.[55] Although expense information is to be collected by discrete vertical stages—i.e., crude petroleum, refining, transportation, and marketing—income statement breakdowns are not required. Consequently, unless the FEA intends to make its own vertically segmented profitability calculations, which is uncertain, the reporting of non-arm's length transfer prices need not cause any special bias.

Again, we find that there are difficult segmental reporting problems in the transfer pricing realm, but there are ways of dealing with them. How serious the remaining potential distortions will be after one has done one's best to cope is likely to be known only through the kind of research contemplated by the FTC staff.

TRADE-OFF THREE: COMMON-COST ALLOCATION

A third hurdle to be surmounted in segmental financial reporting entails the handling of costs and assets common to multiple lines. Basic research in a diversified chemical company may, for example, yield substances or know-how useful to divisions marketing quite different

---

50. FASB, 1975, N. 22 *supra*, p. 4.

51. FASB, 1976, N. 22 *supra*, p. 6.

52. Ibid., p. 13.

53. Ibid., p. 5.

54. Department of Defense, "Profit '76 Study," pp. 12–14.

55. FEA, "Petroleum Company Financial Report," p. 43615.

TABLE 1-3

Common costs as a percentage of sales	*Number of companies*	*Percent of companies*
1–2	47	18.4
3–4	54	21.2
5–8	71	27.9
9–12	37	14.5
13–16	19	7.4
17–20	11	4.3
21–24	7	2.7
25–30	6	2.4
Over 30	3	1.2
Total	255	100.0

products. Other costs, such as the compensation of an executive vice president overseeing several lines, might conceivably be assigned to the lines through a careful analysis of how he spent his time, but the accounting effort would outweigh any possible benefits, and so the cost is treated as if it were common. Still other costs are common by virtue of conceptual impasses. For instance, it is difficult to tell what the right allocation of interest to a division is because if the division were freestanding, it might pay higher interest rates than does the risk-pooling corporation to which it belongs.

Until the results of the FTC's 1974 LB survey are published, the only systematic evidence available on the magnitude of common costs comes from a 1964–1966 survey of several hundred companies by Mautz.[56] Defining common costs to include general and administrative expense, research, product development, institutional advertising, and interest expense and perhaps also bonuses and profit-sharing outlays, he found the following distribution of companies according to the ratio of noninventoriable common costs to organizational unit sales, as shown in Table 1-3. The average is 7.83 percent. In my opinion, this estimate is on the high side because much if not most research and product development (amounting to about 2 percent of manufacturers' sales) is directly attributable to individual lines of business and because interest costs, which in 1965 were about 0.75 percent of all manufacturers' sales, have often been singled out for nonallocation.

If common costs were truly common in the strictest sense, a compel-

56. Mautz, op. cit., p. 363. These figures exclude income taxes. For a larger sample of 317 companies, Mautz finds the ratio of common costs, including income taxes, to sales to be approximately 10.2 percent; see pp. 31, 227. At p. 220 he reports that for 62.3 percent of the companies, assets identified with organizational units amounted to 90 percent or more of total company assets. For 11.8 percent of the companies, identifiable assets were less than 50 percent of total assets.

ling argument could be advanced for not allocating them to individual lines of business because if any given line were eliminated, the costs would nevertheless continue, and so any allocation must necessarily be arbitrary. My own research on multiplant firms suggests that this view is more wrong than right. In particular, it seems clear that such items as central office costs do tend to rise as the size of an enterprise increases.[57] The principal problem is not that no links exist between divisional operations and the magnitude of central office costs, but that it is most difficult to measure the relationships. Therefore, some rough-and-ready allocation is needed if one is to approximate reality.

There is also a more pragmatic reason for attempting to allocate many ostensibly common costs. Different companies organize the same functions in divergent ways. Some, for example, may locate payroll processing at a central office; others choose to decentralize it. In both cases the function exists and its size probably varies closely with the number of employees. If the centralized companies elect to call its costs common and not to allocate them, their divisions will appear more profitable, all else equal, than the divisions of the decentralized company. And yet there may be no real difference in their efficiency and profitability.

Although I believe the weight of evidence favors an attempt to allocate ostensibly common costs, the case is far from ironclad. A hedge option is to do one's segmental accounting both ways—that is, to report a "contribution margin" reflecting profitability before the deduction of allocated common costs and then to calculate another net income margin after all or selected common-cost allocations are made. This is the approach adopted by the FTC. It was also favored by the Financial Accounting Standards Board in its September 1975 exposure draft, but the FASB's final statement of segmental reporting standards waives the contribution margin requirement because of perceived difficulties in distinguishing between truly common and directly traceable costs.[58] Thus, only an operating profit figure is required. Both the FTC and the FASB have prescribed that when allocations are made to compute the net operating profit or loss, interest expenses, income taxes, extraordinary items, nonoperating income, and the cumulative effect of accounting changes *not* be allocated and deducted. Their approaches differ on the handling of central office expenses, the FTC favoring allocation and the FASB leaving unallocated any part not connected with the operation of industry segments.[59]

In its Profit '76 study, the Department of Defense opted for relatively full allocation of costs, including central office and interest costs but

---

57. Scherer et al., *Economics of Multi-Plant Operation*, pp. 323–324; and F. M. Scherer, *Economics of Scale at the Plant and Multi-Plant Levels* (limited Multilith edition, 1975), pp. 184–188.

58. FASB, 1976, N. 22 *supra*, p. 36.

59. Ibid., pp. 6–7.

excluding income taxes. The FEA's proposed Petroleum Company reporting plan, on the other hand, generally avoids allocations by focusing on cash flows directly identifiable with the various lines of business. The Securities and Exchange Commission's 1969 and 1970 segmental reporting rules were geared toward "contribution to income before taxes and extraordinary items," but companies have been accorded wide interpretational leeway. As a result, the segmental profitability data in 10-K reports are quite heterogeneous, with some companies allocating all costs including interest, others all costs but interest, and still others retaining certain noninterest costs in a common corporate pool.

If the allocation of ostensibly common costs is to be attempted, the question remains, what allocation formulas shall be used? And in particular, should all companies be required to use the same formulas, or should each be free to choose its own approach?

Permissiveness has been the predominant strategy among agencies fostering segmental reporting. The SEC has no explicit rules. The FASB has mandated that costs and assets be allocated "on a reasonable basis."[60] Its earlier *Exposure Draft* noted that "those responsible for preparing an enterprise's financial statements are in a position to make more informed allocations than are financial statement users. . . ."[61] The FTC instructed companies completing its 1974 Form LB to use the allocation procedures they considered most appropriate but to describe them in an appendix. And in its Profit '76 study, the Defense Department indicated that the contractor should use "whatever system of allocation he believes will best reflect the nature of his business."[62] However, it went on to specify formulas suggested as being "acceptable."

This permissive approach is in my opinion proper. If, as I believe, crude linkages exist between the incurring of ostensibly common costs and segment activities, company accountants are in the best position to devise allocation systems that approximate them. Still two problems remain. To the extent that those linkages are weak or inexact, differing cost allocation method choices by different firms will introduce an unavoidable element of arbitrariness into reported profitability figures. Also, the permissive approach lends itself to possible abuses. If a company wanted to conceal or diminish profitability differences among reporting segments, it could do so by emphasizing a magnitude such as the gross margin or (even more strongly) the contribution margin as its allocation base.

That the choice of allocation methods does make a significant differ-

---

60. Ibid.

61. FASB, 1975, N. 22 *supra,* p. 27.

62. Department of Defense, "Profit '76 Study," p. 21.

ence is shown by the only quantitative research on the problem. Mautz analyzed the sensitivity of calculated net income to five disparately defined methods for allocating noninventoriable common costs for 30 segments of six corporations.[63] The range of calculated net income values—that is, the highest calculated value minus the lowest calculated value—was related in percentage terms to the value of net income calculated using the company's preferred allocation method. The range for 30 cases was from 2 to 912 percent of income calculated by the preferred method, with a median on the order of 16.5 percent. The high values in Mautz's sample suggest very serious possible inaccuracies.

However, there is reason to believe his methodology overstates the severity of the problem. As noted earlier, he included as common costs interest expense, whose allocation is not contemplated by most proposed segmental reporting systems, and R&D costs, whose commonality is arguable. Also, it appears that at least five of the seven sensitivity range values exceeding 100 percent involve lines of business with low or negative "preferred allocation method" profit margins.[64] Thus, the denominator with respect to which the range percentages were calculated was small, causing the calculated percentages to be large. But a loss or a small profit margin continues in most cases to be a loss or a small profit margin even when large percentage error factors are applied, and so the economic significance of these large reported potential error ranges is slight.

Broader and more conclusive insight on this issue will be provided when the first results of the FTC's 1974 LB survey are published. The Commission's approach to common cost allocation has heeded the wise counsel of Mr. Dooley: 'Thrust ivrybody—but cut th' ca-ards."[65] In addition to having companies use the allocation methods they consider most appropriate, the Commission has stated its intention to follow Mautz's example and reallocate the reported common costs according to a variety of plausible alternative methods.[66] The sensitivity of reported operating income figures will thereby be tested and communicated to potential data users. This, it seems to me, is by far the most sensible way of dealing with an intrinsically tough and largely unexplored problem. It is conceivable that sensitivity to allocation criteria will turn out to be so great that retreat to a standardized contribution margin approach by both the FTC and other organizations, such as the FASB, will prove advisable. On this, only time and experience will tell.

---

63. Mautz, op. cit., pp. 357–373.

64. This can also be seen in Professor Benston's Table 2-12 data, which have been reprocessed from Mautz's original figures but show the same patterns. Only Segment 6 of Company C has a "preferred method" return approximating what one could earn on a savings bank deposit in the mid-1960s.

65. Finley Peter Dunne, *Mr. Dooley on Iverything and Iverybody,* ed. Robert Hutchinson, Dover, New York, 1963, p. 154.

66. FTC, 1975, N. 40 *supra,* pp. 5–6.

ORGANIZATIONAL ALTERNATIVES

I have tried to lay out the main technical problems that must be mastered in implementing segmental financial reporting. In my view, the problems are solvable, albeit imperfectly, and it is important to solve them because the need for good segmental performance information is broad and deep. It is not yet clear in detail what the best technical solutions are. Although the persistence of uncertainty implies that some pluralism of approaches is desirable, it is not too early to ask whether certain organizational approaches are superior to others in meeting the needs for segmental performance information. One might ask too, is there any way of avoiding an already visible proliferation of reporting programs, each with its own special features that impose an extra burden on business firms?

A preliminary grip on the issue can be gained by dividing the "market" for segmental financial reports into three submarkets: the investment community, largely oriented toward individual company data; the heterogeneous collection of government agencies, businessmen, and scholars needing a comprehensive, generalized set of industry-oriented performance data; and the government agencies requiring specialized information on particular industries or groups with which they interact. The third group, I believe, could impose by far the greatest burden if permitted to proliferate out of control. I do not know how to constrain the proliferation of costly special industry surveys except through a tough-minded ad hoc clearance process. The problems in administering such a process are very difficult, mainly because agencies (or more importantly, bureaucracies within agencies) tend to consider their own information needs compelling, because considerable technical competence is needed on the part of clearance reviewers to sort out specious from valid complaints by industry opponents, and because the tendency of industry to resolve matters politically is strong. Unable to solve the problem, I evade it and turn to one only slightly more tractable.

The burden on business enterprises would be reduced if the general segmental reporting programs for investors and industry analysts could be reconciled. The FTC would, I suspect, budge a fair amount in its approach to reporting category formation and its detailed category definitions if the SEC, FASB, and industry would accept and take seriously the notion of reporting at profit-center levels approximating as closely as possible a set of standardized industry categories. An "ideal" consolidated program would then operate roughly as follows. Adhering to accounting rules promulgated by the FASB, companies would include in their annual or 10-K reports breakdowns of sales, gross margin, contribution margin, operating income, and assets for domestic profit centers conforming to a standardized category list developed by a joint industry-government-universities committee. They would also publish a qualitative description of the products or services included in each profit center and a specialization ratio indicating what fraction of reported profit center sales in fact fell within the standard category's defined ambit. Agencies such as the FTC (as well as individuals and private financial analysis organizations such as Investors Management Sciences) could then aggregate or otherwise analyze the published data to their hearts' content. The FTC might also, as it currently does with its *Quarterly Financial Report* program, seek from companies supplemental unpublished information for the reporting profit centers and from nonpublic corporations, presenting the resulting data to the public in aggregated form. It would accept the profit centers defined by the companies even though they match the standardized categories imperfectly, just as it currently accepts some secondary product "contamination" under its LB program. Some enforcement mechanism would be needed to ensure that companies do not adopt overly broad categories—e.g., because their lower-level profit centers closely matching the standard categories lack one or two reportable data elements that could nonetheless be accurately estimated. Logically, an executive subcommittee of the category-definition committee could perform this function if it were given the necessary authority, although the FTC or SEC might serve instead.

If this compromise is to be adopted, industry and the financial standard-setting agencies will have to swallow the bitter pill of standardized categories. Otherwise, I see no alternative to dual programs, unless Congress or the courts prevent the FTC from seeking industry-oriented data. The segment definitions adopted in response to the SEC's 1970 rule yield data virtually worthless for analyzing industrial performance. The FASB's 10 percent and 10-category rules make it almost inevitable that large corporations will report at a more aggregated level of industry detail than small companies. It is unlikely that CPA firms entrusted with enforcing the FASB's standards will do much to ensure the formation of categories sufficiently homogeneous to permit interfirm comparisons or industry analyses. Unless there is movement, the FTC will, I hope, persist in its LB program, estimated to cost $24,000 per average large reporting corporation during its start-up years, or approximately $12 million per year in total.[67]

One possible objection to my compromise proposal is that it would disclose large amounts of information considered confidential. Business firms have made the confidentiality issue a cornerstone of objections to the FTC's LB program, which seeks data somewhat richer than proposed in my compromise for a set of industry categories 80 percent more finely subdivided than the three-digit SIC level originally favored by the FASB. I doubt whether this quantitative difference is large enough to transform the issue qualitatively. If this surmise is correct, I venture only three further observations, given the fact that Chapter 7 takes up the subject of data confidentiality.

---

67. Federal Trade Commission, Bureau of Economics, Staff Memorandum, *1974 Form LB Revision*, July 1, 1975, pp. 6–10.

First, my own belief that the world would not end if such disclosure occurred is evidently not just that of a mad economist; it is supported *inter alia* by the authority of the Financial Accounting Standards Board, which wrote:

> Several respondents to the Discussion Memorandum cited harm to an enterprise's competitive position as a basis for opposing disclosure such as this Statement requires. In the Board's judgment, however, the usefulness to investors and creditors of the information required to be reported by this Statement makes those disclosures essential.[68]

Second, it is important to recognize the asymmetry of disclosure requirements under existing SEC and impending FASB rules. The typical small, specialized public corporation discloses more about detailed line of business activities today in its *consolidated* income statement than General Electric, Textron, and Bendix disclose in their SEC-mandated 10-K breakdowns. Even more insight into small and medium-sized corporations' operations is provided by 10-K segmental disclosures. Mallory & Co. (number 550 on *Fortune's* 1975 list) currently provides a 10-K profit breakdown on its battery operations. Does Union Carbide? Varian Associates (number 492) breaks out its electron tube and device profits. Does General Electric? Carpenter Technology (number 524) segregates its stainless, tool, and special alloy steel profits from one another. Does United States Steel?[69] If disclosure truly had an adverse impact on competitive position, the existing system would work to the relative disadvantage of smaller companies who already enjoy more than their fair share of handicaps, for example, in the capital markets.

Third, one must be clear about the distribution of effects when disclosure does have an impact on competitive position. The problem may be likened to a zero-sum game: the discloser loses and competitors gain. A better approximation, however, would be a three-person variable-sum game: the discloser loses, perhaps appreciably; competitors gain slightly; and society gains significantly through invigorated competition and better-informed resource allocation. One can of course identify situations in which disclosure could stifle competition and impose losses on society rather than improving matters. Open price arrangements are the classic example.[70] Premature disclosure of detailed research and development plans might also inhibit innovation under some circumstances, especially when the would-be innovator is not

---

68. FASB, 1975, N. 22 *supra*, p. 25. See also FASB, 1976, N. 22 *supra*, pp. 32–33.

69. These comparisons are not the result of an extensive search. I sampled six medium-sized-company 10-Ks to find them.

70. See Scherer, *Industrial Market Structure and Economic Performance*, pp. 208–210 and 449–543.

already well-established in the market.[71] But despite a diligent effort, I have had great difficulty finding plausible injury to *society* from the kinds of data reporting contemplated by the FASB and FTC. For my closest approximation to the nature of the disclosure game, a fourth person—management—must be introduced. Managers would clearly lose some insulation from criticism if detailed segmental performance data were published. But I believe a fair amount of open accountability for performance is on balance a healthy thing.

Suppose, however, I am wrong—if not on the substance of my argument, then on the politics. Suppose there is no way of getting industry-oriented segmental financial data without a confidentiality quid pro quo: that the data will not be disclosed publicly except in aggregated form. How should the job be done? Who should do it?

The debate over generalized industry reporting usually juxtaposes the Bureau of the Census against the FTC.[72] But first a digression on the Defense Department's Profit '76 approach is warranted. Data for the study were prepared by industrial contractors' in-house accountants, reviewed by the companies' CPA firms, and then transmitted to the Coopers & Lybrand accounting firm. Coopers & Lybrand processed the data, aggregated them, and prepared reports summarizing the findings. It was charged, *inter alia,* with ensuring that neither the Defense Department nor any other party can deduce the position of any individual data contributor. The approach is an interesting one and warrants further consideration, particularly if the alternatives are ultimately rejected.

Let us, however, think more conventionally in terms of the Bureau of the Census–FTC dichotomy. Elemental fairness argues for the FTC. It pioneered industry-oriented financial reporting when the Bureau of the Census made it clear repeatedly that it had no interest. Yet fairness is not a criterion on which a great deal of weight is likely to be placed in such matters. Also favoring the FTC is its experienced LB cadre—a point to which I shall return again. The FTC's main disadvantage is that, given its antitrust enforcement responsibilities and its vulnerability to Congressional pressures, industry simply doesn't trust its possession of segmental performance information, no matter how assiduously it pledges to keep data-gathering and antitrust functions separate and no matter how consistently it has done so in the past in its *Quarterly Financial Report* program.

This distrust has at least three unfavorable side effects. One is costly,

---

71. See F. M. Scherer, "Research and Development Resource Allocation under Rivalry," *Quarterly Journal of Economics,* vol. 81, no. 3, Aug. 1967, pp. 359–394 (especially pp. 381–385); F. M. Scherer, "Was the Nuclear Arms Race Inevitable?" *Co-existence,* vol. 3, no. 1, Jan. 1966, pp. 59–69; and Morton Kamien and Nancy Schwartz, "Potential Rivalry, Monopoly Profits and the Pace of Inventive Activity," Northwestern University Graduate School of Management, Evanston, Ill., Feb. 1976.

72. *Hearings on Departments of State, Justice, Commerce, the Judiciary and Related Agencies Appropriations, Fiscal Year 1977,* Senate Committee on Appropriations, 94th Cong., 2d Sess., April 27, 1976.

time-consuming litigation. Second, the litigation in turn inhibits flexibility in dealing with accounting and economic problems, especially in an organization dominated by lawyers. It is difficult to be bold and innovative when every significant action visible to the outside world must be cleared with counsel and when industrial counterparts communicating through their own lawyers are less than honest in revealing what data they can and cannot readily supply. Third, although companies challenging the FTC's LB program have suffered several visible defeats in attempts to stop the program through political action, they have also scored some quiet victories. Specifically, funds and especially personnel allotments to support the program were withheld by Congress for fiscal year 1975 and by the OMB for the succeeding two years. Every staff position used for the program had to be cannibalized from other Commission functions. This posed no significant problems in the first two years. But resource constraints began to bite hard in 1976, and when (if?) the Commission secures judicial enforcement of accumulated reporting orders for 1974, 1975, and 1976, it will be buried under an avalanche of paper from which public reports will not emerge for years unless it has better luck in future appropriations struggles.

The Bureau of the Census' principal advantage is that industry knows the Bureau can never take any substantive enforcement action based upon data it receives. Also, the Census Act provides unambiguous protection against congressional demands for the release of data collected under a pledge of confidentiality. Whether this is important depends upon the answer to a question I cannot answer: Does industry's opposition to the LB program primarily reflect unwillingness to let the FTC staff have segmented individual company performance data, or is there a strong element of residual opposition to industry-oriented financial reporting per se? If the former, a census-based program would untie some critical knots. If the latter, the program is unlikely to succeed at the Bureau. Both by tradition and to avoid adverse spillover effects on programs for which it has no power to compel compliance, the Bureau of the Census has taken great pains to maintain harmonious relations with its industrial data sources. Unwillingness to jeopardize that support is one reason why the Bureau showed no early interest in highly controversial segmental financial reporting. If it were assigned a line of business program and industry brought pressure to bear, I believe the Bureau would find ways of letting the program atrophy. The key question is, would industry bring such pressure to bear? I know no way of getting an honest answer without imitating the Gingerbread Man's experiment in letting the fox ferry him across the river.

A further consideration argues strongly against the Bureau of the Census. As I have made clear, segmental performance data have research uses with crucial public policy implications. The data will be gold, and even if hidden, they should be thoroughly mined. The Industry Division of the Bureau of the Census has neither a research tradition nor a significant research capability. On this dimension I have seen few signs of improvement over more than a decade of observation.[73] If anything, the situation has worsened. There was a time when selected independent scholars were allowed confidential access to industry census data for their private research.[74] I am told this is no longer done—whether because of the inherent unfairness in awarding such monopoly franchises, industry opposition to the weakening of confidentiality bars, or other reasons, I know not. In any event, internal mining of the data is improbable unless major attitudinal and organizational changes occur. The Bureau makes much of its willingness to carry out tabulations and analyses for outsiders, disclosing the results in aggregated form only. This has an appealing ring, but it is a poor substitute for an internal research capability. The best way to do good quantitative research is to immerse oneself in the raw data so one knows their possibilities and limitations and can detect such anomalies as a keypunching error that biases the entire set of results. The next best way is to work from outside with inside researchers who have access to the data and who understand both the substance of the problem and the relevant statistical methodology. By far the worst way is to play blindman's bluff with data one cannot see on a problem one's inside programmer doesn't understand. That is the way most if not all scholarly research with industry census data must currently be done. It is very unsatisfactory, and as a consequence a precious national resource is wasted. The waste would be magnified if the Bureau of the Census were assigned the task of collecting and then keeping confidential in perpetuity segmental financial performance data.

One of the things to which I attached highest priority while at the FTC was building in the LB program office a research capability to ensure that full advantage of the data could be taken by both insiders and (subject to confidentiality restraints) outsiders. The seed was successfully planted. Whether it thrives will depend upon the climate of the next two years. If it does thrive, the FTC would in my view be the best organizational locus for a generalized industry-oriented financial reporting program. If the FTC fails in its legal struggle or its attempt to build a viable LB program organization, I would recommend as a second-best alternative the CPA-firm approach used by the Defense Department. Transferring the program to the ill-prepared, unresponsive bureaucracy at the Bureau of the Census would in my opinion be a poor third-best plan.

---

73. In a letter commenting on an earlier version of this paper, Associate Census Director Shirley Kalleck wrote, *inter alia:* "Although our professional resources to support economic research has in the past been somewhat limited, we are currently in the process of supplementing our staff to achieve a more desired research capability, and have recently added several economists with skills at the doctoral level." I remain unpersuaded, in part from experience, that a few Ph.D.s do not a research capability make. The only strategy with a reasonable chance of success would be to begin with a nucleus of persons with demonstrated research talent and to insulate them, along with their junior associates, from political pressures and day-to-day operating responsibilities.

74. Gort, *Diversification and Integration*, p. 3.

APPENDIX A—Form 10-K and Three-Digit Industry Structures of 20 Leading Diversified Corporations

Company	*Number of 10-K groups*	*10-K category description*	*Percent of 1975 sales*	*Number of 3-digit codes*	*Description of three-digit activities*
General Electric	5	Aerospace	12	32	Small arms; household furniture; commercial printing; industrial inorganic chemicals; plastic materials and synthetics; misc. plastic products; pressed or blown glass; misc. nonmetallic mineral products; iron and steel foundries; nonferrous rolling and drawing; fabricated structural metal products; metal forgings and stampings; misc. fabricated metal products; engines and turbines; construction and related machinery; metalworking machinery; special industry machinery; general industry machinery; refrigeration and service machinery; misc. machinery; electric dist. equipment; electrical industrial apparatus; household appliances; electric lighting equip.; radio and TV equipment; communication equipment; electronic components; misc. elec. equipment; aircraft and parts; railroad equipment; measuring and controlling devices; watches and clocks
		Consumer	21		
		Industrial components and systems	29		
		Industrial power equipment	18		
		International	21		
		G.E. Credit Corp. (separately reported)	—		
International Telephone and Telegraph	9	Telecommunications	26	31	Meat products; preserved fruits and vegetables; bakery products; fats and oils; misc. foods; logging camps; millwork and plywood; misc. wood products; pulp mills; books; plastic materials and synthetics; agricultural chemicals; misc. plastic products; misc. nonmetallic mineral products;
		Natural resources	5		
		Industrial products	17		
		Food products	10		
		Automotive and consumer products	11		
		Hotels and business services	8		

APPENDIX A (*Continued*)

Company	*Number of 10-K groups*	*10-K category description*	*Percent of 1975 sales*	*Number of 3-digit codes*	*Description of three-digit activities*
IT&T (Cont.)		Defense and space	4		basic steel products; iron and steel foundries; nonferrous rolling and drawing; cutlery, hand tools, and hardware; plumbing and heating products; fabricated structural metal products; metal forgings and stampings; misc. fabricated metal products; general industrial machinery; office and computing machines; refrigeration and service machinery; electric distributing equipment; electric lighting and wiring equipment; communication equipment; electronic components; motor vehicles and equipment; measuring and controlling devices
		Hartford Casualty & Life	14		
		Other insurance and finance	5		
Gulf & Western Industries	8	Manufacturing	29	27	Lead and zinc mining; sugar and confectionary products; fats and oils; misc. food products; cigars; public-building furniture; industrial inorganic chemicals; misc. plastic products; concrete gypsum and plaster products; iron and steel foundries; primary nonferrous metals; nonferrous rolling and drawing; misc. primary metal products; cutlery, hand tools, and hardware; fabricated structural metal products; metal forgings and stampings; misc. wire products; misc. fabricated metal products; metalworking machinery; general and industrial machinery; refrigeration and service machinery; communication equipment; elec-
		Food and agricultural products	8		
		Natural resources	5		
		Paper and building products	13		
		Leisure time	12		
		Automotive replacement parts	8		
		Consumer products	8		
		Financial services	17		

					tronic components; misc. electrical equipment; motor vehicles and equipment; aircraft and parts
Litton Industries	4	Business systems and equipment Defense, commercial, and marine systems Industrial systems and equipment Professional services and equipment	30 35 19 15	26	Office furniture; partitions and fixtures; paper; paperboard; misc. converted paper products; periodicals; books; commercial printing; fabricated rubber products; nonferrous rolling and drawing; cutlery, hand tools, and hardware; construction machinery; metalworking machinery; general industrial machinery; office and computing machines; refrigeration and service machinery; electric distributing equipment; electrical industrial apparatus; household appliances; electric lighting and wiring; communication equipment; electronic components; misc. electrical equipment; shipbuilding; medical instruments and supplies
Textron	5	Aerospace Consumer Industrial Metal product Creative capital	38 27 18 17 —	25	Preserved fruits and vegetables; misc. food products; yarn and thread; household furniture; misc. converted paper products; paints; misc. plastic products; pottery products; iron and steel foundries; nonferrous foundries; screw machine products; metal forgings and stampings; wire products; misc. fabricated metal products; metalworking machinery; general industrial machinery; office and computing machines; electrical lighting and wiring equipment; aircraft and parts; misc. transportation equipment; measuring and controlling devices; ophthalmic goods; jewelry and silverware; pens, office, and art goods

APPENDIX A (*Continued*)

Company	Number of 10-K groups	10-K category description	Percent of 1975 sales	Number of 3-digit codes	Description of three-digit activities
Beatrice Foods	5	Dairy products	28	23	Meat products; dairy products; preserved fruits and vegetables; bakery products; grain mill products; fats and oils; beverages; misc. foods; household furniture; printing trade services; industrial inorganic chemicals; leather tanning and finishing; luggage; iron and steel foundries; nonferrous foundries; plumbing and heating; screw machine products; misc. fabricated metal products; farm and garden equipment; misc. transportation equipment; misc. manufactures
		Grocery products	35		
		Specialty meat products	8		
		Agriproducts and warehousing	5		
		Manufactured and chemical products	24		
American Can Co.	7	Container and packaging products	54	22	Misc. food products; logging; millwork and plywood; pulp; paper; paperboard; misc. converted paper products; paperboard containers; books; commercial printing; industrial inorganic chemicals; plastic materials and synthetics; drugs; misc. chemical products; misc. plastic products; basic steel; secondary nonferrous metals; metal cans; misc. metal services; misc. fabricated metal products; metalworking machinery; jewelry and silverware
		Consumer products	20		
		International container and packaging products	15		
		Chemicals	9		
		Printing	1		
		Information technology	0.3		
		Miscellaneous businesses	—		
Westinghouse Electric	5	Power systems	37	21	Ordnance and accessories; household furniture; misc. plastic products; pressed and blown glass; pottery and related products; nonferrous rolling and drawing; plumbing and heating; fabricated structural metal products; engines and turbines; construction machinery; special industry
		Industry products	38		
		Public systems	22		
		Broadcasting	2		
		Other	0.6		

					machinery; general industry machinery; refrigeration and service machinery; electric distributing equipment; electrical industrial apparatus; household appliances; electric lighting equipment; communication equipment; electronic components; misc. electrical equipment
Rockwell International	10	Automotive operations	22	20	Ammunition (including missiles); misc. plastic products; iron and steel foundries; nonferrous foundries; misc. primary metal products; plumbing and heating; metal forgings and stampings; wire products; misc. fabricated metal products; farm and garden machinery; metalworking machinery; special industry machinery; electrical industrial apparatus; radio and TV equipment; communications equipment; electronic components; motor vehicles and equipment; aircraft and parts; measuring and controlling devices
		Aircraft	11		
		Space systems and rocket engines	17		
		Other aerospace	2		
		Guidance and control, avionics, and telecommunications	16		
		Calculator products	3		
		Utility products	5		
		Textile machinery, graphic arts, and industrial components	12		
		Home entertainment and household appliances	10		
		Power tools	2		
Bendix	5	Automotive (including recreation)	51	19	Sawmills, wood containers; misc. mineral products; misc. fabricated metal products; construction machinery; metalworking machinery; general industry machinery; office and computing machines; misc. machinery; electric lighting and wiring; communication equipment; electronic components; misc. electrical equipment; motor vehicles and equipment; aircraft and parts; misc. transportation equipment; measuring and controlling devices; engineering and scientific instruments
		Aerospace—electronics	27		
		Shelter	13		
		Industrial—energy	9		
		Sundry and eliminations	−0.6		

APPENDIX A (*Continued*)

Company	*Number of 10-K groups*	*10-K category description*	*Percent of 1975 sales*	*Number of 3-digit codes*	*Description of three-digit activities*
Consolidated Foods	6	Home products and services	23	19	Meat products; dairy products; preserved fruits and vegetables; grain mill products; bakery products; sugar and confectionary products; fats and oils; beverages; narrow fabrics; men's and boys' furnishings; household furniture; misc. furniture and fixtures; commercial printing; soaps, cleaners, and toilet goods; paints; misc. plastic products; household appliances; pens, office, and art goods; misc. manufactures
		Commercial products and services	5		
		Apparel	7		
		Frozen and processed foods	32		
		Food services	22		
		Soft drinks and confections	10		
General Motors	5	U.S. automotive products	65	18	Misc. fabricated textile products; iron and steel foundries; nonferrous foundries; misc. primary metal products; cutlery, hand tools, and hardware; plumbing and heating; metal forgings and stampings; engines and turbines; construction machinery; metalworking machinery; general industrial machinery; household appliances; electric lighting and wiring; communication equipment; misc. electrical equipment; motor vehicles and equipment; railroad equipment
		Nonautomotive products	6		
		Defense and space	1		
		Canadian	11		
		Overseas	18		
Borden	4	Foods	33	18	Meat products; dairy products; preserved fruits and vegetables; bakery products; sugar and confectionary products; fats and oils; beverages; misc. food products; misc. textiles; misc. converted paper products; industrial inorganic chemicals; plastic materials and synthetics; soaps, cleaners,
		Dairy and services	28		
		Chemicals	22		
		International	17		

					and toilet goods; paints; agricultural chemicals; misc. chemical products; misc. plastic products; primary nonferrous metals
W. R. Grace	7	Specialty industrial chemical	27	17	Misc. nonmetallic mineral mining; preserved fruits and vegetables; grain mill products; fats and oils; misc. food products; misc. textile goods; misc. converted paper products; industrial inorganic chemicals; plastic materials and synthetics; soaps, cleaners, and toilet goods; agricultural chemicals; misc. chemical products; misc. plastic products; footwear; misc. nonmetallic mineral products; motor vehicles and equipment; misc. transportation equipment
		Packaging and plastics	10		
		Agricultural chemical	14		
		Natural resources	4		
		Fashion and leisure	14		
		Consumer services	12		
		Packaged foods	19		
TRW Inc.	8	Electronic and computer based services	24	17	Ammunition (including missiles); misc. plastic products; nonferrous rolling and drawing; cutlery, hand tools, and hardware; screw machine products; misc. fabricated metal products; metalworking machinery; general industrial machinery; misc. machinery; electric distributing equipment; electrical industrial apparatus; electric lighting and wiring; communications equipment; electronic components; motor vehicles and equipment; aircraft and parts; motorcycles and bicycles
		Domestic car and truck products	10		
		International car and truck products	19		
		Replacement parts—car and truck	10		
		Spacecraft and propulsion products	11		
		Fasteners, tools, and bearings	13		
		Energy products and services	10		
		Other	3		
United States Steel	5	Steel manufacturing	74	15	Iron ore mining; bituminous coal mining; millwork and plywood; industrial inorganic chemicals; agricultural chemicals; misc. plastic products; cement; basic steel products; iron and steel foundries; nonferrous rolling and drawing; misc. primary metal products; fabricated structural metal products; misc. metal services; construction machinery
		Fabricating and engineering	10		
		Chemicals	7		
		Transportation	6		
		Cement and others	3		

APPENDIX A (*Continued*)

Company	*Number of 10-K groups*	*10-K category description*	*Percent of 1975 sales*	*Number of 3-digit codes*	*Description of three-digit activities*
United Aircraft	5	Power	53	15	Ammunition (including missiles); fire control equipment; misc. plastic products; nonferrous rolling and drawing; wire products; misc. fabricated metal products; metalworking machinery; electric distributing equipment; electrical industrial equipment; electrical lighting and wiring; communication equipment; misc. electrical equipment; motor vehicles and equipment; aircraft and parts; misc. manufactures
		Systems	23		
		Industrial	19		
		Space	2		
		Other	3		
Minnesota Mining & Manufacturing	8	Graphic systems	22	15	Misc. converted paper products; plastic materials and synthetics; drugs; soaps, cleaners, and toilet goods; paints; misc. chemical products; misc. fabricated rubber products; misc. plastic products; pottery and related products; cut stone and stone products; misc. nonmetallic mineral products; misc. machinery; radio and TV equipment; photographic equipment and supplies; misc. manufactures
		Tape and allied products	16		
		Abrasives, adhesives, building service products, and chemicals	15		
		Advertising services and protective products	12		
		Photographic, printing, industrial graphics, and nuclear products	11		
		Recording materials	9		
		Electrical products	8		
		Health care products and services	7		

Sperry Rand	4	Business equipment	46	15	Ammunition (including missiles); office furniture; partitions and fixtures; commercial printing; business forms; farm and garden machinery; construction machinery; general industrial machinery; office and computing machines; electrical industrial apparatus; household appliances; communication equipment; electronic components; aircraft and parts; engineering and scientific instruments
		Machinery products	28		
		Guidance and control equipment	22		
		Other	4		
Georgia Pacific	2	Building products	63	15	Grain mill products; logging camps; sawmills; millwork and plywood; misc. wood products; household furniture; pulp; paper; paperboard; misc. converted paper products; paperboard containers; commercial printing; industrial inorganic chemicals; plastic materials and synthetics; concrete gypsum, and plaster products
		Pulp, paper, and chemicals	37		

APPENDIX B — Industry Category List for FTC Form LB (1974)

FTC code	Description	Related 1972 SIC or census codes
	MANUFACTURING CATEGORIES:	
	Food and Kindred Products	
20.01	meat packing, sausages, and other prepared meat products	2011, 3
20.02	poultry dressing, poultry, and egg processing	2016, 7
20.03	fluid milk	2026
20.04	dairy products except fluid milk	202, x 2026
20.05	canned specialties	2032
20.06	frozen fruits, fruit juices, and vegetables	2037
20.07	frozen specialties	2038
20.08	canned, dried, dehydrated, and pickled fruits and vegetables including preserves, jams, jellies, dehydrated soup mixes, vegetable sauces and seasonings, and salad dressings	2033, 4, 5
20.09	cereal breakfast foods	2043
20.10	dog, cat, and other pet food	2047
20.11	prepared feeds and feed ingredients for animals and fowls, not elsewhere classified	2048
20.12	flour and other grain mill products, rice milling, blended and prepared flour	2041, 4, 5
20.13	wet corn milling	2046
20.14	bread, cake, and related products	2051
20.15	cookies and crackers	2052
20.16	cane sugar	2061, 2
20.17	beet sugar	2063
20.18	confectionary products	2065
20.19	chocolate and cocoa products	2066
20.20	chewing gum	2067
20.21	fats and oils	207
20.22	malt beverages	2082
20.23	malt	2083
20.24	wines, brandy, and brandy spirits	2084

FTC code	Description	Related 1972 SIC or census codes
20.25	distilled liquor	2085
20.26	bottled and canned soft drinks	2086
20.27	flavoring extracts and syrups not elsewhere classified	2087
20.28	roasted coffee	2095
20.29	misc. foods and kindred products, except roasted coffee	209, x 2095
	Tobacco Mnaufacturing	
21.01	cigarettes	211
21.02	cigars	212
21.03	chewing and smoking tobacco	213
21.04	tobacco stemming and redrying	214
	Textile Mill Products	
22.01	weaving mills—cotton, synthetics, and silk	221, 222
22.02	weaving and finishing mills, wool	223
22.03	narrow fabric mills	224
22.04	hosiery	2251, 2
22.05	knit outerwear mills	2253
22.06	knit underwear mills	2254
22.07	knitting mills not elsewhere classified, including circular and warp knit fabric mills	2257, 8, 9
22.08	textile finishing, except wool and knit goods	226
22.09	floor covering mills	227
22.10	yarn and thread mills	228
22.11	tire cord and fabric	2296
22.12	misc. textile goods, except tire cord and fabric	229, x 2296
	Apparel and Other Fabric Products	
23.01	men's and boys' suits and coats	231
23.02	men's and boys' furnishings	232
23.03	women's and misses' outerwear	233
23.04	women's and children's undergarments	234

APPENDIX B (*Continued*)

FTC code	*Description*	*Related 1972 SIC or census codes*
23.05	children's outerwear	236
23.06	misc. apparel and accessories, including hats, caps, and millinery and fur goods	235, 237, 238
23.07	misc. fabricated textile products	239
	Lumber and Wood Products, except Furniture	
24.01	logging camps and logging contractors	241
24.02	sawmills and planing mills	242
24.03	millwork, plywood, and structural members	243
24.04	wood buildings and mobile homes	245
24.05	misc. wood products, including wood containers	244, 249
	Furniture and Fixtures	
25.01	mattresses and bedsprings	2515
25.02	household furniture, except mattresses and bedsprings	251, x 2515
25.03	office furniture	252
25.04	public building and related furniture	253
25.05	partitions and fixtures	254
25.06	misc. furniture and fixtures	259
	Paper and Allied Products	
26.01	pulp mills	261
26.02	paper mills, except building paper	262
26.03	paperboard mills	263
26.04	paper coating and glazing	2641
26.05	envelopes	2642
26.06	bags, except textile bags	2643
26.07	sanitary paper products	2647
26.08	stationery, tablets, and related products	2648
26.09	converted paper and paperboard products not elsewhere classified, including die-cut paper, paperboard, and cardboard, and pressed and molded pulp goods	2645, 6, 9

FTC code	Description	Related 1972 SIC or census codes
26.10	paperboard containers and boxes	265
26.11	building paper and board mills	266
	Printing, Publishing, and Allied Industries	
27.01	newspapers	271
27.02	periodicals	272
27.03	books	273
27.04	misc. publishing	274
27.05	commercial printing	275
27.06	manifold business forms	276
27.07	greeting card publishing	277
27.08	blankbooks and bookbinding	278
27.09	printing trade services	279
	Chemicals and Allied Products	
28.01	industrial gases	2813
28.02	inorganic pigments	2816
28.03	industrial inorganic chemicals, except industrial gases and inorganic pigments	2812, 2819
28.04	plastic materials and resins	2821
28.05	synthetic rubber	2822
28.06	organic fibers	2823, 4
28.07	drugs, ethical	pt. 283
28.08	drugs, proprietary	pt. 283
28.09	perfumes, cosmetics, and other toilet preparations	2844
28.10	soap and other cleaning preparations	284, x 2844
28.11	paints and allied products	285
28.12	gum and wood chemicals	2861
28.13	industrial organic chemicals, except gum and wood chemicals	2865, 9
28.14	fertilizers	2873, 4, 5
28.15	pesticides and agricultural chemicals not elsewhere classified	2879

APPENDIX B (*Continued*)

FTC code	*Description*	*Related 1972 SIC or census codes*
28.16	explosives	2892
28.17	misc. chemical products, except explosives	289, x 2892
	Petroleum Refining and Related Industries	
29.01	petroleum refining	291
29.02	paving and roofing materials	295
29.03	misc. petroleum and coal products	299
	Rubber and Miscellaneous Plastics Products	
30.01	tires and inner tubes	301
30.02	rubber and plastics footwear	302
30.03	reclaimed rubber	303
30.04	rubber and plastics hose and belting	304
30.05	fabricated rubber products not elsewhere classified	306
30.06	misc. plastics products	307
	Leather and Leather Products	
31.01	leather tanning and finishing	311
31.02	footwear, except rubber; and boot and shoe cut stock and findings	313, 314
31.03	luggage	316
31.04	leather goods not elsewhere classified, including leather gloves and mittens, and handbags and personal leather goods	315, 317, 319
	Stone, Clay, Glass, and Concrete Products	
32.01	flat glass	321
32.02	glass containers	3221
32.03	pressed and blown glass not elsewhere classified	3229
32.04	products of purchased glass	323
32.05	cement, hydraulic	324
32.06	structural clay products	325
32.07	vitreous plumbing fixtures	3261

FTC code	Description	Related 1972 SIC or census codes
32.08	porcelain electrical supplies	3264
32.09	pottery and related products, except vitreous plumbing fixtures and porcelain electrical supplies	326, x 3261, 4
32.10	concrete products, including block and brick	3271, 2
32.11	ready-mixed concrete	3273
32.12	lime	3274
32.13	gypsum products	3275
32.14	cut stone and stone products	328
32.15	abrasive products	3291
32.16	asbestos products	3292
32.17	mineral wool	3296
32.18	nonmetallic mineral products not elsewhere classified, including gaskets, packing and sealing devices, ground or treated minerals and earths, and nonclay refractories	3293, 5, 7, 9
	Primary Metal Industries	
33.01	blast furnace and basic steel products	331
33.02	iron and steel foundries	332
33.03	primary copper	3331
33.04	primary lead	3332
33.05	primary zinc	3333
33.06	primary aluminum	3334
33.07	primary nonferrous metals not elsewhere classified	3339
33.08	secondary nonferrous metals	334
33.09	aluminum sheet, plate, and foil, aluminum extruded products, aluminum rolling and drawing not elsewhere classified	3353, 4, 5
33.10	nonferrous rolling and drawing (including copper) not elsewhere classified	3351, 6
33.11	nonferrous wire drawing and insulating	3357
33.12	nonferrous foundries	336
33.13	misc. primary metal products	339

APPENDIX B (*Continued*)

FTC code	Description	Related 1972 SIC or census codes
	Fabricated Metal Products, except Machinery and Transportation Equipment	
34.01	metal cans	3411
34.02	metal barrels, drums, and pails	3412
34.03	cutlery	3421
34.04	hand and edge tools, except machine tools	3423, 5
34.05	hardware not elsewhere classified	3429
34.06	enameled iron and metal sanitary ware	3431
34.07	plumbing fixture fittings and trim (brass goods)	3432
34.08	heating equipment, except electric and warm air furnaces	3433
34.09	fabricated structural metal	3441
34.10	metal doors, sash, frames, molding, and trim	3442
34.11	fabricated plate work (boiler shops)	3443
34.12	misc. metal work, including sheet metal, architectural and ornamental metal work, and prefabricated metal buildings and parts	3444, 6, 8, 9
34.13	screw machine products, bolts, etc.	345
34.14	metal forgings, ferrous and nonferrous	3462, 3
34.15	automotive stampings	3465
34.16	crowns and closures	3466
34.17	metal stampings not elsewhere classified	3469
34.18	metal coating, engraving, and allied services	347
34.19	ordnance and accessories, except vehicles and guided missiles	348
34.20	valves and pipe fittings, except plumbers' brass goods	3494
34.21	misc. fabricated metal products, except valves and pipe fittings	349, x 3494
	Machinery except Electrical	
35.01	turbines and turbine generator sets	3511
35.02	internal combustion engines not elsewhere classified	3519
35.03	farm machinery and equipment	3523

FTC code	*Description*	*Related 1972 SIC or census codes*
35.04	lawn and garden equipment	3524
35.05	construction machinery and equipment	3531
35.06	mining machinery and equipment, except oil field machinery and equipment	3532
35.07	oil field machinery and equipment	3533
35.08	elevators and moving stairways	3534
35.09	conveyors and conveying equipment	3535
35.10	hoists, industrial cranes, and monorail systems	3536
35.11	industrial trucks, tractors, trailers, and stackers	3537
35.12	machine tools, metal cutting types	3541
35.13	machine tool accessories and measuring devices	3545
35.14	power-driven hand tools	3546
35.15	metalworking machinery not elsewhere classified, including metal forming machine tools, special dies and tools, die sets, jigs and fixtures, industrial molds and rolling mill machinery and equipment	3542, 4, 7, 9
35.16	food products machinery	3551
35.17	textile machinery	3552
35.18	woodworking machinery	3553
35.19	paper industries machinery	3554
35.20	printing trades machinery	3555
35.21	special industrial machinery not elsewhere classified	3559
35.22	pumps and pumping equipment	3561
35.23	ball and roller bearings	3562
35.24	air and gas compressors	3563
35.25	blowers and exhaust and ventilation fans	3564
35.26	speed changers, industrial high speed drives, and gears	3566
35.27	industrial process furnaces and ovens	3567
35.28	mechanical power transmission equipment not elsewhere classified	3568
35.29	general industrial machinery and equipment not elsewhere classified including industrial patterns	3565, 9

FTC code	*Description*	*Related 1972 SIC or census codes*
35.30	typewriters	3572
35.31	electronic computing equipment	3573
35.32	calculating and accounting machines, except electronic computing equipment	3574
35.33	scales and balances, except laboratory	3576
35.34	office machines not elsewhere classified	3579
35.35	air conditioning and warm-air heating equipment and commercial and industrial refrigeration equipment	3585
35.36	service industry machines not elsewhere classified, including automatic merchandising machines; commercial laundry, dry cleaning, and pressing machines; and measuring and dispensing pumps	358, x 3585
35.37	misc. machinery, except electrical	359
	Electrical and Electronic Machinery, Equipment, and Supplies	
36.01	transformers	3612
36.02	switchgear and switchboard apparatus	3613
36.03	motors and generators	3621
36.04	industrial controls	3622
36.05	welding apparatus, electric	3623
36.06	carbon and graphite products	3624
36.07	electrical industrial apparatus not elsewhere classified	3629
36.08	household cooking equipment	3631
36.09	household refrigerators and freezers	3632
36.10	household laundry equipment	3633
36.11	household vacuum cleaners	3635
36.12	household appliances not elsewhere classified, including electric housewares and fans and sewing machines	3634, 6, 9
36.13	electric lamps	3641
36.14	residential, commercial, industrial, and institutional electric lighting fixtures	3645, 6
36.15	vehicular lighting equipment	3647

FTC code	Description	Related 1972 SIC or census codes
36.16	lighting equipment not elsewhere classified, including current-carrying and non-current-carrying wiring devices	3643, 4, 8
36.17	radio and TV receiving sets	3651
36.18	phonograph records	3652
36.19	telephone and telegraph apparatus	3661
36.20	radio and TV communication equipment	3662
36.21	electron tubes, receiving and transmitting types	3671, 3
36.22	cathode-ray television picture tubes	3672
36.23	semiconductors and related devices	3674
36.24	electronic capacitors, resistors, coils and transformers, connectors and components not elsewhere classified	3675, 6, 7, 8, 9
36.25	storage batteries	3691
36.26	primary batteries, dry and wet	3692
36.27	engine electrical equipment	3694
36.28	x-ray apparatus and tubes, electrical equipment and supplies not elsewhere classified	3693, 9
	Transportation Equipment	
37.01	passenger cars	37111, 37115
37.02	trucks	37112, pt. 3713
37.03	buses	37113, pt. 3713
37.04	combat vehicles, tanks	37114, 3795
37.05	motor vehicle parts	3714
37.06	truck trailers	3715
37.07	aircraft and aircraft equipment not elsewhere classified	3721, 8
37.08	aircraft engines and engine parts	3724
37.09	ship and boat building and repairing	373
37.10	railroad equipment	374
37.11	motorcycles, bicycles, and parts	375
37.12	guided missiles, space vehicles, and parts	376

APPENDIX B (*Continued*)

FTC code	Description	Related 1972 SIC or census codes
37.13	travel trailers and campers	3792
37.14	transportation equipment not elsewhere classified	3799
	Measuring, Analyzing, and Controlling Instruments; Photographic, Medical, and Optical Goods; Watches and Clocks	
38.01	engineering and scientific instruments	381
38.02	measuring and controlling devices	382
38.03	optical instruments and lenses	383
38.04	dental equipment and supplies	3843
38.05	surgical and medical instruments, appliances, and supplies	384, x 3843
38.06	ophthalmic goods	385
38.07	photocopying equipment	38612
38.08	photographic equipment and supplies, except photocopying equipment	3861, x 38612, 38616-25, 38617-31, 32 & pt. 38618-11
3809	watches, clocks, and watchcases	387
	Miscellaneous Manufacturing Industries	
39.01	jewelry, silverware, and plated ware	391
39.02	musical instruments	393
39.03	sporting, and athletic goods not elsewhere classified	3949
39.04	dolls, games, toys, and children's vehicles	394, x 3949
39.05	pens, pencils, office and art supplies	395

FTC code	*Description*	*Related 1972 SIC or census codes*
39.06	costume jewelry and notions	396
39.07	hard-surface floor coverings	3996
39.08	misc. manufacturing, except hard-surface floor coverings	399, x 3996
	NONMANUFACTURING CATEGORIES:	
1.01	agricultural production—crops	01
2.01	agricultural production—livestock	02
7.01	agricultural services	07
8.01	forestry and fishing	08, 09
10.01	metal mining	10
11.01	anthracite mining and bituminous coal and lignite	11, 12
13.01	oil and gas extraction	13
14.01	mining and quarrying of nonmetallic minerals, except fuels	14
15.01	construction	15, 16, 17
40.01	transportation and public utilities	40, 41, 42, 43, 44, 45, 46, 47, 48, 49
50.01	wholesale trade	50,51
52.01	retail trade	52, 53, 54, 55, 56, 57, 58, 59
60.01	finance, insurance, and real estate	60,61, 62, 63, 64, 65, 66, 67
70.01	services	70, 72, 73, 75, 76, 78, 79, 80, 81, 82, 83, 84, 86, 88, 89

THE FTC'S LINE OF BUSINESS PROGRAM: A BENEFIT-COST ANALYSIS

George J. Benston, *Professor of Finance and Accounting, University of Rochester Graduate School of Management; Director, Center for Research in Government Policy and Business*

BACKGROUND AND DESCRIPTION

The Federal Trade Commission's line of business (LB) program would require some 400 to 450 large, diversified manufacturing corporations to report detailed income, expenses, assets, and supplementary accounting data assigned to lines of business annually. The lines of business are based, essentially, on the Standard Industrial Code (SIC) classifications: 261 such categories have been designated.

The LB program originated with an April 10, 1970, staff report to the FTC that was transmitted to the Subcommittee on Monopoly of the Senate Small Business Committee.[1] In December 1970 the FTC submitted a line of business report form to the Office of Management and Budget for clearance, a necessary procedure since OMB was charged with the responsibility of determining whether the expected benefits of such programs are likely to exceed the costs. After considerable opposition by the intended respondents, the proposal was withdrawn. In August 1973 the proposal was revived[2] and again submitted to OMB for clearance. Again, the potential respondents objected strenuously, claiming that the program offered no benefits but would impose considerable costs. An amendment to the Alaska Pipeline Act transferred approval authority for the program from OMB to the General Accounting Office. Although concluding that the data "would be unreliable at

1. "The Role of Giant Corporations in the American and World Economies," *Hearings before the Subcommittee on Monopoly of the Senate Small Business Committee*, 92d Cong., 1st Sess., Nov. 1971 (published as an appendix).

2. Federal Trade Commission, *Statement of Purpose: Annual Line of Business Report Program*, Aug. 1973 (hereinafter cited as FTC, 1973).

best, and may be seriously misleading,"[3] and that the FTC had underestimated company compliance costs, the GAO nevertheless approved the form because it did not believe that these considerations were within the scope of its authority.

The 1973 version of the program called for data from 2,000 corporations who were to report on 357 LB categories.[4] The 1974 version of the LB program differs from the 1973 version in several important respects. In the face of severe criticism (or perhaps because it came to realize the magnitude of the undertaking), the FTC reduced the number of respondents and LB categories. It also abandoned its instructions for product-oriented data.[5] A December 1973 revision to the August 1974 form instructed companies to report according to establishments rather than products, apparently because the Commission found that companies do not maintain product records defined by SIC codes.[6] The 1975 version (released on August 3, 1976) permits companies to choose among alternative reporting units: "A line of business is composed of one or more basic components. Some LBs will include only one basic component while others may contain many. Basic components may be establishments, product lines, profit centers, organizational units, or other parts of the LB Reporting Section."[7] However, restrictions are placed on the degree to which data relevant to different LBs may be aggregated or combined.

In addition to descriptive material, the form requires companies to report the following type of data for each of their FTC-defined lines of business:

- profit and loss data (from which gross margins, contribution margins, and operating income are obtained):
  - revenues (broken down by transfers and sales to domestic and foreign outsiders)
  - cost of operating revenue
  - media advertising (traceable and nontraceable)
  - other selling expense (traceable and nontraceable)
  - general and administrative expense (traceable and nontraceable)

---

3. Phillip S. Hughes (Assistant Comptroller General), *Report to the Comptroller General of the United States in the Evaluation of the Federal Trade Commission's Proposed Annual Line of Business Report (Form LB)*, approved May 1974, p. 15.
4. FTC, 1973, N.2 *supra*.
5. "For the purpose of this report, create lines of business by combining all business segments from those listed in the company's report which have the same FTC code" (FTC, 1973, p. 11).
6. See Betty Bock, *Line-of-Business Reporting: Problems in the Formulation of a Data Program*, The Conference Board, New York, Nov. 1974, for an excellent critique of the 1973 and first 1974 versions of the LB program.
7. Federal Trade Commission, *1975 Form LB*, Instructions, Aug. 3, 1976, p. 6.

- asset data:
  - plant, property, and equipment (gross and accumulated depreciation, etc.) (traceable and nontraceable)
  - inventories (traceable and nontraceable)
  - all other assets (traceable and nontraceable)
- supplementary data:
  - payrolls
  - materials used
  - depreciation, etc.
  - research and development (company and billed to federal government and to other outsiders)
  - percentage of ending inventory valued on alternative bases
  - percentage of depreciation, etc., calculated with alternative methods
  - percentage of plant, property, and equipment acquired in different years
  - percentage of transfers valued at alternative prices
- reconciliation of profit and loss and asset data with the SEC's 10-K report

Since few (if any) companies maintain internal records by the lines of business defined by the FTC and with the specific detail demanded, the cost to them of complying with the program may be considerable. Furthermore, over 150 of the approximately 440 companies whose participation was commanded have refused to comply and have sued in federal court to have the program discontinued. In testimony at the first public hearing held by the FTC in May 1975, attorneys for some of these companies criticized the LB program as follows.

> [It] is simply wrong—wrong because the [FTC's] Bureau [of Economics] says it needs "market" data but its forms do not ask for market data; wrong because the Bureau says it needs economic data but its forms do not ask for economic data; wrong because the Bureau says it can and will use aggregates of accounting data, but its forms ask for noncomparable, distorted and statistically invalid data that can only result in totally meaningless aggregates [that] have neither accounting validity nor economic validity; and wrong because the Commission cannot secure the confidentiality of individual company data, the disclosure of which could have adverse effects on competition.[8]

In addition, the companies claim they cannot provide the economic data the FTC wants, even at a very high cost, because economically

8. Weil, Gotshal & Manges, "Statement on Behalf of Aluminum Company of America [and twelve other companies]," *United States before Federal Trade Commission on the Matter of Proposed 1974 FTC Form LB,* May 16, 1975, p. 2 (hereinafter cited as Weil, Gotshal & Manges).

meaningful profit rates for individual products cannot be measured by their accounting systems.

The FTC disputes the companies' objections on all grounds. Despite the strenuous objections, the Commission has steadfastly refused to abandon the program. It also has not conducted any benefit-cost analyses of the LB program or any pilot studies of the reporting problems that respondents might have. It has, however, recognized some problems and consequently has restated some reporting requirements to reduce the companies' compliance burden somewhat. In essence, though, the Commission apparently agrees with its Executive Director, R. T. McNamara, who said, "I believe that much of the corporate opposition to the public disclosure of aggregate line of business profitability is because they [corporations] know precisely their sales, costs and profits by products and lines of business."[9]

A resolution of this issue is sought by delineating and examining the costs and benefits of the program.

EXPECTED BENEFITS FROM THE LB PROGRAM

The FTC's Stated Motivation for the Program

The FTC states that it "was motivated to initiate the LB program by numerous developments, of which two stand out. First, American manufacturing corporations have become increasingly diversified." As a consequence "it has become increasingly difficult to obtain a clear picture of financial developments in specific industries . . . because all or most of the leading producers are highly diversified corporations whose financial reports are not broken down to provide such information." Second, the FTC expects the data collected to aid its law enforcement responsibilities with respect to antitrust law enforcement and consumer protection from frauds, misrepresentation, anticompetitive practices, etc. Its ability to determine which industries to investigate for these purposes has "been hampered by the decline over time in the quality of the information available," a condition which the LB data is expected to correct.[10]

In addition, an earlier *Statement of Purpose* mentions the FTC's historic role in the reporting of business information.[11] This role includes publication of a long list of reports of data on business balance sheets and income statements, including the *Quarterly Financial Report*

---

9. R. T. McNamara, "FTC Line of Business Reporting: Fact and Fiction," *Financial Executive*, vol. 42, no. 8, Aug. 1974, p. 25.

10. Federal Trade Commission, *Supporting Statement: FTC Form LB, 1974 Survey Version*, July 1, 1975, pp. 1–2 (hereinafter cited as FTC, 1975).

11. FTC, 1973, N. 2 *supra*, pp. 3–4.

for Manufacturing Companies (QFR) and *Rates of Return in Selected Manufacturing Industries* (no longer published). The LB program is expected to supplement and improve these statistics and give rise to new and better economic studies.

Specific Benefits Expected

The FTC claims that the LB reports will yield benefits to government, economists, business, labor, investors, and consumers. The following list of benefits is as complete as I could glean from the FTC's statements of purpose.[12] The benefits claimed are given in the FTC's words, where possible. At this point, the benefits are stated without criticism.

GOVERNMENT ANTITRUST POLICY

As mentioned above, the FTC has claimed that the LB data will improve the effectiveness with which it allocates its resources by enabling it "to choose as wisely as possible which industry-wide investigations best serve the public interest."[13] The aggregate data are believed to be relevant because "both the determination of what factors explain high profits and the discovery of how important those factors are relative to each other are key inputs in decisions about which industries to investigate and what to do when sub-standard performance is discovered."[14] Though the FTC denies that it will use *individual* company data for antitrust investigations or proceedings, several corporations which oppose the program believe that the data collected may be used (directly or indirectly) to support antitrust and other actions against them.

MACROECONOMIC POLICY

"Line of business data will improve the quality of data used in the Government's efforts to control inflation and unemployment."[15]

> Without much better data on individual industries than those which now exist, it will be impossible to analyze the structure and dynamics of those changes [in the economy] and to pinpoint the reasons why inflation

12. The most complete document supporting the LB program is the FTC's 1973 *Statement of Purpose*. Later statements, i.e., the FTC Bureau of Economics Staff, *FTC Form LB: Supporting Statement,* March 1974, and FTC, 1975, N. 10 *supra,* repeat and in some instances amplify the 1973 statement. Since it is the latest document, the 1975 statement is quoted. The other statements are referred to on the assumption that the FTC did not intend to drop a benefit from consideration because it was not repeated.

13. FTC, 1975, N. 10 *supra,* p. 2.

14. FTC, 1973, N. 2 *supra,* pp. 5–6.

15. Ibid., p. 6.

> persists or is dampened. Line of Business reporting will facilitate such analyses and (perhaps even more important) will mobilize public scrutiny as a check on industrialists who might be tempted to exploit their unleashed [post price and wage controls] market power to raise prices and profits unconscionably.[16]

The data are expected to supplement the statistics used by government agencies. The FTC has explained that various agencies use the FTC's QFR data and that the LB data will "provide a means for the adjustment of the QFR data which [these agencies] use as inputs in their estimation and prediction procedures."[17] In particular, the LB data are expected to provide better predictions of segments of the GNP statistics.

EFFICIENT ALLOCATION OF RESOURCES

"One impact of LB will be to help point out those industries in which demand is inadequately satisfied and as a consequence profits are particularly high. Thus, it will show where existing companies can profitably invest in expanded capacity and new competitors can enter."[18] Lack of LB data is presumed to dull the discipline of the market for investment capital since "the ability of stockholders to exercise this indirect form of discipline is severely impaired by the scrambling of returns for stagnant with dynamic industries in conglomerate corporation reports. Publication of the Line of Business profit data would help stock analysts and ultimately investors make decisions which force managers to use the resources at their command efficiently."[19]

ECONOMIC STUDIES OF INDUSTRY PERFORMANCE

The LB data are expected to be useful for the following analyses:

1. "the efficiency with which markets allocate resources to meet consumer demands" for which "gross margin, contribution margin, and operating income figures [are expected to] measure various dimensions of price structure and profitability"[20]

---

16. Bureau of Economics Staff Report, *Federal Trade Commission Line of Business Reporting Program* (authors identified as Keith Anderson, James M. Folsom, William Levin, William F. Long, Russell Parker, and F. M. Scherer), May 1974, p. 10 (hereinafter cited as Bureau of Economics Staff Report, 1974).

17. FTC, 1973, N. 2 *supra*, pp. 6–7.

18. Bureau of Economics Staff Report, 1974, N. 16 *supra*, p. 7.

19. Ibid., p. 8.

20. FTC, 1975, N. 10 *supra*, p. 2.

2. firms' competitive strategy and conduct in markets which can be discerned with data on media advertising expenditures and other selling expenses[21]
3. the economic performance of industry and its relationship with expenditures on research and development[22] and
4. descriptions of industries, particularly with respect to (*a*) capital intensity, (*b*) cash flows, (*c*) the impact of differing accounting conventions on reported performance measures, (*d*) linkage with census information and the national income accounts through payroll and materials costs[23]

BUSINESS

The LB data are expected to provide information that can be used for the following purposes:

1. evaluation of performance: "Managers and directors of corporations will be able to evaluate the performance of their own enterprises against industry averages."[24]
2. identification of new opportunities: "By pinpointing industries of persistently high profitability, the LB reports will help trigger the search process from which new competitive entry decisions emerge, and thereby contribute to the long-run efficiency of resource allocation."[25]
3. aiding small business firms: "If reliable data were available from a public source . . . small firms would be able to make use of them at minimal cost."[26]
4. aiding buyers of goods and services: "With data on sales, costs, profits and assets, buyers are able to form judgments concerning the appropriateness of price/cost margins and profit rates."[27]

LABOR

The LB data will "facilitate comparisons of labor's share [of total sales and receipts] among different industries. . . . For those companies where laborers are organized on a product, or craft, basis, data on sales, costs, and profits on a line of business basis are essential to the efficient

---

21. Ibid.

22. Ibid.

23. Ibid.

24. Ibid., p. 3.

25. Ibid.

26. FTC, 1973, N. 2 *supra*, p. 2.

27. Ibid.

working of the bargaining process. Organized farm groups have the same need for information in dealing with suppliers and processors."[28]

INVESTORS

"Investment analysts and investors are likely to find the LB reports useful in evaluating the prospects for particular industries."[29] But "when the returns of both profitable and unprofitable ventures are scrambled together in conglomerate corporations' reports, it is much harder for investors to exercise this selectivity so important to the proper allocative functioning of capital markets."[30] (It should be noted that investors presently holding stock in large firms would lose if suppliers, competitors, and labor benefited from the data made public in the LB reports.)

CONSUMERS

Consumers may benefit from the LB reports, if the markets for goods and services and capital are made more efficient. Presumably, these markets do not operate efficiently in the absence of these data.

EVALUATION OF EXPECTED BENEFITS—DATA MEASUREMENT PROBLEMS

To evaluate the benefits expected of the LB program, a series of questions should be answered: (1) Can the specific data the FTC proposes to collect be used to achieve the benefits expected? (2) Can any data of the type the LB program is designed to collect be used beneficially? (3) Are the benefits claimed actually benefits, regardless of data availability and problems? Logically, it would be preferable to answer these questions in reverse order, for if the asserted benefits are not really benefits, data problems are of no consequence. But answers to the questions in the order posed are derived increasingly from philosophically based judgments or empirical assumptions about which equally competent and objective people can disagree. Therefore, it seems preferable to begin with an analysis of the measurement problems that beset the LB program.

Three types of measurement problems can be delineated. First, since the FTC must aggregate the data of a number of firms into clearly defined lines of business, the categories chosen must be sufficiently homogeneous to provide useful data and yet not be so narrow and

---

28. Ibid., p. 3.

29. FTC, 1975, N. 10 *supra*, p. 3.

30. Bureau of Economics Staff Report, 1974, N. 16 *supra*, pp. 7–8.

numerous that they impose excessive burdens on the reporting companies. This is the "classification" problem. Second, since few if any companies record sales, expenses, and assets according to the lines of business defined by the FTC, presently recorded data would have to be allocated meaningfully. This is the "allocation" problem. Third, accounting numbers often provide poor measures of economic values. This is the "valuation" problem. Each of these problems is considered in turn.

Classification Problems

Most of the specific benefits outlined above call for profit data, rates of return, etc.—that is, numbers that refer to markets rather than to industries. In particular, market data are clearly needed for the "antitrust benefit." A good description of this requirement is given by Professor Scherer in his IBM antitrust case testimony: "When we are interested in defining economically meaningful markets we are really interested in defining the boundaries within which competition takes place or does not take place. That is to say, we are concerned with defining the boundaries within which buyers and sellers meaningfully interact in a competitive way."[31] Industry data, which report profit rates, etc., earned by companies who make products that are substitutable in production but not in consumption, clearly would be useless and even misleading. Thus, to use some examples derived from Professor Scherer's IBM testimony,[32] though asphalt paving material and roof shingles may be produced in the same plant and grouped in the same industry, these materials are not substitutes for consumers of road-building materials. For road-building, cement and asphalt are substitutes, but for this comparison, one must take transportation costs into consideration. Thus, relatively high or low rates of return in the paving and roofing materials industry (FTC code 29.02) and in the ready-mixed concrete industry (FTC code 32.11) can tell antitrust investigators little that is not potentially misleading about whether or not to conduct an in-depth investigation.[33]

Market data (as defined by Professor Scherer, above) also are required for macroeconomic inflation studies,[34] efficient allocation of

---

31. F. M. Scherer, "Testimony" in *United States* v. *IBM,* Civ. No. 72-344 (S.D.N.Y. filed Jan. 17, 1969), June 16, 1975, p. 2312.

32. Ibid., pp. 2516–2521, 2668–2672 for examples.

33. However, the ability of producers to enter an industry may provide information about potential competition. For this purpose, knowledge about goods that are substitutes in production may be useful. But without additional information on conversion costs, transportation costs, etc., such data are likely to be misleading.

34. For the moment, the claim that market studies are relevant for the study and control of inflation is not challenged.

resources by producers and investors, economic studies of market performance, evaluation by businessmen of new opportunities, estimates of market profitability by small businessmen, determination of the appropriateness of prices by buyers, and decisions by investors. Indeed, for most of the purposes that the LB data are presumed to serve, the data should refer to specific products and services.

As an example, consider the position of a food manufacturer who is considering entering the market for frozen waffles. The FTC LB category 20.07, frozen specialties, is a relatively homogeneous grouping of products.[35] However, in addition to frozen waffles, it includes other frozen products such as baked foods, dinners, pies, pizza, soups, and spaghetti and meatballs. A high (or low) profit rate on sales or assets for the group might be the result of a very high rate for frozen bread, pizzas, etc., combined with a low rate for frozen waffles because the former markets had few competitors and the latter was declining in consumer favor. If the food manufacturer used these data, a serious mistake to enter or not enter the frozen waffle business would result. Similarly, if others took the data seriously, an antitrust agency would misallocate resources, investors would make poor decisions, food store buyers would feel cheated, and labor leaders might make demands that are contrary to their members' interests. It is vital, therefore, that the data reported be related to markets that are meaningful to the people for whom the data are intended.

The FTC evidently recognized the necessity of collecting and reporting data on markets composed of products and services that are substitutes in consumption. Its 1973 *Statement of Purpose* lists three criteria that should determine the LB categories: "(1) the extent to which they correspond to meaningful economic markets; (2) their competitive significance, as indicated by important dimensions of market structure, such as concentration, and by absolute size; and (3) compatibility with other data sources and with the needs of other public and private users who will use the LB data in conjunction with other data sources." The *Statement* continues: "Of paramount importance in establishing reporting categories is economic meaningfulness. The individual goods and services produced by the company segments which are included in the category should be perceived by buyers as close substitutes for each other. And buyers should view this set of goods or services as poor substitutes, or not substitutes at all, for other goods and services."[36]

---

35. The related 1972 SIC code is 2038. The relative homogeneity of this group may be illustrated by examining the adjacent LB groups. The preceding group (in "Industry Category List for Form LB, 1974"), FTC code 20.06 (SIC code 2037), includes frozen fruits, fruit juices, and vegetables. The next listed group, FTC code 20.08 (SIC code 2033, 4, 5), includes canned fruits and vegetables; preserves, jams, and jellies; diced and dehydrated fruits; vegetables and soup mixes; pickled fruits and vegetables; vegetable sauces and seasonings; and salad dressings.

36. FTC, 1973, N. 2 *supra*, p. 9.

TABLE 1-4

5	(2%)	five-digit or combinations of five-digit SIC categories
132	(48%)	four-digit SIC categories
28	(10%)	combinations of two or more four-digit SIC categories
91	(33%)	three-digit SIC categories
5	(2%)	combinations of two or more three-digit SIC categories
14	(5%)	two-digit and combinations of two or more two-digit SIC categories

Nevertheless, the FTC adopted the SIC classification system to define LB groups even though it recognized that the system had severe limitations. In the words quoted in the *Statement of Purpose:*

> The classification system is not based exclusively on the usage of the product [which] is somewhat of a limitation, since in the economic concept of a market it is immaterial whether products which are substitutable for each other are produced by the same processes or made from the same materials. In some cases, the industry and product definitions are too broad; that is, there are included in the same category products which do not serve the same function and are thus not substitutable for each other. In other cases they are too narrow; that is, a single category fails to include products which are substitutable, for example, metal and glass containers.[37]

However, in order to satisfy the other criteria for selection of LBs (particularly criterion 3, compatibility with other data sources) and perhaps because a manual describing industry and product groups already existed with which many economists and business persons were familiar,[38] they accepted the SIC classification system, with some regroupings.

The latest version, "Industry Category List for FTC Form LB (1974)," calls for companies to report data in 261 manufacturing and 14 nonmanufacturing categories. The categories delineated are combinations of SIC categories, as shown in Table 1-4.[39] Thus, half the LB categories are at the rather high level of aggregation implied by combinations of four-digit, three-digit, and two-digit SICs. The FTC did not require a greater amount of disaggregation because it recognized the burden this would place on respondents and the increased problem of assigning costs and assets. In the FTC's opinion: "The Line of Business categories have

37. Ibid.

38. *Standard Industrial Classification Manual 1972*, Office of Management and Budget, Statistical Policy Division, 1972.

39. The fewer the number of digits, the greater the level of aggregation.

been carefully drawn to strike an optimal balance between richness of detail and minimization of burden."[40]

At least one important expert in the field disagrees strongly. Dr. Betty Bock, Director of Antitrust Research for the Conference Board, analyzed the 223 manufacturing LB categories published by the FTC in April 1975 for the 1974 Form LB. She states that "a detailed analysis of the LB categories made up of single four-digit SIC codes would be likely to show that few, if any, could be directly correlated with markets whose boundaries are not open to serious debate." Since the three-digit and combinations of four-digit groups are even broader, she concludes: "I have come to believe that published data for the LB categories would cause the Commission and all other users to make errors so serious that, if the Commission were to proceed with the program, such users would be well advised to behave as if the data did not exist."[41]

One need not simply take the word of this authority. A reading of the *Standard Industrial Classification Manual* (1972) of the Office of Management and Budget reveals that the categories are rather broad and are based essentially on production rather than consumption similarities. Since the SIC Manual may not be readily available to the reader, Tables 1-5 and 1-6 provide brief descriptions of randomly selected FTC LB categories. To avoid any selection bias, the codes described were chosen from "Industry Category List of FTC Form LB (1974)" as follows: For Table 1-5, the first code was chosen randomly from among the first 20; thereafter every twentieth code was sampled until the list was exhausted. Since this procedure may have inadvertently included too many broad or catchall categories, a sample of four-digit codes only was drawn (Table 1-6). The procedure used was similar to that used for Table 1-5, except that the first observation was chosen randomly from among the first 10 codes; thereafter every tenth observation was sampled.

I hope the reader will agree with me that the condensed descriptions reveal few FTC-defined lines of business that could be considered economically meaningful groupings of products that are substitutes in consumption. Hence, it seems very doubtful that any statistics that relate to those lines of business could provide the benefits envisioned by the FTC.

However, some of the benefits described earlier would relate to production or industries rather than to markets. These presumed benefits would include more efficient allocation of resources if the LB data gave investors better information about the profitability of industries, enhanced economic studies of industry performance, better evaluation

---

40. FTC, Bureau of Economics Staff Memorandum, *1974 Form LB Revision*, July 1, 1975, p. 11 (hereinafter cited as Bureau of Economics Staff Memorandum, 1975).

41. Weil, Gotshal & Manges, N. 8 *supra*, (Affidavit of Betty Bock with respect to proposed 1974 FTC Form LB), p. 8.

TABLE 1-5 Condensed Description of Products Included in Sampled FTC Codes

FTC Code	*Related SIC Code*	*Title*
20.11	2048	prepared feeds and feed ingredients for animals and fowls not elsewhere classified poultry and livestock feed and feed ingredients, such as alfalfa meal, feed supplements, and feed concentrates and feed premixes (pet foods not included)
21.02	212	cigars cigarillos, cigars, stogies
23.06	235, 237, 238, 239	misc. apparel and accessories millinery (womens', misses', childrens', and infants'), hats and caps (of various materials), fur goods (coats, accessories, and trimmings), dress and work gloves except knit and all-leather, robes and dressing gowns (men's and women's), raincoats and other waterproof outer garments (including diaper covers and aprons), leather and sheep-lined clothing, apparel belts, misc. apparel (such as arm bands, academic gowns, garter belts, and prayer shawls), curtains and draperies (fabricated), fabricated house furnishings (such as bedspreads, boat cushions, shower curtains, dust cloths, carpet linings except felt, sheets, slip covers, etc.), textile bags (including laundry and sleeping), canvas and related products (including air cushions, awnings, sails, and tents), pleating and tucking for the trade (decorative, novelty, looping, quilting, stitching, etc.), automotive trimming, apparel findings, etc. (including hatters' fur, luggage linings, shoulder pads, printing and embossing on materials, and trouser waistbands), Schiffli machine embroideries, and other fabricated textile products (such as flags, hammocks, parachutes, pennants, and seat belts)
26.08	2648	stationery, tablets, and related products (made from purchased paper) correspondence-type tablets, desk pads, looseleaf book fillers, notebooks, stationery, boxed writing paper and envelopes, etc.
28.08	part 283	drugs, proprietary a very large number of products primarily advertised or otherwise promoted to the general public
31.02	313, 314	footwear, except rubber; and boot and shoe cut stock and findings

FTC Code	Related SIC Code	Title
		bindings, bows, buckles, heel lifts, laces, soles, house slippers, men's, women's, children's, infants', and babies' footwear, including dress, casual, and work shoes, boots, sandals, etc.
32.18	3293, 3295, 3297, 3299	nonmetallic mineral products not elsewhere classified gaskets, grease retainers, oil seals, packing, washers, ground or otherwise treated minerals and earths (such as barium, blast furnace slag, clay, graphite, mica, shale, and talc), nonclay refractories (clay refractories are classified in FTC code 32.06), and misc. nonmetallic mineral products (such as factory-produced architectural sculptures, art goods, magnesite floor compositions, laminated mica, synthetic stones for gem stones and industrial use, and urns)
34.07	3432	plumbing fixtures fittings and trim (brass goods) plumbers' brass goods, drinking fountain bubblers, metal faucets, lawn hose nozzles, shower rods, metal spigots
35.06	3532	mining machinery and equipment, except oil field machinery and equipment coal breakers, mine cars, mineral cleaning machinery, concentration machinery, core drills, coal cutters, portable rock drills, and rock crushing machinery
35.26	3566	speed changers, industrial high speed drives, and gears power transmission gears, reduction gears and gear units for turbines, speed changers and torque converters, all except for motor vehicles and aircraft
36.09	3632	household refrigerators and freezers home and farm freezers, iceboxes, refrigerator cabinets, and refrigerators
37.01	37111, 37115	passenger cars knocked down or assembled chassis for sale separately, passenger car bodies (trucks and buses are excluded)

TABLE 1-5 Condensed Description of Products Included in Sampled FTC Codes *(Continued)*

FTC Code	*Related SIC Code*	*Title*
38.07	38612	photocopying equipment photocopying equipment (photographic equipment is excluded)
	40, 41, 42, 43, 44, 45, 46, 47, 48, 49	transportation and public utilities line-haul operating railroads, switching and terminal railroads, railway express service, local and suburban passenger transportation, miscellaneous local transportation service (including ambulance service and sightseeing buses), taxicabs, intercity and rural bus lines, bus and car charter services, school buses, bus terminal and maintenance operations, local and long distance trucking services with and without storage, warehousing and storage (refrigerated, household, general, and special)

Source: Selected from "Industry Category List for FTC Form LB (1974)" as follows: first observation selected randomly from first 20 FTC codes on the list; thereafter every twentieth code was sampled until list was exhausted.

of business performance by managers of corporations, pinpointing of profitable industries as investment opportunities, more accurate targeting of industries by labor union bargainers, and better evaluation of a company's performance by present and potential shareholders.

As is the case for market data, production data should be sufficiently homogeneous for the users' purposes. A reading of the contents of the FTC's LB codes, though, reveals that this requirement is not generally met. While many of the products included in an LB code can be made in the same plant or by the same company, few if any plants or companies make all these products. And most plants and companies make other products that are not included in the FTC-defined lines of business. How then can investors use the reported data to decide to invest in nonexistent industries? How can managers compare their plant's performance with industry performance? How can small (or large) corporations decide to enter a high-profit industry or labor unions push hard for wage increases when the reported high profits may be the result of an unknown portion of an FTC-defined "industry"? How can stockholders compare a specific company's performance against the FTC-reported industry performance when no company reports its data publicly according to FTC or SIC codes? It seems unlikely, therefore, that these claimed benefits can be achieved (assuming, for now, that they

TABLE 1-6 Condensed Description of Products Included in FTC Codes—Sampling of Four-Digit SIC Groups

FTC code	*Related SIC code*	*Title and condensed description*
20.10	2047	dog, cat, and other pet food bird food, dog and cat food, horse meat, pet food, slaughtering of nonfood animals
20.23	2083	malt malt, malt by-products, malthouses, sprouts made in malthouses
26.04	2641	paper coating and glazing book paper, bread wrappers, cellophane adhesive tape, coated paper, fancy paper, flypaper, gummed paper and tape, labels, litmus paper, premoistened towelettes, waxed paper, and wrapping paper
28.12	2861	gum and wood chemicals (synthetic organic chemicals and dyes are classified in FTC code 38.13) acetone, calcium acetate, charcoal except activated, dyestuffs, ethyl acetate, dying and tanning extracts, gum naval stores, hardwood distillates, methanol, pine oil, wood patch, rosin, tar and tar oils, turpentine, wood creosote
32.15	3291	abrasive products abrasive buffs, wheels, etc., diamond dressing wheels, emery abrasives, soap-impregnated scouring pads, polishing rouge, sandpaper, steel shot abrasives, whetstones
34.02	3412	metal barrels, drums, and pails (paper containers are classified in FTC code 26.10) shipping containers (barrels, kegs, drums, packages), fluid milk shipping containers, shipping pails other than tinned
34.16	3466	crowns and closures stamped metal bottle caps and tops, jar crowns
35.08	3534	elevators and moving stairways automobile lifts, dumbwaiters, passenger and freight elevators and elevator equipment, passenger and freight escalators
35.19	3554	paper industries machinery bag- and envelope-making machinery, paper-box-making machines, die cutting and stamping machinery, paper folding machines, paper mill machinery, pulp mill machinery, sandpaper manufacturing machines
35.30	3572	typewriters typewriters and parts, including coded media and specialized composing typewriters
36.05	3623	welding apparatus, electric (gas welding apparatus is classified in FTC code 35.15 along with a large variety of metalworking

TABLE 1-6 Condensed Description of Products Included in FTC Codes—Sampling of Four-Digit SIC Groups *(Continued)*

FTC code	*Related SIC code*	*Title and condensed description*
		machinery; laser, electronic beam, and ultrasonic welding apparatus are classified in FTC code 36.20 with radio and TV communication equipment) arc welders and generators, electrodes, resistance welders, transformers, welding wire
36.18	3652	phonograph records and prerecorded magnetic tape phonograph records, preparation of master tapes, prerecorded tapes, record blanks, recording studios
37.08	3724	aircraft engines and engine parts (including research and development) starting vibrators, engines and parts, engine heaters, external power units for hand inertia starters, jet-assisted takeoff devices, aircraft rocket motors, aircraft starters

Source: Selected from "Industry Category List of FTC Form LB (1974)" as follows: first observation selected randomly from first 10 four-digit SIC groups on the list; thereafter every tenth code was sampled until list was exhausted.

are benefits). There remains one further possible benefit from the FTC-SIC line of business data: improved economic studies of industry performance. This possibility is considered further on pages 109–110 below.

Even if proponents of the FTC's LB program insist that the LB categories are sufficiently homogeneous for some purposes, they must contend with the fact that the data actually reported by companies will be even more heterogeneous than the FTC-SIC descriptions. Contamination of the data reported arises because companies do not maintain their accounting records according to SIC categories. The FTC came to understand that the cost to companies of coding sales, transfers, expenditures, assets, etc., by SIC codes would be prohibitive. Therefore, it changed its August 1973 requirement that data be reported by product lines to a requirement that data be reported by basic components. In the FTC's words: "The basic components can be establishments, product lines, profit centers, or other organizational units—which ever strikes the best balance between accuracy of reporting and compliance burden."[42]

This change gives rise to overstatements and understatements of data for individual FTC categories. Where several lines of business are

42. FTC, 1975, N. 10 *supra*, p. 12. The FTC has not stated explicitly how differences of opinion will be resolved about what is the "best balance."

produced by a basic component (as I believe is typical), a company may include a secondary with a primary line, which overstates the primary and understates the secondary line of business. The extent of these overstatements and understatements, at least with respect to revenue, is reduced by an FTC requirement that the primary line's revenues be no less than 85 percent of total establishment revenues.[43] Nevertheless, the actual degree of contamination may be great. Though the Commission's staff reports that its analysis of 1973 LB reports reveals average sales contamination of only 5.6 percent,[44] Betty Bock shows that this figure is misleading, "since it is an average of averages of overstatements in reporting net operating revenues due to primary-secondary product overlap in a limited sample."[45] She estimated separately the degree of overstatements and understatements in the FTC's 261 manufacturing LB categories.[46] Dr. Bock's estimates are reproduced in Table 1-7. This table shows that over a quarter of the categories are likely to be contaminated (overstated, understated, or both) by more than 15 percent with respect to sales. Almost half the categories are likely to be contaminated by more than 10 percent.[47]

Rigorous enforcement of its 85 percent maximum-contamination rule by the FTC may reduce this source of contamination. However, the FTC is not interested in obtaining sales data by lines of business: these data already are available in greater detail than are called for by the FTC's LB categories. Rather it wants to get net profits and assets by lines of business. But there is no way of knowing the extent to which these data will be contaminated as a consequence of permitted primary-secondary product overlap based on net operating revenues.

The hypothetical example in Table 1-8 of a two-product dairy illustrates the problem.[48] Cottage cheese is a dairy product (FTC Code 20.04), but because cottage cheese sales are less than 15 percent of the total, all the sales, production costs, advertising, net profits, and assets of the dairy may be reported under the FTC code for fluid milk (FTC Code 20.03). Even if the FTC knew that fluid-milk sales were overstated

---

43. The specific requirement is much more complex.

44. Bureau of Economics Staff Memorandum, 1975, N. 40 *supra*, p. 13.

45. Betty Bock, "Line of Business Reporting: A Quest for a Snark?," *The Conference Board Record*, vol. 12, no. 11, Nov. 1975, p. 17.

46. The estimates are based on the assumption that all manufacturing companies would report their net operating revenues on an establishment basis. The data used for the analysis are the values of shipments and transfers by four-digit SIC categories as reported by the Bureau of the Census for 1972.

47. Dr. Bock notes that these percentages are likely to be underestimates since they are based on data from all manufacturing companies while the reporting companies will, on the average, be more diversified. Bock, "Line of Business Reporting," pp. 17–18.

48. The example is taken from George J. Benston, "The Baffling New Numbers Game at the FTC," *Fortune*, vol. 92, no. 4, Oct. 1975, p. 176.

TABLE 1-7 Estimates of Primary-Secondary Product Overstatement and Understatement in 261 FTC Manufacturing Categories

	Cumulative percentages of number of categories contaminated		
Degree of contamination, %	*Overstatement*	*Understatement*	*Overstatement, understatement, or both*
More than 25	1	7	8
21–25	5	10	15
16–20	12	18	26
11–15	28	36	48
6–10	64	62	74
2–5	89	82	90
0–1	93	92	93
Not available	7	7	8
Total	100	100	100

Source: Betty Bock, "Line of Business Reporting: A Quest for a Snark?," *The Conference Board Record*, vol. 12, no. 11, Nov. 1975, p. 18.

TABLE 1-8

	Sales	*Production costs*	*Advertising*	*Net profit*	*Assets*
Cottage cheese	$1,000	$870	$10	$120	$1,200
Fluid milk	150	90	30	30	100
Total	$1,150	$960	$40	$150	$1,300
Cottage cheese ÷ fluid milk	15%	10%	300%	25%	8%

Source: George J. Benston, "The Baffling New Numbers Game at the FTC," *Fortune*, vol. 92, no. 4, Oct. 1975, p. 176.

by 15 percent, it could not know that production costs were overstated by 10 percent, advertising by 300 percent, and net profits by 25 percent, or that the profit rate on assets used in making cottage cheese is 30 percent.

Nor are these the only types of contamination. The fact that companies are vertically integrated in different degrees presents the FTC (and other users of corporate data) with serious problems. The intermediate products of a vertically integrated company are similar to final products made by other companies (particularly when similarity is defined as belonging to a specified FTC LB category). Because many vertically integrated companies do not record the costs of these intermediate products as if they were final products, the FTC permits them to combine lines of business. With some exceptions, the rules allow companies to include all data from an earlier (upstream) operation that otherwise would be reported in an LB category in a later (downstream) final manufacturing category. This contamination is permitted if more than 50 percent of the earlier (upstream) category's net operating revenues come from transfers to the later (downstream) category. A similar combination and contamination of data is permitted for backward transfers. Data that otherwise belong in a later (downstream) FTC category beyond the manufacturing level (such as wholesaling) may be combined with data from an earlier (upstream) final manufacturing category. This contamination is permitted if more than 50 percent of the downstream category's net operating revenues are due to the upstream final manufacturing FTC line of business category. As a consequence of these permitted contaminations, not only are the data for a reported LB category contaminated, but also data on other categories may not be reported at all.

Thus, the potential for misleading data being reported is considerable. Dr. Bock used data from a relatively small company having two manufacturing operations, one wholesaling operation, and four FTC-defined lines of business as an illustration.[49] The company manufactures ornamental iron castings, nuts and bolts, and ornamental iron lawn and garden furniture. The castings and furniture are sold wholesale and also are used, with the nuts and bolts, in the furniture manufacture. The company therefore operates in four of the FTC's LB categories: iron and steel foundries (33.02), screw machine products (34.13), household furniture (25.02), and wholesale trade (50.01). It may use any one or a combination of options to report its data in these categories: primary-secondary product combinations (nuts and bolts can be combined with iron and steel foundries); forward integration (ornamental iron castings and nuts and bolts can be reported with household furniture, since the value of the transfers is more than half the net operating revenue of these lines); backward integration (wholesale trade can be reported with household furniture, since more than half the net operating revenues relate to the sale of household furniture); and all options (which permit all revenues to be reported as household furniture). The effect of these options is shown in Table 1-9. Using the actual product data as a base, the permitted reporting options result in net revenues being contaminated by the following percentages: primary-secondary combination—100 percent understatement (nothing reported) of one line and 7 percent overstatement of one line; forward integration—100 percent understatement of two lines and 35 percent overstatement of one line; backward integration—understatements of 100 percent of two lines and 17 percent of one, and 63 percent overstatement of one line; and all options—100 percent understatement of three lines and 73 percent overstatement of the remaining line. Aside from these distortions, the total net revenue reported is greater than the 27.6 of actual revenue by from 27 to 46 percent, except in the "all option"

49. Bock, "Line of Business Reporting," pp. 14–17.

TABLE 1-9 Effect of Alternative Permissible Options on the Reported Net Operating Revenues (Sales plus Transfers) of a Company

		FTC LB category			
Reporting opinions	*Total**	*Iron and steel foundries (FTC 33.02)*	*Screw machine products, etc. (FTC 34.13)*	*Household furniture (FTC 25.02)*	*Wholesale trade (FTC 50.01)*
Actual product data	51.2	18.0	1.2	16.0	16.0
Primary-secondary product combination	51.2	19.2	0.0	16.0	16.0
Forward integration	37.6	0.0	0.0	21.6	16.0
Backward integration	41.2	15.2	0.0	26.0	0.0
All options	27.6	0.0	0.0	27.6	0.0

*Sales outside the firm (excluding intracompany transfers) are 7.2 for ornamental iron castings, 0.4 for nuts and bolts, and 20.0 for furniture, a total of 27.6.

Source: Betty Bock, "Line of Business Reporting: A Quest for a Snark?," *The Conference Board Record,* vol. 12, no. 11, Nov. 1975, p. 15.

case, where there would be no overstatement. Furthermore, there is no way of estimating the effects of these options on the net profits and assets reported for lines of business.

Allocation Problems

Allocation problems arise because multiproduct companies are not simply aggregates of independent single-product companies. Consequently, many operations are jointly organized and there is no conceptual way to assign or allocate many costs to the individual subunits (divisions or departments) and product groups. Activities also tend to be commonly undertaken, with a consequence that there is no practical means of allocating the expenses commonly incurred.

The severity of the allocation problems depends on the nature and organization of production in a particular company. The more a company is vertically integrated, the more critical is the price at which products are transferred from one unit to another. The more it is centralized, the greater is the proportion of expenses that cannot conceptually or practically be allocated to subunits and individual products. Each of these problems is considered next.

INTRACOMPANY TRANSFER

The importance of the price at which intracompany transfers are priced for line of business reporting is described so well in the FTC's 1973 *Statement of Purpose* that it is quoted in its entirety:

> How to handle the pricing of transfers from one part of a company to another part of the same company has been recognized almost universally

as one of the stickiest problems in line of business reporting. It is clearly a problem in the context of the needs of the FTC for line of business data. The reason is that the transfer pricing procedure which is chosen has a direct effect on the relative profits of the two lines of business affected, and, consequently, an indirect effect on measurements of the relative extent to which price exceeds cost.

The choice of a transfer pricing procedure must depend on the expected use of the profit data, of course. *Given the needs of the FTC, it appears that the use of market prices is appropriate. The use of any alternative procedure would distort the measurement of relative profitability.* [Emphasis added] The use of competitive price or cost would have the effect of shifting profits from the industry where they were earned to some other industry.

One difficulty with the use of the market price rule is that the market may be very thin, in the sense that only a small percentage of all the intermediate products in question are exchanged in the market. In fact, there may not be an external market at all. It could be that each producer of a product at a higher stage produces all of some lower stage product which it needs.

Where no market exists, the reason may be that there are such significant real economies of vertical integration that separate production is so inefficient that no one does it. But real economies are not the only conceivable cause for vertical integration, and each situation must be evaluated separately.

There is no question that the problem of the pricing of transfers within a company is theoretically important. Of equal importance is the question of how important the problem is in the real world of business. That question can be answered only with empirical data. Fortunately, one study which contains such data has been published. This study, published by the Financial Executives Research Foundation in 1968, was conducted by Robert K. Mautz. Questionnaires concerning line of business reporting were sent to a large number of companies, with 412 being returned. The number of companies with over one hundred million dollars in sales was 240; 10 to 99 million dollars, 133; 1 to 9 million dollars, 17; and sales not available, 22. The number of companies which were in the Fortune 500 list in manufacturing in 1967 which also responded to the questionnaire was 212. And 26 of Fortune's list of 46 most diversified companies for 1967 were among the respondents.

Responses to a question concerning the magnitude of transfers among organizational units within the reporting company indicated that for 62 percent (of the 404 companies answering the question) the ratio of inter-unit sales to total company sales was between one and five percent. An additional 16.8 percent of the companies reported a ratio between six and ten percent. For all 404 companies, it appears that the average ratio is on the order of seven percent.[50] [Footnote added]

More current data are given in the Bureau of Economics Staff Memorandum, 1975, p. 2: "For the first 224 companies filing 1973 LB reports, transfers amounted to 6.9 percent of total (i.e., internal plus external) sales on the average. For only 24 companies were they more than 15 percent."

The observation that only about seven percent of sales are internal may be misleading. One purpose of the LB Program is to publish data on profitability. Therefore, the impact of internal transfers on profit is also very important. The impact on profits will generally be much larger than the impact on sales.

To illustrate this point, consider a company with two lines of business, one of which transfers some of its output to the other. [See Table 1-10. Since the following text is not very easy to follow, the table was constructed from the data given.]

Call the lines A and B; let the sales of the two lines be 100 and 230, respectively (using market values of the transfers); let the profits of the lines be 10 and 14, respectively; and let A ship 30 percent of its output to B. The ratio of internal sales to external sales would be 10 percent (30 divided by the sum of 70 and 230). For line B to have sales of 230 and profits of 14, its total costs must be 216, of which 30 is for the transfer from A. And the total costs of line A must be 90.

In these circumstances, if the goods which go from A to B are transferred at the cost of 27 instead of the market value of 30, line A will show profits of 7. Its ratio of profits to sales will be shown as 7.2 percent (profits of 7 divided by sales of 97), instead of the correct value of 10 percent. And for line B,

TABLE 1-10 Illustration of the Effect of Alternative Transfer Pricing Methods on Net Profits

	Line of business A		*Line of business B*	
	Market	*"Cost"*	*Market*	*"Cost"*
Amounts				
Sales:				
Outside firm	$ 70	$ 70	$230	$230
Transfer to B	30	27	0	0
Total	$100	$97	$230	$230
Expenses:				
Value added	$ 90	$ 90	$186	$186
Transfers from B	0	0	30	27
Total	$ 90	$ 90	$216	$213
Net profit	$ 10	$ 7	$ 14	$ 17
Assets	$ 67	$ 94	$ 67	$ 94
Percentages				
Net profit/sales	10.0	7.2	6.1	7.4
Net profit/assets	14.9	10.4	14.9	18.1
Percentage changes:				
NP/sales	−2.8/10.0 = −28		1.3/6.1 = 21	
NP/assets	−4.5/14.9 = −30		3.2/14.9 = 21	

Source: Hypothetical example from Federal Trade Commission, *Statement of Purpose: Annual Line of Business Report Program*, Aug. 1973, p. 12.

costs will be reduced to an apparent value of 213, and profits increased by 3, to a value of 17. It will show a ratio of profits to sales of 7.4 percent, whereas the correct value is 6.1 percent.

In this particular illustration, then, the internal sales to external sales ratio of 10 percent is associated with a potential variation of 2.8 percentage points, or 28 percent, for line A, and a potential variation of 1.3 percentage points, or 21 percent, for line B. If the transfer price used fell between cost and the market price, the variations from correct ratios of profits to sales would be smaller, of course.

The result of this crude analysis of the empirical impact of the transfer pricing problem is that the choice of prices can have a significant influence on the measures of performance that are of interest to the FTC. It follows that the specification of a standard pricing technique is essential."[51] [Emphasis added.]

The effect on profit rates of transferring intermediate products at other than market prices among lines of business can also be shown analytically. For a line of business that "sells" an intermediate product, the following symbols are defined:

S = sales to markets outside the firm, in dollars

T = transfers to other line of business, in dollars, when goods are transferred at market prices

m = markup or markdown from market price, in percentages (i.e., if transfer is at average cost and average cost is 80% of market, m = 0.8)

C = costs of goods sold and transferred, in dollars

ps = profit rate on sales

$$ps = \frac{S + Tm - C}{S + Tm} \qquad (1)$$

where t = transferred goods as a percentage of sales to outside markets, when transfers are priced at market ($m = 1$).[52]

$$t = (T/S)|m = 1 \qquad T = tS \qquad (2)$$

where c = cost as a percentage of sales when transfers are priced at market ($m = 1$).

$$c = C/(S + T)|m = 1 \qquad C = c(S + T) \qquad C = c(S + tS) \qquad (3)$$

Substituting eq. (2) and eq. (3) into eq. (1) yields:

$$ps = \frac{S + tSm - c(S + tS)}{S + tSm}$$

---

51. FTC, 1973, N. 2 *supra*, pp. 11–12 (emphasis added).

52. The ratio of transfer sales to total sales ($S + T$) can be used in the analysis by substituting $t/(1 + t)$ for t in the equations.

$$ps = \frac{S(1 + tm - c - ct)}{S(1 + tm)}$$

$$ps = 1 - c\left(\frac{1 + t}{1 + tm}\right) \tag{4}$$

Thus, the key variables are seen to be m, the percentage deviation from market, and t, the relative amount of goods transferred. The larger is t and the less (or more) is m than 1, the greater is the reduction (or increase) of the measured profit rate on sales, ps, and its "true" value.

The effect of nonmarket price transfers on the asset yield (net profit/assets = pa) is related to the profit rate on sales, ps, by the ratio of total sales ($S + T$) to assets (A): $pa = ps \cdot (S + T)/A$, when $m = 1$. As the following formula shows transfers priced at less than market ($m < 1$) that reduce ps, reduce pa additionally:

$$pa = \frac{ps(S + Tm)}{A}$$

$$pa = \frac{ps(S + T)}{A} - \frac{psT(1 - m)}{A} \tag{5}$$

The additional effect on pa, though, is likely to be small.

As an illustration of the application of eq. (4), consider a line of business where the profit rate on outside sales is 0.20 ($ps = 0.20$, $c = 0.80$), transfer "sales" amount to 0.30 percent of outside sales ($t = .3$), and transfer prices are set at variable costs, which amount to 0.60 of total costs ($m = 0.60 \cdot 0.80 = 0.48$). Plugging these values into eq. (4) yields a reported profit rate of 0.09, a reduction of 55 percent of the "true" (outside) net profit/sales. If transfer prices were set closer to market, at, say, full costs ($m = c = .80$), the reported profit rate on sales would be 0.12 rather than 0.20, a reduction of 40 percent. Thus, transfer prices below market can change an apparently high to an apparently low or moderate profit rate line of business.

The transfer price also affects the reported profit of the line of business to which the goods are transferred. The formula that can be used to analyze this effect is developed with the symbols defined above plus the following:

C = cost of goods sold

$C = T + V$

where T = transferred costs from other lines of business, in dollars, when goods are transferred at market prices ($m = 1$) (same definition as above).

V = value added, in dollars

x = the percentage of cost of goods that are transferred costs

$$x = T/C \qquad T = xC \qquad V = (1 - x)C \tag{6}$$

ps = profit rate on sales

$$ps = \frac{S - C}{S}$$

or

$$ps = \frac{S - Tm - V}{S} \tag{7}$$

Substituting eq. (6) into eq. (7) yields

$$\begin{aligned} ps &= \frac{S - xCm - (1 - x)C}{S} \\ &= \frac{1 - xCm}{S} - \frac{(1 - x)C}{S} \\ &= 1 - xCm - (1 - x)C \end{aligned} \tag{8}$$

(Since the relationship between net profits/assets, pa, and net profits/sales, ps, is not affected by transfer prices, the percentage effect of nonmarket transfers is the same for both profitability measures.) Thus, the key variables are m and x, the relative deviations of transfer prices from market and the relative amount of transferred goods used in production. As an example, consider a line of business where $m = 0.48$ (as above), $x = .30$ and $c = .80$. The reported profit rate on sales, ps, then would be 0.32 rather than 0.20, were transfers priced at market. Net profits/assets, pa, also would be reported as 60 percent higher. Were the transfers priced at average cost, $m = c = 0.80$, the ps reported would be 0.25. Thus, a less-than-market transfer price may significantly increase the reported profit rate on sales or assets of a receiving line of business. It seems likely that these distortions in performance measures would be significant for many companies from whom line of business reports are demanded.

Although the FTC clearly is aware of the impact of non-market-derived transfer prices on performance measures, it permits companies to use any method of pricing transfers they wish. This concession was made because many (perhaps most) companies do not transfer goods at market prices, in part because market prices are not available for many intermediate products. The FTC hopes to adjust the data for this distortion in two ways. First, to "minimize any distorting effects of divergent intracompany, interline transfer pricing conventions, instructions are provided concerning the integration of vertically related activities. These permit integration where the majority of an activity's sales are to other company units. For certain industries with especially significant vertical transfer volumes, specific integration guidelines are stated."[53] Second, the amount of transfers and the percentages priced at "market," "cost plus mark up," "cost,"[54] and "other—specify" is called for in the reports. Apparently, these data will be used to estimate the importance and magnitudes of transfer pricing alternatives. Since the FTC has not specified how it intends to make these estimates, their effectiveness cannot be evaluated.[55]

In any event, it is doubtful that these procedures can correct the transfer pricing problem without creating possibly even more serious problems. Required integration of lines of business will eliminate the distorting effect of nonmarket transfer prices, but also will eliminate the information on intermediate lines of business. The sales that permit backward (upstream) and forward (downstream) integration of lines of business also obviate the need for pricing transfer but, as discussed earlier, also eliminate or distort the data reported on the lines of business affected. The contamination that results from these "solutions" may be more serious than the distortions that would have been caused by nonmarket transfer prices. In addition, companies who fear that their reported figures will be used against them might use the permissible reporting options to obviate this danger.

ALLOCATIONS OF COMMON AND JOINT EXPENSES AND ASSETS

Though all multiproduct companies may not transfer products at other than market prices, all incur costs that apply to more than one line of business. Indeed, were it not for economies of common or joint production and distribution, it is doubtful that there would be multiproduct companies. The FTC recognizes this situation, but it states: "The underlying assumption is that operating profit is a useful and informative magnitude for analyzing segmented performance, that allocations must be made to derive it."[56] Before the FTC's "solution" is evaluated, the nature of the problem is outlined.

Common and joint costs are found at several levels of a company. Corporate headquarters expenses are incurred to manage the entire company. If the company is organized into divisions, divisional headquarters expenses are incurred to manage plants, general product lines, geographical areas, etc., depending on the particular organization form or forms adopted. Even within a plant, the cost of maintaining and

---

53. FTC, 1975, N. 10 *supra*, p. 13.

54. "Cost" is not further defined. (It could refer to average, variable, prime, direct, marginal, etc.)

55. An analysis of the effectiveness of dummy variable statistical techniques and of sensitivity analysis for correcting measurement errors and biases is presented below, pp. 109–110.

56. Bureau of Economics Staff Memorandum, 1975, N. 40 *supra*, p. 5.

using the building may be common to the individual products produced therein. Concurrently, investments in the shared facilities relate to the several products.

Though it is conceptually impossible to allocate joint costs to individual activities or products, some common costs, such as the services of headquarters staff, could be charged to the products or lines of business for which the costs were incurred. This direct assignment is not done often in practice because, at the margin, the cost of analysis and bookkeeping often exceeds the value of the information to the company. Even when direct assignment of common costs is worthwhile, the amount charged should be the opportunity cost of the services, the amounts that would not have been incurred had the headquarters services, etc., not been called for. Where the incurrence of these common costs is subject to economies of scale and externalities, the amounts that should be charged to individual products, etc., would not equal the total common costs incurred. (The existence of scale economies and positive externalities is expected, since these are reasons for the existence of multiproduct companies.)

Other common costs, such as most general and administrative expenses, cannot be unambiguously charged to products (or lines of business) because companies usually do not know their functional relationship. While these costs may vary generally with output over time and over wide ranges of output, the extent to which a given element or group of expenses is incurred because a specific product is produced is very difficult, if not conceptually impossible, to measure. Direct engineering-type measurements are difficult and often impossible to make, and, generally, too few observations are available for statistical analysis.

Joint costs are of two types, those that are measured when products are produced in fixed proportions, and fixed period costs that are incurred regardless of the type or amount of production. The first type occurs as a consequence of the requirements of a production process, as where coke and coal tars are jointly produced from coal. In these cases there is no conceptual way to assign the cost of production to one product or another since both *must* be produced. The second type of joint cost (such as the cost of lighting and heating a multiproduct factory that can only be totally opened or closed) also cannot be assigned by concept to the products produced if, within a range of production, the cost will not vary as a consequence of a change in the production of the individual products.[57]

---

57. The FTC incorrectly states: "There are instances in which two or more distinguishable products are produced jointly by a single production process. When that is the case, it *may* not make good economic sense to attempt to assign to each of the products a share of the costs of the resources which are used in the joint production." See FTC, 1973, N. 2 *supra*, pp. 12–13 (emphasis added).

In practice, companies often arbitrarily assign common and joint costs to divisions and units of output. The primary reasons for these allocations are the rules imposed by the Internal Revenue Service, the SEC, and other authorities who require allocations of all manufacturing costs to inventories. Although a large body of professional accounting opinion supports only the assignment of variable (direct) costs to inventories, in general this practice is not accepted by the regulatory authorities. A secondary reason for allocations is control. Many companies apparently believe that they can better inform divisional and production managers of the importance of common and joint "overhead" costs and give them an incentive to monitor these costs if the cost items appear on the managers' budgets and accounting reports. However, many companies do not allocate common or joint costs to divisions and products, because they recognize that there is no conceptual basis for the allocations.

In any event, where common and joint costs do not vary in a measurable way with respect to output, assignment of these costs to output is dysfunctional, particularly for pricing decisions. It is not true, as the FTC states, that because "it is necessary to price the products separately, . . . some procedure *must* be developed to apportion the common costs among the products."[58] Furthermore, the profitability of a line of business cannot be determined by allocating nontraceable common and joint costs. When a multiproduct company is not just a linear combination of separate lines of business, this calculation can be made only by estimating the revenues and expenses that would be foregone were the line of business dropped or expanded. The results of this calculation will differ among companies and at different times for the same company since neither the existence nor the effect of alternative opportunities is stable. In addition, one must know and be able to quantify the consequence of the alternative opportunities to calculate the profitability of a segment of business.

Considering the conceptual impossibility of allocating common and joint costs meaningfully to lines of business, it would seem preferable to call only for the lines' contribution margins to the enterprise (revenues less directly chargeable expenses). Indeed, this is the approach currently permitted by the SEC. However, companies follow dissimilar practices in charging expenses directly to lines of business. In general, the more decentralized a company is, the more likely it is to charge such expenses as accounting, marketing, and general administration to lines of business. Some companies charge departments for central services on a usage basis; others do not allocate these expenses at all. Therefore, contribution margin profits are likely to differ among companies solely because of their form of organization or accounting practices.

---

58. FTC, 1973, N. 2 *supra*, p. 3 (emphasis added).

The only answer to the objection raised above would be an empirically based conclusion that there really is no problem, that nondirect costs are so small a proportion of total costs that reported net profits would not be significantly distorted by arbitrary allocation procedures. At present, the only publicly available data on this question is provided by Robert Mautz and Fred Skousen.[59] Their findings of the amount of noninventoriable common costs (excluding income taxes) and of net income relative to sales for the 255 companies surveyed are presented in Table 1-11.

The average percentage of common costs to sales is 7.8 percent, and the average percentage of net income to sales is 6.3. Thus, the data presented in the table indicate that common costs are likely to be significant. Furthermore, the Mautz and Skousen definition of common costs used may understate the problem. While interest is included in noninventoriable costs (which the FTC does not ask companies to allocate to lines of business), common and joint manufacturing costs that are allocated arbitrarily to inventory are not included. In addition, the lines of business defined by the companies surveyed are likely to be broader than the FTC's LB categories, hence proportionately fewer overhead costs have to be allocated.

Dr. Mautz's survey also provides evidence that many companies do not allocate common costs to product lines and those that do follow divergent procedures. Of the companies for whom the costs are "relevant and common," 40 percent do not allocate general and administrative expenses, 44 percent do not allocate research expense, 46 percent do not allocate product development expense, and 52 percent do not allocate institutional advertising.[60] The balance of the companies use a large number of bases and combination of bases to allocate common costs. The most prevelant base is sales, used by 31 percent of the companies to allocate general and administrative expenses, by 22 percent to allocate research, by 19 percent to allocate product development, and by 30 percent to allocate institutional advertising.[61] Some nine other bases are listed by Mautz, including assets, specific costs or expenses, and physical measure, plus a large "other" category.

Because there is no conceptually correct or practical way to allocate common costs to product lines, the FTC permits companies to use whatever bases they wish. It states: "The staff intends to place great stress on testing the sensitivity of reported operating income to the

---

59. Robert Mautz and Fred Skousen, "Common Cost Allocation in Diversified Companies," *Financial Executive,* vol. 36, no. 6, June 1968, pp. 15–17, 19–25. This is the same data as given in Robert Mautz, *Financial Reporting by Diversified Companies,* Financial Executive Institute, New York, 1968.

60. Mautz, op. cit., schedule 38.

61. Ibid., schedule 39.

TABLE 1-11 Ratios of Noninventoriable Common Costs (Excluding Income Tax) and Net Income to Sales for 255 Companies

Common costs and net income as a percentage of sales	*Percentage distribution of companies*			
	Common costs		*Net income*	
	Percentage	*Cumulative*	*Percentage*	*Cumulative*
1–4	40	40	34	34
5–8	28	68	45	79
9–12	14	82	14	93
13–16	7	89	5	98
17–20	5	94	1	99
21–24	3	97	1	100
25–30+	3	100	0	100

Source: Robert Mautz and Fred Skousen, "Common Cost Allocation in Diversified Companies," *Financial Executive,* vol. 36, no. 6, June 1968, table 1-A, p. 17.

application of plausible alternative formulas."[62] The Mautz and Skousen study provides data from which one can calculate the sensitivity of net profits/sales and net profits/assets to alternative allocations of common costs. Since these costs include interest but exclude income taxes and inventoriable common and joint costs and since the business segments probably are broader and more homogeneous than those chosen by the FTC, the data speak but imperfectly to the question. But they are all that now are available.

Mautz and Skousen obtained data from six companies that permitted them to measure the effect on net income (before income taxes) by company-determined business segments from using alternative bases to allocate noninventoriable common costs. Though the sample was not randomly selected, they state: "Together the six companies represent a broad cross-section of American industry. They illustrate various degrees of management centralization, differing kinds and extent of diversification, and different approaches to segmentation for internal reporting purposes."[63] Table 1-12 gives the net profit amounts as a percentage of assets that result when common costs are allocated according to commonly used alternative bases.[64] The second column of the table provides a measure of the relative effect of the range of the different net profits/assets divided by the net profits/assets determined by the companies (marked with asterisks).[65]

---

62. Bureau of Economics Staff Memorandum, 1975, N. 40 *supra,* p. 15.

63. Mautz and Skousen, op cit., p. 19.

64. Assets by line of business are not given in Mautz and Skousen, op. cit., but can be estimated from their data. A table of net profits/sales by line of business also was constructed. Since the numbers are very similar in relative magnitudes to those presented in Table 1-12, it is not reproduced here.

65. Since the allocation base used by the companies does not always yield the lowest rate of return, the measure of relative range presented is not as great as it could be.

TABLE 1-12 Net Profits before Income Taxes on Assets (NP/A) in Six Companies

		Bases for allocating noninventoriable common costs					
						Other*	
Net profits/assets	*Range as % of net profits/assets per company*	*Sales*	*Total assets*	*Number of employees*	*Gross profit*	*Type 1*	*Type 2*
Company A—Overall 13%							
Segment 1	41.5	8.9	12.3*	13.5	13.8	12.9	
Segment 2	29.1	11.9	11.7*	8.5	8.8	10.1	
Segment 3	23.1	19.2	15.6*	18.9	18.2	17.2	
Company B							
Segment 1	12.6	12.8	12.8	14.1		12.7*	12.5
Segment 2	472.2	1.3	1.6	(5.3)		1.8*	3.2
Segment 3	481.1	(2.8)	(4.7)	(20.6)		(3.7)*	(3.7)
Segment 4	152.8	(5.8)	(4.2)	(9.1)		(3.6)*	(4.2)
Company C							
Segment 1	10.9	22.0	22.0	23.2	20.9	21.1*	
Segment 2	8.5	32.7	34.6	35.6	33.0	34.1*	
Segment 3	842.9	3.3	2.9	2.1	6.6	0.7*	
Segment 4	30.7	26.8	26.5	22.3	26.8	32.2*	
Segment 5	52.8	6.4	7.2	5.9	9.4	12.5*	
Segment 6	260.5	(1.0)	(2.0)	(6.1)	0.0	3.8*	
Segment 7	409.1	5.6	2.5	2.9	4.6	1.1*	
Segment 8	10.6	22.3	22.0	21.8	23.0	20.8*	
Segment 9	181.9	17.5	22.6	23.6	16.4	(27.6)*	
Company D							
Segment 1	7.6	15.9	17.2		16.9	17.1*	17.2
Segment 2	3.3	15.4	15.1		14.9	15.1*	15.2
Segment 3	2.5	15.9	15.8		16.2	15.8*	15.9
Segment 4	3.1	20.0	19.6		19.7	19.6*	19.4
Company E							
Segment 1	7.4	7.8	7.8	8.4	8.4	8.1*	
Segment 2	12.4	8.7	8.5	9.6	9.3	8.9*	
Segment 3	18.3	23.5	24.8	20.6	23.5	23.0*	
Segment 4	7.4	9.6	9.3	9.5	10.0	9.5*	
Segment 5	15.1	11.5	11.5	10.9	9.8	11.3*	
Company F							
Segment 1	12.7	19.2	20.2	21.3		22.0*	20.6
Segment 2	10.2	18.8	19.2	17.7		19.6*	19.7
Segment 3	36.0	4.0	5.1	3.3		5.0*	4.9
Segment 4	11.6	8.5	9.6	9.1		9.5*	9.0
Segment 5	73.7	3.3	2.5	3.1		1.9*	2.4

*Other methods: Company A, capital investment in segment for current year; Company B, Type 1, combination of effort and selected payroll dollars; Type 2, fixed assets; Company C, amounts proportionate to directly related expenses; Company D, Type 1, combination of sales and investment; Type 2, net profit (before taxes); Company E, Massachusetts formula; Company F, Type 1, percentage of sales which varies for different segments; Type 2, investment.

Source: Robert Mautz and Fred Skousen, "Common Cost Allocation in Diversified Companies," *Financial Executive*, vol. 36, no. 6, June 1968, tables 3, 6, and 7.

Several conclusions can be drawn from Table 1-12.[66] First, the use of alternative, acceptable bases for allocating common costs yields a considerable variance in net profits/assets. Taking each of the thirty lines of business as an observation, the differences expressed as a percentage of the amount determined by each company's preferred allocation base may be summarized as follows: 0–5%—3 lines (10%); 6–10%—4 lines (13%); 11–20%—9 lines (30%); 21–40%—4 lines (13%); 41–60%—2 lines (7%); 61–80%—1 line (3%); 141–843%—7 lines (23%). However, Company D has an unusually low percentage of common costs to sales of 0.5 percent.[67] (The other companies' percentages range from 5.2 to 2.0 percent.) Also the divisor of Company C's line 3 is very small, which results in a very large percentage difference over the company's preferred allocation method. With these five observations removed, there are no observations in the 0–5 percent category, three instead of four lines in the 6–10 percent category, and six instead of seven lines in the over 141 percent category. Second, the use of alternative allocation bases is likely to affect adversely decisions based on the numbers. When one considers that a difference of a few percentage points may determine whether funds are borrowed and a project undertaken or whether or not a company is charged with monopolistic or predatory pricing behavior, the differences revealed in Table 1-12 appear significant. Finally, the generally wide range of net profits/assets over lines within each company, no matter which allocation method is used, indicates that the accuracy and meaning of this sort of data should be questioned. In particular, is it likely that a company would continue to operate lines of business that yield negative rates of return? Either these data are seriously incorrect or there are unstated joint demands and costs among lines that make the negative return lines actually profitable and the high rate of return lines not as profitable as they appear. If a user of the data did not realize this, very poor decisions might be made. If the user did realize this, of what value would these data be?

Aside from the probable understatement of the magnitudes of the common cost allocations that would be required for the FTC's LB program, the Mautz and Skousen data do not include another, possibly even more important measurement problem: allocation of assets among lines of business. Since a major purpose of the LB program is measurement of comparative profitability of lines of business, it is clear that a most (perhaps *the* most) important number is net profits/assets. (Differences in net profits/sales among lines of business and companies may reflect only differences in vertical integration and differences in the

---

66. The conclusions also apply to net profits/sales, which were calculated but are not presented.

67. The percentage for the two years prior to the study is 1 percent. Mautz and Skousen, op. cit., table 3.

amount of assets invested per unit of time.)[68] But this calculation requires companies to assign directly used assets and to allocate commonly used assets to the FTC-defined lines of business.

Allocation of assets presents companies with an even greater problem than the requirement that they report product sales and costs by lines of business since productive assets (such as machinery and buildings) rarely are recorded as "belonging" to specific products (unless they produce only one product). Furthermore, commonly used facilities (such as plant-site roads and railroad tracks) rarely can be meaningfully related to specific products produced. In addition, corporate headquarters facilities and current assets may not be assigned or assignable to individual lines of business. For a fairly large proportion of assets, then, allocations to lines of business must be arbitrary. As a result, the reported net profits/assets of individual lines of business must be arbitrary.[69]

An additional problem is that the reported assets are year-end numbers. Many businesses end their fiscal year at the time when their inventories and/or receivables are lowest (at the trough of their annual business cycle). For these companies, the year-end-asset amounts understate the investment to which net profits should be related, thus overstating the profitability measure, net profits/assets.

Accounting Numbers and Economic Values

The "specific benefits" described previously are based on the assumption that the LB data provide meaningful estimates of economic values. Expenses should reflect the opportunity costs of earning the revenue reported. Assets should be stated at the cost of replacing their productive potential.[70] It is well known, though, that many of the accounting numbers that will be reported in the LB reports measure economic values very poorly. Therefore, unless the magnitudes of the divergence between economic values and the numbers reported is relatively small or can be adjusted, the LB figures will be misleading or meaningless.

Two of the variables on which the FTC apparently intends to concentrate, advertising and business promotion (A&BP) and research and development (R&D), are among those accounting-based measurements that most seriously diverge from economic values. Accountants charge virtually all expenditures for these items (and other expenditures for

---

68. For example, though the profit margin (net profits/sales) of a piano retailer is greater than that of a food retailer, it would be incorrect to conclude from this number that one is and the other is not "profitable."

69. The effect on net profits/assets of a measurement error in assets is $1/(1 + e)$ where e is the percentage error in measuring assets. Thus a 20 percent understatement of assets results in a 25 percent overstatement of net profits/assets.

70. These economic values will be referred to as the "correct" numbers.

intangibles) to current expenses even though it is recognized that much of the expenditures have future value, i.e., they are assets. Consequently, a company that engaged heavily in past A&BP and/or in R&D will understate its assets and overstate its current expenses. Its current profit, therefore, will tend to be higher than it would be were the accounting "correct," unless the expiration of past expensed amounts exceeded current expenditures. But since past A&BP and R&D were expensed, the assets of such companies would be lower and net profits/assets could be higher or lower than would be the case were the numbers "correct," depending on the magnitudes and timing and past and present expenditures and the periodic decline in their present values.

The valuation of inventories at historical cost is another important divergence between accounting numbers and economic values, particularly in a period when prices are not stable. If prices are increasing and if inventories are recorded at first-in first-out (FIFO), the asset (inventory) will be stated approximately at its economic value, but the cost of goods sold will be understated. If inventories are stated at last-in first-out (LIFO), the reverse will be the case, and if inventory costs have been increasing for a number of years, the asset value can be very seriously understated. Though companies subject to the Securities Exchange Act of 1934 now have to disclose the replacement values of their LIFO inventories, the FTC has not required them to record inventories at current values: The companies only have to indicate the percentages of their inventories that are recorded on different bases. Perhaps one reason for the FTC's instructions may be that many (possibly most) companies can only estimate the replacement values of total inventories, since they record their product inventories at FIFO or average cost and reduce total inventories to the LIFO basis with a central "inventory adjustment" account.

The amounts recorded for fixed assets and depreciation is a third major divergence between accounting numbers and economic values. These long-lived assets are recorded at the amounts expended for them at the price levels in effect at the time they were purchased. The amounts charged to annual production costs and expenses are determined by depreciation rules that often poorly reflect the economic cost of using assets (the change in the assets' present values). While the SEC is attempting to correct this situation somewhat by requiring large[71] companies to state their fixed assets at replacement cost, it is not at all clear that this can be done. Many assets would not be replaced as they were originally produced, and determining the value of alternative

---

71. Companies whose inventories and gross property, plant, and equipment (i.e., before deduction of accumulated depreciation, etc.) are more than $100 million and more than 10 percent of total assets (Securities and Exchange Commission, Accounting Release No. 190, March 23, 1976).

assets that would produce an equivalent quality and quantity of output may be impossible or very expensive. A price index procedure, therefore, is favored by many companies, although they recognize that the results of its application might be very inexact. It is generally acknowledged, though, that a restatement of fixed assets as some estimate of current value is likely to have a significant effect on reported net profits and net profits/assets.

The recording of assets and expenses at historically determined amounts also is responsible for another serious error: The costs of using natural resources or goods supplied subject to a fixed long-term contract are recorded at their original (historical) cost, not at their present (opportunity) cost. Hence, a coal mine operator records cost of coal sold as a function of the original cost of the mine; a company that uses natural gas supplied in accordance with a pre-OPEC-boycott-negotiated price records its cost of use at noncurrent prices, etc. Therefore, a user of the FTC's LB data may draw the misleading conclusion that an industry (such as coal mining or petrochemicals) is earning supernormal operating profits, when actually the reported profits are the result of a windfall caused by an unexpected change in some aspect of the economy.

These divergences of accounting numbers from economic values (and many others that could be listed) may seriously bias the reported LB data. It is not sufficient for the FTC to point out that business publications, such as *Forbes* and *Business Week,* publish accounting reports or draw inferences from them.[72] Aside from the fact that there is no evidence that these "authorities" present accounting data in meaningful ways, the numbers published generally compare individual firms as wholes over time. The FTC could have mentioned that business executives also use accounting numbers to evaluate the performance of their subordinates and to make pricing, output, and capital budgeting decisions. However, it then would have to recognize that business executives can informally adjust the data to account for divergences from economic values, because they are intimately familiar with their enterprise, its accounting system, and environment.

This familiarity is not usually shared by the government economist or other similar potential user of the LB data. Therefore, though the FTC correctly states, " . . . in using financial performance information, a government agency does have an obligation to understand its limitations,"[73] it is not clear how this knowledge can be obtained.

The only remaining procedure for dealing with the accounting data problem and the measurement problems discussed above is to correct the data judgmentally or statistically or hope that the errors are rela-

---

72. Bureau of Economics Staff Memorandum, 1975, N. 40 *supra,* p. 15.

73. Ibid.

tively small. Before consideration is given to the adjustment procedures mentioned by the FTC, some indication of the magnitude of the errors will be attempted.

Magnitude of the Data Measurement Problems

The data measurement problems to which the FTC's LB program is subject may obviate the program's presumed benefits. Since the data requirements for industry studies are the least stringent, and since the SIC contamination problems (discussed above) least affect this "benefit," it appears best to begin with it. If the expected measurement problems are of too great a magnitude for industry studies, they would be too great for the other "benefits."

Though contamination problems affect industry studies less than those analyses requiring market data, the LB categories of the FTC-SIC have serious shortcomings. First, the categories are very imperfect descriptions of "industries" in which goods included are substitutes in production (see previous discussion and Tables 1-5 and 1-6). Second, industry studies require a comparable time series for longitudinal studies so that time-determined random measurement errors can be averaged out and cross-sectional analyses replicated. However, the SIC categories are not stable over time. Dr. Bock compared the Department of the Census' 1947 SIC codes with those for 1972. She reports: "Although the Bureau of the Census reported data for 439 industry categories both in 1947 and in 1972, only 146 categories [33 percent] remained definitionally comparable over the period."[74] The further contamination of FTC-SIC groups permitted by the FTC (up to 85 percent for sales plus unknown amounts of costs and upstream and downstream combinations) results in additional problems, including the shifting of companies from one "industry" to another as the production in a plant changes from one type of output to another.

Some economists and others who want to do industry analyses appear willing to overlook the classification and contamination problems which others believe invalidate studies based on SIC data.[75] But even if the SIC definitions of industries are accepted, the problems of measuring net income and assets by these lines of business remain. The seriousness of the measurement errors can be estimated by reference to the magnitudes of the numbers used by economists in industry studies. The number of these studies is quite large: Leonard Weiss outlines 47 studies of industrial industries in his comprehensive review of the

---

74. Betty Bock, "New Numbers on Concentration: Fears and Fact," *The Conference Board Record*, vol. 13, no. 3, March 1976, p. 20.

75. Examples of this criticism may be found in Ibid., and in John S. McGee, "Efficiency and Economies of Scale," Harvey J. Goldschmid, M. Michael Mann, and J. Fred Weston (eds.), *Industrial Concentration: The New Learning*, Little, Brown, Boston, 1974, pp. 101–104.

literature, mentions eight more in a footnote, and adds a new study presented in his paper.[76] Therefore, the findings of only a few of the more prominent, wide-ranging, or recent studies are reported here.[77]

The yields on equity (net profits after tax/equity) as a function of concentration (*CR*) is analyzed in a number of studies. Table 1-13 summarizes six of these.

The coefficients of *CR* computed are multiplied against three possible changes in concentration. The first value, 76 or 50, is the extreme value of *CR* in the data analyzed (except for Weiss's regressions, where the distribution of the data is not given). The other values illustrate fairly large changes in concentration. Thus, an extremely concentrated (compared to a nonconcentrated) industry might have as much as a 9 percent difference in net profits after tax/equity.

Other studies provide additional data on the possible magnitudes of differences in equity yield and asset yield (net profits after tax plus interest/assets). The data from five studies covering seven time periods that compare the average yields on equity and assets associated with industries grouped according to concentration ratios are displayed in Table 1-14. The maximum differences in equity yields range from 4.3 to 5.3 percent. The maximum differences in asset yields are 1.3 and 4.2 percent. Table 1-15 displays a similar comparison derived from four studies of the relationship between barriers to entry and the after-tax yield on equity. The maximum differences range from 1.2 to 6.5 percent.

Most of these data are derived from periods before the conglomerate movement that the FTC says masked corporate data and motivated it to undertake the line of business program. Though they are not completely comparable to the LB data (neither interest, taxes, or equity is allocated to lines of business), these data may provide some indication of the magnitudes against which measurement errors might be compared. If before-tax yields are approximated by doubling the maximum differences in yields given in Tables 1-14 and 1-15, the maximum overall difference in concentration between industries with "very high" and "moderate to low barriers to entry" is 13 percent. The regression studies summarized in Table 1-13 show a maximum before-tax equity yield difference of 18 percent associated with an increase in concentration of 76 percent. These numbers are extremes.

---

76. Leonard Weiss, "The Concentration-Profits Relationship and Antitrust," in Goldschmid et al. (eds.), op. cit., pp. 201, 204–220.

77. Relatively large-scale studies by Stigler and Brozen are not summarized because they did not find a significant or positive difference in yields associated with greater concentration ratios. George J. Stigler, *Capital and Rates of Return in Manufacturing Industries,* National Bureau of Economic Research, Princeton, N.J., 1963, and Yale Brozen, "Concentration and Profits: Does Concentration Matter?" in J. Fred Weston and Stanley I. Ornstein (eds.), *The Impact of Large Firms on the U.S. Economy,* Lexington Books, Heath, Lexington, Mass., 1973, pp. 59–70.

TABLE 1-13 Regression Studies of Net Profits after Taxes/Equity as a Function of Concentration (CR = Eight-Firm Concentration Ratio)

		Predicted effect of concentration on performance measure		
Study	*Period and data*	*ΔCR = 76**	*ΔCR = 50*	*ΔCR = 25*
Weiss [1971]†	1947–1951 Bain's [1956] 20-industry data	4.6 to 8.9‡	3.0 to 6.0‡	1.5 to 3.0‡
	1900–1960 Mann's [1966] 30-industry data	3.6 to 7.7‡	2.4 to 5.2‡	1.2 to 2.6‡
Sherman [1968]	1958 20 two-digit industries	7.6	5.0	2.5
Weiss [1963]	1948–1958 22 two-digit industries	§	4.5	2.3

*Since the concentration ratios used are not given by Weiss or Bain, the maximum difference found by Sherman is used.

†The regression that uses Bain's pre-World War II data is not shown.

‡The regressions include three dummy variables which equal one or zero depending on whether barriers to entry are low to moderate, substantial, or high. The numbers given are for the extreme values.

§The range of *CR* (a weighted average) is 53.4. The other variable in the regression is output growth, 1947–1959. A regression for the period 1948–1949, which shows an insignificant coefficient for *CR*, is not given here.

Source: J. S. Bain, *Barriers to New Competition*, Harvard University Press, Cambridge, Mass., 1956; Michael M. Mann, "Seller Concentration: Barriers to Entry, and Rates of Return in Thirty Industries, 1950–1960," *Review of Economics and Statistics*, vol. 48, Aug. 1966, pp. 296–307; Howard J. Sherman, *Profits in the United States*, Cornell University Press, Ithaca, N.Y., 1968; Leonard Weiss, "Average Concentration Ratios and Industrial Performance," *Journal of Industrial Economics*, vol. 2, July 1963, pp. 233–254; Leonard Weiss, "Quantitative Studies of Industrial Organization," in Michael D. Intrilagator (ed.), *Frontiers of Quantitative Economics*, North-Holland Publishing, Amsterdam, 1971, pp. 362–403.

An additional indication of significant magnitudes may be taken from the proposed Industrial Reorganization Act (the Hart bill).[78] The bill declares "a rebuttable presumption that monopoly power is possessed—(1) by any corporation if the average rate of return on net worth after taxes is in excess of 15 per centum over a period of five consecutive years out of the most recent seven years preceding the filing of the complaint."[79]

An indication of the likely degree of measurement error can be derived from Table 1-12, which gives the effect of alternative, acceptable though essentially arbitrary, methods of allocating noninventoriable common costs. In more than three-quarters of the lines of business, the range of difference in net profits/assets divided by the companies' preferred method (not the smallest number) is greater than 10 percent. Considering that the FTC's definition of a line of business is narrower than that used by companies and often tracks a company's divisions very poorly, it would seem that these percentage differences are under-

78. See Goldschmid et al., op. cit., pp. 444–448.

79. § 101(b).

TABLE 1-14 Rates of Return Associated with Differences in Concentration*

Study	Period	Sample size	Degree of industry concentration: High	Moderate	Low	Maximum difference
I. Concentration						
A. Net profits after tax/equity						
Mann [1966]	1950–1960	30 two-digit	13.3	9.0		4.3
Qualls [1972]†	1947–1951	20 two-digit	16.3	11.0		5.3
	1950–1960	30 two-digit	13.3	9.0		4.3
Orr [1974]	1960–1969	71 four-digit (Canadian)				4.4‡
B. Net Profits after tax and interest/assets						
Meehan and Duchesneau [1973]	1954–1963	32 four-digit	3.5	5.4	4.1	1.3
C. Net income plus interest/assets						
Demsetz [1973]	1963	95 three-digit	12.5	8.3	9.2	4.2

*Eight-firm concentration ratio except for Demsetz, who uses a four-firm ratio.

†The analysis that uses pre-World War II data is not shown.

‡The difference was computed from a regression, where a dummy variable equaled one when the industry was in the highest fifth of the distribution of concentration ratios and zero otherwise.

Source: Harold Demsetz, "Industry Structure, Market Rivalry, and Public Policy," in J. Fred Weston and Stanley I. Ornstein (ed.), *The Impact of Large Firms on the U.S. Economy*, Lexington Books, Heath, Lexington, Mass., 1973, pp. 71–82; Michael M. Mann, "Seller Concentration: Barriers to Entry, and Rates of Return in Thirty Industries, 1950–1960," *Review of Economics and Statistics*, vol. 48, Aug. 1966, pp. 296–307; James W. Meehan, Jr.; and Thomas D. Duchesneau, "The Critical Level of Concentration: An Empirical Analysis," *Journal of Industrial Economics*, vol. 22, Sept. 1973, pp. 21–36; Dale Orr, "An Index of Entry Barriers and Its Application to the Market Structure Performance Relationship." *Journal of Industrial Economics*, vol. 23, Sept. 1974, pp. 39–49; David Qualls, "Concentration, Barriers to Entry, and Long Run Economic Profit Margins," *Journal of Industrial Economics*, vol. 20, April 1972, pp. 146–158.

TABLE 1-15 Net Income after Tax/Equity Associated with Differences in Barriers to Entry

			Barriers to entry			
Study	*Period*	*Sample size*	*Very high*	*Substantial*	*Moderate to low*	*Maximum difference*
Mann [1966]	1950–1960	30 two-digit	16.4	11.3	9.9	6.5
Sherman [1968]	1958	20 two-digit	7.3		5.7	1.6
Orr [1974]	1960–1969	71 four-digit (Canadian)	6.1	4.9	5.2	1.2
Qualls [1972]*	1947–1951	20 two-digit	19.0	13.4	11.6	7.4
	1950–1960	30 two-digit	16.4	11.3	9.9	6.5

*The analysis that uses Bain's pre-World War II data is not shown.

Source: Michael M. Mann, "Seller Concentration: Barriers to Entry, and Rates of Return in Thirty Industries, 1950–1960," *Review of Economics and Statistics*, vol. 48, Aug. 1966, pp. 296–307; Howard J. Sherman, *Profits in the United States*, Cornell University Press, Ithaca, N.Y., 1968; Dale Orr, "An Index of Entry Barriers and Its Application to the Market Structure Performance Relationship," *Journal of Industrial Economics*, vol. 23, Sept. 1974, pp. 39–49; David Qualls, "Concentration, Barriers to Entry, and Long Run Economic Profit Margins," *Journal of Industrial Economics*, vol. 20, April 1972, pp. 146–158.

stated. Given the focus of some antitrust analysts on particular magnitudes of profit rates as significant—with "high" rates possibly indicating monopoly or collusion and "low" rates possibly indicating predatory conduct or the inefficiency of the "sloppy monopolist"—measurement errors in profit rates of even 1 percent or less, especially over time, can be critical.

The effect on measures of performance of alternative, arbitrary allocations of joint and common costs and of incorrectly using accounting numbers to represent economic values can be examined analytically.[80] The following symbols are defined for this analysis:

S = sales

C = costs

$P = S - C$ = net profits

$ps = P/S$ = profit rate on sales

d = difference in costs due to arbitrary allocations, etc., as a percentage of costs, C

ps' = reported profit rate on sales when costs are over- or understated by d

$$ps' = \frac{S - C - Cd}{S} \qquad ps' = ps - d + dps \tag{9}$$

80. The effect on net profits/sales and net profit/assets of intrafirm transfers at nonmarket prices is shown by eqs. (4), (5), and (8) on pp. 82–83. Rather than complicate the analysis further, this additional distortion is not included.

Since net profits/assets (*pa*) is equal to net profits/sales (*ps*) times sales over assets and neither sales nor assets are affected by errors in costs, the effect on *pa* is the same as the effect on *ps*.[81]

Table 1-16 shows the reported profit rate on sales or assets (*ps′* or *pa′*) that results from a given percentage error in costs (*d*), compared to the "actual" profit rates. This calculation does not include the effect of nonmarket price intrafirm transfers. Nor does it include the effect on net profits/assets of mismeasurements and arbitrary allocations of assets. These additionally offset net profits/assets by the reciprocal of the percentage misstatement of assets. Thus, it seems evident that data measurement problems are likely to swamp any inferences that otherwise might be drawn from the reported numbers.

The FTC suggests two procedures for "correcting" the data: averaging and statistical analysis. The FTC's staff states:

> Aggregation of performance data prepared according to varying accounting rules is likely on the average to improve the quality of the data, not degrade it. To the extent that differences in accounting conventions intrude on an unsystematic (or in statisticians' language, random) basis, the errors introduced thereby are likely under the law of large numbers to cancel each other out, so that the industry aggregates are more accurate than any individual company observation would on the average be. If on the other hand the differences are systematic, there are statistical methods for detecting them and filtering them out. For example, if profits tend to be lower when the degree of secondary product "contamination" is relatively high, that tendency can be detected through statistical analysis, and appropriate correction factors can be estimated and published.[82]

Where the measurement errors are random deviations around a "true" number, one can rely on the law of large numbers. However, differences due to alternative procedures for allocating common and joint costs are not random. Though an average of these allocated costs obviously would be some numbers between the extremes, the aggregate would not be more accurate than any of the individual company numbers, as the staff claims. It is possible, of course, that within a line of business, the relative amounts of companies' allocated common and joint costs are randomly distributed with respect to some number of interest, such as a concentration ratio. In this event, a statistically significant correlation between concentration ratios and reported net profits would really reflect a correlation between concentration ratios and contribution margins (revenues less direct expenses) or other, unspecified variables. But it is well known that contribution margins depend significantly on companies' organizational structures and accounting procedures. This is the reason that contribution margins are

---

81. The effect on the profit rate on sales or assets also can be expressed as an amount, x', rather than as a percentage. In this event, eq. (9) would be $d(ps - 1) = x'$.

82. Bureau of Economics Staff Memorandum, 1975, N. 40 *supra*, p. 13.

TABLE 1-16 Reported Profit Rate of Sales ($ps' \cdot x$) or Assets ($pa' \cdot x$) When Costs Are Understated or Overstated (d)

Percentage understatement (−) or overstatement (+) of costs (d)	*"Actual" profit rate on sales (ps) or assets (pa)*				
	0.05	*0.10*	*0.15*	*0.20*	*0.30*
−0.30	0.34	0.37	0.41	0.44	0.51
−0.20	0.24	0.28	0.32	0.36	0.44
−0.10	0.15	0.19	0.24	0.28	0.39
−0.05	0.10	0.15	0.19	0.24	0.34
+0.05	0.00	0.06	0.10	0.16	0.27
+0.10	−0.05	0.01	0.07	0.12	0.23
+0.20	−0.14	−0.08	−0.04	0.04	0.16
+0.30	−0.24	−0.20	−0.11	−0.04	0.09

Source: Author.

not used for structure-performance studies. Consequently, neither the FTC nor anyone else can use a statistical procedure to solve a conceptual problem. The conceptual problem is that measuring net profits on a comparable basis among multiproduct companies is not possible. Averaging reported numbers can only mask, but cannot solve, the problem, because there is no "true" net profit, no central tendency, for which the law of large numbers is meaningful.

The statistical procedures the FTC intends to use to account for systematic errors are not specified. Instead, one is told of a search for procedures:

> As economists' knowledge of the conceptual problems has advanced,[83] the Bureau of Economics staff has intensified its efforts to identify and compensate for those limitations. For example, the Bureau presently has a project underway to develop computerized methods which will correct for the "expensing" of advertising and research and development outlays when economic profits would be stated more accurately if such outlays were capitalized and depreciated over an appropriate interval. Further projects of this nature will undoubtedly be pursued as the Line of Business program provides the necessary data base.[84]

I am informed by Dr. William Long, Director of the Line of Business Project, that such procedures have not as yet been specified or tested with actual or simulated data. Considering that the FTC is requiring companies to report for each line of business such detailed and costly information as the percentages of ending inventory valued according to

---

83. It should be noted that many economists, accountants, and managers have been aware of those conceptual problems for quite some time.

84. Bureau of Economics Staff Memorandum, 1975, N. 40 *supra,* p. 16.

different bases, percentages of fixed assets depreciated according to different methods, percentages of transfers out valued at different prices, and the percentages of plant and equipment acquired over different time periods, one would have thought that a logically coherent, empirically validated method for adjusting the data would already have been developed before respondents were asked to supply specific data.

The only reference to a specific procedure that I could find is by Professor Scherer (when he was Director of the FTC's Bureau of Economics), in a detailed letter to the General Accounting Office that speaks to various questions raised about the LB program. He states, "The approach will be similar to some work I have done recently in correcting data on plant sizes covering twelve industries and six nations for systematic international productivity differences."[85] Elsewhere, he has written:

> The analysis analogous to what we will perform to investigate accounting convention effects is concentrated on pp. 115–117 and 224–225, where the most closely analogous variable is the productivity adjustment dummy variable *ADJ* [which equals 1 where plant sizes are measured as employment (which is an overstatement) rather than in output, zero otherwise]. Note that in every case *ADJ* compensates in the proper direction and by reasonable amounts for the biases known to exist in the unadjusted plant size figures.[86]

The effect of including this variable in the regression presented on pages 224 to 225[87] can be determined by computing the values of the dependent variable predicted ($\hat{D}$) with and without inclusion of the dummy variable, *ADJ*.[88] *ADJ* equals 1 for 9 of the 71 observations. With *ADJ* set equal to 1 for these observations, the percentage error in predicting the dependent variable[89] ($[D - \hat{D}]/D$) ranges from −23 to

---

85. F. M. Scherer, Alan Beckenstein, Erich Kaufer, and R. Dennis Murphy, with the assistance of Francine Bougeon-Maassen, *The Economics of Multi-Plant Operation,* Harvard, Cambridge, Mass., 1975.

86. F. M. Scherer, Letter to Carl F. Bogar, Assistant Director, Office of Special Programs, United States General Accounting Office, Aug. 6, 1975.

87. Scherer et al., op cit., pp. 224–225.

88. The data required for these computations are presented in the book, a practice that is unusually complete and honest, for which Professor Scherer should be commended.

89. *D*, the dependent variable, is MP03, the average number of plants operated per firm by the leading three firms. The complete regression is

$$\log MP03 = -0.142 + \underset{(.157)}{1.074} \log CONC + \underset{(.075)}{.936} \log SIZE + \underset{(.197)}{.493}\, ADJ - \underset{(.095)}{.841} \log TOP50/MOS; \; R^2 = .751$$

(standard errors in parentheses)

+79, with a mean, absolute value of 30 percent. With *ADJ* set to equal zero instead, the percentage error ($[D - \hat{D}]/D$) ranges from −69 to +22, with a mean, absolute value of 28 percent. The inclusion of ADJ changes the values of the dependent variable considerably, from −20 to +180 percent, an average of +42 percent. But, on balance, the predicted values of the dependent variable appear to be no better than had *ADJ* not been included in the regression.

In the other application of the adjustment dummy variable mentioned, the dependent variable, relative industry plant size (*TOP50/MOS*), is stated in terms of employment rather than in terms of the preferred measure, productivity, for nine cases. In sixteen additional cases, the employment measured plant size variable could be adjusted to a productivity measure. The balance of 44 observations could be measured in terms of productivity. Seven regressions are presented (four in additive form and three in multiplicative form where the variables are transformed to logarithms) with *ADJ* included as an independent variable, equaling 1 for the nine nonproductivity adjusted observations and zero for the other observations.[90] Since it is known that the adjustments reduce the value of the dependent variable, it is not surprising that the coefficients of *ADJ* are positive, as Professor Scherer says. But none of the coefficients is statistically significant: the t statistics are .56, .80, .24, .18, 1.1, 1.22, 1.28 and 1.29. Since the "true" value of the dependent variables for these nine observations is not known, it is not possible to determine the meaningfulness of the magnitudes of the coefficients estimated. However, for the four additive regressions, the coefficients are .044, .095, .137 and .198, which shows that the magnitudes of the computed adjustments depends considerably on the other independent variables included in the regression. As percentages of the dependent variables, the adjustment factors range from 2 to 7 percent when *ADJ* = .044 and from 9 to 31 percent when *ADJ* = .198. The coefficients of *ADJ* in the three multiplicative regressions are .087, .108 and .109. They imply adjustments of the dependent variable of 22, 38, and 29 percent. Thus, the two formulations (additive and multiplicative) yield rather different adjustments.

Two regressions were computed, permitting one to determine the usefulness of *ADJ* to "correct" the data. In these regressions, the 16 adjusted dependent variables were included at their preadjusted magnitudes. The coefficients of *ADJ*, then, give a computed adjustment that can be compared to the actual adjustment.[91] In the additive regression, the coefficient is .281 (significant at the .05 level), which implies that each dependent variable should be .281 lower were it stated in terms of productivity. The actual adjustments range from .06 to 1.44 and average

---

90. Scherer et al., op. cit., pp. 118–119.

91. The adjustments made to *TOP50/MOS* were computed with the reciprocal of the values given in Scherer et al., op. cit., table 3.9, p. 73.

.47. The percentages by which the computed adjustment of .28 falls short of the "actual" adjustments range from +460 to −80, with a mean absolute percentage difference of 99. In the multiplicative regression, the coefficient of *ADJ* is .263 (significant at the .01 level), which implies that each dependent variable should be 83 percent lower were it stated in terms of productivity. Expressed in percentage terms, the "actual" adjustments range from 5 to 335, with a mean of 107. The amount by which the computed percentage adjustment of 83 exceeds or falls short of the "actual" percentage adjustment ranges from +78 to −252, with a mean absolute percentage difference of 67. Thus, it does not appear that the multiple regression, dummy variable procedure was a very effective method of estimating the biases known to exist in the plant size variable. Of course, it might be more effective in a larger sample and with different variables, but the example cited by Professor Scherer does not provide much support for this expectation.

EVALUATION OF EXPECTED BENEFITS—CONCEPTUAL DATA PROBLEMS AND SUMMARY EVALUATIONS OF SPECIFIC BENEFITS

Even if the FTC's economists and statisticians somehow could "solve" the data measurement problems that confront the LB program, they must face the basic conceptual and philosophical problems that undermine the program. These may be delineated as conceptual measurement problems, aggregation effects on presumed benefits, and doubts as to whether the presumed benefits are, in fact, benefits.

Conceptual Measurement Problems

Though they have been discussed previously, the conceptual measurement problems that beset line of business data are so severe that they should be emphasized. First, the joint and common costs of producing, distributing, administering, etc., products or lines of business *cannot* meaningfully be allocated to them. Furthermore, the relative amount of joint and common costs vary among companies. Multiproduct companies are organized in diverse ways reflecting their pasts, their managements, and the economies of production, distribution, and management that they are able to and hope to achieve. It is unusual for two such companies to be very similarly organized. Therefore, the contribution margins (revenues less direct expenses) of products made by different companies rarely are comparable. In addition, where the production or sales of one product line affects the costs or revenues of another, it is conceptually impossible to measure separately net profit or return on investment of each.

Second, the economic values of many important assets and expenses cannot be measured adequately. In particular, the present values of many fixed assets cannot be determined without market transactions, which do not occur until the assets are sold. Intangible assets, such as the future value of past research and development and advertising expenditures, similarly cannot be measured very well, if at all.[92] The amount of expenses recorded is a function of the asset values recorded: a corollary of the conceptual impossibility of measuring fixed assets is the conceptual impossibility of measuring depreciation.

Third, even when accounting numbers are not severely subject to measurement problems, they rarely provide complete estimates of the opportunity costs of decisions. To use the numbers effectively, the decision maker must know much more about the context in which the decision is to be made. While this knowledge can be obtained by the managers of a company, it cannot be reported to an agency such as the FTC for communication to users of the LB data.

Aggregation Effects

The nongovernment users of the LB data are presumed to benefit from observing the line of business profit rates on sales and assets reported. To protect the confidentiality of the respondents' reports, these numbers will be aggregates and averages of the data reported. However, it is of no benefit to the businessperson, customer, labor leader, or shareholder to learn that on average, or in the aggregate, profit rates are higher or lower in some line of business. The aggregates obviously have no meaning; since they reflect only the composition of the sample or well-known facts (e.g., total sales and net profits are greater in the passenger car industry than in the frozen specialties industry). Aside from the data limitations discussed above, the average profit rate on sales or assets are algebraic sums of low and high rates. The user of the data has no reason to believe that the average is a relevant number. Furthermore, even if some distribution statistics are provided, users of these data will not know which companies are in the higher ranges and which are in the lower ranges. Consequently, there will be no way for users to review the circumstances in which the reported rates of return were "earned" so that they may attempt to judge the relevance, to them, of the numbers reported.

Summary and Additional Doubts about the Specific Benefits Claimed

GOVERNMENT ANTITRUST POLICY

The general failure of the FTC-SIC categories to group products that are substitutes in use make the LB data essentially useless for antitrust proceedings. In addition, the conceptual and practical measurement

---

92. Accounting for price level changes is a very difficult, though perhaps not a conceptually impossible, problem.

problems discussed above make it unlikely that the reported profit rates, etc., will be meaningful. Indeed, if a monopolistic company recorded a "high" accounting profit, it might elect to choose a cost allocation or asset measurement procedure that would enable it to report a low profit rate for its monopolized line of business. In addition, the data do not enable the FTC or anyone else to distinguish between high profit rates due to economies of scale, externalities in production, superior efficiency, favorable purchase contracts, luck or accident, historical costs, reporting conventions, etc., and those due to monopoly practices. At best, then, the data are useless. If they are taken seriously, the FTC is likely to misuse its and the public's resources.

MACROECONOMIC POLICY

The data problems discussed similarly affect this presumed benefit negatively. In addition, there is considerable doubt that data of the type the FTC wants to collect are relevant for macroeconomic policy. Though it is alleged that line of business data will make it possible "to analyze the structure and dynamics of [price and unemployment] changes [in the economy] and to pinpoint the reason why inflation persists or is dampened,"[93] it seems clear that the LB categories are too broad to support such an analysis. Casual observation should be sufficient to demonstrate that the prices of individual goods and services do not change by the same or even similar proportions. Even studies of aggregate price changes[94] show great diversity of changes. It is also doubtful that there is any meaningful relationship among inflation, unemployment, and profits or concentration by lines of business,[95] and there is no reason to believe that the FTC's LB data would be useful in clearing up any remaining doubts.

An illustration of the difficulty (if not impossibility) of drawing meaningful inferences from these type of data is a recent, generally well done, FTC staff economic report, *Price and Profit Trends in Four Food Manufacturing Industries.* The study addressed the following questions: "Did retail food prices [which increased by 37 percent between 1971

---

93. Bureau of Economics Staff Report, 1974, N. 40 *supra,* p. 10.

94. See, for example, Phillip Cagan, "Changes in the Recession Behavior of Wholesale Prices in the 1920's and Post-World War II," *Explorations in Economic Research,* vol. 2, no. 1, Winter 1975.

95. See Willard F. Mueller for a contrary view; see also J. Fred Weston and Steven Lustgarten, and Ralph E. Beals for what I believe to be far superior analyses that essentially discredit the cost-push and market power hypotheses apparently assumed by the FTC: Willard F. Mueller, "Industrial Concentration: An Important Inflationary Force" (pp. 280–306), and J. Fred Weston and Steven Lustgarten, "Concentration and Wage-Price Changes" (pp. 307–332), in Goldschmid, Mann, and Weston (eds.), *Industrial Concentration;* Ralph E. Beals, "Concentrated Industries, Administered Prices and Inflation: A Survey of Recent Empirical Research," prepared for the Council on Wage and Price Stability, unpublished manuscript, May 15, 1975.

and 1974 compared to a 22 percent increase in the Consumer Price Index] rise in part because of enhanced profits at intermediate stages? . . . Has the pattern of price increases been influenced by seller concentration?"[96] The report answers these questions by comparing the after-tax profit on stockholders' equity in meat packing, fluid milk, bread, and beer with all food manufacturing and all manufacturing. Data for the four industries studied were taken from the Quarterly Financial Reports filed by some 507 companies which had a high percentage of sales in one of the industries. The comparison of annual (1958–1972) after-tax profit on stockholders' equity shows a maximum average difference between any of the four industries and either of the two manufacturing percentages of −1.7. The maximum differences in any year are −2.4 and +1.2.[97] The rates of return are not meaningfully different when the firms are grouped by asset sizes. Masson and Parker conclude: "In none of the four industry samples . . . has the after-tax return on equity been palpably excessive." However, had they based their conclusions on line of business numbers reported by multiproduct companies, they would not know whether or not the average annual maximum difference of −1.7 percent was due to data measurement errors and allocation choices adopted by the companies. Alternatively, if they found a difference of, say, +5.0 percent or more, they would not have been justified in concluding that the industries had been "tempted to exploit their unleashed market power to raise profits and prices unconscionably."

In fact, most of the study was unnecessary. The authors find that after-tax quarterly profits on sales average 0.9 percent for meat packing, 0.8 percent for fluid milk, 1.3 percent for bread, 3.8 percent for beer, and 2.7 percent for all food manufacturing, with no evident trend over the period (third quarter 1972 through first quarter 1975). Lacking measurement errors, these numbers are overstated because the factor return on equity is not deducted. Retail prices over this period, though, increased by 21.4 percent (meat), 33.2 percent (milk), 51.3 percent (bread), 22.4 percent (beer), and 40.2 percent (food at home). It is clear that excessive profits had almost nothing to do with the price increases. This conclusion could have been drawn simply by reviewing the annual financial statements of companies in the industries.

Indeed, were the factor return to equity (measured on a market, not an accounting basis) deducted from net profits reported by most corporations in most industries, it would be clear that this adjusted net profit amount as a percentage of sales cannot account for the price increases

---

96. Alison Masson and Russell C. Parker, *Price and Profit Trends in Four Food Manufacturing Industries,* Staff Report to the Federal Trade Commission, Washington, D.C., July 1975, p. 1.

97. Ibid., Table 6. The quarterly data are more variable. The average maximum difference is −7.0. In any quarter, the maximum differences are −10.2 and +4.9 (ibid., Table 4).

experienced in an inflation. Therefore, it seems wasteful and needless to collect line of business data for this type of analysis.

EFFICIENT ALLOCATION OF RESOURCES

Given the broad, nonhomogeneous, non-market-oriented FTC-SIC categories, the data measurement biases and the aggregated and nonidentified data that will be reported, it is difficult to imagine how a user can determine which are the "industries in which demand is inadequately satisfied and as a consequence profits are particularly high." Nor does it seem possible that the data "will show where existing companies can profitably invest in expanded capacity and new competitors can enter."[98] Furthermore, by the time the data are published, they will be "stale," since it is unlikely that superior investment opportunities would go unnoticed for several years. Therefore, companies would be well advised to ignore the LB reports lest they be misled into making unprofitable or even disastrous investments.[99] (The benefits to analysts and stockholders are discussed below.)

BUSINESS AND LABOR

For the same reasons outlined above, the LB data are unlikely to be useful to small or large businesses for evaluation of performance or for pinpointing new opportunities. Both of these important problems require much better, more precise data than would be provided by the LB reports. Indeed, the LB data are much more likely to provide misleading than useful signals.

The LB data would also be dysfunctional were they used by buyers of goods and services or labor unions to evaluate the fairness with which they are treated. At best, the data may give rise to needless arguments. At worse, buyers or union leaders may make decisions that are contrary to their own and the companies' best interests.

INVESTORS

Stockholders and analysts, in particular, are unlikely to find the LB data useful. Even were none of the problems mentioned above serious, they would be unable to compare the LB ratios with those reported by individual corporations, because few, if any, corporations report their sales, expenses, etc., by the FTC/SIC-defined lines of business. Therefore, the LB data would not "help stock analysts and ultimately inves-

---

98. Bureau of Economics Staff Report, 1974, N. 40 *supra,* p. 7.

99. Were the FTC a private data collection company, I wonder if a consumer protection agency (such as the FTC) or users of the LB reports could sue it successfully for false and misleading advertising.

tors make decisions which force managers to use the resources at their command efficiently," as is asserted in the FTC Bureau of Economics Staff Report.[100]

The belief that LB data are necessary or even meaningful for investors also is contrary to the findings of studies on the efficiency of the stock markets. These studies[101] find that the publication of corporations' financial data is not followed by reevaluations of the corporations' shares, either because the data are not meaningful or because they are known or fully anticipated before publication.[102] These studies also are consistent with the hypothesis and subsequent finding that required publication of data by the SEC did not measurably affect investors' expectations.[103] To my knowledge, only one defensible study found evidence to the contrary. Daniel Collins[104] developed a trading rule model to determine whether investors might have benefited from knowing the segment profit data that the SEC first required companies to report beginning with fiscal year 1970. (These data were reported in 1971 retrospectively for the years 1968, 1969, and 1970). His findings were mixed. He reports average positive abnormal (compared to investments in alternative, equivalently risky shares) returns (18 percent) for 1968 and 1969, small and statistically insignificant abnormal returns for 1970, and no significant abnormal returns for the period as a whole. The question was further examined by B. Horwitz and R. Kolodny, who tested for the effect on security prices and market measures of risk of companies who reported segment income data for the first time during 1971, with those of a sample of companies that did not. They conclude: "Thus the authors' results provide no evidence in support of the universally accepted contention that the SEC required disclosure furnished investors with valuable information."[105]

It is generally concluded, then, that the securities markets are efficient with respect to publicly available information, in the sense that share prices very quickly incorporate this information and are unbiased estimates of intrinsic values.[106] Therefore, it is very doubtful that publi-

---

100. FTC, 1974, N. 40 *supra,* p. 8.

101. Reviewed in George J. Benston, *Corporate Financial Disclosure in the UK and the USA,* Lexington Books, Heath, Lexington, Mass., 1976, chap. 4.2.6.

102. Inadequacy of the models, specifications, and/or data is another, always possible explanation of insignificant findings.

103. See George J. Benston, "Required Disclosure and the Stock Market: An Evaluation of the Securities Exchange Act of 1934," *American Economic Review,* vol. 63, no. 1, March 1973, pp. 132–155.

104. Daniel W. Collins, "SEC Product-Line Reporting and Market Efficiency,' *Journal of Financial Economics,* vol. 2, no. 2, June 1975, pp. 125–164.

105. B. Horwitz and R. Kolodny, "Line of Business Reporting and Security Prices: An Analysis of a SEC Disclosure Rule," *Bell Journal of Economics,* vol. 8, no. 1, Spring 1977, p. 247.

106. This conclusion is based on an extensive review of research in Benston, *Corporate Financial Disclosure,* chaps. 4.2.5 and 4.2.6.

cation of LB data by the FTC, a year or more after the period to which these data pertain, in a form that cannot be directly related to individual corporations, would be useful to investors. Furthermore, considering that the LB categories do not conform to the business segments in corporate published reports and that corporations are now required by the FASB and the SEC to publish product-line data, the FTC's LB data would seem to be of no value to investors.

ECONOMIC STUDIES OF INDUSTRY PERFORMANCE

The FTC's Bureau of Economics staff has taken note of criticism of market structure studies:

> One argument advanced by several LB program critics is that the program is based upon a questionable premise: that there are systematic relationships between industrial structure on the one hand and economic performance on the other. It is true that reference has been made to such relationships in previous Bureau of Economics statements concerning the Line of Business program as well as in other work of the Bureau. It is not true, however, that the value of the LB program hinges upon the existence of those relationships. Rather, a thorough understanding of the postulated relationships, including knowledge of their possible non-existence if that is the case, is vital to the well-informed formulation and implementation of antitrust policy concerning mergers and market dominance. At present there is great uncertainty and disagreement over these matters.[107] A paramount reason for the present knowledge void is the dearth of reliable information on various aspects of industry performance. The Line of Business program is designed to fill that information void. With LB data, it will be possible to carry out the studies needed to establish a solid basis for understanding whatever links may exist between industrial structure and economic performance. Whatever the studies show, the results will be important to antitrust policy-making.[108]

However, there are many reasons to believe that the LB data is not "reliable information" that may be used to "carry out the studies needed to establish a solid basis for understanding whatever links may exist between industrial structure and economic performance." As is discussed (and I believe, demonstrated) above, the LB data are rife with biases that are a result of unsolvable conceptual and practical measurement problems, and the FTC/SEC-designated lines of business do not define relatively homogeneous markets. Furthermore, many of the economic market-performance questions to which the LB data seem directed have been "answered" by researchers who used much better data. For example, the universally acknowledged problem that

---

107. Here the authors cite Goldschmid, Mann, and Weston (eds.), *Industrial Concentration.*

108. Bureau of Economic Staff Memorandum, 1975, N. 40 *supra,* p. 10.

expensed advertising results in an understatement of recorded assets and equity has been corrected by researchers who used time series data or stock market values for equity and bonds.[109] Though there still are some unanswered questions, there is no reason to expect them to be answered by a greater quantity of inappropriate data.

In any event, the industrial structure-market performance questions to which the LB data might be applied have not been specified by the FTC. In response to a question in September 1976, William Long told me that models which identify the variables and their presumed functional relationships have not been developed. Even without the models, it seems clear that the data cannot speak to the issues outlined by Franklin Edwards in his essay which closes *Industrial Concentration: The New Learning,* entitled "Issues for Further Study: Where Does the Researcher Go From Here?" The "concentration, economies of scale, and profits debate" cannot be reduced, since economies of scale cannot be measured with the data requested by the FTC. The "advertising debate" cannot be advanced since, for one thing, there appears to be no way that past advertising expenditures can be capitalized with the data reported. Resolution of the "concentration and innovation debate" falters on the same problem. "Concentration and inflation" is discussed at length above, where it was concluded that the LB data are insufficient to answer the question, if indeed there is a meaningful question. The "distributive effects of monopoly" question does not appear to be one that the LB data can answer, if for no other reason than the probability that the data are too variable and biased to measure monopoly returns. Finally, the "monopoly-costs inefficiency issue" cannot be considered with the LB data since there is no way to determine the reason for the magnitudes of the expenses reported.

In summary, the benefits claimed for the LB program fail to emerge from this examination. Since the program yet may yield benefits that I have not adequately considered, I turn now to a specification of its costs.

COSTS OF THE LB PROGRAM

The costs of the FTC's LB program, were it implemented, would be borne by three groups: the taxpayers, the respondents, and consumers. For each of these groups, two types of costs can be distinguished—direct and indirect. Though indirect costs often are not measurable, they often are of considerable magnitude and therefore should be considered.

---

109. See references in Yale Brozen, "Entry Barriers: Advertising and Product Differentiation," in Goldschmid, Mann, and Weston (eds.), *Industrial Concentration,* pp. 115–137.

Costs to the Taxpayers

The FTC estimated that the annual cost to the Commission might be $198,000 for fiscal year 1975 and $413,000 for fiscal year 1976 (exclusive of legal costs in 1976). Thereafter, "annual costs are expected to increase to accommodate users of the data."[110] These direct costs are overstated to the extent that they include allocations of overhead that would continue in the absence of the program. However, if past experience is a guide, they are more likely to be understated. For example, it would be remarkable if the FTC could transcribe the data in machine-readable form, check it thoroughly for recording and reporting accuracy, and program the data files and analyses for the $413,000 per year estimated. It also is doubtful that the costs of checking out apparent reporting errors, including field visits to respondents, have been estimated fully. Nor does it appear that the costs of extending the program to additional companies and for additional data have been included.[111]

An additional direct cost to other branches of the government (not mentioned in the FTC's estimates) is the amount of income taxes that the respondents would not pay, since the costs to the companies of complying with the program are deductible. Hence, the amounts estimated as paid by the respondents actually should be charged in large measure to the United States Treasury.

If the LB data is taken seriously by the FTC or by other governmental agencies (such as the Justice Department), the cost of dysfunctional investigations should be charged to the program. Should the agencies rely on these data to determine which industrywide investigations best serve the public interest, the cost of their failure to investigate meaningful areas of monopoly and fraud also should be included as an indirect cost of the program.

Costs to the Respondents

There is considerable dispute about the direct cost to companies of complying with the FTC's demand for LB data. The companies' estimates are higher than those estimated by the FTC, perhaps because the companies are more concerned than is the FTC about the reliability of the data. It is not that the companies care more about the LB reports than does the FTC. It is that the companies' officials have to sign the reports, and they are aware that they may be required to substantiate the numbers they report. While the FTC's staff may be willing to have

---

110. FTC, 1975, N. 10 *supra*, pp. 16–17.

111. Some support for this expectation may be derived from the FTC's estimate in 1973 of the cost of administering the program when it was supposed to apply to 2,000 companies. The direct cost were estimated to be $283,000 for the first year and $187,000 annually for succeeding years (FTC, N. 2 *supra*, pp. 27–28).

the companies estimate or even "guesstimate" the numbers, company officials are justifiably fearful that the numbers that are accepted as reasonable estimates at one time or by one staff member may appear in the future to be deliberately misleading.

The FTC states that 11 companies estimated direct costs of from $6,000 to $400,000 with a median value of $40,000 for completing the now defunct 1973 form. For an earlier version of the 1974 form, 25 companies are said to have estimated costs of from $5,000 to $1.8 million, with a median value of $56,000.[112] Because it believes that the newest version of the form and the instructions "will reduce anticipated burden about a third," the staff concludes that "this median compliance cost for companies similar to those filing burden affidavits in the fall of 1974 would be on the order of $37,000."[113] Since it does not believe that the companies filing in 1974 are representative, having more lines of business than would the average respondent, the staff estimates an annual compliance burden of $24,000 per company.[114] With 450 companies required to file, this amounts to $10.8 million per year.

It seems likely that the direct costs of compliance, whether the FTC's annual average of $24,000 per company or the companies' estimates of more than $56,000 (according to the FTC), may not be nearly so great as the indirect costs. The respondents must be concerned that the data will be used to support investigations about their activities. If undertaken, such investigations often require extensive use of very valuable executive talent, financial and technical analyses, and legal fees. Perhaps even more important is the cost of worrying about an investigation rather than about the operations of the enterprise. In addition, the companies may have to defend themselves from nongovernmental users who take the LB data seriously. These include investors who attempt to enter markets where the profits actually are not excessive, customers who become upset at what they believe are unjustifiably high prices, labor unions who demand more than they otherwise would, and shareholders who mistakenly believe that management is not competent. In those few cases where the LB data actually do give users useful data, the respondents must contend with foreign producers who do not have to provide similar data.

It should be noted, however, that the compliance cost of the LB program falls partially on the U.S. Treasury and eventually on con-

---

112. Bureau of Economics Staff Memorandum, 1975, N. 40 *supra*, p. 7.

113. Ibid., p. 8.

114. This number is based on a compliance cost of $2,650 per line of business and an average number of nine lines per company. An indication of the staff's ability to estimate compliance cost may be derived from their estimates for company compliance with the 1973 version, which was abandoned in large part because it was too difficult to complete. A cost of $200 per line of business, or $1,800 for a nine-line company, was the estimate for this version (FTC, 1973, p. 28).

sumers. Initially the companies (that is to say, the shareholders) bear the burden.[115] But as is the case with all taxes, the cost largely falls on consumers.[116]

Summary of Costs

The total annual direct costs of the program are estimated by the FTC to be $413,000 + $10,800,000 = $11,213,000. Even if these amounts are not seriously underestimated, past experience indicates that they are likely to grow over time. Since the FTC originally wanted the program to include 2,000 companies who were to report on 357 lines of business (261 are now required), it seems reasonable to assume that the agency will move to expand the program should it be permitted to implement it. In addition, for the reasons outlined above, it will have to expand its requests for data considerably as it realizes how poor the numbers reported are. Thus, the compliance costs to the companies and the program costs to the FTC are likely to increase considerably over time. The growth rate may be estimated by reference to the growth of the FTC's budget. Over five-year periods, in constant dollars, the FTC's average annual budget increased by the following percentages: 1971–1975, 6.4 percent; 1966–1970, 5.0 percent; 1961–1965, 13.2 percent; 1956–1960, 6.2 percent. Since most of the cost of the LB program will be borne by the respondents, for which the Commission need not request congressional appropriations, it would seem very conservative to estimate a 6 percent annual growth in cost. A further conservative assumption is that the program's costs will increase at 6 percent for only five years and then remain stable (in constant dollars). However, if past experience with government-mandated reporting programs is a guide, once the LB program is begun, it will never cease, no matter how obvious it becomes that the data are essentially worthless. Nevertheless, the program is assumed to be terminated after 40 years. Therefore, the annual direct costs of $11,213,000 are expected to have increased to $15,005,523 after five years. The present value of the program's cost then would be $209,802,067 if the costs were discounted at 6 percent or $162,041,152 if the costs were discounted at 8 percent.[117]

---

15. Because the market for corporate shares is efficient, it is doubtful that any investors who are misled by the LB data bear any costs other than the transactions costs of unnecessarily buying or selling shares.

16. The relative amounts borne by owners of capital and the intermediate and final consumers of the companies' products depend on the elasticity of demand they face and the time over which adjustments take place.

17. The magnitude of this cost should be compared not to the sales or net profits of the respondents, but to the present value of the benefits that this expenditure of the nation's resources is expected to purchase. The analyses above indicate that these benefits are likely to be nonexistent.

The direct costs, even though probably greatly understated by the FTC, are most likely the least expensive part of the LB program. The indirect costs to the companies and, therefore, to the economy, are considerable. Unfortunately, these costs are not recorded as a tax or even as a direct charge to some account. Therefore, they are likely to be underestimated, even by the companies. Nevertheless, they represent a dead-weight cost to the economy.

SUMMARY AND CONCLUSIONS

The FTC proposes to collect detailed data from large multiproduct companies according to designated "lines of business." The benefits claimed for the program are delineated and analyzed in prior sections. These benefits include more efficient government antitrust activity, improvement of macroeconomic policy (particularly control of inflation), a more efficient allocation of resources in the economy, improved studies of economic performance, and the provision of useful information to business, labor, and investors.

Analysis of the data that would be collected reveals serious and perhaps fatal measurement problems. First, the products included in the FTC-designated lines of business, which are based on SIC categories, generally are not substitutes in demand. Hence, they do not relate to markets and are of little value for many of the benefits claimed (such as antitrust policy and evaluation of markets by potential entrants). There also is doubt that the categories contain products that are substitutes in production, and this obviates other benefits, such as industry studies and yardsticks against which managers can measure their performance. Second, the reporting rules the FTC has promulgated permit contamination of the data with respect to the LB categories. Consequently, users of the data will be unable to know the extent to which the categories actually refer to their labels and to what extent some possibly important categories have been collapsed into others. In particular, there will be no way for users to estimate the degree of cost or asset contamination. Third, allocation problems beset the data. Intracompany transfers not stated at market values (as is likely) distort the profit rates on sales or assets that are reported. Common and joint expenses and assets may be allocated according to whatever procedure each company chooses. There is reason to believe that these expenses are nontrivial and that the use of alternative, acceptable (though essentially arbitrary) allocation procedures will significantly alter the reported profit rates. Fourth, the acounting numbers reported do not reflect economic values well in many important instances. For example, expenditures for intangible assets, such as advertising and research and development, are completely expensed. Fixed assets and depreciation are recorded at original cost, unadjusted for changes in the purchasing power of money. Inventories may be recorded at LIFO or FIFO. Expenses incurred may reflect special, nonreproducible situations, such as favorable supply contracts. The assets that are divided into net profit are year-end amounts which may be very poor estimates of the average amounts employed during the year.

The magnitude of the errors in measuring profit rates may be compared to the profit rates that studies have shown to be those which distinguish concentrated from unconcentrated industries, industries with presumed high barriers to entry from those with presumed low barriers to entry, and monopoly firms from competitive firms. This comparision indicates that the measurement errors probably exceed these differences by a significant margin.

Furthermore, many of the data measurement problems cannot be "solved." Although the FTC claims that it can adjust and correct the data for measurement errors, it has not stated the procedures it plans to use. The only reference to a particular procedure I could find was to a method used by Professor Scherer.[118] Examination of the dummy variable method he employs, however, shows that it produces widely varying, significantly different amounts. When compared with the adjustments that Professor Scherer made to his data directly, the amounts computed with the dummy variable are as bad as or worse than those computed without the dummy variable. This example, at least, does not justify the belief that the FTC can successfully adjust the data for measurement errors.

Of greater importance, though, is recognition of the conceptual impossibility of calculating meaningful profit rates by line of business in a multiproduct company. Conceptually, there is no correct way to allocate joint and common costs, in the sense that the allocated amounts are the cost of producing or the assets used to produce the individual products. Differences in the amounts of common and joint expenses and assets allocated to lines of business by one necessarily arbitrary method or another are not random numbers. There is no "true" number; hence, it is incorrect to say that "under the law of large numbers the errors will cancel each other out, so that industry aggregates are more accurate than any individual company observation would on the average be."[119]

Indeed, while aggregation of the data received from many companies would reduce apparent (though not actual) measurement errors, it also would obscure meaningful differences that users would need (assuming that the individual company data were meaningful). An industry average (assuming that the FTC-SIC categories are industries) is of little value to businesspersons who are considering whether or not to enter a

---

118. Scherer et al., *The Economics of Multi-Plant Operation.*

119. Bureau of Economics Staff Memorandum, 1975, N. 40 *supra,* p. 13.

market. Without knowledge of the particular environment within which the numbers were generated, any benefits the data might have bought cannot be obtained. Furthermore, aggregates that "average-out" measurement errors present users with misleading data. As Dr. Bock points out in her discussion of LB category contamination:

> Although the absolute value of the overstatements and understatements for a given FTC category may appear to offset each other, such an apparent reduction in "contamination" is an arithmetic mirage. The offsets are not effected by matched data covering the same products (or the same categories), but by a mechanical offsetting of overstatements and understatements for different compositions of reported data for different lines of business.[120]

When the specific benefits claimed for the LB data are considered in the light of the data problems enumerated, it becomes clear that the benefits are not achievable. Government antitrust policy requires market data that are reliable. Assuming that profit data are relevant for inflation control, the expected measurement errors in the LB data far exceed the tolerance required for determining if profits are "excessive." The benefit from efficient allocation of resources probably is negative, since the LB data are more likely to give misleading signals to managers, labor leaders, and buyers. Investors would not find the data useful since the reported numbers could not be related to corporate reports and, more importantly, the data would not be published until long after they might have been meaningful. Finally, though the FTC now says the LB program was instituted in part to enable its economists to conduct improved industry structure-performance studies, the reliability and type of data that would be collected would not serve this purpose. Such problems with past studies as expensed advertising and R&D expenses would be present in the LB data. The data cannot distinguish between higher profits earned because of superior efficiency or those due to restrictive market practices. Most importantly, because of the measurement errors and biases built into the data as a consequence of the FTC's definitions of lines of business, the disparity between accounting numbers and economic values, and the conceptual impossibility of allocating joint and common expenses and assets, there is little reason to expect that meaningful economic studies will emerge from the LB data.

Though the benefits from the LB program may be negligible, the costs would not be. The initial direct annual costs to the government (excluding legal costs) for handling data from 450 companies are estimated by the FTC to be $413,000. This amount is likely to be under-

---

120. Bock, "Line of Business Reporting," p. 17.

stated.[121] Aside from the fact that proponents of programs tend to understate costs, the program probably will increase in scope and detail over the years. The direct costs to the respondents are now estimated by the FTC to be $24,000 annually for the average company or $10.8 million for the 450 companies to whom the forms are directed.[122] The companies believe the costs will be higher, in part because they must sign the forms and are concerned that they will be criticized for estimates that appear misleading in the light of future events. The total annual amount of $11,213,000 estimated by the FTC no doubt will grow larger over time. If the annual growth rate is about the same as the FTC's annual rate of budget increase and continues for five years, the annual direct cost will be $15 million. Assuming, based on past experience, that once established the program will continue for at least 40 years, the present value of the LB program discounted at 6 percent is $209 million and, at 8 percent, $162 million. In addition, the companies probably will have to incur considerable indirect and other opportunity costs for such activities as defending themselves from misdirected antitrust and other investigations. Considering that these costs and the costs of other people using bad data, etc., are not included, and that the program may expand at an even greater rate in the future, these amounts appear to be considerable understatements of the program's total cost.

It is unlikely that the program will achieve any benefits for the costs that will be imposed on the economy. In addition to the conclusion drawn above that most, if not all, of the benefits claimed by the FTC cannot be achieved because of conceptual and data measurement problems, one should question whether companies who could record profits that might be considered "unfair" in some quarters would choose to report such numbers. As is discussed above in greater detail, relatively high or low profits on a product or line of business may be recorded simply because of arbitrary procedures for allocating joint and common costs, accounting conventions that charge intangible assets to expenses and that record assets at their historical costs, random fluctuations, etc. Therefore, companies might choose to incur the expense of setting up their records to report under different but equally permissible rules yielding lower recorded profit rates. While this can be done, it is likely to be very expensive. The cost of these activities to the company and to the economy might be considerably greater than the direct costs of filing the reports.

Because it seems clear to me that the costs of the FTC's LB program exceed its expected benefits and that the program should be aban-

---

121. In 1973, the FTC estimated that the cost of processing more detailed data from 2,000 companies would be $187,000 annually, based on an estimate of $800 per company.

122. In 1973, the FTC estimated a direct cost of $1,800 for a similar-sized company to complete a more difficult form.

doned, I do not understand why the program was adopted by an agency that is charged with protecting consumers. Obviously, consumers will eventually bear the direct and indirect costs of the program. Would they (or anyone else) have given a grant of this magnitude to researchers who presented them with a proposal similar to the one presented by the FTC? The proposal does not contain any clear specification of how the data are to be corrected or used. Pretesting and analysis apparently did not precede the decision to require the specific data asked for on the forms. The benefits claimed are simply asserted. No critical analysis appears to have been done. I find it shocking that this waste of resources could be seriously contemplated by government officials who claim to be acting in the public interest.

COMMENTARY

Frederic M. Scherer

A paper as negative as Professor Benston's tells me more about debating technique than it does about the substance of the issues being debated. I am puzzled as to why Benston focuses only on the FTC's program, even though our assignment was much more broadly couched.

In choosing such a narrow perspective, namely just the FTC's LB reporting program, Professor Benston leaves unanswered two fundamental questions. First, if the benefits from segmental financial data are so meager, why have so many financial reporting programs, both public and private, emerged in the last half-dozen years? Second, if the FTC's program, in particular, is so bad, what distinguishes it from other programs Benston doesn't mention and that industry has opposed less vigorously? I submit that these are questions he could not address without undermining his argument fatally.

Let me say a few words, first, about the benefits issue. Professor Benston doesn't seem to think that segmental performance data would be of much value to investors. This is a bit hard to reconcile with the findings of the staff of the SEC's Advisory Committee on Corporate Disclosure. A memorandum the committee made public on October 21, 1976, begins with this observation:

> From the interviewing completed to date, it appears that one of the fundamental categories of information which analysts seek for use in investment decision-making is detailed information with respect to the various lines of business of the companies which they analyze. It appears that much of their time is spent gathering, or attempting to gather, this information, because in their view the Line-of-Business information in SEC filings often combines too many segments to be useful.

The memorandum goes on to recommend that the SEC become involved in setting uniform industry reporting categories, and that the segmental financial performance information thus reported "is so important to the understanding of a business that it should be placed in the front part of the disclosure document which is filed with the Commission, rather than in a less conspicuous place." Now, how can one conclude that this kind of information is of no value to an analyst?

Also, Benston makes much of the harmful consequences that might flow from the use of the FTC's aggregated LB performance reports. He argues, for example, that one might be burned entering the frozen waffle business on the basis of performance information on the FTC's "Frozen Specialties" category. In this and other examples, he seems to assume that businessmen are stupid, unable to recognize when data do or do not provide the necessary support for a decision.

I have talked to many businessmen, and I don't find them stupid in that way. They know what they can do with data; they know what they can't do; and they are not likely to make stupid decisions on the basis of broadly aggregated data.

It has always seemed to me that an appropriate analogy is to the use of a Geiger counter in prospecting for uranium. A frequency of clicks reveals that there is treasure buried. It does not, however, give you information about the magnitude of the lode; it doesn't tell you how deep you are going to have to dig for it. Much more work is required in order to find out exactly what is needed to mine the ore. What the Geiger counter does is narrow the costly—and it is costly—search process, not end it. So also with LB data. It is a useful instrument, but not the end of analysis.

Let me turn now to some of the key technical issues related to segmental reporting. In attacking the FTC's LB program, Professor Benston views as vices problems of establishing what he calls economic values. Now, that is a problem generic to all accounting data and not just to the problem of segmental reporting.

Granted, such problems exist, but are they really as hopeless as Benston suggests? Are the many analysts who try to squeeze segmental inferences out of accounting data all to be judged mentally incompetent for their attempt? I think not, because there is, in fact, much meaning in the numbers that accounting data provide, even though they have their limitations.

This is, perhaps, the most fundamental point on which we disagree. And, again, let me stress, this is a generic problem of accounting data in general, not of accounting data as used for segmental performance reporting.

Let me, therefore, focus on the problems which are unique to segmental performance reporting. One is transfer pricing. Here, Professor Benston attempts to have his argument both ways. He says that where it is difficult to set an arm's-length price, the problem of transfer pricing is a horror. And, indeed, it may be. But when the FTC tries to do something sensible about the problem, such as integrating lines with extensive transfers, Benston criticizes the Commission for permitting "contaminations."

Now, I don't see how one can legitimately view it that way. If you look, for example, at General Motors' operations, and you find it has a foundry, a sheet-goods stamping plant, and an automobile assembly plant and if it is difficult to establish an arm's-length transfer price, then it seems to me it makes a lot of sense to integrate those three operations together and view them as an integrated automobile manufacturing operation. That is not contamination. That is just viewing the operation as it is. In their segmental reporting programs, the FTC and the Department of Defense have tried very hard to make these kinds of distinctions. If they have failed, Benston should come forward with specific, constructive suggestions as to how they can improve their vertical integration rules.

Similarly, it is clear that common costs are problematic. But my experience—and I have interviewed in my multiplant study maybe 70 or 80 multiplant, multiproduct companies—suggests that most of the difficulty here is the problem of imprecision in measurement, not the kind of conceptual impasse, the impossibility of measuring, that Benston talks about.

If this is the problem, the question is one of how close and how robust an approximation can be achieved. On this the only source of evidence, as Benston correctly points out, is Professor Mautz's study of six companies.[1] The data are summarized in Table 1-12 of Benston's paper. He looks at the table and finds that there is a high incidence of important measurement inaccuracies.

What are the different numbers that emerge? For Company A, Segment 1, for example: by one allocation formula, 8.9 percent; by another, 12.3; by another 13.5; by another 13.8; by another 12.9. They are all in the same ballpark—all middling rates of return.

You can go through the illustrations one by one and find they tend to fall into three classes with only two exceptions. First, all returns are high by any criterion; second, all returns are low, a lot lower than you could get in a savings bank; and third, all are in the middling area.

The only clear exception is Segment 9 of Company C, and I have looked pretty hard at why that is so wildly inconsistent. There seem to be at least two reasons. One is that that particular segment accounts for about one-half of one percent of the employment of the reporting company. It is very small. And the second reason is that the company uses a very strange allocation criterion. I have been trying for a year and a half to figure out what it is. It is "amounts proportionate to directly related expenses." It is just very strange and gives you wild results, as it does for other results of Company C.

---

1. Robert K. Mautz, *Financial Reporting by Diversified Companies*, Financial Executives Institute, New York, 1968.

But, I submit that most of the data, in fact, suggest that you are not going to reach seriously misleading results, no matter what criterion you use.

In the section on *Evaluation of Expected Benefits—Data Measurement Problems,* Benston discusses Mautz's data and notes that ambiguities yield prediction errors on the order of 20 percent or so of profits. He then develops a mathematical profit-error-analysis model, assuming that errors of this magnitude creep into *costs*—not profits, costs—and as a result he gets very, very high *profit*-prediction errors. But this is nothing more than sleight of hand. For Mautz's sample, costs were roughly sixteen times the profit margins on which Mautz's analyses, and hence Benston's analyses, were focused. So, again, I really don't think the inaccuracy problems are anything like what Benston has suggested.

Let me say a few words now about the third major problem of segmental reporting, category definition. The FTC's definitions have been much criticized, and I will concede readily that there are some pretty bad examples. But you can always find horror stories. The key question is: How good are they on the average?

The second issue here involves what criterion one is going to use. Dr. Betty Bock and Professor Benston have persistently said: "These categories have to be economic markets."

In its very first position paper on this, the FTC said: "Yes, we would like the data to be on markets, but it would be very difficult to accomplish that." The FTC has gradually backed away from markets because it has, indeed, recognized it was difficult to obtain LB data by markets. But the Commission concluded that data on industries would also be very useful. Well, of course, I was involved in that decision-making process, but despite that bias, I truly believe that from an industry standpoint the LB categories are extremely meaningful.

Let me give an example. I spent four or five years working on a book which is summarized in the Center for Law and Economic Studies' work on industrial concentration.[2] It was an intensive investigation on twelve industries. I had no influence whatsoever that I know of on the formulation of the FTC's 1973 reporting categories, and yet, seven of the twelve were identical to the categories that I found meaningful for purposes of my research project. The other five differed for the most part only in minor respects. I would have loved to have had performance data arrayed by each and every one of those twelve industry categories. I could have done a much better job in my book analyzing the structure-performance relationships in those industries if I had had such information.

Let me say a word also about this problem of contamination. Benston

---

2. Harvey J. Goldschmid, H. Michael Mann, and J. Fred Weston (eds.), *Industrial Concentration: The New Learning,* Little, Brown, Boston, 1974.

talks about the 85 percent rule which, in effect, allowed 15 percent so-called contamination.

That is only a part of the rule. The rule is double-edged. It says that contamination may not be greater than 15 percent, but also not greater than the average level of contamination in the company's plants. These latter data we have from the Bureau of the Census, and we know they are on the order of somewhere between 6 and 8 percent. So the problem has again been overemphasized. I think contamination of 6 to 8 percent is quite acceptable compared to the enormous data problems we currently have.

Finally, let me say a few words about confidentiality. Here, I believe, the FTC's approach is deficient. I see no reason other than power politics for keeping confidential the kinds of individual company data that the FTC is collecting.

Under SEC rules, the data that small companies are required to publish are issued at a more detailed level than the FTC's categories. For the small companies you get very, very narrow segment categories. For the large companies you get very, very broad categories under the SEC's rules.

Now if, in fact, this disclosure of detailed individual company data by narrowly defined segments is harmful, it must be the little companies that are getting harmed, because they are, in fact, already disclosing data generally at a finer level of detail than the FTC requires. If, therefore, there is real harm—and I don't think there is—then the existing SEC system is unfair to small companies. Their ability to hold their own despite such detailed disclosure regulations suggests to me, at least, that the consequences of individual company data disclosure have been grossly exaggerated.

In sum, the problems of segmental financial reporting are undeniably difficult. But from the fact that the Strategic Planning Institute, a private organization, has seen fit to collect segmental performance data without any government prodding at all, and from much other evidence, I am convinced that there is a genuine demand for segmental performance information. I have analyzed all the various programs, and I see no indication that the FTC's solutions are less sensible than those of other organizations, public and private, which Benston has not criticized, and with which industry is cooperating.

DIALOGUE

DAVID MARTIN: Professor Benston, how would you respond to Professor Scherer's commentary?

BENSTON: I will be brief. The reader should realize that I am not saying all I could. What disturbs me about Professor Scherer's comments is that he seems to think of this as a debate and uses debating tools. I don't want to cloak myself with some mantle of academic responsibility, but the truth is I don't see this as a debate. I am not trying to make points. I am not trying to find something good to say about the other side because I think that will make me seem a more balanced person. I am trying to get at the truth as best I am able to do. I would have said something good about the LB program if I could have found it. I didn't deliberately stack the deck.

The problem is if some things are not useful, they are not useful. If they are conceptually impossible, then they are. It is not a matter of sitting back and saying there is a better way of doing it. It can't be done.

I can understand the reasons for the economists

The session was chaired by William K. Jones, Professor of Law, Columbia University School of Law. For further biographical information, see Appendix 1.

at the FTC or business people, or whoever did it, putting together this program. If you have read the work in industrial organization, you realize something better can be done. So you say, "I want better data." But if a doctoral student of mine had come to me with the LB proposal, I would have rejected it as not being a conceivable project. If he had insisted, I would have suggested he move to another school. There are ideas that just cannot fly, and the FTC's LB program happens to be one of them.

ELEANOR FOX: Professor Benston, you expressed serious concerns about contamination and the problem of fitting data into prefitted categories. If you had access to the data from any number of companies in a market, could you, using that data, draw conclusions that would be useful in any one of the seven or so areas that you outlined as possible areas of benefit?

BENSTON: For some of them, yes. Basically, what one has to do and what was not done, to my knowledge, by the FTC, is to state clear hypotheses first: What is it you are trying to answer? What question are you asking? Once you have a specific question in mind, then you can get the data that speak to that question. And when the data are insufficient, then you will know it.

FOX: I wonder if you think anything useful could be gleaned from such data on how industry structure and performance relate?

BENSTON: Let me speak to my own experience. One of my fields of intensive work is banking. Banking data are by magnitudes of ten better than accounting data from other firms. I am doing a study at the Federal Reserve. We are trying to look at exactly that question in banking markets—and banks are restricted to a particular market. I must say that even with excellent data, we are not getting answers that are meaningful because we can't measure what a bank's market is, and every time we change it slightly we get a different answer. The question is: Can you find out something with market performance data? The answer is: Very little, very little.

WILLIAM LOVETT: If we assume the Carter Administration is serious about doing more toward prodding the economy to full employment and, therefore, that wage-price monitoring of a much more comprehensive nature may be needed in a few years, to what extent would the LB program, if we assume it is implemented as the FTC would like, have to be supplemented by much stronger data acquisition to achieve adequate wage-price monitoring for concentrated industries?

SCHERER: Well, again, I would say that the correct analogy is to a Geiger counter. You've got data on 261 manufacturing industry sectors. That is rather finely subdivided. Having gone that far, however, you might be interested in some narrower sector. In that case, you would focus your inquiry and say: "How about telling us something more about antifreeze?" Antifreeze does not happen to be one of the LB industry sectors.

Let me add one further comment that is obliquely related to the question. I have just reviewed what I think are the best articles on the relationship between industry structure and wage-setting behavior. The best article is based on data from about fifteen or twenty companies. It is highly aggregated so that you really cannot draw proper structure-performance links.

We suspect that there is a link between profitability and wage bargaining, but I do not believe I err in saying that economists do not understand the nature of that link. We don't have adequate data with which we can link profitability on the one hand and wage-change data on the other. If we don't understand that, we do not have the conceptual background to implement a policy of trying to bring the economy to full employment without inflation.

FRANKLIN EDWARDS: As an economist, when I approach the subject of the need for regulation or the need for government intervention, I immediately start searching for some concept of market failure or injustice which I seek to remedy by government intervention. Why doesn't the free market result in companies collecting that data which is useful, first; and secondly, if companies do collect it, why doesn't the free market result in its disclosure?

SCHERER: The first thing I would say is I disagree rather strongly with Professor Benston on his assertion that companies do not collect data that correlate with the FTC's LB categories. There are, of course, some exceptions, but by and large things fit pretty well, as nearly as we can tell, from the initial implementation of the LB program. So, to answer your first question, I believe the companies do have the data.

As to the question about disclosure, let me address it by the most extreme of analogies. In Finland, there is one petroleum refining company. It is a nationalized company. It is owned by the people of Finland. Last week I was talking to an official of the Finish Government who was telling me about the enormous difficulties the Finnish government experienced trying to get cost and profit information from its nationalized petroleum refining industry. Why did the government have difficulty? Because knowledge is power.

I liken the situation in my paper to a zero-sum game. This happens to be a game that under the law is stacked in favor of the companies. If they don't want to give out the data, unless there is some kind of compulsion, they won't. And that, I think, is the market failure.

BENSTON: I'd like to speak to Professor Edwards's question about market failure. I don't see a failure here. I have looked at the evidence with reference to the stock market. I have done some of the work with reference to the accounting data and stock market prices. I was the reviewer, as a matter of fact, of the piece by Collins that was referred to, and another piece to be published by the *Bell Journal*.

The evidence that publication of financial data has any effect on stock data at all is practically nonexistent. The evidence is that it has practically no effect. That is not because the data are not useful, but they are used by people in specific ways, and other data are used before they become public. The FTC's LB data won't have any public usefulness. It won't solve problems. It won't give people information. It will be expensive, though. I don't see the public purpose in the whole thing.

SCHERER: As I understand the evidence, there are two papers specifically to the point we are dealing with, one unpublished which I haven't seen, and one by Collins which I have seen. The article by Collins is the lead article in a most prestigious journal.[1] If that is zero evidence, I guess I don't know what evidence is.

Also, it may be true that investors take into account, before reports are formally issued, the information that those financial reports are going to make available to the public. Nevertheless, if those reports were not issued sooner or later, one would lose a feedback process which allows investors to reconcile their expectations with the new and revised information. So even if Professor Benston is right on his point, I don't think you can say that the information has no value to investors.

BENSTON: I was the reviewer of Collins's piece. I approved it for publication. He does not prove his points. It is a good paper; the results are not, however, statistically significant.

WILLIAM K. JONES: Let me ask a technical question to clear up one point that Professor Scherer made. He referred to General Motors and the problems of collapsing various stages of automobile production into a single unit. In order to do that in a meaningful way, would you have to apply the same approach to other companies in the same industry? That is, could you have General Motors providing information on a fully integrated basis and have other automobile manufacturers providing information by different segments? Is that a problem?

---

1. Daniel W. Collins, "SEC Product-Line Reporting and Market Efficiency," *Journal of Financial Economics*, vol. 2, no. 2, June 1975.

SCHERER: Sure, it's a problem. I engaged in a minor research project in my early days on the decision-making and organizational structure of the automobile companies. The FTC's guidelines for integration are based on knowledge of that structure and what kinds of activities could be integrated by all of the companies and what kinds of activities are those for which transfer prices could be set on a meaningful basis and, therefore, for which disintegration was possible.

BENSTON: The companies will have a choice, and depending upon how they exercise it, you will have different numbers. That is inevitable. Maybe the choice should have been mandated, and maybe eventually it will be. But the difficulty is that these problems are not solvable. So you have various arbitrary alternatives to solving the problems.

I think a lot of what we are discussing now should also come up in the discussion of the meaning of numbers. The problem we face is we can't measure some things we would like to measure.

LOUIS SCHWARTZ: I find myself puzzled about the reach of Professor Benston's argument. It seems to me that his comprehensive attack on LB reporting, as requiring impossible allocations and so on, must lead him to the conclusion that all businessmen running conglomerate enterprises are just blundering. He must assume, for example, that AT&T doesn't know whether more investment in its Western Electric division or in its Long Lines Division would be a good thing; that the petroleum companies have no idea whether they need more refineries, retail establishments, or production; and that all the companies which pretend to have profit centers are deceiving themselves and others.

BENSTON: Yes, I think that is a very good point. The key word you said was "more." And the key analysis is *incremental* analysis. Surely companies try to solve these problems by saying: "If we do this, what will happen?"

But the LB data we are discussing do not refer to that. They refer to accounting for past decisions made where depreciation has been taken on an essentially arbitrary basis. So people look at return on investment, but when they do, it is with reference to that number in exactly the same circumstances within that company over some past period, and then they adjust it. Companies do use internal data, but they have to look at incremental analyses essentially, and you have to know how those data arose and what the biases are, and if you are in the company, you know.

SCHWARTZ: They do it by line of business, do they not?

BENSTON: They do it by departments and control aspects. These are not the same as lines of business.

SCHWARTZ: Not exactly.

BENSTON: No, not at all. There is no point in keeping your books according to SIC codes.

HARLAN BLAKE: I didn't take Professor Benston's argument to reach quite as far as Professor Schwartz did, but does it not reach to the use by outsiders, such as antitrust enforcement agencies and courts, of market-based standards of concentration as bases for enforcement policy or rulings of illegality?

BENSTON: I think you can look at the terms of observable, measurable market prices. As to cost accounting data, as an accountant, I believe I am capable of proving anything I want with cost accounting data. If I can't, I will turn in my CPA. Because I have available to me a whole set of arbitrary allocation rules, any one of which is acceptable by authorities, I can make the numbers come out the way I want them to come out within some range. And anyone who looks at my data and thinks he knows something is a fool. But market prices are different. You have to sell something and buy something.

MARK GREEN: As to nondisclosure by a foreign firm, does either of you know whether foreign countries or the European Economic Community requires LB reporting within their jurisdictions? Have they attempted it?

BENSTON: I don't know of any.

SCHERER: There is none that I know of. Visitors from a variety of foreign countries have come and talked to the FTC's staff to find out how one does it. There is interest.

ELLIOTT WEISS: At the meeting of the SEC's Advisory Committee at which segment reporting was discussed, there was a panel of company representatives. Every one of them mentioned that their companies, in fact, did keep some kind of segmented books for their operations. The greatest concern of this group of representatives of five or six companies was that they would be forced to abandon their systems of bookkeeping for some other system imposed by government.

Professor Scherer, I wonder how much importance you attach to standardization of categories as opposed to a system whereby the breakdowns could be along the lines the companies use, with an explanation of accounting principles somewhat comparable to that now included for overall financial reporting. Would this be an acceptable substitute for the kind of standardized categories you mentioned?

SCHERER: I suspect your approach would be wonderful if companies would take the mandate seriously and define their categories as narrowly as they have them defined internally. The study of conglomerates that the FTC made early in the 1970s showed that on the average the companies had something like thirty or thirty-five internal categories on which they collected profit, loss, asset, and other data. They reported, on the average, on about five categories. I suspect the LB problem could be solved very simply if companies would really be willing to disclose what data they already have internally.

JONES: Is there a difference between reporting which is going to be made public and reporting from which the FTC or some other governmental body is going to seek to produce aggregate figures? How do you produce aggregate figures with each company reporting on its own basis?

SCHERER: If the companies, in fact, published at the narrow level of detail for which they collect internally, I suspect you would find sufficient homogeneity that the problem of aggregation would not be very great.

BENSTON: I don't wish to state this as a survey, but I have over some time been involved with looking at a number of companies' internal records for a variety of things, and what I find is an enormous diversity. You see reporting internally on profit centers and on cost centers; sometimes a division is organized geographically (e.g., the Midwest division sells all the products there), and sometimes according to product lines, with the marketing geographical. Sometimes within the same company, different divisions will account different ways. Some will use standard costs; others will not. And segments will change over time as a different manager takes over a particular segment of a company.

The problem we have here is we are dealing with a diverse universe of companies that are constantly changing their procedures as the world changes and as they attempt to adapt to that world. To try to ram them into some sort of pigeonhole is to damage, very seriously damage, the meaningfulness of anything you get out.

FREDERICK ROWE: I have two questions. First, inasmuch as Professor Scherer wishes to validate the thesis of a positive correlation between structure and performance and Professor Benston fears that the LB program is done at an extravagant cost both directly and indirectly, can the thesis be validated at a lesser cost by collecting historic data, i.e., data twenty or thirty years old, as empirical material pertinent to the thesis?

Second, Mark Green asked if there is foreign experience with similar endeavors. I would like to ask whether there is experience in transportation or other regulated industries in this country upon which one could draw as a parallel to demonstrate either the utility or futility of the LB enterprise?

SCHERER: On the first question, when one analyzes structure-performance relationships, the best studies typically do use data that are about twenty years old or so. One reason for use of historical data is that industry was much less complex and diversified in those days. Therefore, you get somewhat cleaner data. Also, only for 1950 do we have adequate data on individual company market shares as a result of a 1950 FTC survey. The FTC is trying to repeat the survey for 1972, and although apparently every company complied voluntarily in 1950, for some reason the companies have found they can't supply the data in 1972.

One further point. Although I have emphasized the research use of LB data, that is by no means the only use. A company contemplating entering the paint industry—and we have had inquiries from would-be paint manufacturers—is not going to be helped much by 1950 profit data on the paint industry.

Labor markets have changed. Those who are trying to understand the links among profitability, demand changes, labor changes, and degrees of unionization are not going to be helped much by 1950 data when, again, the financial structure of the American economy was rather different. You can do some things with old data, but you can by no means do all you would wish. Also, the longer you go back in history, the more difficulty companies are likely to have retrieving data, and that would create additional problems.

BENSTON: I would suggest to anyone considering entering the paint industry that he consider the market prices. The prices paints sell for are available, and any company contemplating entry had better do a market survey. Unless they can get to a company's books and look at the cost of raw materials, look at the machinery it is using, the depreciation, etc., you will be terribly misled. No company would rely on aggregate data. Companies make projections: "If we do this, then what will happen?"

As to regulated industries, I think that is a very good point—uniform accounting has been pushed and tried a variety of times. The net result is that most of the numbers are useless and nobody uses them. The darned things are all the same and don't mean anything. I might say Germany experimented with uniform accounting in 1928 and destroyed its accounting system.

DAVID MARSH: May I point out for the record that before this whole thing left the GAO, there was considerable testimony and views, not just by larger companies but by various smaller and medium-sized ones. There are some medium-sized companies that are very diverse, and they are affected as suppliers, subcontractors, and so forth, right down the pike.

SCHERER: Sure, there has been lots of testimony. I think the FTC's LB program is a nice case study in administrative procedure. I must say it opened my eyes.

Two kinds of things opened my eyes. One is that the companies came on the record and said all sorts of things. And I would go out and speak at conferences and sit down with the accountants of those companies, and they would tell me a completely different story about the feasibility of LB reporting. They would say on the record: "We can't do it." In private, face to face, they would say they could do it—sure, they had a few problems, but they could do it.

Second, we have literally hundreds of documents from companies—1970, 1973, and so forth. I have read a large quantity of them and found that documentation produced in the context of open hearings, and the like, is largely useless. Where we really began to find out and zero in on what was feasible and what was not feasible was when we actually implemented the 1973 LB reporting program.

At that point, a wave of motions to quash came in, and the FTC did one of the smartest things it has done throughout the LB reporting program. It said: "Okay, we deny the motions you have filed, but we give you leave to file renewed motions to quash, provided you address in detail the inconsistencies between your accounting system and the FTC categories." That, by the way, was Cal Collier's idea, I think, and it's one of the best ideas that's been had in this whole thing.

If you look at those renewed motions to quash and the underlying documentation, you will find an extraordinarily different story being told than the story that was told in the summaries that were presented in the context of hearings on this.

MARSH: That was a little different time frame, perhaps, though.

LEONARD WEISS: First, a brief point with regard to the usefulness of standard accounting. There is no industry that has been so thoroughly and systematically studied as the electric power industry, and I think it's precisely because it does have standard accounting. And the results, I think, are very well accepted.

My main point is that we have, for generations, had LB reporting at the Bureau of the Census. It is classified by the SIC system. You have the problem of transfers. Most of the transfer problems that Professor Benston raised are also applicable to the Census industry statistics. And those Census industry statistics have been very widely used. I feel that in many statistical studies they have yielded expected results and often very close to precisely expected relationships. There is, for example, the relationship between price-cost margin and gross fixed assets or the relationship between price-fixed margin and advertising. That goes a little bit beyond Census. It includes the input-output tables.

We have had a great deal of experience with something that is very closely analogous to LB reporting already, and I don't think it's been disastrous at all.

BENSTON: That is a tautological analysis. The fact that people have used data in ways in which they shouldn't have bothered isn't much of an argument, I think. I don't comprehend the analysis that says, "Because we have had some bad studies, we should have more bad studies."

The new LB data will not improve the situation. They have the same limitations as the old data but more of them. What is the use of going to the expense and flooding—if someone is foolish enough to publish more of this—the journals with misinformation? I don't understand it.

CARL AUERBACH: I have two questions. First, how rigid is the SIC classification system? If classifications change over time, won't it be a devil of a job to try to get meaningful comparable data over time? You will always be collecting data which can't be compared as time goes by.

Second—and this bothers me somewhat—I don't see what sense it makes for public policy to make decisions based on data which each company itself could manipulate (by accounting conventions) for whatever purposes it deems desirable at the time it has to report. And for all of the public policy purposes which are outlined in the papers—setting aside the confidentiality point which we ought to consider separately—wouldn't it make more sense simply to require the submission of data about direct or variable costs by product lines? Then you would be able to compare it with price and you would be able to compare it with overall profitability. And do you really need anything more for any of these public policy purposes which you have in mind?

BENSTON: I agree with your first half. All I want to do is refer you to a study that Betty Bock did (I am constantly referring to her, but she has done such good work, what can I do?) looking at the changes of the FTC categories from 1947 to 1972.

BETTY BOCK: We have Mr. Biles of the Bureau of the Census here, of course. I found there was about a two-thirds turnover from 1947 to 1972 in the definitions of the manufacturing categories.

ELMER BILES: That sounds about right. Of course, you must keep in mind that the Bureau itself does not determine the structure. There is an office of OMB which actually promulgates this system at the four-digit level. The Bureau itself has structured product classes, of which we have some 1,300. This is for the annual survey of manufacturers when we collect information. We also publish information on general statistics, and, of course, we have information on the degree of coverage for these categories.

There has been a definite shift since 1947. I think one of the considerations that does enter into decisions by the SIC technical group is what impact a given change would have. One is very reluctant to change just for change's sake. Of course, there have been technological changes that have occurred.

SCHERER: Let me deal with both of these points. I have used the Census data very frequently, and yes, there are over a period of thirty years fairly substantial incomparabilities. What usually happens is that something that once was aggregated gets broken out, or a couple of things get put together. If you are very inventive, you can piece together a long series, but even so, you have continuity at least for five years, and typically for ten years, and very frequently even for a longer span of years, so you can do some pretty good time-series analyses. Moreover, you know how the things have changed so you know how to relink them if you want to do a time-series analysis, especially if you have raw data.

As to whether companies should publish their direct or variable costs, make that suggestion to a drug company that testified before the Kefauver committee!

BENSTON: A problem with publishing data about variable costs is that they will vary from time to time, sometimes not very much, other times very considerably. A second problem is that you can look at one company over time, perhaps, but you cannot aggregate companies. It is not meaningful.

DAVID HULETT: On the confidentiality point Professor Scherer mentioned, perhaps we at OMB were the engineers of the power politics that made this information confidential. The reason for that, just to state my personal view, was that unless we leaped that hurdle, the program was not going to get off the ground.

ALICE TEPPER MARLIN: I have been working over the last seven or eight years with data that have been relatively new in their release to the general public from corporations, and every single argument that has been raised today is equally valid for many other areas of disclosure, for instance, EEO-1 reports, reporting on effluent emissions, air and water data, even 10-Ks and annual reports. Today, I believe Professor Benston stated that 10-Ks and annual reports were wastes of money and shouldn't be bothered with.

There seems to be an assumption that because data are complex and not completely comparable, we can't trust individuals or the government to use these data with some degree of wisdom and sophistication, and that across-industry comparisons will be made when they are not valid.

There are frequently misuses of data. I think I could take almost any disclosure requirement that has been proposed and think of three or four ways I'd like to improve it to make the data more useful and more accurate. But I get very weary seeing the response to these data problems being suggestions for elimination of any general disclosure. Private interests do continually have access to these data.

My background is as a security analyst on Wall Street. While working as an analyst, I had access to most of the data we are talking about today on a confidential basis. I never would have thought of making it available to the general public. It would have been against my own interests and cut me out of my job.

SCHERER: I think the speaker has put her finger on precisely the difference between Professor Benston and myself. I know there are problems in using data. The FTC knows there are problems. Everybody else who has been involved in segmental reporting knows there are problems.

I think, however, and I believe a lot of people think, that one can nevertheless do the kinds of things one needs to do to make intelligent use of these data, understanding their limitations, and also understanding their potentialities. The disagreement, it seems to me, is that simple.

You have the same kinds of problems with all sorts of other data. Professor Benston, for example, computes the discounted present value of the FTC's LB program costs over a forty-year period and comes up with a figure of something like $200 million. Well, anybody can play that kind of game. And I went to Dave Hulett's report on the cost of the federal government's statistical programs and found by similar assumptions that the discounted present value of only the intragovernment costs of collecting labor statistics is $1.28 billion.

Now, that is a lot of money to be spending on a program when we don't even know how to measure unemployment. And, yet, I'm sure that one can make very, very good use of the kinds of labor statistics that are collected, even though there are conceptual difficulties.

BENSTON: I think that Alice Tepper Marlin and Professor Scherer have summed up the thing very well. Basically, my problem with the LB program is that the numbers coming out are so bad that I cannot see how they can be useful. I didn't say, if a number is not perfect it therefore has no use. I said when a number is useless, it has no use. When a number cannot be interpreted at all, it has no use. There is a difference! And so the problem with the LB program is that it has no measurable benefits other than, perhaps, to some of the individuals involved.

Maybe it has some benefit for gross national product. That has never been spelled out very clearly. Maybe if it had been and I had looked into it more closely, I might have changed my mind.

But against that, one has to put the cost—and that is true not only of this program but of the labor statistics program and any program in which a government involves itself. If their benefits do not exceed the costs, then we ought to consider very carefully whether we are missing something, and if we are, we ought not carry out the program.

Somebody bears the cost of all these data-dredging programs. And the somebody is us. And the question is, don't we have something better to do with our resources than waste them? I think so, and I think every program should be subjected to scrutiny.

In general, I am against any mandated anything. I hate to put this on a philosophical level because we get instant disagreements, but I am philosophically concerned that we ought not mandate things unless we can demonstrate that benefits will be incurred.

TEPPER MARLIN: Is there, therefore, no mandatory disclosure that you would support, Professor Benston?

BENSTON: My studies of the SEC's mandated disclosure led me to believe that it's unnecessary and, therefore, not useful. I would not have supported it at the time and do not now. One reason is that there was voluntary disclosure at the time, and the other is that all the security markets are efficient. The mandated disclosure will not make the markets more efficient.

TEPPER MARLIN: Is there any mandated disclosure you would support?

BENSTON: I think there are many things which the public has a right to know and where there are benefits. The problem is, however, we are swamped with data that nobody knows what to do with but that somebody—at real cost—has to produce. And simply saying, "I would like to know" is not a sufficient reason for mandating disclosure.

CHAPTER TWO

Uniform Reporting Dealing with Corporate Ownership

EDITOR'S NOTE

Reporting dealing with corporate ownership has a faintly 1930s ring. Images of Berle and Means and of TNEC monographs jump quickly to mind. But Vic Reinemer's paper demonstrates that ownership reporting is very much a contemporary concern. A host of regulatory agencies (e.g., Civil Aeronautics Board, Federal Communications Commission, Federal Trade Commission, Interstate Commerce Commission, Securities and Exchange Commission), with responsibilities for issues as varied as industry concentration, management conflict-of-interest, interlocking directorates, and foreign control over sensitive industries, have important ownership-reporting programs.

Reinemer points to the difficulty of obtaining accurate ownership information because of nominees, depositories, and shares held by brokers in "street names"—the problem of so-called anonymous shareholders. He urges no new legislation; instead, he proposes that agencies make more effective use of their existing authority and promulgate already developed "model corporate disclosure regulations."

Hans H. Angermueller agrees that a composite reporting model for multiagency use is desirable. He fears, however, that when legislators apply the concept of uniform reporting to ownership disclosure "what they are really talking about is uniformly *more*—not uniformly *less*." In his view, the case for the reporting of additional ownership information has not been established. He is concerned about privacy-chilling "dragnet operations" and the cost of new reporting.

CORPORATE OWNERSHIP AND CONTROL: A PUBLIC POLICY VIEW

Vic Reinemer, *Staff Director, Senate Subcommittee on Reports, Accounting and Management*

INTRODUCTION

According to my dictionary, ownership implies control. Control or potential control of a corporation is not easy to ascertain. But it is that control aspect of ownership which is important from a public policy viewpoint. Accurate and timely information bearing upon control and potential control of corporations can:

- signal wholesale escape from regulation through creation of holding companies which milk regulated subsidiaries . . .
- reveal—and deter—self-dealing and violations of antitrust and conflict-of-interest statutes and regulations . . .
- show the extent and nature of economic concentration, especially in sensitive areas such as broadcasting . . .
- provide regulators and the Congress with timely notice of conditions within key industries and individual companies which, if not corrected, will lead to pleas for bailout by the taxpayers or legalization of violations of ownership concentration limits . . .
- provide the data base upon which continuous and proper Federal surveillance of regulated industries is made manageable. This will reduce the requirements for frantic and disruptive Congressional and agency investigations which reveal primarily the enduring truth of Professor Finagle's Law of Information, to wit:

  The information we have is not what we want,
  the information we want is not what we need, and
  the information we need is not available.[1]

---

1. *Corporate Ownership and Control,* Subcommittee on Reports of Senate Committee on Government Operations, 94th Cong., 1st Sess., S. Doc. No. 94-246, 1975, p. 2.

Discussion of the ownership and control of corporations has suffered from confusing concepts of ownership. Oil companies, for example, claim that they are owned by 14 million hard hats, working women, and senior citizens. Utility and food firms picture widows, farmers, small businessmen and women, blue-collar workers, and college students as their "owners." Tiffany's advertises that "everybody owns the free enterprise system." Professor Peter Drucker, industry consultant and prolific author, maintains that "the employees of America are the only true 'owners' of the means of production," that "through their pension funds they are the only true 'capitalists' around, owning, controlling and directing" the country's capital.[2]

The claims in corporate advertising that minuscule or indirect stockholdings result in ownership and advertisers' omission or downplaying of the role of institutional investors are essentially incorrect. I do realize, however, that few persons expect to receive the whole truth from advertising.

Professor Drucker's situation is different. Unrefuted excerpts from *The Unseen Revolution,* his book on pension funds, received prominent editorial display in publications such as *The New York Times* and the *Wall Street Journal.* Their readers are led to believe that workers actually control the huge and growing pension fund investments. In reality, of course, most of these pension funds are controlled by banks selected by corporate management.

We need not concern ourselves here with disclosure by persons whose ownership is bereft of control, except in those instances where it is necessary to go to such persons—if their holdings are sizable—to learn who does control. They are not the widow who invests through a mutual fund or the college student who was sold a life insurance policy by a company with a large common-stock portfolio. Nor are we concerned here about disclosure by persons whose direct investments in corporations are too inconsequential to give them any potential leverage within the firm. Our focus is on management of the information which bears on control of corporations by principal investors, most of them institutional.

LEVERS OF CONTROL

One lever of control resides with those empowered to vote, buy, and sell significant amounts of voting stock in a firm. I shall discuss voting power, which often but not necessarily accompanies the power to buy and sell stock. A second lever is exercised through the granting—or withholding—of credit, and the attachment of conditions and restrictions on loans. Membership on the board of directors and interlocking directorates constitutes a third lever. A fourth can be termed corporate

---

2. Peter F. Drucker, *The Unseen Revolution: How Pension Fund Socialism Came to America,* Harper & Row, New York, 1976.

structure—the relationship of a firm to parent firm, subsidiaries, and joint ventures.

Control can be exercised by one or a combination of these levers. Controlling action taken by one party can be followed by controlling action by another party, using a different lever. The Anaconda Company's recent history offers a case in point.

Anaconda's Experience

A consortium of banks, led by Chase Manhattan, entered into a credit agreement with Anaconda in 1968. The agreement provided for modification of the lending terms by vote of four institutions holding 60 percent of the total debt, that 60 percent being the amount held by the four major banks. Chase was named trustee under the trust indenture. Chase was assigned broad powers and specifically a seat on the board of directors.

In subsequent years, more credit was granted by the Chase-led banks and more restrictions were placed upon Anaconda as its problems relative to losing its Chilean property mounted. Finally, one of Chase's men on the board was installed as Anaconda's chief executive officer. He brought in a new management team.

Although Anaconda sorely needed funds to maintain its operations in the western United States, the Chase team decided—not surprisingly—that Anaconda's immediate financial duty was to pay off the debt to Chase and the other banks in the consortium. That was promptly arranged. Anaconda's United States operations, thus bereft of necessary modernization capital, were sharply curtailed. Hundreds of Anaconda employees were thrown out of work.[3]

Those trained and willing workers probably would have responded enthusiastically to injection of capital into the firm by an investor. A logical possibility would have been the Anaconda pension fund. Its assets are valued at $144 million. Alas—and contrary to Professor Drucker's thesis—Anaconda workers do not control their pension fund. Nor does Anaconda. Those pension funds are controlled by major banks.

The Anaconda workers are typical. Banks chosen by company management control some 80 percent of pension fund assets. Ironically—but not surprisingly, given its other leverage within Anaconda—the Chase is one of Anaconda's pension fund managers. But the pension fund lever was not pulled in behalf of the Anaconda workers. The banks' control of the pension fund was so complete that even Anaconda's management could not have used it.

---

3. *Hearings on Proposed Offer by Crane Company to Acquire Anaconda Company*, Subcommittee on Reports, Accounting and Management of Senate Committee on Government Operations, 94th Cong., 1st Sess., Oct. 8, 1975.

Subsequently, Anaconda was pursued, sometimes unwillingly, by several suitors—Crane, Tenneco, and Atlantic Richfield (Arco), the last of which eventually enveloped Anaconda. These suitors sought to use the first lever of control I mentioned (i.e., voting stock), which the Chase had not had in any significant amount and had not needed to exercise control, given its firm grasp on other levers.

The apparent interest of these several Anaconda suitors was to use Anaconda's losses to decrease prospective parent's taxes. Then the public and the regulators would lose track of the once mighty Anaconda. Its 10-K and other reports—for what they were worth—would no longer be filed at the SEC. If Arco were successful in its takeover of Anaconda, its line of business reports to the Federal Trade Commission would be so secret—thanks to industry's successful lobbying of both the Congress and the Commission—that not even the FTC's Bureau of Competition could view them. The increasing concentration of economic power would be accompanied by decreasing information regarding a major component of an expanding conglomerate.

The Powers of the Debt Holder

The Anaconda illustration shows how a commercial creditor may hold enormous powers over a company through contractual restrictions contained in loan indentures. The nature of modern corporate organization accentuates the ability of major creditors to control corporate activities.

In a corporation where common-stock ownership is widely dispersed, management has nearly complete autonomy, except for the authority of major stock-voters. Shareholder rights may be altered through mere changes in corporate bylaws. Dissenting shareholders face a series of legal and procedural obstacles in challenging the presumptively valid actions of management.

Generally, shareholders have no right to redeem their shares and get their money back when financial adversity strikes them—or at any other time. On the other hand, debt instruments are designed to protect the lender's capital. Restrictions are placed upon the borrower regarding his financial condition, the disposition of his assets, his management structure, or any other matter which may be governed by a legal contract.

Violation of the provisions in a debt agreement generally lead to default and the activation of remedies the creditor has provided for his benefit in the debt agreement. The most common remedy calls for immediate repayment of the outstanding loan balance, plus a penalty charge in some cases.

Unlike shareholders, creditors can go straight to court over grievances, without first exhausting remedies within the corporate framework. Creditors supplying working capital are in a position of special influence, since they provide a company's lifeblood.

The Information Gaps

Only fragmentary information concerning the ability of lenders to control companies or restrict management's range of options through loan indentures can be found at the SEC. The current, unindexed reports—often unavailable to Congress or the public because they have been checked out to SEC staff—cite key documents, filed in earlier years, by reference. Those pertinent files are in storage, out of town. The SEC staff has no time to find the needle in that haystack; so those seeking information wait for days or weeks until the files have been located and shipped from the record center.

The gathering of information on officers and directors and corporate structure is similarly frustrating. Reporting requirements regarding these matters vary from agency to agency. Standard financial references are deficient, including only data—sometimes partial—which are volunteered by firms. Some major banks have declined to provide the Library of Congress with basic data regarding corporate affiliations of their officers, which are missing from the usual references.

Most of the regulatory commissions have been rigidly paralyzed, for several years, on matters dealing with corporate control. The Federal Power Commission has spent millions of dollars on its much heralded Regulatory Information System (RIS). But RIS does not include ownership and control data. That is because the FPC has delayed for more than two years promulgation of its own proposals for collection of information from electric utilities and gas pipeline companies regarding major stock-voters, debt holders, and interlocks.

The Civil Aeronautics Board's investigation of institutional investors' influence on regulated airlines—which was to encompass stock voting, debt holding, interlocks, and equipment leasing—has been in a holding pattern for almost three years, not having reached even the prehearing conference stage. The Federal Communications Commission last year quietly dropped its five-year study of ownership patterns in the broadcasting industry. In shutting down the operation, the Commission wrapped its findings in a mantle of administrative secrecy, only part of which has been removed by remedies applicable under the Freedom of Information Act.

The SEC will provide impressive computer printouts of interlocks between officers and directors of reporting companies and other firms. But the SEC printouts are deceptively outdated and inaccurate. That is because the SEC feeds information into the computer but never takes out the deadwood—the retired and expired directors. The result is a "Who Was Who" rather than a "Who Is Who." Laborious handwork is essential in order to obtain current, accurate data.

The Department of Justice and FTC do not even use computers to keep track of interlocks. It is the FBI, not the Antitrust Division, which occupies and uses the computer capability within the $126 million J. Edgar Hoover edifice on Pennsylvania Avenue to keep track of millions of *individuals*, rather than hundreds of corporations. The Law Enforcement Assistance Administration grants millions of dollars to state and local governments for similar computerization of records on individuals.

Private corporations keep track of your and my debts, affiliations, health, and even reputed moral condition in retail credit data banks and industry computers. But, contrary to the spirit of campaign rhetoric promising a decrease in the amount of burdensome regulation and reports, the government does not maintain accurate and basic data concerning the control of corporations whose decisions sharply affect our lives.

This regulatory gap exists despite the substantial powers Congress has given the various agencies—including the power to impose sanctions and issue subpoenas—to collect such information and tabulate it so as to "maximize its usefulness to other agencies and the public." And this gap exists despite the statutory and regulatory responsibilities of agencies to impose certain limits on control of corporations.[4]

Major Stock-voters

The darkest corner of the jungle screens the identity of major voting interests within corporations. Regulatory commissions generally

---

4. *Joint Hearings on Corporate Disclosure* (three parts), Subcommittee on Budgeting, Management and Expenditures and Subcommittee on Intergovernmental Relations of Senate Committee on Government Operations, 93d Cong., 2d Sess., 1974; *Disclosure of Corporate Ownership*, S. Doc. No. 93-62, March 4, 1974, by the two subcommittees. See especially in Hearings, Part II, excerpts from statutes relating to authority of Federal Trade Commission and General Accounting Office, pp. 1061–1075, and in S. Doc. No. 93-62, Appendix A, "Reporting Requirements and Dissemination of Information on Corporate Ownership and Structure," pp. 197–230, and "Statutes Authorizing Regulatory Commissions to Collect Certain Data and Sanctions Applicable to Companies which Fail to Provide Data," pp. 230–232.

The Federal Reports Act of 1942 (44 U.S.C. § 3501) provides that "Information collected and tabulated by a Federal agency shall, as far as is expedient, be tabulated in a manner to maximize the usefulness of the information to other agencies and the public."

The Alaska Pipeline Act (P.L. 93–153, 44 U.S.C. § 3512 (1973)), in transferring from the OMB to the GAO responsibility for reviewing information requests of independent regulatory agencies, applies this requirement specifically to independent regulatory agencies.

P.L. 93-556 (1974) (establishing a Commission on Federal Paperwork) directs the Commission in Section 3(b)(4) to ascertain what changes are possible and desirable so that "information held by the Federal Government is processed and disseminated to maximize its usefulness to all Federal agencies and the public."

The Securities Acts Amendments of 1975 (P.L. 94-29) amend Section 13 of the Securities Exchange Act of 1934 (15 U.S.C. § 78m) by adding new subsection (f) which deals with reports to be filed by institutional investment managers regarding equity security holdings, voting rights, and related matters. Paragraph (3) of subsection (f) provides that the SEC "shall tabulate the information contained in any report filed pursuant to this subsection in a manner which will, in the view of the Commission maximize the usefulness of the information to other Federal and State authorities and the public."

require firms subject to their reporting jurisdiction to name a certain number of major holders of voting securities, or those with holdings above a stated percentage of the firm's voting stock. The reporting benchmark may be:

1. the top 30 (railroads reporting to the ICC, communications common carriers reporting to the FCC, water carriers reporting to the FMC);
2. the top 20 (nonexempt utility holding companies, but only in their initial registration with the SEC);
3. the top 10 (electric and gas utilities reporting to the FPC, motor carriers reporting to the ICC);
4. the top 5 (freight forwarders reporting to the ICC);
5. in excess of 1 percent of the voting securities (broadcast companies reporting to the FCC);
6. in excess of 3 percent (cable companies reporting to the FCC);
7. in excess of 5 percent (some companies reporting to the SEC); or
8. in excess of 10 percent (other companies reporting to the SEC).[5]

Cede & Co.

Reports on security holders and voting powers are filed annually. Often the largest or one of the largest reported stockholders is Cede & Co. That is the first tree which has to be removed from the jungle. There is no reason why Cede & Co. should appear on any list of stockholders and their voting powers. Cede & Co. denotes stock held by Depository Trust Company of New York (DTC). This depository was established by the financial community in the late 1960s to simplify settlement of securities transactions among brokers and institutional customers.

At the end of 1975, DTC participants included 29 banks and 219 broker-dealers. They held more than 2.5 billion shares in more than 8,000 companies. DTC accepts stock from these participating institutional depositors and credits it to their accounts. Stock can be transferred within the DTC system by computerized book entry. Cumbersome and costly movement of certificates thus becomes unnecessary. All the stock is registered in the name of Cede (for *Ce*rtificate *De*pository) & Co.

Initially DTC was a wholly owned subsidiary of the New York Stock Exchange. The Exchange is still the majority stockholder. However, the American Exchange and National Association of Security Dealers were each sold 8 percent of DTC stock, which they hold on behalf of broker-dealer depository participants. Other depository participants—principally major banks—bought some 20 percent of the DTC stock. Stock in

---

5. S. Doc. No. 93-62, N. 4 *supra*, Appendix A.

DTC will be reallocated among depository participants pursuant to a formula based upon their participation in the depository.

Table 2-1 indicates the percentage of voting stock in selected, well-known companies held by Cede & Co. in 1972 and 1975. The percentage of Cede & Co. holdings increased for 28 of these 35 companies, decreased for seven companies.

Depository Trust has no power to buy, sell, or vote any of the stock it holds. Each year, at no charge, DTC provides each portfolio company whose stock it holds a Security Position Listing. This listing identifies each bank, brokerage firm, or other depository participant for whom DTC held stock in the portfolio company, as of its record date. The listing also shows the number of shares held, for each depository participant, in the recipient portfolio company.

Use of the Security Position Listing (see Figure 2-1) by corporate secretaries, in filing their annual ownership reports with regulatory commissions, does not necessarily lead directly to identification of those parties empowered to vote the stock held in the depository. Depository participants may or may not have that power, depending upon individual circumstances. However, use of the list in compiling ownership reports does at least reveal the names and holdings of identified institutions, from whom voting information can be obtained. To the extent that an institutional investor holds stock in a portfolio company through Cede & Co. and also in other accounts, its holdings are understated on the portfolio company's stockholder record lists if the Cede & Co. holding is not aggregated with other holdings by the investor in the portfolio company.

Usually, however, companies do not use the Security Position Listing in their report to commissions. They know that the tail-wagging watchdogs at the commissions will not fuss at them if they do not—unless the company has to report to the Interstate Commerce Commission.

Two and a half years ago the ICC told companies reporting to it to list shares registered in the name of Cede & Co. in the name of the appropriate banks and brokerage houses. The companies complied. The old ICC thus accomplished by memorandum what younger commissions have not seen fit to do in years of rule making and handwringing. The DTC, for its part, has been completely cooperative with our subcommittee and with government agencies which seek security position listings. The fault lies with the somnolent or timorous commissions.

The SEC position perfectly suits those companies which do not wish to disclose the Security Position Listing provided them by the DTC. To begin with, the SEC has the least informative stockholder reporting provision of any of the regulatory commissions. Registrants under the Securities Exchange Act of 1934 are required to name only each individual who owns of record or is known by the registrant to own beneficially more than 10 percent of any class of securities. Companies in which 10 percent or more of the voting stock is held by Cede & Co.

TABLE 2-1 CEDE & Co. Holdings in Selected Companies, 1972 and 1975

Company	*1972*	*1975*
Ashland Oil	7.0%	8.1%
Chrysler	12.1	15.8
LTV Corp.*	39.0	34.0
Bethlehem Steel	7.2	8.6
Greyhound	8.1	13.8
United Brands	20.5	16.3
Raytheon	5.5	5.4
Trans World Airlines	10.6	27.4
Pan American World Airways	15.0	23.8
Eastern Airlines	19.0	31.9
Braniff International Corp.†	15.3	30.0
Continental Airlines	17.0	27.0
PSG, Inc.‡	21.3	31.3
North Central Airlines	10.6	13.6
Penn Central	18.9	16.0
Chicago, Milwaukee Corp.§	32.6	39.4
Kansas City Southern	13.9	5.8
Rio Grande Industries	7.7	9.8
Spector Industries	15.1	7.8
American Electric Power	5.5	13.4
General Telephone & Electronics	3.8	7.5
Consolidated Edison	5.4	9.8
Philadelphia Electric	3.9	6.7
American Natural Gas	5.4	11.6
Niagara Mohawk Power	6.9	13.5
Northeast Utilities	3.0	7.9
Union Electric	5.3	8.2
Allegheny Power System	5.9	8.5
Baltimore Gas & Electric	4.2	6.6
Pennsylvania Power & Light	3.8	5.1
Potomac Electric Power	6.1	11.1
Western Union Corp.	6.9	19.6
Cleveland Electric Illum.	3.3	6.2
Grand Union	13.6	1.0
Charter N.Y. Corp.	4.1	7.4

*Formerly Ling-Temco Vought, Inc.

†Formerly Braniff Airways

‡Formerly Pacific Southwest Airlines

§Formerly Chicago, Milwaukee, St. Paul & Pacific

Source: Disclosure of Corporate Ownership, S. Doc. No. 93-62, March 4, 1974, p. 72 (1972 data), and letter to Vic Reinemer from Edward J. McGuire, Jr., secretary, Depository Trust Company, March 9, 1976 (1975 data).

The Depository Trust Company

SECURITY POSITION LISTING

AMER ELECTRIC POWER (SECURITY DESCRIPTION) — 00000000 (CODE) — 025537 10 1 (CUSIP) — 08 25 76 (DATE) — 1 (PAGE)

PARTICIPANT NUMBER	PARTICIPANT NAME	QUANTITY
714	A.E.MASTEN	300
122	ADAMS PECK	940
107	ADVEST CO	42,[illegible]5
201	AG EDWARDS	117,390
573	ALEX BROWN	41,445
31	ARNHOLD	14,747
370	ASIEL CO	363
33	BACHE H.S.	262,858
776	BACON WHIP	1,306
46	BAIRD	1,044
495	BAKER W	4,346
901	BANK OF NY	657,150
903	BANKERS TR	5,933
352	BEAR STERN	67,948
543	BECKCO	2,512
54	BECKER	25,303
709	BELL BECK	379
756	BLUNT	4,436
87	BLYTH EAST	311,578
711	BOETTCHER	32,635
954	BOS SAFE	63,790
135	BRADFORD J	82,566
970	BRADFRD TR	54,279
742	BRANCH CAB	3,534
10	BROWN BROS	11,016
338	BRUNS NORD	40,351
207	BURGESS	6,022
302	BURNHAM	79,748
902	CHASE MANH	420,035
912	CHEM BK	
713	CHRISTOPHR	2,379
1040	CIT FID BK	550
968	CIT SO NB	100
906	CITIBANK	305,694
212	COGGESHALL	8,923
1	COBLIN HOCH	2,963
286	COWEN CO	15,097
797	DE HAVEN	2,086
18	DUFT & CO	1,590
3	DOMINICK	4,502
509	DONALDSON	4,155
176	DRYSDALE	2,116
730	EPPLER G T	7,22[illegible]
233	ERNST & CO	17,005
231	EVANS CO	5,742

PARTICIPANT NUMBER	PARTICIPANT • NAME	QUANTITY
571	FAHNESTOCK	53,111
490	FAULKNER D	2,351
926	FID UN TR.	2,840
987	FIDUCIARY	11,500
73	FIRST MHTN	4,178
194	FOSTER A	6,276
951	FST MER NB	2,020
5	GOLDMAN	94,779
759	GRADISON	9,112
344	GRANGER CO	3,135
593	GRUNTAL CO	37,791
420	GRUSS O	3,736
298	HARDY & CO	13,295
282	HENDERSON	4,404
322	HERZFELD	35,785
768	HILLIARD	5,760
536	HOPPIN W	19,846
545	HORNBLOWER	117,123
452	HUGH JOHNS	5,171
487	HUTTON E F	856,774
985	INDUST N/B	1,230
124	INGALLS	8,364
798	INST EQUIT	2,239
346	INTERSTATE	2,950
967	IRVING TR	
374	JANNEY MS	17,526
234	JESUP & L	3,612
256	JOSEPHTAL	12,933
407	KALB VORHS	823
65	KIDDER P	68,967
142	KINGSLEY	200
455	LASKER S&S	33,000
88	LAWRENCE	20,818
308	LAZARD FR	8,317
277	LEWCO SEC	153,279
965	LNIST ROCH	
271	LOEB RHDES	205,445
202	LOEWI	25,976
136	MASON N CO	15,723
761	MANLEY B M	9,825
918	MARINE MID	223,829
299	MC DONALD	3,835
513	MC MULLEN	15,638
161	MERRILL	4,990,320
727	MESIROW CO	7,695

PARTICIPANT NUMBER	PARTICIPANT NAME	QUANTITY
930	MEGRS HANO	366,402
779	MID-SOUTH	1,300
942	MIDWEST EX	26,454
62	MITCHELL H	4,629
781	MOORE	4,132
114	MOORE S	21,096
923	MORGAN GTY	253
6942	MSTC CUST	13,326
525	MUIR JOHN	4,610
16	MUTUAL	4,557
155	NEUBERGER	9,324
778	NEWHARD	8,316
438	OPPEN & CO	34,660
97	PAC S DTC	22,137
221	PAINE	835,595
503	PARRISH CO	6,488
443	PERSHING	229,929
204	PRESCOTT	40,365
570	PURCELL G	45
701	R ROWLAND	8,753
547	R.W. BAIRD	9,593
700	RAUSCHER P	11,820
725	RAYMOND	4,550
390	REICH CO	1,790
704	REINHOLDT	400
435	REYNOLDS	320,037
712	ROBINSON H	4,940
729	RODMAN&REN	7,948
706	RONEY W C	18,014
116	ROTAN	6,154
411	ROTHSCHILD	45,713
13	S C BRNSTN	12,057
478	S.D.COHN	700
763	SADE & CO	1,144
274	SALOMON BR	22,112
70	SCC-PHILA	2,910
397	SEC SET CP	25,321
436	SELIGMAN	
427	SESKIS	1,112
764	SHAINE	2,931
418	SHERS HAY	318,419
219	SHIELDS	33,878
415	SHUMAN	1,033
6	SMITH	213,331
501	SPEAR L K	3,587

PARTICIPANT NUMBER	PARTICIPANT NAME	QUANTITY
227	STERN L	3,182
793	STIFEL	18,068
187	SUTRO INC	17,369
71	THOMSON	220,057
310	TRASK SPEN	13,518
382	TUCKER A	31,226
931	U S TRUST	6,030
1028	UTD AMER	14
598	VINER EA	2,847
193	WATLING	7,716
94	WEBER HALL	1,332
245	WEEDEN&CO	1,966
314	WELLINGTON	6,577
935	WELLS FRGO	32,400
141	WHEAT	30,497
333	WHITE WELD	74,726
195	WHITNEY HN	1,148
15	WITTER D	639,521
306	WITTER WD	1,370
530	WOOD S W	20,448
740	1ST ALBANY	10,830

TOTAL SHARES 13,749,136 ******

MR W J ROSE VP
AMERICAN ELECTRIC POWER CO INC
2 BROADWAY
NEW YORK NY 10008

FIGURE 2-1 Security Position Listing

generally interpret these instructions as not requiring submission of the specific information provided by DTC regarding the holdings of depository participants.

Stockholders or intervenors in regulatory proceedings who attempt to obtain information regarding Cede & Co. holdings directly from companies encounter a variety of obstacles. Senior financial officers of American Electric Power testified that they did not know and could not find out for whom Cede & Co. held their stock. Niagara Mohawk erroneously informed a customer that Cede & Co. has the highest voting powers in the company, when of course Cede & Co. and its associated DTC have no voting powers. Consolidated Edison and Gulf + Western refused to make the Security Position Listing available to stockholders, with lawyers for the latter firm quoting the Corporation Law of Delaware and nitpicking the imprecision of the request.

Congressional intercession with the FPC led to release of Niagara Mohawk's and Con Ed's Security Position Listing to the stockholders. But the SEC, whose staff was persuaded long ago by the New York Stock Exchange that disclosure of Cede & Co. holdings would not be useful, could not bring itself to help the Sisters of Charity and National Council of Churches obtain Gulf + Western's listing. The church groups were trying to locate and talk to major stock-voters regarding a proposal on the agenda at Gulf + Western's annual meeting.

The position of the SEC was that the Commission is still studying the matter, as part of the extended street-name study, that the matter is still under review in rule making, and that the lawyers just are not sure about the Commission's authority in such matters. Why not, suggested the SEC's Chairman, have people with such problems write another letter to the Commission? Clearly, the solution to the Cede & Co. problem discovered by the ICC in 1974 is too simple and successful for application by the sophisticated SEC.[6]

Unaggregated Nominee Holdings

Another severe distortion of corporate ownership reports stems from use of nominee names, a nominee usually being a partnership formed by institutional investors solely for acting as a record holder of securities. In the first place, reporting companies often fail to identify the institutional investors whose stock in their company is held in nominee name. Secondly, the reporting companies usually fail to aggregate all the holdings in the company by an investor whose holdings are in more than one nominee account.

---

6. Application of Appalachian Power Company for an increase in rates, Case No. 19474, Virginia State Corporation Commission, January 1975, especially cross-examination of Richard E. Disbrow, executive vice president and controller, American Electric Power Service Corporation, and Gerald P. Maloney, vice president, American Electric Power, by Virgil H. Goode, Jr.; letter to Chairman Richard L. Dunham, FPC, from Senator Metcalf, Feb. 24, 1976, and Dunham response, March 12, 1976; letter to Chairman Roderick M. Hills, SEC, from Senator Metcalf, Feb. 23, 1976, and Hills's response, April 7, 1976.

The DTC uses but one nominee—Cede & Co. But Cede & Co. is only one of some 8,000 nominees used by investors and listed in the Nominee List, published early each year by the American Society of Corporate Secretaries.[7]

The top 15 holders of equity securities, with total equity holdings of almost $100 billion as of the end of 1975, use 420 nominees. They are shown in Table 2-2.

Use of nominees simplifies transactions and record keeping for firms and their customers. It affords the institution using them a cost-free mechanism for rewarding faithful employees. "Good ole Schondelmeier—let's immortalize him. Call that new account Schondelmeier & Co."

Perhaps the ingenious nominee system reduces the volume of gold watches which banks and other institutional investors need at retirement ceremonies. But use of nominees in ownership reports utterly confuses regulators and stockholders. For example, in reports filed last year with the FCC, Western Union listed nine nominees, and AT&T 21 nominees, among their top 30 stockholders. For both companies, the listed addresses of the nominees were simply "New York, N.Y." The most enterprising Western Union messenger, or telephone operator, would be unable to deliver messages or queries to these major "stockholders," which are neither in the phone book nor the city directory.

AT&T told the FCC that its largest stockholder, with 8,884,818 shares, was Kabo & Co. Stockholder No. 6 was Sior & Co., with 2 million shares. Stockholder No. 7, with 1,953,651 shares, was Pitt & Co. All three, however, are nominees for Bankers Trust of New York. AT&T also reported that Stockholder No. 4 was Cudd & Co. (2,636,171 shares) and No. 5 was Kane & Co. (2,435,562 shares). Cudd and Kane are both Chase nominees.

It would thus appear that the aggregated holdings of Bankers Trust and Chase in AT&T totaled, respectively, 12,838,469 and 5,071,733 shares, the totals of the above accounts. But, as is usual in ownership reports, appearances are deceiving. The same banks had numerous other holdings in AT&T in other nominee accounts, none of which was big enough to be included among the top 30 stockholders.

These additional holdings amounted to more than 3 million shares for Bankers Trust and more than 1 million for Chase. That brought the total AT&T holdings reported last year—only after AT&T was prodded by the FCC, after *it* was prodded by Senator Metcalf—to 15,843,815 shares for Bankers Trust and 6,133,815 shares for Chase.[8]

---

7. Nominee List, American Society of Corporate Secretaries, 1 Rockefeller Plaza, N.Y. 10020, $25. The Society declined to sell the Nominee List to a regulatory commission, an attorney in a rate case, and a newspaper editor early in the 1970s. The Society began selling it after Senator Metcalf put the 1971 Nominee List in the *Congressional Record* on June 24, 1971 (vol. 117, no. 98, part II).

8. S. Doc. No. 94-246, N. 1 *supra*, pp. 8–9, and appendix C, pp. 340–445.

TABLE 2-2 Nominees of Top 15 Equity Holders

Institution	*Equity holders (millions)*	*Number of nominees*	*Names of nominees*			
1. Morgan Guaranty Trust	$15,744	19	Bicher & Co.	Powers & Co.	Sifone & Co.	TEPE & CO.
			Bucher & Co.	Rose & Co.	Siftu & Co.	TEWES & CO.
			Gavin & Co.	Schmidt & Co.	Sims & Co.	Zande & Co.
			Ince & Co.	Schopp & Co.	Stawis & Co.	Zink & Co.
			Lowell & Co.	Scott & Co.	TEGGE & Co.	
2. Bankers Trust	11,200	50	Alna & Co.	Forbank & Co.	Pitt & Co.	
			Auer & Co.	Guadi & Co.	Pyramid Nominees	
			Bankcan & Co.	Gusbram & Co.	Rejoh & Co.	
			Bankers Nominee	Hemfar & Co.	Ronis & Co.	
			Banlifco & Co.	Hodel & Co.	Ross & Co.	
			Barnett & Co.	Infid & Co.	Rothmayer & Co.	
			Batrus & Co.	Jovert & Co.	Salkeld & Co.	
			Becu & Co.	KABO & Co.	Seena & Co.	
			Bock & Co.	Kellou & Co.	Sior & Co.	
			Boehm & Co.	Lehcor & Co.	Strebew & Co.	
			Borug & Co.	Linvar & Co.	Subse & Co.	
			Cenrus & Co.	MFB Mutual & Co.	Surtic & Co.	
			Comna Co.	Muico & Co.	Varlin & Co.	
			Corag & Co.	Muller & Co.	Var Three & Co.	
			Dobbin & Co.	Naban & Co.		
			Eddy & Co.	Occerg & Co.		
			Enemel & Co.	Patey & Co.		
			Farnum & Co.	Pendiv & Co.		
3. Citibank	11,026	37	Adbon & Co.	Dooling & Co.	NATS CUMCO	
			AULT & CO.	Drake & Co.	NATS DISCO	

			Ball & Co.	Dwyer & Co.	Nimer & Co.
			Barnes & Co.	Foye & Co.	Overseas Nominee Inc.
			BENCO & Co.	Gerlach & Co.	Potts & Co.
			Borden & Co.	Griffin & Co.	Schondelmeier & Co.
			Brad & Co.	Hank & Co.	Stella & Co.
			Cadre & Co.	Hurley & Co.	Storms & Co.
			Camino & Co.	JSCC & Co.	Stuart & Co.
			Chave & Co.	King & Co.	Sweeney & Co.
			Congen 15 & Co.	Kordula & Co.	Thomas & Co.
			DEBRO & Co.	McCary & Co.	Weber & Co.
					Wurtz & Co.
4. U.S. Trust	6,097	10	Atwell & Co.	Lux & Co.	Prime & Co.
			Faust & Co.	Mansell & Co.	TRI & Co.
			Four & Co.	PENY & Co.	U.S. Trust Co.
			Heil & Co.		
5. Manufacturers Hanover Trust	5,905	41	Aulis & Co.	Gustaf & Co.	Norwood & Co.
			Bahr & Co.	Hamilton & Co.	Orion & Co.
			Balsa & Co.	Harrigan & Co.	Price & Co.
			Bane & Co.	Hemp & Co.	Rowe & Co.
			Bird & Co.	Ides & Co.	Rudolph & Co.
			Bober & Co.	Jennifer & Co.	Sarah & Co.
			Chappell & Co.	Jocasta & Co.	Sigler & Co.
			Civet & Co.	Lake & Co.	Sloyan & Co.
			Cook & Co.	Logan & Co.	Suydam & Co.
			Crolius & Co.	Loriot & Co.	Tamp & Co.
			Ewing & Co.	Mancot & Co.	Thirsk & Co.
			Fisk & Co.	Manleg & Co.	Urell & Co.
			Flynn M. & Co.	Manre & Co.	Vanek & Co.
			Grandin & Co.	Matthews & Co.	

TABLE 2-2 Nominees of Top 15 Equity Holders *(Continued)*

Institution	*Equity holders (millions)*	*Number of nominees*	*Names of nominees*		
6. Chase Manhattan	$5,351	27	Andrews & Co.	Elzay & Co.	Reeves & Co.
			Bedle & Co.	Gansel & Co.	Ring & Co.
			Bender & Co.	Gooss & Co.	Round & Co.
			Chase Nominees Ltd.	Gunn & Co.	Ryan & Co.
			Cudd & Co.	JSCC-Clint & Co.	Settle & Co.
			Dell & Co.	Kane & Co.	Taylor & Witt
			Derren & Co.	McKenna & Co.	TIMM & Co.
			Egger & Co.	Padom & Co.	Titus & Co.
			Ehren & Co.	Pickering, L.D. & Co.	White & Co.
7. Prudential Insurance	5,206	30	Aftco	Hasco	PUFCO
			Byeco	JOTCO	QUALCO
			Cadco	KATCO	Quinco
			DEBCO	LATCO	RUNCO
			Ertco	Modco	SAYCO
			Fivco	Ninco	Sevco
			Floco	NUBCO	Sixco
			Forco	Octco	TENCO
			GATCO	OHMCO	TRECO
			Gepco	Oneco	TWOCO
8. Harris Trust	5,115	14	Act & Co.	Gale & Co.	NORBROOK & CO.
			Bivest & Co.	HAAL & Co.	Ord & Co.
			Donson & Co.	HAP & Co.	

			ELD & Co.	HIT & Co.	Wait & Co.	
			EMP & Co.	Mot & Co.	Whimm & Co.	
9. Scudder, Stevens & Clark	5,043	None				
10. National Bank, Detroit	4,984	17	ATEL & Co.	IRON & Co.	Thorn & Co.	
			Brownell & Co.	LILDOW & CO.	Trussal & Co.	
			CUM & Co.	MIFUND & Co.	UNALCO & Co.	
			FGA & Co.	NAB & Co.	UNIPRES & Co.	
			FOMO & Co.	NORWELL & Co.	Woodfort & Co.	
			GREYPEN & Co.	POCON & Co.		
11. T. Rowe Price	4,600	None				
12. Investors Diversified Services	4,452	9	Carothers & Clark			
			Investors Mutual, an IDS subsidiary, uses the same nominee as its parent IDS does—Carothers & Clark. In addition, IDS subsidiaries and affiliates use the following nominees:			
			IDS Life Insurance			Anak & Co.
			IDS Progressive Fund			CEAL & Co.
			IDS Life Insurance Co. Variable Annuity Fund A			Desa & Co.
			IDS Growth Fund, Inc.			Hum & Co.
			IDS Life Insurance Co. Variable Annuity Fund B			Kamus & Co.
			Investors Stock Fund			PERC & Co.
			Investors Selective Funds, Inc.			SEL & Co.
			Investors Variable Payment Fund			VAR & Co.
13. First National Bank, Boston	4,168	141	Abate & Co.	COCO & Co.	Ham & Co.	PRESCOTT & Co.
			ADLER & Co.	COFFIN & CO.	Herald & Co.	Princeton & Co.
			AGAR & Co.	CONWAY & CO.	Holbank	Put & Co.

TABLE 2-2 Nominees of Top 15 Equity Holders *(Continued)*

Institution	*Equity holders (millions)*	*Number of nominees*	*Names of nominees*			
13. First National Bank, Boston	4,168	141	Amlico	COTY & Co.	HOLDEN & Co.	Reading & Co.
			APPLE & Co.	CRAN & Co.	HYDE & Co.	RICHARDSON & Co.
			Arey & Co.	Crest & Co.	IKE & Co.	Rockport & Co.
			ARO & Co.	Crow & Co.	JEROME & Co.	RULE & Co.
			Ashmont & Co.	CURLEY & Co.	Jimmy & Co.	Rutland & Co.
			Babson & Co.	DAVIDSON & Co.	Joy & Co.	SAKS & Co.
			BACON & Co.	Dedham & Co.	LABB & Co.	SALEM & Co.
			Baxter & Co.	Dobbins & Co.	Lamb & Co.	SALTER & Co.
			Beaver & Co.	Dodd & Co.	LAWLOR & Co.	Santoro & Co.
			BEN & Co.	Don & Co.	Low & Co.	Segal & Co.
			BERK & Co.	DOVER & Co.	Lupi & Co.	SHERRY & Co.
			Berlin & Co.	DROWN & Co.	Lusk & Co.	Skelton & Co.
			Biggs & Co.	DUNLAP & Co.	Mace & Co.	Sprague, Julian K. & Co.
			Birch & Co.	EGAN & Co.	MacKay & Co.	Stet & Co.
			BIRMINGHAM & Co.	ELK & Co.	MAJOR & Co.	Sull & Co.
			BISHOP & Co.	EMORY & Co.	Mass. Employees & Co.	SWAN & Co.
			Blanchard & Co.	FADER & Co.	Mass. Teachers & Co.	SWIFT & Co.
			Bob & Co.	FAY & Co.	Medford & Co.	SUSAN & Co.
			Breen & Co.	FEDERAL & Co.	Milford & Co.	TARR & Co.
			BRENDA & Co.	Felix & Co.	Milk & Co.	TULLY & Co.
			BRIM & Co.	FINE & Co.	Milton & Co.	Vera & Co.
			BURMA & Co.	FIR & Co.	Neat & Co.	Vincent & Co.
			Cage & Co.	FIRST CORP. & Co.		
				FORD & Co.		

			Cal & Co.	FROST & Co.	NEB & Co.	WALCO & Co.
			CANER & Co.	Fuller & Co.	Needham & Co.	Walpole & Co.
			CANTY & Co.	GANS & Co.	Norton & Co.	WALSH & Co.
			Carlo & Co.	Gem & Co.	Noyes & Co.	Warren & Co.
			Carney & Co.	Gilco	OXFORD & Co.	Waveco
			Carver & Co.	Glade & Co.	Pamela & Co.	WED & Co.
			Ceylon & Co.	GREER & Co.	PAPER & Co.	WESTON & CO.
			CHAR & Co.	GURNEY & CO.	Phil & Co.	WYLIE & CO.
			Clem & Co.	GUS & Co.	PILGRIM & Co.	ZIMCO & Co.
			CLUB & Co.		Plymouth & Co.	
14. Wilmington Trust	4,102	8	Birch & Bradford	Hirs & Harney		
			Cole & Cannon	Lack & Lindsay		
			Dean & Davis	Mertz & Moyer		
			Flinn & Fairman	Pearch & Pettit		
15. First National Bank, Chicago	3,941	17	Alfund & Co.	Friend & Co.	Searsfund & Co.	
			Bloom & Co.	Investmor & Co.	Serve & Co.	
			Conac & Co.	Merna & Co.	Silo & Co.	
			Dearborn & Co.	Monroe & Co.	Sisco & Co.	
			Eagle Co.	Olen & Co.	UAM & Co.	
			Finat & Co.	Rosley & Co.		
Totals	$96,934	420				

Source: Ranking and equity holdings (over which institutions have *direct* investment responsibility) from *Institutional Investor,* August, 1976, 448 Madison Ave., N.Y. 10022. Nominees from Nominee List.

Illustrative 1976 Ownership Reports

The problems of which I write can perhaps be best visualized by reviewing ownership reports filed by well-known companies with various commissions. For example, in a "Security Holders and Voting Powers" report filed with the FPC by Indiana and Michigan Electric Company, the company flunked even the first, simple question. Asked to give "the names and addresses of the 10 [largest] security holders," it did not identify its one security holder, American Electric Power, the largest public utility holding company in the nation. Utilities long ago learned that they can be casual in filing ownership information with the FPC.

In the response of El Paso Natural Gas to the FPC, you learn that El Paso Natural Gas is controlled by the El Paso Company. You also see the name and address of someone with a trivial seven votes out of every one million in the gas company. But you do not learn who has a significant voting interest in the controlling holding company, the El Paso Company. As recently as 1974, El Paso Natural Gas reported its 10 top stockholders to the FPC. Then, by the simple device of becoming part of a holding company, El Paso Natural Gas escaped that reporting requirement.

The SEC requires utility holding companies to identify their 20 major stockholders only once, at the time of initial registration. Most such reports—filed back in the 1930s and 1940s— are useless. A 1974 ownership report on the parent El Paso Company could be useful. But El Paso—and numerous other holding companies—are exempt from the SEC's utility holding company reporting provisions.

Government files are filled with reports such as those described above. Consider the reports of the nation's largest industry, electric power. Its 213 major investor-owned components include 92 which reported this year that they are controlled by holding companies, whose major stock-voters escape meaningful ownership reporting to both the FPC and SEC.

Railroads that account for two-thirds of the rail industry's revenues escaped ICC reporting jurisdiction by becoming part of conglomerates in the 11 years ending in mid-1973. Many large motor carriers similarly escaped ICC reporting requirements. The stock ownership reports of subsidiaries of these transportation conglomerates at the ICC are as void of information as is the El Paso Natural Gas report at the FPC.

Many of these new conglomerates and holding companies milked the transportation subsidiaries and even transferred land grants, at no cost to the parent companies. Taxpayers and their government did not know who the new owners were, but pumped billions of subsidy dollars into the subsidiaries.

Figure 2-2 shows how a company—Dayton Power and Light— can list 10 top "security holders" without divulging much accurate information and simultaneously disseminating misinformation.

The Dayton Power and Light report states that Cede & Co. was

Annual report of THE DAYTON POWER AND LIGHT COMPANY Year ended December 31, 1975

SECURITY HOLDERS AND VOTING POWERS

1. (A) Give the names and addresses of the 10 security holders of the respondent who, at the date of the latest closing of the stock book or compilation of list of stockholders of the respondent, prior to the end of the year, had the highest voting powers in the respondent, and state the number of votes which each would have had the right to cast on that date if a meeting were then in order. If any such holder held in trust, give in a footnote the known particulars of the trust (whether voting trust, etc.), duration of trust, and principal holders of beneficiary interests in the trust. If the stock book was not closed or a list of stockholders not compiled within one year prior to the end of the year or if since the previous compilation of a list of stockholders, some other class of security has become vested with voting rights, then show such 10 security holders as of the close of the year. Arrange the names of the security holders in the order of voting power, commencing with the highest. Show in column (a) the titles of officers and directors included in such list of 10 security holders.

(B) Give also the voting powers resulting from ownership of securities of the respondent of each officer and director not included in the list of 10 largest security holders.

2. If any security other than stock carries voting rights, explain in a supplemental statement the circumstances whereby such security became vested with voting rights and give other important particulars concerning the voting rights of such security. State whether voting rights are actual or contingent and if contingent describe the contingency.

3. If any class or issue of security has any special privileges in the election of directors, trustees or managers, or in the determination of corporate action by any method, explain briefly.

See Note on Page 107.

4. Furnish particulars concerning any options, warrants, or rights outstanding at the end of the year for others to purchase securities of the respondent or any securities or other assets owned by the respondent, including prices, expiration dates, and other material information relating to exercise of the options, warrants, or rights. Specify the amount of such securities or assets so entitled to be purchased by any officer, director, associated company, or any of the ten largest security holders. This instruction is inapplicable to convertible securities or to any securities substantially all of which are outstanding in the hands of the general public where the options, warrants, or rights were issued on a prorata basis.

5. Give date of the latest closing of the stock book prior to end of year, and state the purpose of such closing .... Not closed - record date of November 7, 1975 for dividend payment.

6. State the total number of votes cast at the latest general meeting prior to the end of year for election of directors of the respondent and number of such votes cast by proxy.
Total 10,800,443
By proxy 10,796,667

7. Give the date and place of such meeting ..... Dayton, Ohio ..... April 10, 1975

Line No.	Name and Address of Security Holder (a)	VOTING SECURITIES — Number of votes as of .... Total Votes (b)	Common Stock (c)	Preferred Stock (d)	Other (e)
1	Total votes of all voting securities	15,403,639	15,403,639	See Note on Page 107	None
2	Total number of security holders	51,325	51,325		
3	Total votes of security holders listed below	2,199,133	2,199,133		
4	1 (A)				
5	Cede & Co., New York, New York	1,194,483	1,194,483		
6	Gepco, Newark, New Jersey	171,000	171,000		
7	Oneco, Newark, New Jersey	145,000	145,000		
8	The Public Employees Retirement Board of Ohio, Columbus, Ohio	141,400	141,400		
9	Main Miller & Company, Akron, Ohio	120,000	120,000		
10	Norton & Co., Boston, Massachusetts	110,000	110,000		
11	Sten & Co., New York, New York	90,000	90,000		
12	The Continental Corporation, New York, New York	79,250	79,250		
13	Pitt & Co., New York, New York	76,000	76,000		
14	SFS & Co., Hartford, Connecticut	72,000	72,000		
15					

FIGURE 2-2 Dayton Power and Light Company Report to FPC

entitled to vote more than 10 percent of the stock that was voted at the last annual meeting. As previously noted, Cede & Co. has no voting power. Dayton Power and Light was one of 79 major electric utilities which did not use the Security Position Listing provided it by DTC in preparing its 1975 ownership report.

Dayton Power and Light's reported stockholders No. 2 and No. 3 are Gepco and Oneco. These are not Ultra Man's monsters or relatives of the long-eared fellow on "Star Trek." They are nominees of one of the many institutional investors which spend millions of dollars advertising their names, yet lose the opportunity for free advertising because of the nominee system. Gepco and Oneco are both nominees of Prudential Insurance, which is not even mentioned in the report. Prudential, of course, has full voting and discretionary rights to both blocks of stock.

The next largest stockholder is written in plain English, "The Public Employees Retirement Board of Ohio." This is an investment of those working men and women who—if you believe Professor Drucker—control the country. In this instance the Ohio board, rather than a bank, manages the pension fund. It is remarkable that an investment managed by public officials is accurately stated, while larger investments managed by private firms are not.

The FPC now proposes to computerize the inaccurate ownership data it collects, rather than adopt its 1974 proposals, mentioned earlier, to improve the accuracy of reports. I do not want to leave the impression that the FPC is the worst agency insofar as collection of accurate stock ownership data are concerned. It is only one of the worst.

The Federal Trade Commission simply does not use its vast powers to collect ownership information on a regular basis. The Federal Energy Administration has yet to follow up on its own finding that requirements for corporate ownership disclosure are ineffective. The Federal Reserve System is still ponderously pondering revision of its own reporting requirements, guided by Chairman Burns's declaration that additional disclosure might not conform with the public interest as he sees it. The Federal Maritime Commission not only has done nothing to improve its stock ownership reports, it labels as *confidential* ownership reports identical to reports filed with the ICC, which routinely makes them public.[9]

---

9. S. Doc. No. 94-246, N. 1 *supra,* pp. 103–104 and noted appendix references. See also FCC Report and Order adopted June 10, 1976, in FCC Doc. No. 20520 (institutional ownership of broadcast and cable companies); FCC Report and Order adopted June 10, 1976, in FCC Doc. No. 20521 (corporate ownership reporting and disclosure by broadcast licensee); "The Passive Communications Commission," 122 Cong. Rec. S9, 159-61 (daily ed. June 14, 1976) (remarks of Senator Lee Metcalf); FPC Notice of Proposed Rulemaking, Corporate and Financial Reports for Class A and Class B Natural Gas Companies, in FPC Doc. No. RM76-33, Aug. 26, 1976, and Corporate and Financial Reports for Class A and B Electric Utilities and Licenses, in FPC Doc. No. RM76-34, Aug. 31, 1976.

Progress at the ICC

The ICC has made the most progress of all federal agencies in improving stock ownership reports. Earlier, I mentioned the ICC memorandum of February 14, 1974, which instructed carriers to list shares held by Cede & Co. in the name of the institutional investor for whom it held stock. The same memorandum told the carriers to aggregate other nominee holdings. This simple and straightforward memorandum, by Director John Grady of the ICC's Bureau of Accounts, is one of the few advances in corporate stock ownership reporting in modern-day Washington. Let us therefore preserve it and the ICC's follow-up letter for historians:

NOTICE

To the Chief Accounting Officers of all Carriers Subject to the Commission's Financial Reporting Requirements:

The forms of annual reports required to be filed by carriers subject to the Commission's jurisdiction include schedules which provide for the disclosure of the identity and other information with respect to the largest holders of the respondent carriers' outstanding capital stock.

There are indications that the carriers are not responding in the manner contemplated in the instructions and are not using all of the means available to identify the person or organizations represented by a "nominee."

The instructions contemplate disclosure of the identity of the "beneficial owners" of the stock and the particulars of any trusts, including voting trusts. Moreover, the carriers should be able by using the "Nominee List," now available from the American Society of Corporate Secretaries, 9 Rockefeller Plaza, New York, N.Y. 10020, to identify the persons or organizations the nominees represent. The shares reported in the name of multiple nominees for individual banks or other investors should be aggregated for the purpose of determining the largest security holders (e.g. thirty for a railroad).

The top security holders should not include the name of Cede & Co., which is the nominee of Depository Trust, a stock exchange device used to facilitate stock transfers. Depository Trust has an obligation to fully inform any issuer of a security of the participants in the depository which hold that security, and the amount of the holdings. Such shares registered in the name of Cede & Co. shall be included in the holdings of the person or organization for whose account they are being held and considered in determining the list of the "largest security holders."

The procedures prescribed in this notice should be incorporated into all 1973 annual reports.

JOHN A. GRADY, *Director*

FOLLOWUP LETTER TO ORIGINAL LETTER DATED FEBRUARY 14, 1974

By notice dated February 14, 1974, the chief accounting officers of all carriers subject to the Commission's reporting requirements were requested to amplify the reporting requirements of Schedule 109, Voting Powers and Elections, by disclosing the identity of the persons and/or organizations voting the largest number of shares of the carrier's capital stock. The primary problem encountered in reporting this information in the past was the identification of the persons or organizations represented by nominees, trusts or brokerage firms.

Your company's 1973 annual report failed to adequately disclose sufficient information relative to voting rights. In order to comply with these reporting requirements regarding stock ownership, the name of the persons and/or organizations having authority to vote the carrier's stock should be listed in Schedule 109, Voting Powers and Elections.

The compilations of holdings by size do not necessarily indicate the voting rights. This is particularly true concerning institutional holdings. In furnishing the required information, the voting rights should be disclosed as follows:

Sole voting rights—The institution alone is responsible for voting shares. The names of the institutions will be adequate disclosure.

Shared voting rights—The institution shares the voting responsibilities with a co-trustee or co-executor. In such instances, the names of the co-trustees or co-executors must be shown.

No voting rights—The institution has no voting authority and all proxies are mailed directly to the beneficial owners or the parties exercising investment control.

In these circumstances, those exercising investment control should be shown.

You are requested to furnish the required information within 30 days from the date of this letter. If you have any questions concerning this request, please do not hesitate to call me.

Issuance of the preceding memorandum followed publication, in January 1974, of the Metcalf-Muskie study, *Disclosure of Corporate Ownership.*[10] That study included the General Accounting Office's finding that the Burlington Northern (BN)—an illustrative example—reported 24 nominees among its 30 largest stockholders, and that the 24 nominees represented two insurance companies and 12 banks.

Figure 2-3 is the BN report filed in 1976 with the ICC. It shows compliance with the 1974 ICC memorandum. There are no nominees. Multiple accounts of a single holder are aggregated. But this 1976 report is still a highly inaccurate identification of—as the instructions in paragraph 9 request—the 30 highest voting powers in the company.

Let's look closely at Figure 2-3.

Reported stockholder No. 1 is Merrill Lynch, the biggest brokerage house (and one of the few which will handle small investment accounts). As a matter of policy, Merrill Lynch tenders 95 percent of its uninstructed vote to corporate managements.

---

10. S. Doc. No. 93-62, N. 4 *supra*.

Merrill Lynch records show that the 5 percent of the votes retained by Merrill Lynch are sufficient to cover any instructions to vote against management. If the brokerage firm receives instructions from clients in excess of 5 percent against management, the initial vote will be revoked and a new vote tendered.

Merrill Lynch operates, of course, under the New York Stock Exchange rules which permit it and other brokers to vote uninstructed shares 15 days before the corporation's meeting, provided that a company supplies its proxy material early enough so that a broker can make distribution 15 days before the meeting.

A combination of circumstances sometimes leads to failure of stockholders to receive proxy materials in time to vote them. And many stockholders pitch the proxy materials away when they deal only with such "routine"—but all-important—issues as election of the board of directors. Merrill Lynch estimates that, on the average, it receives instructions for only 15 to 20 percent of the stock it holds, and most of the instructed vote is cast for management. Thus, the brokerage house typically votes for management some 95 percent of all the stock it holds.

The reasons for the abysmally low turnout of small voters should be mentioned. After all, they reason, why bother to participate in a Soviet-style election?

The single slate of candidates was chosen in advance by management. It also selected all the issues to be decided, except possibly those which tenacious minority interests may have gotten onto the agenda despite the constraints of SEC rules and management decisions.

Typically, a stockholder cannot even vote against that single slate, or against individual directors. He or she votes yes or withholds the vote. So, as a practical matter, Merrill Lynch and other brokerage houses do vote—for management—a substantial block of the stock which they hold.

However, in the BN illustration, the potential voting strength of Merrill Lynch is understated. That is because not all depository holdings for Merrill Lynch in the BN are among the 872,014 shares attributed to the brokerage firm.

The holdings of the big depository—Cede & Co.—are included in Merrill Lynch holdings. But, notice two other, smaller depositories in Figure 2-3. One is stockholder No. 4—the Midwest Stock Exchange Clearing Corporation. The other is stockholder No. 22, the Pacific Clearing Corporation. By looking at back-up data at the ICC, one learns that Merrill Lynch has the largest block of stock—10,238 shares—in Pacific Clearing Corporation. Detail on the holdings of the larger depository, Midwest Stock Exchange Corporation, is not in the file.[11] Profes-

---

11. Memorandum from Pacific Securities Depository Trust to Burlington Northern, Nov. 24, 1975, and related correspondence in BN files at ICC, Washington D.C. After follow-up queries by the subcommittee and the ICC, Midwest reported that it held four blocks of stock, totaling 51,682 shares, for Merrill Lynch.

Road Initials: BN year: 1975

109. VOTING POWERS AND ELECTIONS

1. State the par value of each share of stock: Common, $ NPV per share; first preferred, $10.00 per share; second preferred, $ None per share; debenture stock, $ None per share.

2. State whether or not each share of stock has the right to one vote; if not, give full particulars in a footnote Voting rights on common stock only

3. Are voting rights proportional to holdings? Yes If not, state in a footnote the relation between holdings and corresponding voting rights.

4. Are voting rights attached to any securities other than stock? No If so, name in a footnote each security, other than stock to which voting rights are attached (as of the close of the year), and state in detail the relation between holdings and corresponding voting rights, stating whether voting rights are actual or contingent, and if contingent showing the contingency.

5. Has any class or issue of securities any special privileges in the election of directors, trustees, or managers, or in the determination of corporate action by any method? Common stock only If so, describe fully in a footnote each such class or issue and give a succinct statement showing clearly the character and extent of such privileges.

6. Give the date of the latest closing of the stock book prior to the actual filing of this report, and state the purpose of such closing February 2, 1976 (Record date of common dividend payable March 1, 1976)

7. State the total voting power of all security holders of the respondent at the date of such closing, if within one year of the date of such filing; if not, state as of the close of the year. 12,438,421 votes, as of February 2, 1976 (Date)

8. State the total number of stockholders of record, as of the date shown in answer to inquiry No. 7. 57,538 stockholders.

9. Give the names of the thirty security holders of the respondent who, at the date of the latest closing of the stock book or compilation of list of stockholders of the respondent (if within 1 year prior to the actual filing of this report), had the highest voting powers in the respondent, showing for each his address, the number of votes which he would have had a right to cast on that date had a meeting then been in order, and the classification of the number of votes to which he was entitled, with respect to securities held by him, such securities being classified as common stock, second preferred stock, first preferred stock, and other securities, stating in a footnote the names of such other securities (if any). If any such holder held in trust, give (in a footnote) the particulars of the trust. In the case of voting trust agreements give, as supplemental information on page 13, the names and addresses of the thirty largest holders of the voting trust certificates and the amount of their individual holdings. *If the stock book was not closed or the list of stockholders compiled within such year, show such thirty security holders as of the close of the year.*

List under Footnotes, page 9, Other Securities with Voting Power.

Line No.	Name of security holder (a)	Address of security holder (b)	Number of votes to which security holder was entitled (c)	NUMBER OF VOTES, CLASSIFIED WITH RESPECT TO SECURITIES ON WHICH BASED — Stocks — Common (d)	PREFERRED — Second (e)	PREFERRED — First (f)
1	Merrill Lynch, Pierce, Fenner & Smith	New York, NY	872 014	872 014		
2	Morgan Guaranty Trust Co.*	New York, NY	507 519	507 519		
3	Bank of New York *	New York, NY	498 806	498 806		
4	Midwest Stock Exch.Clearing*	Chicago, IL	198 401	198 401		
5	Cleveland Trust Co. *	Cleveland, OH	130 462	130 462		
6	Irving Trust Co. *	New York, NY	130 219	130 219		
7	Paine Webber Jackson&Curtis	New York, NY	128 531	128 531		
8	First National City Bank *	New York, NY	108 555	108 555		
9	Manufacturers Hanover Tr.Co.*	New York, NY	107 049	107 049		
10	Lazard Freres & Co.	New York, NY	101 450	101 450		
11	Equit.Life Assur. Society	New York, NY	100 000	100 000		
12	Bankers Trust Co. *	New York, NY	87 998	87 998		
13	First Jersey Natl. Bank *	Jersey City, NJ	85 000	85 000		
14	Minn.State Bd.of Investment*	St. Paul, MN	84 700	84 700		
15	Pershing & Co.	New York, NY	72 785	72 785		
16	Loeb Rhoades & Co.	New York, NY	70 411	70 411		
17	Dean Witter & Co.	San Francisco,CA	66 605	66 605		
18	United States Trust Co. *	New York, NY	66 507	66 507		
19	Brown Bros. Harriman	New York, NY	63 780	63 780		
20	Chase Manhattan Bank *	New York, NY	62 111	62 111		
21	E. F. Hutton & Co.	New York, NY	56 850	56 850		
22	Pacific Clearing Corp. *	San Francisco,CA	54 473	54 473		
23	Bache & Co.	New York, NY	53 644	53 644		
24	Pittsburgh Natl. Bank *	Pittsburgh, PA	51 974	51 974		
25	First Natl. Bank of Mpls.*	Minneapolis, MN	49 634	49 634		
26	Bank of America *	Los Angeles, CA	45 824	45 824		
27	West Publishing Co.	St. Paul, MN	45 000	45 000		
28	Northwestern Natl. Bank *	Minneapolis, MN	42 511	42 511		
29	Blyth Eastman Dillon & Co.	New York, NY	41 340	41 340		
30	Marine Midland Bank *	New York, NY	37 562	37 562		

Note: Schedule 109, Voting Powers and Elections, continued on page 9.

Railroad Annual Report R-1

FIGURE 2-3 Burlington Northern Report to ICC

sor Finagle's Third Law of Information, "The information we need is not available," again rules.

BN stockholders Nos. 2 and 3 are reported as being Morgan Guaranty and the Bank of New York. Footnotes on the BN's report say that the banks are not the stockholders of record. Well, who are?

Morgan told the ICC that it had no sole voting rights to any of the

109. VOTING POWERS AND ELECTIONS—(Continued From Page 8)

10. State the total number of votes cast at the latest general meeting for the election of directors of the respondent. 9,794,638 votes cast.

11. Give the date of such meeting. May 8, 1975

12. Give the place of such meeting. St. Paul, Minnesota

NOTES AND REMARKS

Note: Cede & Co., the nominee for the Stock Clearing Corporation, acting for members of the New York Stock Exchange, held as of February 13, 1976 2,228,079 shares. Shares held by Cede & Co. have been included in above listing to the extent applicable.

* Not stockholder of record.
Nominee of security holder is registered owner.
Inquiry has been made regarding voting rights. Replies which have been received are attached.

Railroad Annual Report R-1

FIGURE 2-3 **(*Continued*)**

507,519 shares, and shared voting rights to 3,040 shares. As to the other more than half a million shares—more than 4 percent of the voting stock—Morgan told the BN (which passed the letter on to the ICC), "We feel that our obligation of confidentiality to our clients . . . prevents our disclosing to you [their] identity." That is nonsense.

The principal Morgan client in this instance, which is the Affiliated

Fund, reports its 343,200 shares in the BN to the fund's stockholders. And if you burrow around the SEC long enough, you will also find there the fund's verifying report on that holding, to which voting and discretionary powers attach. Furthermore, such mutual fund investments in hundreds of companies are reported regularly in *Vickers Guide: Investment Company Portfolios.*[12]

It is the same story with the Bank of New York. Among its 498,806 BN holdings are 403,400 shares for the Dreyfus Fund. Yet, the Bank of New York told the BN and the ICC that it would not tell who voted the stock reported in the bank's name, because of the bank's "unique responsibility to maintain private relationships with our customers."

Reporting of voting stock in the name of the mutual fund or other entity which controls it would, of course, diminish what seems—sometimes erroneously—to be extremely heavy bank influence within companies. For some reason, bankers seem unduly protective of mutual funds, which are the dominant voting interests in many corporations, and whose names rarely appear on corporate stock ownership reports.

A report filed by the Southern Railroad goes right to the brink of meaningful reporting, then stops. Holdings of bank nominees and DTC's nominee, Cede & Co., have been aggregated and reported in the name of the ranked investor. But this report still falls one huge step short of identifying the voting interests in the stock.

For example, a major bloc of stock held by Morgan is 200,000 shares listed in the name of Douglass & Co. The Nominee List shows you that Douglass & Co. represents the holdings of the Affiliated Fund. Such mutual funds, or the investment company complexes of which they are a part, vote those shares. Fund managers do not consult with the people who buy stock in the funds. The fund's holdings can be verified by its own public report, its report to the SEC, or in *Vickers Guide, Investment Company Portfolios.*

The Nominee List, unfortunately, does not identify all the institutional investors for whom banks hold stock they do not vote. In some instances, the Nominee List shows that one nominee is used by several funds. An example is Cudd & Co., a Chase nominee which Southern Railroad reported as holding 895,611 shares. The Nominee List shows six mutual funds (which are parts of several different mutual fund complexes) as associated with Cudd & Co.

Laurance Rockefeller and Cudd & Co.

But the Nominee List does not show all the institutions and other investors who use Cudd & Co.'s address, Box 1508, Church Street (New York City) Post Office, as a mailing address. This insufficiency of the

---

12. *Vickers Guide: Investment Company Portfolios (Common Stock),* $215, published and updated during the year by Vickers Associates, 226 New York Avenue, Huntington, N.Y. 11743.

Nominee List as the complete indicator of custodial customers became apparent after the Civil Aeronautics Board published in 1974—at Congressional request—a list of the 30 largest stockholders in major airlines.

Laurance Rockefeller's name was not on the list, although published reports had indicated he was a major Eastern Air Lines stockholder. Investigation by the CAB, the SEC, and Eastern, initiated by the Senate Reports, Accounting and Management Subcommittee, finally found that one block of Mr. Rockefeller's common stock was in his own name, that he had purchased an entire issue of preferred stock which had voting rights, and that his third buy in Eastern was over at the Chase in the custody of Cudd & Co.[13]

Our initial research into the nature of holdings in custodial accounts such as Cudd & Co. indicates that holdings by individuals are relatively small. A survey by the Library of Congress published in May 1976[14] showed that individual and family investments amounted to only from 1 to 5½ percent of the custodial accounts of the three banks which reported the largest common stock holdings in custodial accounts.

Both Chase and Morgan told the Library of Congress that they did not know the market value of the stock in their custodial accounts, and so they were not among the three banks with the largest reported custodial holdings of common stock. Those three—Citibank, Bankers Trust of New York, and State Street of Boston—reported more than $52 billion worth of common stock in custodial accounts.

The significance of this study of custodial accounts, on which the previous literature is exceedingly thin, is in my opinion threefold.

First, common-stock holdings of major banks in custodial accounts are very large—half again as large, on the average, as the stockholdings in their trust departments.

Second, the bulk of the stock is held by the banks for institutional investors—mutual funds, pension funds, endowments, insurance companies, other (including foreign) banks, and other corporations. At least that was the situation with the three banks which reported the largest custodial holdings.

Third, most of these custodial stockholdings are held by institutional investors which either now or soon will be required to report their holdings and voting rights to the SEC, under the Securities Act Amendments of 1975. Reference to that information at the SEC, in conjunction with a company's list of record stockholders, will enable corporate secretaries to readily compile accurate lists of most of the major stockvoters in their companies.

---

13. S. Doc. No. 94-246, N. 1 *supra*, p. 12; *Corporate Disclosure Hearings*, N. 4 *supra*, part III, pp. 934–939.

14. *Institutional Investors' Common Stock, Holdings and Voting Rights*, Subcommittee on Reports, Accounting and Management of Senate Committee on Government Operations, part II, 94th Cong., 2d Sess., S. Doc. No. 94-247.

Some corporate secretaries—or lawyers speaking for their companies—may say that they cannot obtain information on voting interests in their company, or that if they did obtain and disclose it, the companies would be adversely affected in the marketplace. Those arguments recurred at the ICC's informal conference in January 1975 regarding Docket 36141, its proposed adoption of Model Corporate Disclosure Regulations.

Both arguments are devoid of merit. One can even argue that companies whose major stock-voters have been revealed in reports to regulatory commissions are institutional favorites.[15] The CAB already obtains identification of some stock-voters with voting interests to 1 percent or more of regulated airlines' stock—but only if that voting interest is within the portfolio of a record owner of 5 percent or more of the stock. The FCC obtains information on stock-voters with 1 percent or more voting interests. Some broadcasters have problems answering simple questions. RCA warrants, at best, a clothbound set of the *Book of Knowledge* as consolation prize for its bumbling and incomplete reports. The award for good reporting to the FCC goes to Metromedia. Companies looking for quality models should refer to Metromedia reports.

MODEL CORPORATE DISCLOSURE REGULATIONS (MCDR)

The regulatory commissions not only have the authority to collect accurate and timely ownership information and the responsibility to tabulate it to maximize its usefulness to other agencies and the public. They also have before them—and it has been before them since January 1975—a set of model corporate disclosure regulations (the MCDR) developed by their own senior staffs, the General Accounting Office, and our Subcommittee staff.

This model was developed over a six-month period in 1974 by the interagency Steering Committee on Uniform Corporate Reporting. It was established by the GAO after the 1974 hearings on corporate disclosure[16] showed the morass of duplicative but inaccurate and incomplete reports on ownership and control now collected by the commissions and the need for collecting reliable information on a regular basis.

The MCDR consists of four definitions and four short sections dealing with corporate structure, major stock-voters, major debt-holders, and affiliations of officers and directors. The MCDR follows, as Figure 2-4.

Many parts of the model are patterned on regulations already promulgated by a commission, after comment by interested parties, and found to be workable and reasonable. For example, the definition of

---

15. S. Doc. No. 94-247, N. 14 *supra*, pp. 12, 194–226.

16. *Joint Hearings on Corporate Disclosure* (three parts), N. 4 *supra* (throughout).

Definitions

Annual Reporting. The term *annual reporting* means as of December 31 of each calendar year.

Control. The term *control* (including the terms *controlling, controlled by* and *under common control with*) means the possession, direct or indirect, of the power to direct or cause the direction of the management or policies of a person, natural or artificial. Sources of power may include, but are not limited to: equity security ownership; debtholdings; sole or partial voting arrangements; common directors, officers, or stockholders; or lease, purchase, lines of credit, supply, distribution, or operating agreements.

Financing Lease. The term *financing lease* shall refer to any lease which during the noncancelable lease period, either (1) covers 75 percent or more of the economic life of the property or (2) has terms which assure the lessor of a full recovery of the fair market value (which would normally be represented by his investment) of the property at the inception of the lease plus a reasonable return on the use of the assets invested subject only to limited risk in the realization of the residual interest in the property and the credit risks generally associated with secured loans.

Parent of Respondent. Parent of respondent shall refer to every firm, holding company or other person or combination of persons who ultimately control the respondent, as well as any intermediary controlling entity.

Annual Reporting Requirements

I. Corporate Structure.

A. For each respondent, parent of respondent, subsidiaries (and/or organizations controlled) of the respondent, joint ventures involved in by the respondent, and subsidiaries (and/or organizations controlled) of joint ventures involved in by the respondent, the following information shall be submitted:

1. Name and address.

2. Basis of control.

3. Principal business activities.

a. List and describe by 4-digit SIC Code and short title each industry in which the respondent's activities generated 10% of gross revenues or $5 million dollars (during the reporting year). 4-digit industry SIC codes & short titles are listed in the most recent *Standard Industrial Classification Manual* as published by the Executive Office of the President, Office of Management & Budget.

FIGURE 2-4 Model Corporate Disclosure Regulations, January 1975

b. 4-digit SIC Codes and short titles should be listed in order of significance relative to the total activities of respondent, based upon the percentage of gross revenues generated within each 4-digit industry.

4. Copy of the latest balance sheet and income statement and consolidated balance sheet and income statement, if available.

5. A copy of any chart or other graphic material showing the relationship of the respondent to such parents, subsidiaries, and other organizations listed.

B. In addition to subparagraph (A) above, list every corporation, partnership, or other business organization in which the respondent owns more than five percent of the outstanding voting securities or other ownership interests and indicate the percentage so owned.

II. Voting Stock Ownership.

A. In descending order, the 30 largest holders of voting shares (not to include any holder with less than one-tenth of one percent of the outstanding shares) in the respondent, identified as to

1. name

2. address

3. type (bank, broker, holding company, individual or other specified category)

4. the number of voting shares held (as of the end of the calendar year) and its percentage relationship to total outstanding shares. (If some shares—such as preferred issues—carry limited voting rights describe the limitation and the number of shares affected.)

(In determining the number of shares held, all nominee and other accounts of each shareholder, including accounts held by depository trust companies (CEDE & CO., SICOVAM, Pacific Coast Stock Exchange Clearing Corp., Midwest Stock Exchange Clearing Corp.) shall be aggregated and reported as one account in the name of the bank, broker, holding company, individual or other identified shareholder.)

B. With respect to each of the 30 largest holders, the number of shares (and percentage relationship to total outstanding voting shares) over which the holder has

1. sole voting power

FIGURE 2-4 **(*Continued*)**

2. shared voting power (if voting power is shared with any of the thirty largest shareholders, identify the shareholder and the number of shares held)

3. no voting power under any circumstances.

C. With respect to shares over which the stockholder has no voting power, the name and address of the person(s) empowered to vote the ten largest blocks of stock, the number of shares and the percentage of stock in relation to the total outstanding voting shares.

D. With respect to the 30 largest holders of voting shares in any parent, holding company or other organization or person controlling the respondent, provide the information required in subparagraphs (A), (B) and (C) above.

III. Affiliations of Officers and Directors

A. The name, address and social security number of each of the principal officers and each director, trustee, partner or person exercising similar functions, of the respondent and parent together with his title and position with the respondent and with any parent, holding company, person, or combination of persons, controlling the respondent, and with any subsidiary of the respondent and any other company, firm or organization which the respondent controls.

B. For each of the officials named under subparagraph (A) above, list the principal occupation or business affiliation if other than listed in subparagraph (A), and all affiliations with any other business or financial organizations, firm or partnership.

C. A list of each contract, agreement or other business arrangement exceeding an aggregate value of one million dollars entered into between the respondent and any business or financial organizations, firm or partnership named in subparagraph (B) above, identifying the parties, amounts, dates and product or service involved.

D. A list of each contract, agreement or other business arrangement in excess of $600 entered into during the calendar year (other than compensation related to position with respondent) between the respondent and each officer and director listed in subparagraph (A), identifying the parties, amounts, dates and product or service involved. In addition, provide the same information with respect to professional services for each firm, partnership or organization with which the officer or director is affiliated.

FIGURE 2-4 (*Continued*)

IV. Debt Holdings

A. A description of each long-term debt (debt due after one year) of the respondent in excess of one million dollars, including the name and address of the creditor, the character of the debt, nature of the security, if any, the date of origin, the date of maturity, the total amount of the debt, the rate of interest, the total amount of interest to be paid, and a copy of any and all restrictive covenants attached to the indebtedness (where such indebtedness is widely held, such as bonds and debentures, provide the name of the trustee in place of the creditor).

1. With respect to each holder of more than five percent of each issue reported provide the name, address, and type of holder—bank, broker, holding company, individual or other specified category and amount of debt held.

B. A description of each short-term debt (under one year) excluding accounts payable of the respondent, including the name and address of the creditor, nature and character of the liability, period of the debt, rate of interest, total amount of such short-term debt, nature of the security, and date when debt was paid, or date when such debt must be paid, and a copy of any and all restrictive covenants attached to the indebtedness.

C. A description of each financing lease arrangement, equipment trust, conditional sales contract, or major liability with respect to the capital assets of the respondent and involving aggregate payments in excess of one million dollars and a copy of any and all restrictive covenants attached to the indebtedness.

FIGURE 2-4 (*Continued*)

"financing lease" is the one used by the SEC. The $600 benchmark for reporting payments by respondent companies to officers and directors for professional services was initially adopted by the FPC in 1969, upon the recommendation of the Business Advisory Council on Federal Reports. (The $600 cutoff conforms with IRS reporting requirements.)

The Steering Committee recommended that the "top 30" stockholder reporting requirement, already used for one or more regulated industries by three commissions and proposed by a fourth, be used with modification. Procedures for translating nominee names into voting interests are based upon methods used by the ICC since 1974.

The MCDR places upon respondent companies the responsibility to obtain from major stockholders, and report to the commission, the major stock-voters. However, no stockholding or voting interest amounting to less than 1/10 of 1 percent of a company's outstanding voting stock need be reported.

This benchmark is high enough to exclude practically all individual investors in major corporations. But, it is low enough to disclose significant voting interests of those individuals or persons who spread their investments in a single company into several different accounts—the Laurance Rockefellers or the Fidelity Fund group in Boston. (Until recently, Fidelity was the largest stockholder in Anaconda, with 5.6 percent voting interest, divided into four nominee accounts in two banks, but a consolidated report of these Fidelity voting interests is not filed with the SEC.)[17]

The commissions could impose the MCDR selectively, that is, on Class A utilities, Class I railroads, etc.—the larger companies. Exclusion of small firms from the reporting requirement would permit each commission to obtain useful and necessary information from major and medium-sized companies while relieving many small companies of a reporting requirement which would not be of great significance.

The model is intended to replace existing reporting requirements, where applicable. Many major corporations, with subsidiaries subject to reporting jurisdictions of several commissions, now file a variety of ownership reports. Adoption of the uniform MCDR would reduce the reporting burden of such companies.

None of the regulatory commissions or other regulatory agencies whose staff participated in their formation (e.g., Federal Reserve Board, Federal Energy Administration) seem interested in promulgating the model corporate disclosure regulations, except for the ICC. The FCC went to rule making on the MCDR and its own alternatives (not even being able to agree upon common reporting requirements for its Common Carrier Bureau and its Broadcast Bureau, even though in some instances the same corporations report to both on different ownership forms). However, the FCC has decided to wait and see what the SEC does. At one point, the position of the FPC was that it was waiting to see what the ICC did. When it appeared that the ICC would do something, the FPC decided to wait and see what the SEC does. Also waiting is the Federal Maritime Commission (FMC).

The SEC proposed adoption of a modification of the MCDR, but has now taken the position that it wants to wait and see what the Congress does. There is always another bill to talk about, if a commission would rather not use the existing laws which Congress wrote and the President signed for the commission to administer. Perhaps, the government and the corporations it is supposed to regulate are simply following the Golden Rule: Whoever has the gold makes the rules.

---

17. S. Doc. No. 94-246, N. 1 *supra*, pp. 11, 534–557.

NEW DEMANDS FOR OWNERSHIP DISCLOSURE: A REALISTIC LOOK AT THE ULTIMATE PUBLIC INTEREST

Hans H. Angermueller, *Senior Vice President and General Counsel, Citicorp*

INTRODUCTION

Business disclosures, voluntary and required, now figure so prominently in the day-to-day activities of all corporate attorneys that a detailed critical examination of the subject of government information needs is highly desirable. Clearly, the present trend toward greater disclosure of private sector activity has achieved some public benefits. On occasion, it has led to the formulation of constructive regulatory guidelines. However, broad-based and indiscriminate new disclosure demands should be subjected to rigorous cost-benefit and public-interest analyses.

In the wake of deep public resentment over regrettable and highly publicized ethical lapses in American boardrooms, nothing could be easier than to enact sweeping new laws restricting entire areas of corporate discretion. And nothing could be more detrimental to the ultimate public interest.

It is crucial to our national well-being for government to find a better way to ventilate immediate public indignation than institutionalizing that concern through hastily considered placatory legislation.

My assigned subject is "Uniform Reporting Dealing with Corporate Ownership." I must, however, take the liberty of sketching briefly my position with respect to overall legislatively mandated business disclosure, before withdrawing to the narrower focus of corporate ownership.

GENERAL BUSINESS DISCLOSURE

Relentless proposals for additional business disclosure, set forth with missionary zeal by government legislators and regulators, are based on two fallacious beliefs. The first is that every bad judgment by a government regulator is caused by insufficient information. If one accepts that premise, then it is easy to leap to the conclusion that gathering a totality of information will assure achieving infallible judgments. A number of elected officials have made this remarkable leap and are now dutifully designing legislation to compel total information. But the belief is false, both in practice and in theory.

Most managers today will agree that the quality of a business judgment depends on the adequacy, relevance, and timeliness of the information on which it is based. In fact, the managerial dictum has evolved that, given sufficient reliable information, a decision will make itself. As a practical matter, however, managers know that a point is reached in the process of information gathering when a decision must be made—for they will cease to be managers. The cost of gathering a reasonable amount of information is reasonable. The cost of gathering total information is prohibitive. At a certain point, the incremental benefits resulting from further information gathering cease to be worth their cost.

To borrow an analogy from the area of environment, the cost of removing 98 percent of all particulate matter from industrial effluents is high, but manageable. The cost of scrubbing out the remaining 2 percent, to get surgically pure air, is astronomical and unmanageable.

Even though a business manager would make fewer errors if it were available, the manager knows that one cannot hold out for perfect information. The manager knows that costs have to be passed along to consumers, and that consumers will simply turn to more practical, cost-conscious competitors. However, devisers and enforcers of business regulations appear to compete with no one and therefore seem to be free to pursue whatever theoretically perfect information base will relieve them of the necessity of making difficult, discretionary cost-benefit judgments. Yet, there is no such thing as a "free lunch," and there is, indeed, a very real price to pay.

Senator Charles Percy underscored this fact in May 1976 when he opposed S.3151, the Multinational Business Information Act. Taking note of the "staggering new reporting requirement" this bill would place on American companies, he said:

> There is an implicit assumption that this proposed new requirement is free of cost to the American taxpayer but we know this is not true. Fifty percent of the company costs will be borne by the U.S. government in a tax writeoff. The consumer picks up the other costs in the product price and 100 percent of the data processing in Washington will be paid for by the American people. . . . Before any Senator decides on this bill an economic impact statement should be rendered so we can see what the new costs to consumers would be. With the information the costs of the bill could be weighed against the benefits to be received from it.[1]

---

1. 122 *Cong. Rec.* S7,632 (daily ed. May 20, 1976) (remarks of Senator Percy).

Irrespective of costs, it is simply not true that all mistakes made by regulatory officials are caused by a dearth of information. On the contrary, it is entirely possible that more errors derive from an *excess* than a *shortage* of available business information. A deluge of information—some relevant, most not—may discourage even the most diligent and dedicated regulator from extracting the truly relevant in time to exercise effective oversight.

Another fallacious belief now exciting a fair share of disclosure proposals springs from public cynicism. Revelations of wrongdoing by individuals in public and private life have led some to conclude that the only way to preserve what is valued most in America is to trust no one. In lieu of elemental trust, everyone must now disclose everything. In a gross perversion of democratic principle, laws are now being framed on the assumption that all are guilty who have not totally disclosed their innocence.

These self-denigrating laws proceed from the assumption that if one subpoenas enough records and rifles enough files, sooner or later the search for a culpable deed will be rewarded. Perhaps it will, but consider the cost. Long-treasured individual rights are being systematically eroded under this new "doctrine of potential abuse." In essence, the doctrine maintains that an existing private right that could conceivably be exercised against the public interest should be revoked. It is not necessary to produce *evidence* that such a right has actually been abused—only that it can be conjectured.

It is readily understandable that legislators, confident in their own integrity, are often ill at ease when applying this doctrine of hypothetical guilt to others. Thus, we find Senator Edmund Muskie, Chairman of the Senate Subcommittee on Intergovernmental Relations, in his 1974 apologia for the 1973 committee print, "Disclosure of Corporate Ownership," saying:

> . . . a few, very large banks, operating as institutional investors, are in a position to exercise control over the health and welfare of many of the nation's largest corporations.
>
> I want to emphasize that the report, "Disclosure of Corporate Ownership," is not intended to accuse anyone of an outright attempt to gain control of and manipulate the American corporate economy, although it may be that there are such attempts that have been made or that may be made, but the report itself makes no such accusation, although some have misconstrued it that way.[2]

In a stab at summary justification, he concludes that the present system of corporate ownership "radiates at least the appearance of

---

2. *Joint Hearings on Corporate Disclosure,* Subcommittee on Budget, Management and Expenditures and Subcommittee on Intergovernmental Relations of Senate Committee on Government Operations, 93d Cong., 2d Sess., March 21, 1974, p. 9 (opening statement of Senator Muskie).

serious conflicts of interest that, if real, makes a mockery of free enterprise."[3] Perhaps so, but legislating "appearances" instead of "realities" makes a worse mockery of democratic principle and due process.

It is not easy to wedge in a kind word for the traditional concept of mutual trust, even though it has been the basic glue holding together our democratic experiment for the past two centuries. A few persons still try, however. Arthur Burns, former Federal Reserve Board chairman, has argued in opposition to various "sunshine" bills:

> In striving to renew the public's trust in government, we should recognize that such trust ultimately will depend not upon the public's observation of the process of government decision making, but upon their perception that their government is comprised of men and women of intelligence and integrity making reasonable decisions in the public interest.[4]

Despite the present climate of cynicism, intelligence and integrity remain the rule in the private sector, no less than the public sector and the broad population. Enacting "sunshine" laws with implicit assumptions to the contrary, requiring government and business to make costly and redundant demonstration of innocence to unspecified charges, is no service to the nation.

REPORTING OF CORPORATE OWNERSHIP

From my general conclusion above, it follows that specific new legislation requiring additional disclosure of record and beneficial ownership of, or control over, equity securities of publicly owned American companies is unnecessary and against the public interest. In my view:

1. No case has been made for the necessity of comprehensive new corporate ownership legislation.
2. For the public policy purposes advanced, existing legislation is adequate.
3. Any new disclosure powers granted to regulatory agencies should be directed to cases of perceived abuse and not to massive dragnet operations.

For any who may be unacquainted with the particulars of corporate ownership disclosure, let me define the scope of this subject, then sketch in the historical highlights. First, we must ascertain just what is encompassed by the term "corporate ownership."

---

3. Ibid.

4. Arthur Burns, "The Proper Limits of Openness in Government," speech at 1976 International Monetary Conference, San Francisco, June 19, 1976, Federal Reserve System, 1976.

Section 12 of the Securities Exchange Act of 1934 requires most companies whose securities are publicly held to register and file certain basic information with the Securities and Exchange Commission.[5] This requirement applies whether the securities of these companies are traded on a national exchange or over-the-counter. There are approximately ten thousand companies now registered under the Securities Exchange Act. Some of these companies may have as few as five hundred shareholders of record and others may have millions.

As of year-end 1975, the stock of these companies had an aggregate market value in excess of $800 billion,[6] which is about one-third of the value of all debt and equity securities (including those issued or guaranteed by the Federal, state, and municipal governments) outstanding in the United States.[7]

It is estimated that approximately 25 million individuals own securities in these companies representing about 60 percent of total ownership.[8] Financial intermediaries such as banks and brokers acting in various fiduciary capacities and mutual funds acting as investment pooling vehicles probably account for another 30 percent. Foreign investors and others account for the balance.[9]

The companies that issue these securities know their stockholders of record, of course. However, stock records generally show only the names and addresses of the record holders and the number of shares owned. Information as to the nature of the ownership (direct or fiduciary), voting power (direct, delegated, or shared), and the nationality of the owner (whether record or beneficial) is not usually carried in stock books.

Statistics and data regarding such matters are more commonly reflected in the records of financial intermediaries such as banks, brokers, and investment vehicles. These records, however, provide no instant key to ownership because they cover a wide variety of intermediary functions, including trusts, estates, guardianships, agencies, and custodianships. Whereas some beneficial owners may be known, others may be yet unborn, while still others cannot be determined until one or more parties are deceased.

In the case of pension trusts, the beneficial owners are the nearly 50 million employees (well over half the national work force) that are covered by public and private pension plans.[10] It is difficult to imagine

---

5. Securities Act Amendments of 1964, P. L. No. 88-467, 78 Stat. 565 (amending 15 U.S.C. §§78c, 1-p, t, w, ff and 77d (1964)).

6. *Supply and Demand for Credit in 1976,* Salomon Brothers, New York, 1976, table IIIC.

7. Ibid., table I.

8. Ibid., table IIIC.

9. U.S. Treasury Department, *Interim Report to the Congress on Foreign Portfolio Investment in the United States,* Oct. 1975, pp. 77–85.

10. Peter F. Drucker, "Pension Fund 'Socialism,'" *The Public Interest,* no. 42, Winter 1976, p. 7.

any public benefit from disclosing their varied and varying individual ownership interests.

This is further complicated by the fact that from day to day—indeed, from hour to hour—the composition of total corporate ownership fluctuates because of new issues, redemptions or retirements of old issues, and the continuous trading of outstanding stock. On the New York Stock Exchange alone, more than $125 billion worth of stock changed hands during 1975.[11]

Using the latest technology, it may be feasible to provide a reasonably detailed picture of this enormous, complex, ever-changing sea of corporate ownership as of a given moment. But this assumes that the corporate issuers, multiple intermediaries, and ultimate beneficial owners are willing, through legislative mandate or otherwise, to have their picture taken. It also assumes that a vast range of legal, definitional, and technical problems are solvable. Even then, however, the developed picture will always, of necessity, portray the past. The sea of corporate ownership never remains still.

We must bear in mind these very real drawbacks, as we analyze the supposed "benefits" from expanded uniform public disclosure of corporate ownership.

Several years ago, the hoped-for "benefit" was supposed to be evidence that the big banks were dominating United States corporations. A congressional theory arose that the American investor is a unique species that does not respond to ordinary market intelligence and obvious economic conditions like other investors. If American investors took a good look around and pulled their savings out of equities, they could not have done so voluntarily—goes the theory—they must have been squeezed out by large institutional investors.

This notion precipitated intense governmental scrutiny into the specific holdings of institutional investors to determine for what "nefarious" purpose they had set out to corner the market in stocks of declining value. As noted above, advocates of greater disclosure, like Senator Muskie, had a ready answer to this enigma: a few large bank trust departments were preparing to acquire all the major corporations and run American industry.

According to Senator Muskie, hearings held in 1973 and 1974 painted the picture of a United States economy where "billions of dollars in investment capital are under the control of a highly select 'old boy' network virtually closed to the world around it. To recoin an old New England saying, the corporate presidents speak only to the bank directors, and the bank directors speak only to God."[12]

Initially, it was felt that the quickest way to expose such a network was to find out exactly which banks "owned" which industries. And so there followed the first wave of legislative and regulatory responses to

---

11. New York Stock Exchange, *1976 Fact Book,* Department of Public Relations and Market Development.

12. *Joint Hearings on Corporate Disclosure,* N. 2 *supra,* p. 10.

achieve total ownership disclosure. First, the Office of the Comptroller of the Currency in 1974 issued regulations requiring National Banks of significant size to disclose their fiduciary equity holdings.[13] This step, presumably because of its limited applicability, was followed in June 1975 by the enactment of Section 13(f) of the Exchange Act,[14] which required all major "institutional investment managers" to disclose similar holdings. "An enlightened public policy," according to Senator Muskie, "requires nothing less than full public disclosure of corporate ownership."[15]

Careful examination of the mandated (as well as earlier voluntary) disclosures by banks soon revealed, however, that the securities held in trust by banks were actually distributed among a great variety of accounts. Because the beneficial owners of these securities sought diverse investment objectives of their own and retained bank trust managers under contract to pursue those various objectives, the idea of a bank using these holdings to engineer a monolithic takeover of its own proved untenable.

Thus, in his transmittal letter covering publication of a survey of *Institutional Investors' Common Stock Holdings and Voting Rights* in May 1976, Senator Lee Metcalf (cochairman with Senator Muskie of the Joint Subcommittee which held the 1973–1974 hearings on bank disclosure) concluded that the practice of listing the record owners (banks) as the major holders of voting stock in the main category of custodial accounts "overstates the influence of banks."[16]

Running concurrently on a track all its own is the venerable nominee account controversy—"venerable" for age, not relevance. Periodically, some excitable newcomer to the area of corporate ownership rediscovers the long-established practice of using nominee or street-name accounts to facilitate the transfer of stocks. He invariably denounces these traditional accounts as a massive cover-up of securities ownership when he spies nominees of major institutional investors listed among the largest owners of record of many big companies. Each time, an accusing finger is pointed and the curtain is swept aside with a flourish to reveal absolutely nothing new and nothing sinister.

One can easily establish which nominees represent which institutions by consulting an annual directory published by the American Society of Corporate Secretaries. This is still a long way, of course, from identifying the ultimate beneficial owners of the shares registered with

---

13. Comptroller of the Currency, *Regulations,* Pt. 9, §9.1 *et seq.*, Dec. 1, 1974.

14. Securities Act Amendments of 1975, P. L. No. 94-2, §10, 89 Stat. 120 (amending 15 U.S.C. §78m (1968)).

15. *Joint Hearings on Corporate Disclosure,* N. 2 *supra,* p. 9.

16. *Institutional Investors' Common Stock: Holdings and Voting Rights,* Subcommittee on Reports, Accounting and Management of Senate Committee on Government Operations, 94th Cong., 2d Sess., May 5, 1976, p. v (Committee Print) (letter of transmittal from Senator Metcalf).

nominee accounts. The stock of any one company held by a single nominee may be beneficially owned by a large number of trust and investment accounts. Moreover, the shares of one company may be distributed among, and registered with, a number of nominees. It would be a formidable task to track down and add up all the shares of a given company belonging to any one beneficial owner throughout the entire nominee account stock transfer system.

Why, then, is such a complex system tolerated? For the same reason that Churchill "tolerated" democracy—because it is the worst system around except for all the others. This judgment was reaffirmed by the preliminary findings of the SEC study on the use of nominee and street-name accounts.

The SEC analyzed the six most frequently discussed alternatives to nominee registration, including multiple name registration and various centralized mailing, order processing, proxy forwarding, and depository concepts. The study concluded that the present use of nominees "facilitates the transfer of securities and is essential to the operation of the current systems for the clearance and settlement of securities transactions."[17] Chairman Hills summarized this conclusion in his transmittal letter.

> Finally, while the Commission recognized that the practice of nominee registration can be abused, it believes that this possibility is inherent in any securities processing system. It presently appears that assuring improved access to the underlying records for those with legitimate concerns would be a more useful endeavor than the imposition of new reporting systems or the reduction or elimination of the nominee name registration practice altogether.[18]

In other words, the SEC advocates a sharper spear to impale the records of specific violators of securities laws—not a dismantling of the present system. I could not agree more.

Nevertheless, despite these reassurances by regulatory officials, some legislators and others cling to the suspicion that nominees are *really* there not to facilitate, but to hide, stock transactions. Recognizing that it may be futile, I would nevertheless like to reiterate that nominees are used to assure prompt, efficient deliveries and transfers of securities for the convenience of, and with cost benefits to, financial institutions, corporations, the brokerage community, and the ultimate owners of the securities involved. Almost all states have adopted statutes permitting the registration of securities in the name of nominees. In the case of New York banks, nominees are registered with public officials in

---

17. *The Practice of Recording the Ownership of Securities in the Records of the Issuer in Other Than the Name of the Beneficial Owner of Such Securities,* preliminary report of the SEC, Dec. 4, 1975, p. 1 (letter of transmittal from Roderick M. Hills).

18. Ibid., p. 20.

addition to being published annually in the Nominee List which is available for purchase by anyone. Nominees are *not* used for the purpose of hiding ownership. In the legendary words of Ethel Barrymore: "That's all there is. There isn't any more."

Deprived of any evidence that banks intended to take over corporate America with nominee accounts or anything else, conspiracy theorists were forced to look elsewhere for villains. Candidates were soon found overseas.

It is increasingly apparent that the present campaign to mandate wholesale disclosure of beneficial ownership is basically an effort to ferret out the well-funded foreign investor or group of foreign investors. In early 1975, Senator Harrison Williams started recounting frightening statistics on the potential disruptive power of foreign investors—particularly Arab investors—on our national economy. He reported:

> *The London Economist* has made some sobering calculations about Arab economic power. It is estimated, for example, that OPEC could use their surplus oil revenues to buy all companies on the world's major stock exchanges in 15.6 years—at present quotations—all companies listed on the New York Stock Exchange in 9.2 years; all IBM stock in 143 days; all Exxon stock in 79 days; and the Rockefeller family's wealth in only 6 days. These are chilling calculations, the implications of which must be evaluated with the utmost seriousness.
>
> Mr. President, I believe it is time to assess whether our "open door" economic policy should be modified in light of recent and reasonably foreseeable events.[19]

These statistics, together with numerous examples of domestic and foreign "takeovers," were the preamble to Senator Williams's introduction of S.425. This proposed legislation was designed to require disclosure of the *beneficial* ownership of *all* publicly traded United States equity securities and to require *prior* notification to the SEC and the President of the acquisition by any *foreign* investor of 5 percent or more of any equity security of any company, whether publicly traded or not. Senator Williams underscored the timeliness of his bill by stating:

> Mr. President, there is an urgent and manifest need for this legislation. The world is today at a precarious, if not perilous, point. Difficult and complex negotiations are underway to resolve global economic and political problems which threaten to endanger world order and peace. The United States must be in a position of financial independence if we are to play an instrumental role in arriving at permanent and peaceful solutions. This bill will aid us in achieving that result.[20]

---

19. 121 *Cong. Rec.* 1350 (remarks of Senator Harrison Williams).

20. Ibid., p. 1351.

Though S.425 was not enacted into law, its disclosure provisions in modified form reappeared as Title III of S.3084 which was introduced in 1976. Senator Adlai Stevenson, a sponsor of the bill, in May 1976, confirmed that the disclosure provisions were directed toward foreign—particularly Arab—investments.

> Of immediate concern in light of continuing tensions in the Middle East and the accumulation of vast sums in the hands of OPEC (a $60 billion surplus in 1974; $40 billion in 1975) is the possibility that foreign investment from Arab sources will be manipulated for political purposes. The Treasury Department estimates that during the first nine months of 1975, $3.5 billion, or 75 percent, of all the foreign portfolio investment in the United States came from OPEC sources. Such investment could constitute a powerful economic weapon should the Arab states attempt to employ it to achieve political ends.[21]

The government apparently is still in the process of defining its own needs in the area of corporate ownership disclosure. But, its focus seems to have shifted from owners of record to those investors—especially foreign investors—who might acquire dangerous concentrations of beneficial ownership of United States companies, then theoretically use such ownership to the disadvantage of our economy or the disadvantage of particular companies. To judge the seriousness of this threat, we must consider how share ownership actually translates into corporate influence.

THE HOW (AND WHY) OF CORPORATE CONTROL

Investors, whether individual or institutional, domestic or foreign, invest in the anticipation of gain. It is inconsistent with human experience for investors who have acquired wealth through the sale of goods or services to expend that wealth for purposes other than to preserve or increase it.

Broadly speaking, an acquisition of securities falls into one of two categories. It is either a portfolio investment or a direct investment. Insofar as equity securities are concerned, the Treasury Department defines as portfolio investments any purchases of "less than 10 percent of voting securities"[22] "which do not involve any intention on the part of the investor to exercise a significant influence on the management of the enterprise."[23] Thus, portfolio investors are content to rely on the efforts of incumbent management to enhance the value of their investments. If these expectations are not met or are too long in being

---

21. S. Rep. No. 94-917, May 25, 1976.

22. U.S. Treasury Department, *Interim Report*, p. 109.

23. Ibid., p. 2.

realized, investors dispose of such investments through normal market channels.

The second form of investment, direct investment, is defined as acquiring "at least 10 percent of the voting stock for incorporated enterprises."[24] Direct investments are usually made with the intention of assuming some degree of control over the affairs of the enterprise—either by installing new management, instituting new policies, or assuring future transactions with the company.

The manner and extent of control effected through direct investment in voting securities can take many forms depending on the attitude of incumbent management. If the direct investment is welcomed, perhaps even sought, by incumbent management, the desired measure of control may be transferred even though numerous obstacles must be overcome in the process. The direct investment in 1969 by British Petroleum in Standard Oil of Ohio is a good illustration. The announcement was made with the full approval of both boards of directors on June 3, 1969, that British Petroleum would acquire initially 25 percent of the outstanding shares of Standard Oil of Ohio in exchange for BP's oil reserves in Alaska and a number of service stations. Depending on the amount of oil produced by the Alaskan fields, BP was to gradually accumulate over time a majority interest (up to 54 percent) of Standard stock. Obstacles arose to throw off the terms and the timetable for this direct investment. The Justice Department questioned certain antitrust aspects which resulted in divestiture of certain retail stations. Environmental protests delayed construction of the Alaskan Pipeline. The capacity of the pipe was changed. The British government's ownership of 49 percent of British Petroleum raised the investment challenge to the level of international diplomacy. Nevertheless, the investment was made and the progressive acquisition of shares is moving ahead on a revised schedule because incumbent management welcomed the investment and made numerous accommodations to effect it.

Conversely, if the putative control is contested by incumbent management, the desired degree of control can be delayed for long periods of time and, indeed, may be deflected entirely through a combination of legal, public relations, and political processes.[25]

Depending upon a company's structure and management philosophy, the day-to-day operations of most American business enterprises are determined by their senior management. Long-range business policies and objectives are usually set by the directors of these companies, in consultation with senior management. Investors, especially those

---

24. Ibid., p. 109.

25. For examples in this category see the domestic battle for control of Chris Craft Corporation in Walter Guzzardi, "The Casualties Were Staggering in the Battle for Piper Aircraft," *Fortune*, vol. 93, no. 4, April 1976, pp. 90 ff, and the U.S./foreign contest for control of Copperweld Corporation in Rush Loving, "The House of Rothschild Gets a U.S. Wing," *Fortune*, vol. 94, no. 1, July 1976, pp. 164 ff.

holding significant numbers of shares, are always listened to courteously, but they are unlikely to alter the broad operations, policies, and objectives of a corporation for two reasons. First, it is somewhat unlikely that a shareholder, who is usually not engaged in a business similar to that in which he is investing, will come up with a recommended improvement that has not already been the subject of some degree of study and evaluation. And second, every shareholder's interests cannot be separately represented at the director level. Accordingly, to exert control, an investor must at least have some direct effective representation on the board.

How that representation is gained depends on many factors: the nature of the business in which the company is engaged; whether or not that business is regulated; the amount of voting stock acquired; the applicable state laws covering the election of directors; the observance of proxy rules and regulations under federal securities laws; the impact which changed board representation may have on third-party contracts; and, perhaps most importantly, the attitude of incumbent management.

Certainly, the surest defense against surprise shifts of control by American companies is already contained in section 13(d) of the Securities Exchange Act.[26] That section was authored eight years ago by Senator Williams, who is now pressing for even broader disclosure proposals. I submit that section 13(d) is a tested, effective, and fully adequate protection against surprise takeovers by unfriendly investors, domestic and foreign. Section 13(d) of the act requires, among other things, that any person (or group of persons acting in concert), domestic or foreign, who acquires directly or indirectly more than 5 percent of the outstanding shares of any class of a registered security must, within 10 days, notify both the issuer and the SEC, specifying:

1. the background and identity of the ultimate purchaser;
2. the source of funds or other considerations used to make the purchase;
3. the purpose of the purchase, including any plans to acquire control, liquidate, sell assets, merge, or make any other major change in the business of the company issuing the security;
4. the number of shares beneficially owned by the purchaser as well as any rights to purchase further shares; and
5. a catchall provision spelled out as follows:

> . . . information as to any contracts, arrangements, or understandings with any person with respect to any securities of the issuer, including but not limited to transfer of any of the securities, joint ventures, loan or option arrangements, puts and calls, guaranties of loans, guaranties against loss or guaranties of profits, division of losses or profits, or the

---

26. Act of July 29, 1968, P. L. No. 90-439 §2, 82 Stat. 454 (amending 15 U.S.C. §78m (1964)).

giving or withholding of proxies, naming the persons with whom such contracts, arrangements, or understandings have been entered into, and giving the details thereof.[27]

The objection is sometimes raised that a stock purchaser, for reasons of his own, may not file the required information with the issuing company or the SEC when his holdings exceed 5 percent. This is true enough. But it does not follow that he will begin to comply with the law merely because the threshold amount is lowered to 1 or 2 percent or ½ percent. The point is that less than 5 percent ownership provides no muscle at all, and when anyone owning more than 5 percent attempts to flex even that little muscle without having complied with section 13(d), then his ownership is susceptible to prosecution for violation of law and can be neutralized. Injunctive powers inherent in the Securities Exchange Act[28] could probably be invoked to deny that person the right to vote his illegally acquired shares; so the threat of exercising control effectively evaporates until final compliance has been achieved.

What *will* happen if the threshold is lowered is that those intent on evading the law will be unaffected, while ever-tighter reporting nets will draw in enormous schools of small fish whose routine stock transactions are no threat to anyone—except perhaps the recipients of the reports who will be deluged with inconsequential data.

Former SEC chairman Ray Garrett, when testifying on the beneficial ownership disclosure aspects of S.425, the Foreign Investment Act of 1975, alluded to this administrative burden:

> We are concerned about the substantial costs that would be imposed on brokerage firms, banks, trust companies, and especially, transfer agents, as well as the issuing companies, if the precise provisions of S.425 were enacted, since the bill would apply to all beneficial owners, even the owner of one share of common stock. The burden of receiving so much material would also be severe on the Commission. Computer print-outs of stock records of widely-held companies can easily fill a large file drawer, and there are some 9,000 companies presently registered under the Exchange Act. It is not unusual for a large company to have over 100,000 record holders of its common stock. AT&T has millions. So much data is too expensive to collect and more than anyone can effectively and properly use.
>
> If the intention of this section of the bill is to elicit significant information regarding beneficial owners, the Congress should consider less burdensome, alternative means of accomplishing this goal. At the very least, the disclosure in filings should be limited, perhaps to the 20 or 30 largest holders, or any holder of more than some percentage such as 2 percent or 1 percent.[29]

---

27. Ibid., §(d) (1) (E).

28. Securities Exchange Act of 1934, 15 U.S.C. §§77 b–e, j, k, m, o, s, 78 *et seq.* (as amended).

29. *Hearings on Foreign Investment Act of 1975, S.425,* Subcommittee on Securities of Senate Committee on Banking, Housing and Urban Affairs, 94th Cong., 1st Sess., March 5, 1975, pp. 97–98 (statement of Ray Garrett, Jr., SEC Chairman).

Similar caution was urged in June 1976 by the then SEC chairman, Roderick M. Hills, when commenting on the Bank Secrecy Act of 1970. Chairman Hills dealt with the effectiveness of section 13(d) as follows:

> The Commission is currently considering the adoption of a package of rules and form changes which would modify our requirements for the disclosure of beneficial ownership. This proceeding is the culmination of a study which began with a public fact-finding investigation in the fall of 1974 and which included extensive public comment on the Commission's proposals in this area published in August 1975. Our proposals will be the first major exercise of the Commission's rule making authority under the Williams Act and will include rules, form changes, and guidelines for determining when a person is a beneficial owner in certain situations. The proposal will also require additional disclosure from beneficial owners in required filings in takeover and acquisition situations. These proposals will be helpful to our enforcement efforts in the areas we have discussed this morning. *We believe that the Commission and the Congress should consider the operations of these new rules before recommending any additional legislation in this area.*[30]

When two successive chairmen of the federal agency charged with primary responsibility for the proper functioning of our securities markets caution against additional disclosure requirements and suggest that existing laws may be adequate, it would seem appropriate to listen, especially in view of the potential expense of meeting new requirements.

COST FACTORS

This brings us to a consideration of the probable cost of proposed legislation requiring additional record and beneficial corporate ownership disclosure. I have already mentioned the monumental quantities of data which might be involved, as well as the fact that all such data will be reported after the fact. These represent heavy collection and reporting costs to the private sector. However, in the last analysis, these costs will presumably be spread among many institutions to be borne by their respective customers and shareholders. The greater and more concentrated burden will fall upon the particular governmental agency charged with the receipt, assembly, storage, and retrieval of this staggering quantity of information, if it is to serve any meaningful objective. The question is whether the objective is truly meaningful. Senator Lee Metcalf, one of the staunchest proponents of corporate disclosure, in a letter sent late in 1975 to the SEC suggests that the real purpose of

---

30. *Oversight Hearings into the Operations of the IRS: Administration of the Bank Secrecy and Reporting Act,* Subcommittee on Commerce, Consumer and Monetary Affairs of House Committee on Government Operations, 94th Cong., 2d Sess., June 28, 1976, pp. 14–15 (statement of Roderick M. Hills) (emphasis added).

disclosure is to fulfill a "special need" for investors to determine "who controls the policies of a corporation." Senator Metcalf states:

> Investors have special need for the information to be disclosed under the model. Without such information, they are unable to determine who controls the policies of a corporation. Direction of corporate policies is the most significant factor affecting the value of an investment over a period of time, yet, current and proposed SEC disclosure regulations do not reveal the ultimate persons or institutions who can exercise control. . . .
>
> One of the primary problems regarding voting stock ownership is the intertwining of information on voting stock control with information on beneficial ownership. . . .
>
> A breakdown of voting rights is also necessary to analyze the proposed reporting provision which requires the respondent to identify those who hold voting authority for the securities where the respondent has no voting rights. The ability to control corporate activities derives from voting authority rather than mere record ownership. Identification of voting rights by type is an integral part of any disclosure regulations.[31]

Apparently, Senator Metcalf assumes that, without extensive new data on the record and beneficial ownership of publicly traded securities, investors have no way to determine the policies of the underlying corporations. This ignores the fact that, without question, the American investing public is by far the best informed and advised group of investors in the world. The vast, detailed, and frequent corporate reporting requirements of the federal securities laws, supplemented by the flood of analytical reports and analyses furnished at little or no charge by the securities industry, provide infinitely more useful information on policies, control, and operations of publicly owned United States corporations than would a mind-boggling series of raw ownership statistics reflecting total shares held of record and beneficially, together with voting rights held, delegated, or shared.

When an individual investor goes out to buy a share of stock, he does not ask who owns the company. He wants to know what it earns and what its prospects are. The "special need" detected by Senator Metcalf for investors to know the company's owners is not evident from surveys, stockholder communications, or investors meetings.

We should also consider the intangible "cost" of invading the privacy of an *existing* investor in order to provide some measure of information to a *prospective* investor. Even if additional ownership information were to prove useful, current, and material to a prospective investor (a proposition I seriously doubt), the question remains whether the trade-off, in the long range, is worth it.

In the post-Watergate world, disclosures of governmental and corporate venality share the limelight with equally disturbing examples of

---

31. 121 *Cong. Rec.* E6,734 (daily ed., Dec. 17, 1975) (statement of Senator Metcalf).

governmental invasions of privacy. I believe that if anyone proposed a general disclosure of individual earnings by throwing open the federal income tax return files, there would be an enormous public outcry. Why should not the same objections which apply to disclosure of earnings apply to disclosure of assets? Probably because fewer people are affected. Nevertheless, fundamental doubt remains: whether there is a sufficiently *compelling* public need to further the already disturbing trend toward universal "sunshine."

Apart from the loss of privacy, a further cost will be incurred if broad disclosures of corporate ownership deter the flow of capital—particularly foreign capital—into United States equity securities. The usual rebuttal to this argument is, of course, "What do these investors have to hide?" Admittedly, the desires and needs for individual privacy are not equally shared throughout the world. However, many U.S. citizens believe they enjoy Justice Brandeis's famous "right to be left alone—the most comprehensive of rights and the most valued by civilized men."[32] Citizens of many other countries not only share that belief, but grew up in cultures where it is even more firmly protected by their laws than ours. Any measures which impair the privacy of investors will have some detrimental effect upon the flow of savings into equity markets—markets which already have been losing ground relative to debt markets. Obviously, the detrimental impact of additional detailed disclosure of record and beneficial corporate ownership cannot be proved before it happens; however, it is a "cost" that should certainly be well considered before it is incurred.

CONCLUSION

I have been invited to comment on particular applications that have been made or might yet be made of the concept of uniform reporting of ownership to one industry or another—down to this or that percentage of shares. But, as I hope I have made clear, before we can discuss the "how" we have to deal with the "why." When there is less dependence on the "doctrine of potential abuse" and more tangible evidence of a need for greater ownership disclosure, then the search for application techniques—uniform or otherwise—will gain relevance. Until then, I am not persuaded that sifting through industries for likely targets is a productive exercise.

Just assume for the moment that a system were designed and programmed to deliver an accurate printout at any given moment of the names, addresses, and national origins of every beneficial owner—born and unborn—as well as the possessor of voting rights for every last share issued by every public corporation engaged in any industry in the United States. Suppose that all this wealth of computerized

---

32. *Olmsted* v. *United States*, 277 U.S. 438, 476 (1927).

information could be delivered to the appropriate governmental agency simply by pushing a function button.

Would there be some manifest public benefit derived from pushing it? Would that benefit bear any sensible relationship to the cost of such an apparatus? Could it conceivably justify to rational minds the awesome sacrifice of personal privacy—"the right to be left alone"?

We are asked to believe that the supreme overriding benefit would be the assurance that no one is secretly gaining control of these companies in order to destroy them or in some other manner to harm our country or its economy.

Laws are already on the books restricting, or requiring reporting of, various degrees of ownership of our banking, insurance, shipping, airline, broadcasting, and utility industries. As indicated above, a U.S. corporation engaged in virtually any industry will, if publicly owned, require reporting of 5 percent or more concentrations of domestic or foreign ownership. I feel that our federal securities laws generally provide adequate tools to prevent counterproductive takeovers of individual companies or industries. I have no argument, however, with the suggestions made by former SEC Chairman Hills to sharpen these tools to a surgical level in order to deal with foreign investors who disregard our laws. This would permit our courts to "restrict transfer of shares, prohibit payment of or impound dividends, or require public sale of the securities involved."[33]

My colleagues at Citibank and I recognize the virtues of uniformity in reporting. Indeed, we have frequently urged greater uniformity to minimize the unnecessary expense of supplying substantially the same information to separate agencies in different formats, or of providing it at staggered intervals when the data are just different enough to require redoing. The opportunity to program a computer to respond to various agencies concurrently would be a welcome step.

The Interagency Steering Committee on Uniform Corporate Reporting has made commendable progress in this direction by designing a composite reporting model for multiagency use. The specific features of the model are subject to refinement, but the precedent for approaching government informational needs on a cooperative basis is sound. It should clarify present reporting, which has been trivialized and weighed down with excessive details.

The final design of a uniform reporting model presumably would accommodate more information than is needed by any one regulatory agency, but encompass enough information to meet the requirements of all. When legislators apply the concept of "uniform reporting" to *ownership* disclosure, however, I get the uneasy feeling that what they are really talking about is uniformly *more*—not uniformly *less*. And in my view, no need for additional ownership information has been established.

---

33. *Oversight Hearings,* p. 12.

DIALOGUE

ALICE TEPPER MARLIN: I was interested in Mr. Reinemer's comment that banks were particularly protective of the holdings of mutual funds, because, from my days on Wall Street, I remember that the holdings of mutual funds were the easiest to identify. They are published in *Vickers Guide,* which comes out quarterly. Have you access to *Vickers?* Why is there a keen interest in mutual fund holdings on Wall Street, and yet a keen interest in protecting that list?

REINEMER: It has been especially puzzling. We finally got hold of a Nominee List—the American Society of Corporate Secretaries refused to sell the nominee list to, for example, the FPC—and Senator Metcalf put it in the *Congressional Record.* It took ninety-four pages, but it was then in the public domain.

ANGERMUELLER: The issue of the so-called protection of mutual funds, I think, is a little bit of a misnomer. Mutual funds, under the Investment Company Act, generally have to have a bank custodian for their securities. A custodian has no voting rights. He is basically a safety deposit box.

This session was chaired by William L. Cary, Professor of Law, Columbia University School of Law. For further biographical information, see Appendix 1.

Again, for liquidity purposes, he will register his holdings in nominee name.

The record owner—because the beneficial owner is actually the holder of the mutual fund shares—has to report its holdings at least quarterly to the SEC. I guess it would not be a terribly difficult thing to have the SEC expand its regulations and tell the mutual funds, which are subject to the SEC's regulation, to notify the company of its ownership of particular securities so it can appear in the lists. But it would be an enormous burden if banks had to try to track down all the persons for whom they are holding securities in custody and to disclose such persons. That would raise confidentiality issues.

The fact is I do not think any mutual fund is trying to hide its securities holdings. It is already a matter of public record. Statements of holdings are sent to the mutual fund holders quarterly, if not more frequently.

ROSWELL B. PERKINS: With the emphasis on continuous reporting, it would seem there is some merit in trying to rely on the SEC's records. I do, however, fully understand the frustration of not being able to find (e.g., because they are buried in a warehouse) the SEC's records. But, assuming SEC record keeping can be improved, what is there about the 10-K that would need beefing up in order to meet the same standards as the proposed Model Corporate Disclosure Regulation? In what particular respect do you feel the 10-K is inadequate? Take, for example, the whole section on debt instruments that is in the proposed Model Regulations; it seems to me to duplicate the 10-K in that it would require a copy to be filed of all material debt instruments. It seems to me the arguments for relying on the 10-K, and maybe doing some minor tinkering as needed, are very strong.

REINEMER: There are three parts to my answer. First, the 10-K is deficient; you don't get the full view of other business affiliations of officers and directors. Secondly, on debt-holding information, there is the admitted problem the SEC has in managing information. The last three chairmen of the SEC and Senator Metcalf have had conversations about the sorry state of the SEC's files. They simply have not developed a sensible management system at the SEC.

Third, as to voting securities, 10 percent is simply an insufficient benchmark if you want some idea of where the control of a company lies. The Model Regulations require the reporting of the thirty top stockholders down to 1/10 of 1 percent.

ANGERMUELLER: I don't think SEC disclosure requirements are limited to percentages. Both the 1933 and 1934 Acts deal with the requirement to report control, irrespective of percentages. I think trying to define a percentage limit, whether it be the thirty largest or 5 percent or 10 percent, is something of a self-defeating move. I think dealing with the concept of "control" is the right way to approach the subject.

FRANK R. EDWARDS: This is really a question directed to Mr. Reinemer; it goes to the basic argument for uniform reporting of corporate ownership.

As I interpret your discussion and paper, you advance two reasons for uniform reporting. First, you suggest it is necessary for the intelligent enforcement of a number of regulations. And you seem to be talking as if you believe that the regulatory agencies are acting in the public interest, and if they only had the right information, they would do a better job. Well, if I assume that the regulatory agencies are doing their best to act in the public interest, I see no inconsistency between nonuniform reporting and good regulation. Each regulatory agency has different objectives. The regulation is different. It would not surprise me if they needed different information for the enforcement of different regulations.

That leads me to the second argument, which is one I think you make more forcefully, and that is that the regulatory agencies are not doing a good job. You make references to "if they got off the dime, etc."—that type of argument suggests to me that your major thrust is to argue that if we had uniform reporting it would make regulation better than it is now.

My question is: Do you really believe that uniform reporting can be more than a superficial palliative for the problems we have with regulation? Are not the problems of regulation—and of regulatory bureaucracies—much deeper than a mere information problem?

REINEMER: Let me say that one of the most important things about having this information reported is that it becomes available not only to the commissions, but also to the public. What we are talking about is not really the kind of information which needs to be protected. We are not talking about confidential information.

And getting that information collected by the commissions into the public domain opens the whole regulatory process to people who see for the first time accurate information, and then they can use it. So often the commissions have assumed that, "Gee, if we just could get certain information which would be useful to us, and we sort of keep it to ourselves, we are going to be able to protect the public interest." Well, that is a very impractical view of how government works.

Government is so big, our whole information management system is so poor, that we need to concentrate on making accurate information available to the using public.

Also, I don't want to underestimate the value to firms that now have to make numerous reports on these various reporting requirements—the value to them of uniform Model Regulations.

ANGERMUELLER: Vic, how many people who make investment decisions do you think would be influenced by knowing, or not knowing, the thirty largest stockholders in a corporation?

REINEMER: Well, of course, I am thinking more of shareholder groups concerned about the decisions of a particular company. How are they going to be able to have any influence whatsoever at an annual election, in the selection of the board of directors, in voting or in deciding how votes are going to be cast, unless they can find out in advance of the meeting who the major voting interests are and talk to the people in those funds or banks and try to persuade them. What we are talking about here, really, is something that is basic to corporate democracy. We wish to make the voting process work a bit better so that the average stockholder or fund manager, who might not agree with management, can have his input into corporate decisions.

GEORGE J. BENSTON: Mr. Reinemer, I gather one of the reasons for wanting this type of disclosure is because of your concern about the power that individuals or institutions may have on large corporations that influence all of our lives. Would you extend this concern to wanting to know the investment interests—i.e., the ownership of various enterprises and the various sources of income—of people who have considerable power over the lives of citizens, namely, senators, representatives, and their staffs?

REINEMER: We have pretty good disclosure as to those people right now.

BENSTON: Is there complete public disclosure of the holdings of the members of committee staffs?

REINEMER: Staff people above a certain salary limit report fairly completely. But it is the old business. It goes to the comptroller general, and he seals it up so the public does not have it.

BENSTON: Would you be in favor of this information being made public?

REINEMER: Definitely. And this was part of the Watergate reform bill that did not get through. I do think and hope that the next Congress will require pretty good reporting on congressional staff as well as members.

ELLIOTT WEISS: This is a question for Mr. Angermueller. I have perceived what seems to be a hole in the disclosure system with respect to corporate ownership. It involves primarily pension funds which are managed by money management houses. Every banker I have ever spoken to who holds that kind of stock as a custodian says, as you did, "We don't vote custodian stock." Of course, you do have to stamp the proxy card because it is in your nominee name and then it gets shipped out to somebody.

I have never talked to a money manager who says that he votes the stock. It seems to me somebody either votes the stock or those cards you stamp go into a trash basket somewhere.

ANGERMUELLER: It may be the latter. As a custodian we have no voting power; we get the proxy card and we ship it out to the person we perceive has that voting power. It may be the investment manager does dump it in the trash basket, which accounts for the fact that in corporate meetings about 10 percent of the stock is never voted. It may be the managers or individuals or the inefficiency of the Postal Service, I don't know, but the fact is we don't do the voting.

WEISS: But is there some way Mr. Reinemer or other interested people can find out what, in fact, those people do? Is there some way to design the system to find out what happens? We are talking about a very substantial block of investment capital.

ANGERMUELLER: In many cases those investment managers may very well be investment advisers who have to file under the Investment Advisers Act. It may be. What actually happens, to be candid, I don't know.

WILLIAM L. CARY: When Morgan Guaranty, Bankers Trust, or Citibank invests funds for these large pension funds or trusts, I assume the banks would vote the stock. That is clear.

ANGERMUELLER: We usually vote it alone. In some cases, we share responsibility with the settler corporation. But we do exercise voting rights.

CARY: Am I right that some banks feel rather uncomfortable doing so?

ANGERMUELLER: That is correct.

CARY: In other words, it is not necessarily anything that you are seeking.

ANGERMUELLER: We would like to find somebody to take away the burden, but generally the corporation does not want to do it. As to the multitude of potential beneficiaries—we don't know how to select them.

ROBERT W. HAMILTON: Have you ever voted stock against management?

ANGERMUELLER: Yes, we have.

HAMILTON: When?

ANGERMUELLER: I do not remember. We get asked that particular question at each annual meeting, and there are certain percentages. I can find out. It is a matter of public record. I just do not recall the percentage at the present time.

CARL A. AUERBACH: I think it's proper in this gathering to evoke the names of Berle and Means. If it is the purpose of public disclosure to contribute to public education, wouldn't it be misleading to give the impression that the thirty largest holders of voting shares, defined as including those who own more than 1/10 of 1 percent, really control a modern corporation?

REINEMER: I guess I have not made my point clear: voting control of stock is simply one of the possible levers of control. I have not suggested what the reporting limits should be. We are trying to improve a grossly inaccurate reporting system so that regulators and the public have information on the actual potential leverage in four different areas.

I have pointed out in my paper how in a number of instances an institution—and not necessarily a large institution—or some individuals, will have stock in a particular company in a number of different accounts. And if you don't go down to this kind of level, to 1/10 of 1 percent, you are not going to pick up significant voting interests.

FREDERICK ROWE: I would like to ask Mr. Angermueller what cost or detriment he perceives in making this information available?

ANGERMUELLER: Since Citibank is subject already to the Federal Reserve, the Comptroller of the Currency, the SEC, and various state regulatory authorities, the additional burden that this would impose in describing, for example, the short-term debt that we have outstanding, the long-term debt that we have outstanding, the various contracts in excess of $1 million—it would prove an enormous burden for us. I seriously question whether there would be any real benefit to the investing public.

CHAPTER THREE

The Information Required for Indicative (Noncompulsory) National Planning

EDITOR'S NOTE

This chapter presents a subject matter of fundamental importance. Although, as this note is written, references to the Humphrey-Javits Balanced Growth and Economic Planning Act seem dated, the underlying dialogue on the value and practicability of planning remains vibrant. At issue are questions such as: Can the kinds of planning information that, for example, Professor Leontief seeks be collected at tolerable cost? How useful would the information be in government's policymaking process? Would the collection or disclosure of such information conflict with antitrust enforcement or other regulatory goals?

Dean Michael I. Sovern, who chaired the dialogue on planning, wisely and wittily set forth the following précis of the Leontief-Scott debate:

> The jargon and the blandness of the session's title nonetheless fails to assuage the views of some who see the subject as unleashing bureaucrats who have never met a payroll to tell those in the private sector when, where, and what to produce.
>
> There are others who, at the very least, see the need for the government to coordinate its own policies and actions. For them, planning is congenial and easy to accept.
>
> "National planning" obviously has many meanings. In the sense of truly comprehensive planning, the idea evokes the summary of France's planning experience, attributed to Giscard d'Estaing. He said, it is alleged, "We have simply substituted error for chance." Professor Scott analyzes that experience with greater detail and subtlety.
>
> Whatever meaning of planning one emphasizes, an indispensable prerequisite is obviously a reliable data base, which raises the question whether

quality information, to the extent necessary for broad-based planning, can really be collected by a government. Critics point to the complexity of international markets, the presumed unwillingness of private companies to provide government with unbiased, up-to-date data, and they conclude that the collection of quality information is a hopeless but very costly enterprise.

Professor Leontief, as you know, disagrees. Indeed, he makes so bold as to tell us that a staff of between 200 to 250 persons can carry out his data-gathering and research program. And his eloquent case for the need for such an effort reminds me of Adlai Stevenson's description of the human animal as a peculiar animal unable to read the handwriting on the wall until its back is against it.

For me, as I suspect for many of you, the toughest question is whether Professor Leontief's autonomous professional data-gatherers and analysts can operate neutrally in a political environment. He will say yes; Professor Scott will doubtless be skeptical.

AN INFORMATION SYSTEM FOR POLICY DECISIONS IN A MODERN ECONOMY

Wassily Leontief, *Professor of Economics, New York University*

INTRODUCTORY OBSERVATIONS

The design of a statistical or any other data system should obviously be controlled by specification of purposes that it is intended to serve. In the course of their historical development, the contents and organization of government statistics gradually adjust themselves to change in the use that is being made of them. As in any other political or administrative process, this adjustment occurs, however, with a considerable lag. Thus, it is not surprising that users of official statistics both within and outside the government tend to view even the latest facts and figures offered to them as being already obsolete. To keep an information system up to date, one has to look ahead.

In this paper, I endeavor to describe the demands that the United States government statistical service should be expected to meet five or ten years from now, and to suggest some of the steps that would have to be taken in the immediate future so as to enable it to satisfy these crucial, long-term needs.

Because of greater familiarity with the economic scene, I will center my attention on economic statistics. The same considerations, however, apply to population, health, environment, and all other areas of social statistics as well.

Without the driving force of private enterprise operating within the flexible setting of a free market economy, this country could never have attained the high level of economic well-being that it enjoys today. The invisible hand of the competitive price mechanism cannot, however, maintain the balance of the system and secure the satisfaction of rapidly expanding social needs without the guiding and supporting action of that other, highly visible public hand.

Over 27 percent of our GNP now passes directly through federal, state, and local government budgets, and most, if not all, private economic activities are subject to direct or indirect governmental control. The extension of public involvement in all aspects of economic and social life represents a natural and unavoidable response to the rise of modern large-scale technology; the rapid growth of the demand for public, as contrasted to private, goods; and, last but not least, the increasing concern for social and economic equity as contrasted to simple efficiency.

The present patchwork pattern of governmental action in the economic field grew, step-by-step, out of the necessity to provide immediate remedies to particular exigencies. Only in the case of regularly recurring or persistent problems such as cyclical unemployment or the stubborn inflationary trends, has there been a semblance of systematic anticipatory policies. The present government involvement in the operation of our economy presents a confusing picture of a sprawling labyrinth rather than a blueprint of a rationally designed edifice.

In an advanced industrial economy like ours, any action intended to meet a problem confronting one particular industry, one particular geographic area, or one particular group of citizens is bound to affect—whether intended or not—many other industries, other regions, and other citizens. Moreover, many, if not most, of the decisions, private as well as public, arrived at and carried out today can be expected to affect the economy and the state of our society not only next year, but five, ten, and even twenty years from now.

The troubleshooting approach to formulation of government policies, at least in the economic field, is bound to be ineffectual and inordinately costly under such conditions. Measures devised to meet one particular problem turn out to create new problems or, at least, to aggravate the already existing ones.

An alternative to the troubleshooting, trial-and-error approach is one in which the country's economy is viewed as a system of interrelated activities (which it actually is) and the economic policies of the federal, state, and local governments are conceived as a combination of well-coordinated rules and actions designed to facilitate the day-to-day operation and, to some extent, steer in a desired direction the development of the system as a whole.

Some recent legislative reforms and administrative changes can be interpreted as tentative moves in this direction. The time has now come to take a decisive step: A strong autonomous research organization should be established to provide all branches and agencies of the government with technical support required for developing a systematic coordinated approach to development, evaluation, and practical implementation of national, regional, and local, general and sectoral economic policies. The proposed organization could also strengthen the quality and compatibility of privately gathered data (e.g., by associations and research groups) by providing suggested statistical standards and guidelines.

This organization should also be responsible for monitoring in great detail developments in all parts of the United States economy, with emphasis on changes in their interrelationships and, whenever necessary, on their dependence on anticipated changes in the structure of the world economy. In doing so, it should be able to identify and perhaps anticipate the potential trouble spots. In looking ahead, the analytical capabilities of that organization should be engaged not so much in crystal ball predictions of the future, but rather in systematic elaboration of alternative scenarios each describing, with emphasis on sectoral and regional detail, the anticipated effect of a particular combination of national, regional, and local economic policies. This is, in fact, the only means by which the government and the electorate at large will be able to make an informed choice among alternative policies.

While providing research support to legislators and administrators engaged in the overall direction of national economic policies and assisting in the choice of appropriate methods for their practical implementation, the proposed technical organization should not be directly involved in either process any more than is, for instance, the Bureau of Labor Statistics (Department of Labor) or the Bureau of Economic Analysis (Department of Commerce). In order to be able to discharge effectively the responsibilities assigned to it, it should, however, have a decisive voice in determining the direction and scope of the data-gathering activities of the federal and, in some instances, even of the state and local governments.

THE MODELING APPROACH

The scientific tool best suited to the task of analyzing the operations of large economic systems is the model. A model is not so much a small-scale replica of the real thing as it is a surveyor's map, a blueprint of its structure and of the interrelationships between all its different parts. The modeling approach can be considered today to be practically indispensable for systematic understanding of the functioning or, as the case may be, the malfunctioning of a modern economy, for tracing the actual or potential sources of trouble and for deciding what adjustments should be made, what actions could be taken—to set it right.

The model-building approach is widely used both by government and private business. It has been recognized as an effective monitoring device and decision-making aid in dealing with complex production, transportation, or distribution systems, as well as in market analysis. Large government agencies—such as the Energy Research and Development Administration, the Environmental Protection Agency, and the Department of Transportation and their state and local counterparts—resort to model building. Large oil companies and chemical concerns, both in the United States and abroad, use economic models to assess alternative patterns of corporate development. Several hundred economic models are operated in the government, and certainly a much larger number are used by members of the private sector.

Formally, a model is a system of equations. Some of the variables entering into it describe inputs, outputs, and prices of different goods and services, the levels of income and of employment in various industries and regions; others represent, for example, the levels of investment in new productive capacities or the quantities of exports and of imports. The *parameters* entering into the description of individual equations describe the structural characteristics of the various parts of the economy. Large sets of *technical coefficients* describe, for example, the "cooking recipes" of the individual industries—relationships between the quantities of labor, materials, or energy used and the amounts of finished goods produced. Others reflect the composition of the typical shopping basket of different income groups, or the breakdown of various kinds of governmental expenditures. Still others describe the tax rates determining the level of government revenues.

As time goes on, the magnitude of these relationship parameters must be expected to change, reflecting new methods of production, shifts in consumer tastes, or, say, introduction of new environmental regulations.

LARGE OR SMALL MODEL

Models differ in the scope of their coverage and detail. There are models of particular sectors of production, such as United States agriculture or the petrochemical industry; there are models of particular geographic areas as, for example, the state of Texas or the city of Philadelphia; and, of course, there are models of the United States economy as a whole.

Detailed models such as those used by commercial market analysts may have one variable representing coarse gray cotton fabric and another for printed cotton cloth. In a highly aggregative model, on the other hand, all types of cotton goods or even all kinds of textiles may be lumped together and represented by a single annual sales variable. The size of a model (i.e., the total number of equations, variables, and parameters it contains) depends, not unlike the complexity of a road map, on the magnitude of the geographic area it covers and the level of detail with which it is depicted.

A model describing the entire United States economy can be very simple if the picture it presents is drawn sketchily in terms of a small number of aggregative variables such as the total GNP, investment and consumption, total employment, total government revenues and outlays, the total money supply, and the average levels of wages and prices. The total number of equations describing such a system might be as small as ten. On the other hand, a detailed model of a single sector, say petroleum refining, can contain several hundred variables identifying separately each one of the different types of crudes and of the intermediate and finished products. The system of equations describing in minute detail the structure of production would, in this case, contain a separate description of each one of alternative processes that might be used to produce the same good.

Models used for management purposes in the private sector, and more recently in the public sector as well, are mostly of the second type: detailed, but offering narrow coverage. Those used for description of general economic conditions and projection of business trends belong mostly to the first, aggregative kind. They are broad in coverage, but short on details. This is largely because most of the theoretical thinking in this area for many years has been and still is dominated by the aggregative Keynesian approach. According to it, the economy can be controlled effectively through skillful manipulation of a few strategic variables of the aggregative kind—the total government revenue and outlays, the total supply of money, and the rate of interest. A small aggregative model could be expected to contain all the information required for managing as large and as complex an economy as that of the United States.

The experience of past years has shown that this is not the case. Moreover, a small aggregative model cannot possibly incorporate the factual information and provide the analytical understanding required for the handling of innumerable problems with which the government has to cope from day to day, from year to year, from one decade to the next. Questions raised by the energy crisis, potential shortages of some of the basic raw materials, and the problems of the environment cannot be treated or even posed in aggregative terms. Hence, it is not surprising that specialized models, narrow in coverage but rich in detail, are being used now not only in the private corporate sector, but by governmental agencies as well. Such separate, one might call them departmental, models, while helping an individual agency to organize and interpret facts and figures pertaining to the limited area lying within its immediate purview, obviously cannot be used for purposes of interagency coordination. In fact, "adversary fact-finding" is being replaced nowadays with "adversary model building."

The more complex the economy, the greater the mutual interdependence of its parts. The greater such interdependence, the more complete, the more detailed must be the model needed to describe it. The integrating model of the United States economy must be a large set of equations, and it has to be detailed. Far from discouraging the construction of other models, it would facilitate it by providing their developers with large sets of well-organized, calibrated data.

PREDICTIVE MODELS AND OPERATIONAL MODELS

Most of the existing large models of the United States economy are used mainly, although not exclusively, for forecasting purposes: for anticipation of what might be loosely referred to as the general state of business three or six or, say, twelve months ahead. The primary data employed in construction of such predictive models come in the form of time series—most of them of a highly aggregative kind—showing the past behavior and relationships of the economic variables that enter into an equation. The forecasts are obtained through extrapolation of past statistical relationships among these variables estimated on the basis of their observed behavior in the past with emphasis on apparent leads and lags. While some of these relationships could be interpreted unequivocally as describing direct observable connections between cause and effect, in most instances, however, this is not the case.

Models of the operational type depend to a lesser extent on formal extrapolation of statistical relationships observed in the past. Being usually more detailed than predictive models, they can assimilate directly large sets of detailed factual information of a technical and organizational kind. For instance, the estimate of the use of fertilizers or pesticides per acre by different cultures on different soils can be obtained from agronomists; estimates of the capital requirements of the copper mining industry might involve a survey of operating or projected mines; and an estimate of the demands for primary school teachers would require a systematic study of teacher-pupil ratios in selected school districts.

To be sure, such information can be of little use for the purposes we have in mind unless it is combined within the framework of the model with other data of similar specialized kinds: To know how much fertilizer is required per acre of corn or how much investment is necessary to bring out an additional ton of copper in a particular type of mine does not suffice for estimating the total amount of fertilizer used for corn production or the investment requirement of the copper mining industry at some future point in time. The missing total output figures can be determined only within the framework of a large model covering all sectors of the national economy. Moreover, to be capable of absorbing concrete specific information of the kind described above, that model has to be not only comprehensive but detailed. In spite of their size, such models, or at least the results of computation based on them, will be more comprehensible to those familiar with growing corn, mining copper, or teaching school from firsthand experience.

Some corporate users of an aggregative model of the United States economy do, indeed, undertake the task of "disaggregating" that part of it in which they happen to be particularly interested, using additional specialized information which the builders of the model could not handle. Some builders of aggregative models supply to their customers what might be called special disaggregation kits as optional equipment. Needless to say, the results of such makeshift operations are bound to be inferior to those that would have been obtained if all details had been incorporated in the original analytical design.

FACTS AND FIGURES

One of the great advantages of choosing the modeling approach is that it would provide an impetus and, at the same time, the means for modernizing and streamlining our entire statistical system.

The lack of effective coordination in the general area of policy formation and implementation is matched by the absence of a clear, overall design in gathering, organizing, and presenting the facts and figures on which both public and private decision making so critically depend. While the Bureau of the Census might have been originally intended to function as our "Central Statistical Office," by now there is hardly any department or federal agency that has not been put in charge of collecting and publishing statistics pertaining to its particular domain. The Department of Labor is mainly, but not entirely, in charge of employment, wage, and cost-of-living statistics. Information on railroad and trucking freight is collected by the ICC, and information on air shipments is collected by the FAA. The FPC is the principal collector of data for the electrical and power companies, while the Department of the Interior is the primary gatherer of coal and oil output data. While the Standard Industrial and Commodity Classifications are commonly adhered to, each agency feels free to use its own classification and definitions and to determine on its own the frequency and timing of its statistical operations.

As every user of government statistics knows, to secure a modicum of comparability and compatibility between figures emanating from different agencies or even from different offices within the same agency is a trying task, absorbing an inordinate amount of time and money. Much valuable information falls inevitably by the wayside. The time elapsing between collection and the actual release of urgently needed figures is, in many instances, too long. An official input-output table describing the flow of goods and services between all sectors of the American economy in the year 1972, a table based mainly on census figures, will, for example, be ready for release only in 1978. In the absence of a comprehensive statistical plan, data-gathering crash programs are initiated which are both inefficient and costly. Much more complete and reliable information would be on hand at the time of a crisis if the need for it were anticipated and detailed basic data were collected year-in and year-out.

Construction of a large integrating model of the national economy, while serving the immediate needs of analysts and policymakers, would also make an important contribution by transforming our obsolete statistical services into a modern, well-integrated information system. According to preliminary estimates (supported, incidentally, by some of the most outspoken opponents of national economic planning), the sum total of present federal budgets should be increased by some $450 million. The modeling approach can be used as a device for securing a reasonable order of priorities in allocating these additional funds.

Most of the well-deserved criticism of the existing large economic models used by the government, and in private sectors as well, is directed not at their potential capabilities, but at the rather obvious weaknesses of their data base. Even when the analytical design is criticized, it is because it often reflects a desperate attempt to compensate for the lack of reliable factual information by recourse to sophisticated but, nevertheless, very dubious estimating procedures. Instead of permitting the technical advice that the policymaker needs so badly to be distorted by the lack of indispensable data, determined efforts should be made to upgrade our national statistical system so that it would be capable of meeting the legitimate demand for complete and reliable figures.

Most of the difficult problems confronting the country—energy, environment, natural resources—are partly economic, partly technical, and partly social. The conventional distinctions between economics, engineering, geology, and even biology gradually disappear. This is bound to be reflected in the structure of the model and of the data requirements as well. It is also the reason why agencies possessing technical competence in certain areas should continue to collect specialized information pertaining to these areas. They should, however, do so in strict compliance with standards established by the organization charged with the responsibility for construction and maintenance of the master model.

Much emphasis was placed in recent years on summary indexes, such as the general price level, total level of unemployment, and so on. Not to be outdone by the economists, other social scientists are pressing for compilation and publication of summary measures of environmental disruption and even of a number describing the "general quality of life." Such figures might assist an individual researcher to summarize the subjective impression gained from careful examination of long arrays of heterogeneous data. They should, however, not be interpreted as meaningful objective measures of observed facts, and, certainly, such broad indexes cannot be used as viable substitutes for large sets of detailed data which they are often supposed to represent. Reliance on broad index numbers is more often than not a sure sign of missing analytical insight or of a lack of detailed factual information and, in most instances, of both.

FUNCTIONAL ORGANIZATION

The limited success of numerous reorganization schemes for increasing the efficiency of our government seems to be owing, in part, to the fact that too little attention has usually been paid to specification of methods and techniques by which the function assigned to different units shown on fancy organization charts could actually be accomplished. This is particularly true of legislative and administrative functions pertaining to economic questions. Dealing with the formal institutional and legal aspects of a new setup is not enough.

The magnitude and complexity of the task involved in constructing and running a comprehensive computerized model of the largest economy in the world should not be underestimated. It is bound to be a formidable task comparable not so much to that of the research department of the Federal Reserve Board or the National Bureau of Economic

Research, but rather to that of a major scientific-technical facility such as the Linear Accelerator Center established at Stanford.

Economic research is usually carried on like traditional handicrafts. Each analyst works on his own assignment, employing with greater or lesser skill a kit of standard hand tools. A large economic model is, on the contrary, one single complex piece of equipment; its operation and maintenance involve systematic division of labor and, at the same time, disciplined cooperation among members of a large, differentiated crew. One team takes charge of the formal design of the model, another of mathematical programming and computation, and still another organizes and stores the numbers fed into the machine. By far the largest part of the professional staff has, however, to be concerned with substantive economic and technical problems involved in collection and interpretation of these data.

The entire field covered by the model, in other words all parts of the United States economy, has to be mapped out thoroughly and evenly. The most recent input-output tables describe its structure and its operation in terms of some 400 different sectors. For general monitoring purposes, these can be consolidated into 60 to 80 groups with at least one expert in charge of each. Moreover, regional, metropolitan, environmental problems or questions of employment or capital functions that cut across the entire sectoral spectrum will have to be tended by separate teams. Staff members working on special sectoral and cross-sectoral problems can be expected to maintain close working relationships with experts in other parts of the government, in the business sector, and in various public and private research institutions as well.

A special section (corresponding to the Statistical Policy Division in the Office of Management and Budget) will have to be made responsible for the establishment of statistical standards for all data-gathering activities throughout the government, for initiation of new programs and integration of all data flows.

The activities and responsibilities of the proposed research organization will thus comprise:

1. serving the research needs of the Economic Development Board (to be established in the Executive Branch of the federal government).
2. preparing special research reports at the request of congressional committees and various departments and committees in the Executive Branch.
3. monitoring the state of the United States economy and its relationship to the rest of the world; preparing and publishing, on its own initiative, technical reports on problems confronting it.
4. coordinating data-gathering activities throughout the government.

The size of the professional staff needed to carry out such a program can be estimated to be between 200 and 250 persons. The very nature of the operation requires that it be performed on a sufficiently large scale.

NATIONAL ECONOMIC PLANNING

Bruce R. Scott, *Professor, Harvard Graduate School of Business Administration*

National economic planning is attracting increasing interest in the United States, in part because of the disappointing performance of the American economy since 1970 and in part because of the poor results of government efforts to improve this performance. There is a growing awareness that the accepted tools of macroeconomic management are inadequate to solve our problems, particularly those of simultaneous unemployment and inflation. Despite unused capacity and high unemployment, prices and wages continue to rise, especially in some sectors such as housing. As a result, possible government interventions to supplement or manage market forces are attracting increasing attention. National planning, as proposed in the Humphrey-Javits bill, is perhaps the most comprehensive and significant of the proposed innovations designed to bring harmony into the current array of often conflicting state interventions at sectoral and macroeconomic levels.

The current interest in national planning arises at a time when the United States public has little experience or understanding of it, although academicians have discussed it for at least half a century and two industrial democracies, France and Japan, have practiced planning since the end of World War II. During the war, a limited form of planning—i.e., the allocation of strategic materials—was also practiced in the United States. Nevertheless, U.S. interest in the subject declined after the war and the return to a free market. Interest revived again, but only briefly, at the start of the Kennedy administration, again because of concern with recent poor economic performance.

Unfortunately, such debate as there has been about planning suggests that the most important issue to be weighed is that of potential economic gains versus potential political costs. More precisely, the debaters have asked whether better management of the economy is worth the risk of increased centralization of power for the government at Washington. I should like to suggest, however, that there is a more serious and a more subtle problem to consider: one that hinges on the fact that the economics and politics of planning cannot really be separated. Where national economic planning points up important choices to be made, it brings to light problems which are *both* economic and political. A plan to deal with inflation, unemployment, or both, for example, is part economics and part politics. As a result, political control of the planning process can and will be used to shape the economic alternatives considered for desired political purposes. Thus, the critical issues to be evaluated are not so much those of economic gains versus political costs as those of how economics and politics mix in the process of formulating and administering a plan. It is essential to give explicit attention to the proposed institutional arrangements if we are to understand how national planning is likely to work in the United States. Since we do not now have comprehensive economic planning as proposed in the Humphrey-Javits bill, we cannot examine or research direct U.S. experience with the proposed institutional framework. This leaves several choices. One can, for example, analyze the role of planning in other American organizations and then analogize to the situation facing the federal government; it is also possible to analyze the experience of other industrial democracies with national planning. I propose to do some of each, beginning with brief analogies to simpler organizations while reserving most of the analysis for a comparison between the American situation and the experience of France and Japan.

The French deserve credit for pioneering in the field of indicative planning. Since World War II, they have developed a set of institutions and planning methods which are consistent both with democracy and with a market economy open to private enterprise. It should be no surprise, therefore, that when the top economists of the Kennedy administration became interested in national planning, they invited Pierre Masse, the French Commissaire au Plan, to come to Washington to explain how the French system worked. Likewise, it should be no surprise that the sponsors of the Humphrey-Javits bill thought of France as the prime model for the type of indicative planning they had in mind.[1] For these reasons, plus the fact that my own experience with national planning is based mainly on research in France, French experience will serve as the primary basis for evaluating the proposed framework for national planning.[2]

---

1. Symposium on *Our Third Century: Directions,* Senate Committee on Government Operations, 94th Cong., 2d Sess., Feb. 4–6, 1976 (testimony of Senator Jacob K. Javits).

2. In company with a colleague, Professor John McArthur of the Harvard Business School, I was involved in a five-year study of national planning in France from 1963 to 1968. During that period, we interviewed top management in some 50 French companies, high government officials in the Ministries of Finance and of Industry, and the staff of the Planning

French experience to date should give pause to those who advocate national planning in the United States. France has established a clear position of leadership among democratic countries in this field, not only in terms of seniority but also in terms of creation of a sophisticated set of institutional arrangements, the employment of an elite group of planners, and the development of successive models and other methods of planning; at the very same time, however, national planning has declined in influence in France. This decline in influence is of particular significance because France is a highly centralized country compared to the United States, and thus the centralization implicit in planning has never been an important ideological issue. Furthermore, leadership in this field has been a point of some pride among public officials at least since the return of stable government under de Gaulle. From a peak of perceived influence in the early 1960s, the Fifth, Sixth, and Seventh Plans have drawn progressively less attention from business and government alike. The situation is now one where there is open debate, even among top French planners, of the utility of the French approach in light of the strategic choices facing the government. Thus, while all agree that the need for more effective economic policy making is increasing, the French approach to national economic planning seems to be unable to rise to this challenge.

I believe that there are two basic reasons for the declining influence of French planning. The first is an excessively centralized set of institutional arrangements which have allowed the government to use the national planning process largely as a public relations device. The second is a shift of the French economy from being essentially closed prior to entry into the Common Market to being essentially open since then. Experience suggests that it is much more difficult to plan in an open economy than in one which has tight controls on foreign trade and capital movements.

In light of this French experience and its obvious relevance to the present situation in the United States, I propose to give particular attention to these two key areas, namely institutional framework for planning and the challenge of planning in an open economy. My basic question concerning national planning in the U.S. is not so much one of potential economic gains versus potential political costs as whether an appropriate institutional framework can be developed for effective national planning in an open economy. My concern is the risk that

---

Commission in order to analyze how national planning worked and what influence it had on large companies in a selected sample of industries. The results of that study were published in 1969 in a book titled *Industrial Planning in France*, Harvard Graduate School of Business Administration, Division of Research, Boston. This research has been supplemented by a consulting project for the French Planning Commission, "Strengths and Weaknesses of French Industry," as well as by continuing personal contact with top business managers and planning officials. For example, I have had an opportunity to discuss how planning worked with each of the six French Planning Commissioners, beginning with Jean Monnet and including Jean Ripert.

national planning will soon become a public relations activity here as in France and that, as a result, it will not yield much in economic gains.

The analysis which follows begins with an examination of some analogies between national planning and planning in simpler organizations. Next, it considers the institutional framework proposed in the Humphrey-Javits bill, and particularly the relationship between the planning board, the White House, and the Congress. This is a first opportunity to consider the possible blends of economics and politics which are likely to emerge in the planning process. Then, I propose to consider the content and concepts of national planning so as to focus attention on those areas where innovations seem most feasible, given the present state of the art. Following this overview of concepts and content, I propose to look in more detail at the three areas where the prospects seem highest for innovation, namely coherence planning of demand and supply, structural planning, and incomes planning. These three sections will draw heavily on French, and to a lesser degree Japanese, experience with national planning. Next, we will consider the informational questions involved, including availability, confidentiality, and possible conflicts with other considerations such as antitrust. A final section will consider some possible improvements in the prospects for national planning, including possible amendments to the Humphrey-Javits bill.

ANALOGIES AS A FRAMEWORK FOR ANALYSIS

If the 1970s have brought increasing recognition of the need to make government intervention more effective, perhaps by national economic planning, what are the problems involved in moving ahead? Given our lack of experience with planning, we are tempted to say simply that it is better to plan than not to plan. We support this statement by drawing analogies between governing a state and such relatively simple activities as driving a car, building a bridge or an office building, or managing a household. In each such case, a plan of "where we are going and how to get there" is obviously useful.

These analogies are of little value, however, because they simplify the situation so much as to distort it more than clarify it. Obviously, it is advantageous to know where we are going when we drive a car, especially if one person controls the steering wheel, another the gas, and a third the brakes. But, if three people are in the car, where to go is a political as well as a technical decision. The choice of the options or routes to be followed in reaching our destination may also be partly political. And while a technician might delight in evaluating all the options, a politician might very well decide to exclude some of them because he does not want to know how they compare with his own favorite alternative. Former President Ford's exclusion of a much higher gasoline tax as an option for dealing with the energy crisis might be an example of an instance where those who did not understand the political constraints were eliminated from the planning process altogether.

A more sophisticated case for planning is sometimes made by drawing an analogy between governing a state and managing a business. Big companies plan. Superior forecasting and planning are increasingly seen as key ingredients in effective business performance. How can government, with far greater responsibilities than business, do less planning than a large corporation?

The analogy between government and business planning is an attractive one, especially in a country where large corporations have long made major contributions to our economic progress and growth. In addition, corporate planning has not violated the traditional American values associated with a decentralized, pluralistic society. In short, corporate planning is consistent with our goals of both a strong economic performance and of personal freedom.

It is tempting to allow the similarities between corporate and state planning to obscure such important differences as the need in the latter for centralized power, the probable need for a quasi-public process, and the priority likely to be given to short-term politics versus long-term public interests in the choice of national goals. The analogy with planning in the large corporation still allows national planning to be treated largely as a technical problem, a problem for experts, models, and computers. Planning is viewed as a neutral process managed by impartial experts who cast up options or scenarios from which politicians select the one that they believe is best for the country. Based on this point of view, another easy step is to focus on the types of information needed, on methods to manipulate this information, and on means to safeguard it from abuse. In a way, this approach fits in nicely with the framework of Professor Leontief's paper, which examines the informational aspects of national planning.

To accept such an antiseptic view, however, is in my opinion to miss some major issues that need to be explored. The major issues are not those of the availability of information or its manipulation via models and computers; the major issues are the relationship of the planning process to the political and administrative structures of the state, the secrecy or openness of the process, the planning goals to be pursued, and the scope of planning in terms of how much of the economy it attempts to cover or "plan for."

National planning is an attempt to develop a more rational process of policy formulation and implementation so as to improve the performance of the economy. It is an attempt to increase the amount of economic and mathematical logic in the policy-formulation process. By implication, it is also an attempt to increase the emphasis on medium- and long-term considerations as opposed to short-term ones, and likewise to increase the emphasis given to broad common interests as opposed to narrow special interests. Planning is a structural device aimed primarily at making changes in the way the government operates, and each of the intended changes has political as well as economic or technical implications.

The shortcomings of evaluating national planning via an analogy with corporate planning stem directly from differences in the legal framework affecting government and business, from the differing processes through which political and corporate power are achieved and exercised, and from differences in the sets of goals that guide the public and the private planning tasks. Sovereignty in the American corporation derives from the stockholders or owners, and not from the community of people served by the corporation or from its employees. Corporate sovereignty does not rest with all the interest groups affected by the company, but rather with the owners of the property.

Moreover, the political process within the corporation reflects the legal framework. Management is "elected" by the shareholders, not by the customers or by the employees. In practice, a corporation is managed as a self-perpetuating oligarchy where management selects the board of directors and the board "elects" the management. The exercise of power in a strong from-the-top-down manner reflects management's power over and lack of accountability to the employees in the organization. The contrast between this situation and the political process of appealing for votes in a democratic system where sovereignty rests with the people is obvious and fundamental.

Another fundamental difference between national and corporate planning lies in the nature of the goals to which planning is addressed. Some discrepancies may exist between the goals of corporate management and stockholders, but the economic objective of the company is to maximize a reasonably consistent set of shared objectives such as growth, earnings, and financial security. The distribution of resources within the corporation via salary levels and so forth is done by management on the basis of its own logic, usually without any accountability to employees, and usually in a confidential if not a secret manner. (Exceptions are a few top managers in publicly held corporations and workers whose pay is set by collective bargaining.)

Government, on the other hand, deals with a multitude of competing or conflicting interests, many of which are equally legitimate. National goals may well benefit one group at the expense of another. "Stable food prices," for example, may benefit the consumer at the expense of the farmer. And while economic growth may broadly benefit the entire population, government is the legitimate focus for efforts to change the distribution of the fruits of that economic growth. In the corporation, income distribution may be a technical question to be solved in secret according to performance-oriented criteria, but for government, it is a political question to be dealt with in a quasi-public political forum on the basis of what can be accepted as just or fair.

To highlight this contrast, just imagine what the five-year plan of a major corporation would read like if it were prepared for mass distribution to employees, customers, and competitors instead of to a small, closely defined group of executives with a "need to know." The first kind of plan would doubtless be a public-relations document of little real interest to corporate top management. The very idea of making a plan public is enough to guarantee that its content will differ dramatically from that of a confidential plan. And yet, our process of government is based on open access to information by the press and the public. Under these circumstances, one might well ask, what would a national plan be, a "real" one or a public-relations document?

To argue that planning is better than no planning is a little like being in favor of God, the flag, and motherhood. Various fragments of national planning already exist at various levels in our government. The question before us is whether comprehensive, indicative national planning along the lines of the Humphrey-Javits bill would yield a significant improvement in the management of our economy. Would it help both government and business do their planning and thereby their managing in a more effective way? Perhaps the simple most important test is the degree to which the proposed planning process would result in a real plan as contrasted to a sophisticated public-relations document. To establish and finance a new agency and an elaborate planning process only to end with a public-relations plan would surely be a disappointment.

To evaluate how planning might work in the United States and what impact it might have requires a look at the proposed institutional framework. This framework will have a very strong influence on how the planning process works, and, in a very real sense, it is the planning process that is important. The resulting plan makes an interesting reference document, but the real impact—if any—of national planning is to be found in the process of formulating the major options, working out the necessary compromises, and harmonizing the efforts of various agencies. It is essential, therefore, to consider the proposed institutional structure for planning and try to understand how this would impact upon the existing structure of government. This inquiry will provide some assistance in trying to assess how useful a planning process the proposed structure is likely to yield.

INSTITUTIONAL FRAMEWORK FOR PLANNING

The Humphrey-Javits bill proposes an institutional framework for planning which is similar in several respects to that found in other large organizations, for example, large business corporations. The planning board will be part of the executive office of the President; hence, in broad outline it will be analogous to the long-range planning department of any number of large firms. Its mandate to coordinate the long-range planning activities of the major departments and agencies of the executive branch is likewise analogous to the planning function in a large corporation. The bill, however, envisions some checks and balances which make the structure much more complex and much more subtle than the planning structure of any corporation with which I am familiar. The proposed structure is also similar to that used by the

French government, except that it gives Congress the right to delete or disapprove specific segments of the plan and forbids the executive branch to implement any such segments. Thus, the plan restricts the executive branch, at least in the sense that it cannot implement portions which are not approved.

The Humphrey-Javits bill provides that the planning board shall not only develop a balanced growth plan but also review the major programs and activities of other government departments and agencies to determine their consistency with the plan. The board is not given any specific powers to achieve compliance from government departments, but it is given the power to demand an explanation of variances. This is not a function commonly given to corporate planning departments, nor is it one given to the French Commissariat du Plan. It suggests increased power, of a subtle sort, for the U.S. planning board.

Moreover, the bill also provides that the plan is to be submitted to an economic council comprised of department and certain agency heads for its approval, prior to submission to the President for his approval. As a result, department and agency heads will have an opportunity to shape and reshape the plan in its formative stages. If the council functions successfully, it will act like a Cabinet in dealing with the pulling and hauling of special interests as expressed by the different Cabinet officers. The outcome should be just what is desired, namely a negotiated overview, established at the Cabinet level, which will bring the sometimes parochial interests of the departments into line through a process of negotiation and compromise.

If the planning process were to work as envisioned in the bill, the situation would be analogous to that of a corporation which required its long-range plan to be submitted to a council of division managers and staff department heads prior to submission to the chief executive. The process would be one characterized by checks and balances, with the outcome supposedly representing an overall point of view, even though the department and agency heads represented their respective constituencies. Subsequently, the planning board would monitor the departments and agencies to see if they were following the agreements reached in the process of formulating the plan.

Such, at any rate, is the theory. There are more subtle elements in this structure. The plan is to be submitted to Congress, where it is to be approved or disapproved by joint resolution. The plan is not a law, however; nor is it a budget. It is a statement of intent by the executive branch, which is reviewed by the legislative branch. It does not commit either branch to specific programs or specific spending levels, since such commitments require congressional authorization and a subsequent appropriation of funds to support them. The congressional authorization and appropriation process may be guided by the plan, but it is not controlled by the plan in any way. The present bill is aimed at encouraging the executive branch to get its house in order, almost as though "order" were a "management problem" independent of the influence of Congress and congressional subcommittees on the departments and agencies involved. Given the powers of Congress to shape the activities of the agencies through its control of the purse and given the power of special interests to influence the Congress, it is not at all clear how much the plan would influence the programs and activities of the departments and agencies, despite the formal powers of review rested in the planning board. In short, it is not at all clear how the planning process or the plan would influence Congress.

Perhaps there is a still more basic subtlety in the proposed structure. It seems to assume somehow that the President and his staff want to develop an explicit overview or "balanced economic growth plan" to guide themselves and the various agencies and departments. Is this really desirable? If so, why? And if so, why has it not been done already, perhaps by expanding the activities of the Council of Economic Advisers to serve as a planning board, and by having the advisers report to the same modified Cabinet which the bill refers to as the economic planning council? Do we really need new legislation to provide a new structure and a new information-gathering process, or is there a deeper question of whether or not an elected President really wants a formal long-range plan spelled out in a public document?

> As I see it . . . no procedural changes of any consequence are necessary to improve the government's work developing long-range objectives and policies, certainly no new organizational structures. What is required is that both the executive and legislative branches more strongly perceive the value in doing so, and then just do it. There is nothing at the moment that precludes them from doing so.[3]

I wish it were clear that a comprehensive public plan would help the President. To me it is not at all clear that it would, despite the obvious attractions of the idea. In fact, I find it uncomfortably easy to believe that a plan would *not* be useful—that is, a plan that had to be threshed out through a process involving so many people and so many representatives of special interests would not be useful. Under the arrangements proposed in the Humphrey-Javits bill, the President might well find it desirable to use this quasi-public process to develop not a bona fide plan but a public-relations document.

Consider the context, the environment into which the document would emerge. The power of the purse rests with Congress. Congress is not directly controlled by the plan. Congress remains the battleground of special interests. It is in this battleground of special interests that the President must attempt to win passage of budgets as well as new legislation. It is not clear to me that a national plan, with its focus on balanced growth and an overall national interest, will help the President and his staff in bargaining with special interest groups for their

---

3. Symposium on *Our Third Century: Directions,* (testimony of Roy Ash).

support. Rather, the opposite would seem more likely. Indeed, the plan, if it were real, would require spelling out some key proposals far in advance of required congressional or administrative action. This would give any disadvantaged special interests additional time to mount a counterattack as well as a clearer target to shoot at.

This concern might have little relevance for certain of the plan's major objectives: for instance, it might not hinder stating such goals as full employment, price stability, balanced economic growth, and stable international relations. Although Republicans and Democrats differ sharply on the meaning and importance of full employment, and likewise, on the desirability of price stability when it involves a trade-off with employment, we have no strong interest groups promoting unemployment, inflation, unbalanced growth, or unstable international relations. On the other hand, each of the remaining areas where the plan must set objectives invites the battling of special interests. For example, the plan is required to establish objectives for such controversial matters as the equitable distribution of income, balanced urban and regional development, and the efficient utilization of public and private resources; it must also provide for meeting essential needs in transportation, energy, agriculture, raw material supplies, housing, education, essential public services, and research and development. The problems with an "equitable" distribution of income are obvious, yet these are among the most important problems to be faced, because the ultimate success or failure of planning will depend on arriving at some form of incomes policy. This can be an implicit policy if we muddle along, but it must be explicit if it is to be included in a plan. Similarly, what constitutes an adequate supply of food, raw materials, or energy? Are we to consider the consumers' point of view or the suppliers'? And what about the views of the foreign competitor?

Where such conflicts of interest exist, and where they are legitimate in a market economy, national planning may well deal with them in terms of slogans and platitudes, avoiding or even suppressing the basic issues. Our present energy policy is suggestive of how this might happen. The present policy has, with considerable merit, been labeled a "Drain America First" policy. America has done less than any other major industrial country to conserve energy. Our relatively low gasoline price is eloquent testimony to this fact. Gasoline in America costs about one-third what it costs in Europe or Japan. And yet, we continue our policy of low gasoline taxes and low retail prices in order to maintain jobs in the auto industry, the tire industry, the oil industry, and the highway construction industry. We do not point out the opportunity or the need for dramatic conservation measures, even though we use about one-third of each barrel of oil for gasoline while other industrialized countries use about 10 to 15 percent of each barrel for this purpose.

A United States conservation program similar to those in force in other industrial countries would entail genuine economic dislocations. It would also invite another look at our foreign policy in the Middle

East. Our aversion to being dependent on Arab sources for oil might then be examined in terms of its economic cost in this country as well as the loss of economic security it entails for a country such as Saudi Arabia. With both the United States and Saudi Arabia having much to gain from a stable, long-term supplier-customer relationship, the question of "Why not?" would come up. Again, however, economics would confront politics—in this case, the strong domestic political support for United States sponsorship of Israel. The essentials of our energy problem, I suggest, are not ones requiring sophisticated analysis or computerized models to understand. We continue a "Drain America First" policy because it is good short-run economics and good short-run politics. And, instead of facing the obvious increase in our dependence on foreign sources of oil, we launch a public-relations campaign called "Project Independence."

National planning could all too easily become a vehicle for doing just this same kind of thing in many areas, combining them all into a consolidated public-relations document. Moreover, the proposed planning structure, which gives the President control of the planning process yet leaves Congress immune from making any real commitment in support of the plan, and which requires wide-ranging consultation with business, labor, and state and local government, is a structure which invites public-relations planning. One distinguished expert in this field has taken a more optimistic view, saying:

> The material set-up of the organization responsible for the preparation of alternative scenarios, and the elaboration of the national economic plan and its subsequent revisions, had to be dictated by the requirements of its technical, non-political task. One can visualize it as autonomous public body loosely affiliated with the executive branch of the federal government.[4]

Perhaps this is the technical imperative, but the proposed legislation reads otherwise.

To argue the merits of national planning as though the plan were being formulated in an antiseptic, nonpolitical institution or structure is utterly to miss one of the fundamental issues to be dealt with, namely, the relationship between the general and special interests in the institutions through which a plan is first formulated and later implemented. If the special interest groups retain their bases of political power, not only will the planning reflect those interests, it is quite likely that the planners will be prohibited from even studying scenarios which conflict with important special interests.

This view might seem cynical to some. To those who have had extensive exposure to public life and large organizations, I trust it will not sound unduly so. To anyone who recalls our recent experience with

---

4. Wassily Leontief, "National Economic Planning: Methods and Problems," *Challenge Magazine*, vol. 19, no. 3, July–Aug. 1976, p. 9.

what Schlesinger has called the "imperial presidency," I believe it will sound all too familiar. In addition, from observing the national planning process in France, one can hardly escape the conclusion that politics has dominated economics[5] and that the political leadership has exerted strong control to exclude the study, and sometimes even the open discussion, of alternatives which it did not want studied.[6]

The planning structure proposed by the Humphrey-Javits bill is a complex and subtle one. While housed in the executive branch, it would be much influenced by Congress. Indeed, one of its most vulnerable aspects is that it does not seem to provide much relief from the dominance of special interests that characterizes so much of our legislative process. There is the strong possibility, therefore, that national planning would yield little of real substance, owing to Presidential and congressional preoccupations with special interests.

With this basic caveat about the efficacy of the whole process, let us turn to the more technical and economic aspects of national planning. Let us take a "bottoms-up" point of view, so to speak, and see what the planners might do if they were allowed full reign to work on the real problems.

THE CONTENT AND CONCEPTS OF NATIONAL PLANNING

If we turn to the content of national planning, the activities to be planned range over a number of levels, from the macroeconomic at one end to an individual industry at the other. Some levels are more

---

5. For example, as we pointed out in our 1969 study, in the case of the Fifth French Plan:

> A credibility gap developed about certain of the assumptions, policies, and programs outlined in the published text of the Fifth Plan. (Apart from the practicability of some of the cutbacks proposed for the initial growth targets and low anticipated rate of inflation, questions have been raised as to whether the plan achieved a prediction of almost full employment by envisaging suspiciously low gains in productivity.) On a more restricted scale, questions have been raised as to whether the plan made the prospects for the coal-producing and steel-producing regions look better than they were by understating the rate at which coal would decline as a source of energy and overstating the rate at which steel could be exported at profitable prices. Still another question was whether the plan over-stated the investment to be made in chemicals by the French producers, this time with a view to discouraging invasion of the industry by foreign capital. Doubt has also been cast on the plan's estimate for growth in the building materials field, not so much on the grounds of a systematic bias for political reasons as on the grounds that the sources from which the estimates were taken comprised some companies which were ignorant and some which were seeking to fool their competitors.

See Scott and McArthur, op. cit., pp. 459, 460.

6. For example, President de Gaulle prohibited study of options based on inflation rates over 1.5 percent for the Fifth Plan, despite the French record for the highest rate of inflation among major European countries for the preceding decade. As a result, none of the projections were realistic with respect to inflation, and the planners had to compensate as best they could for this politically imposed constraint.

important to discuss than others. Macroeconomic planning, which is concerned with overall growth, cyclical ups and downs, inflation and unemployment, would not be very much affected by the creation of a new United States agency for national planning. The Council of Economic Advisers does macroeconomic forecasting now, and there is little reason to expect that the concepts and processes already used would necessarily change. On the other hand, any commitment to a particular combination of goals for growth rate, unemployment, and inflation would represent an important political choice to be made by the highest political levels, not by the planners. This supremacy of the politicians also characterizes the French and Japanese experiences, even though both countries have adopted formal national economic planning. The goals for growth, employment and inflation are political choices made by governments, albeit on the basis of forecasts by the economic advisers.[7]

When it comes to planning the division of the fruits of economic expansion, the Humphrey-Javits bill would require an explicit incomes policy rather than the implicit and partial one that we have today. If a real incomes policy were to be adopted (not just guidelines for price increases or for an average annual wage increase, but a policy designed to change and "improve" the present pattern of income distribution), it would represent a major change. This is an area where we can make only a tentative estimate of what national planning might mean or what data it might require. Not only is the complexity of the problem too great, but also relevant foreign experience upon which we might draw is lacking. We will return to this question after we explore other aspects of national planning.

As we move away from the macroeconomic level of our economy, another basic distinction must be made. About one-third of all United States economic activity depends directly on the federal government, especially on government spending programs. Neither the level of government spending nor the allocation of expenditures to particular programs would be much affected by the new planning process as outlined in the Humphrey-Javits bill. The Office of Management and Budget already does this type of planning, and it would continue to have chief responsibility for this activity under the proposed national planning process. In addition, the Chief Executive can already implement spending plans, at least to the extent of proposing outlays to Congress and expending whatever amounts are actually appropriated.

Major innovations are implied, however, by the adoption of plan-

---

7. As pointed out in a recent Brookings study, it has even been argued that the planned Japanese growth targets—always far exceeded in practice—were deliberately set low, the government's alleged purpose being "to generate low targets for the expansion of investment in social overhead" (T. Watanhbe, cited by Gardner Ackley and Horomitsu Ishi in "Fiscal, Monetary, and Related Policies," in Hugh Patrick and Henry Rosovsky (eds.), *Asia's New Giant: How the Japanese Economy Works,* The Brookings Institution, Washington, D.C., 1976, p. 235, n. 75).

ning in the nongovernment or so-called productive sectors, such as commerce, manufacturing, agriculture, transport, and communications. National planning would create a new level, or perhaps levels, of planning for these activities. It would disaggregate these productive segments into their component parts, such as industries and services, and it would develop plans by industry. It would not, however, plan for specific firms, except implicitly in cases where a single firm had a monopoly or near-monopoly in an industry (as in telecommunications or regional utilities). Planning for the productive sectors implies many innovations in both the formulation of the plan and in its implementation. Here, we find government attempting to plan for the private sector, and, quite literally, trying to supplement the marketplace as an influence on the development of various industries and regions. Implementation would have to particularly subtle in this area, because government planners would not have financial responsibility for the impact of their plans, yet business managers who would supposedly be influenced by the plans would also have to consider their fiduciary responsibility to their stockholders.[8] If implementation were purely voluntary, planning would be just a technical exercise in forecasting and would have little impact on anyone. If, on the other hand, businessmen were in some sense induced or required to follow the plan, then planning at the industry level would indeed be a significant innovation. In practice, implementation would require *some* sort of incentives to induce *some* degree of compliance. Here, we find the area in which the business managers' fear of excessive political interference and control runs squarely into the economists' enthusiasm for improving on the marketplace. It is essential, therefore, to understand the degree of detail included in the proposed plan, and likewise, the power of the incentives or regulations which might be used to implement the plan.

Broadly speaking, three types of issues are involved in planning at the industry level: one centering on demand and supply by industry; a second on industry structure; and the third on income distribution. Following an exploration of these issues, we will look specifically at the information requirements for national planning.

COHERENCE PLANNING, OR THE PLANNING OF SUPPLY TO MEET DEMAND

Coherence planning is aimed at reducing the incidence of gluts and shortages; the idea is more nearly to balance supply and demand through (1) forecasting demand several years ahead; (2) estimating the productive capacity required to meet that demand; and finally, (3) subtracting existing capacity from the forecast requirements to arrive at an estimate of the new investments required by the particular industry.

---

8. While in most cases the guiding force in the firm is its "corporate strategy," the threat of shareholder lawsuits requires respect for a decision maker's fiduciary responsibility.

Reducing shortages minimizes the disruption of other industries which depend on a given industry for particular items of supply. Reducing excess capacity minimizes waste, whether this takes the form of idle plant capacity or unemployment. As a result, coherence or supply planning improves the functioning of the whole economy as well as the efficiency of the particular industry in question.

Demand forecasting is part of the regular economic planning which most large private firms do already. Several differences exist, however, between company and national planning. National planning presumably would draw upon more sources of information and, hence, do a better job. For example, through the division of economic information, the planning board would be authorized to secure information from all government departments and agencies. As a result, the planning board might have access to some sources not ordinarily available to a corporation. In addition, planners might sponsor the development of new sources of information, the more timely collection and compilation of existing data, and the development or further enrichment of methods used for processing data. For example, the planning board might well wish to use an input-output matrix to link the various sectors, and it might be able to afford a more detailed matrix than any now available to industry, or perhaps one using more timely information, or both.

In undertaking coherence planning, the planning board would be supplementing not only the planning of private firms but also that of various industry associations and of the recently formed private firms, such as Data Resources, Inc., that engage in economic forecasting. Data Resources, Inc., works with industry, utilizing confidential information in what the firm describes as the largest computer-modeling installation in the world. Its customers subscribe to a service which includes industry seminars as well as regular economic forecasts. Thus, in the area of coherence planning, the planning board would be establishing a new organization and data-collection process which would compete with a private economic forecasting industry already using input-output analysis to cover our major industries and to link them to one another.

The national planning board might or might not do a better job than the private firms. It seems likely that the private forecasting firms would have more intimate, more up-to-date information from subscribing customers, because it would be in the interest of the customer-firms to supply such information in order to improve the data base and, thus, the derived forecasts. The planning board would probably have better data from government, but it would almost surely have a more cumbersome, bureaucratic relationship with private companies.

The quality and timeliness of the forecasts is only a start, however. The next question is, how does the forecast become a plan? What happens, for instance, if the forecast is for excess capacity in an industry over the next three or four years? The private forecasters can only point this contingency out to their clients and leave it to their clients to scale down their investment plans or risk the inevitable losses associated with idle capacity. The private forecasters have no way to influence industry except through industry's own more informed, more enlightened response. What about the planning board?

The planning board could establish a capacity goal for a particular industry: so many tons of steelmaking capacity, for example. Moreover, under section 208a(3), the board could also:

> —recommend legislative or administrative actions necessary to achieve the objectives of the Plan, including recommendations with respect to money supply growth, the Federal Budget credit needs, interest rates, taxes and subsidies, anti-trust and merger policy, changes in industrial structure and regulation, international trade, and other policies and programs of economic significance.

Although at the outset, the planning board would have no powers of implementation, it could seek such powers through legislation, or it could ask other government agencies and departments to use their powers to influence business to implement the plan. The steel industry is one that comes to mind in this connection. The planning board could ask other agencies to offer incentives to induce the steel industry to reduce its planned investments and avoid prospective over-capacity. Conversely, the Board could arrange incentives to spur additions of plant capacity if the industry appeared to be underbuilding. But, if the planning board and the industry leaders could not somehow agree, either on the appropriate forecast or on the appropriate market response by company, then we would have the planners trying to foist their view upon those individuals who have the ultimate financial responsibility, namely, management.

If industry and the planning board have similar forecasts and similar conclusions on how to develop capacity, national planning helps to confirm industry planning but has little other impact. If industry and government disagree, however, national planning has an opportunity to exert influence. This might (1) lead various firms in the industry to rethink and revise their forecasts and plans spontaneously, or (2) lead the government to influence particular firms to increase or reduce their investment plans. There is no way for an "industry" to respond to projected overcapacity; firms must respond. And, if they do not do so spontaneously, government must try to exert influence on specific firms. To allow "the industry" to settle the matter would violate the antitrust laws in a given situation and if practiced with any regularity, encourage the formation of cartels. When tried in the United States under the National Industrial Recovery Act in the 1930s, there was considerable concern about the ability of industry to adequately stifle the natural competitive instincts. In addition, there was a landmark Supreme Court decision which declared that this self-regulation by industry represented an excessive and unconstitutional delegation of governmental powers to industry.[9] While the administrative framework proposed by the Humphrey-Javits bill might well overcome both of the problems encountered in the 1930s, the practical problems of implementing a plan among privately owned firms remain.

These problems are so significant that in France the government has all but abandoned coherence planning. It is worth reviewing this experience in some detail, since the lessons for the United States are so clear.

Coherence planning has been truly effective under only two conditions: general shortages and a closed economy. Without *both* of these conditions, planning has exerted only occasional influence. Even then it has not been at all clear that the influence was beneficial.[10] More often and more recently, coherence planning has suffered a dramatic decline in influence. In France it has been abandoned for most sectors in the 1970s.

France had a semiclosed economy from 1944 through 1958, when a successful devaluation plus participation in the Common Market led to the abandonment of import quotas and to the scaling down of tariffs in line with the Rome Treaty. From 1944 into the early 1950s, France also had an economy characterized by shortages, not only because French productive capacity had been destroyed by the war but also because France lacked the foreign exchange needed to buy sufficient quantities abroad to relieve domestic shortages. In these circumstances, France had to produce or do without. The problem was quite literally one of production. On the other hand, few firms had developed much planning expertise, and the French government did not yet have a working set of national income accounts to help organize the necessary information.

In these circumstances, the planners worked with industry to help forecast demand for a selected group of basic industries—initially only six—and to allocate scarce resources to augment capacity in those key industries. To implement the plans was a matter of encouraging industry to *increase* its investment plans, in aggregate as well as in particular subcategories. The planners were able to help implement their plans because the United States government had insisted that the French develop a plan for using Marshall aid, and had also insisted that the aid be used to implement the plan. Thus, the planners could not only encourage industry, they could offer supplementary financing on preferential terms. Aggressive firms stood to benefit financially by implementing the plans.

Since the six sectors were interlocked by inputs and outputs, the respective industry plans had to be coherent. For example, steel was needed for railroad cars and locomotives, and rolling stock was needed

9. *A.L.A. Schecter* v. *Poultry Corp.*, 295 U.S. 495 (1935).

10. Scott and McArthur, op. cit., chap. XII.

to move coal and iron supplies to make the steel. Similarly, more electricity was needed to run the steel plants, and steel was needed to expand the electric generating capacity. It was important to produce not only more steel but the right mix of steel products. It was important to avoid an excess of boxcar steel and a shortage of steel for generators. Similarly, it was important to make steel for the six basic industries in preference to allocating it to automobiles or electric mixers. Under these circumstances, national planning was both influential and successful in improving the coherence of French investments to avoid excess capacity in some areas while acute shortages existed in other, closely related areas.

With the achievement of adequate supplies, equilibrium in the balance-of-payments position, and the opening of the frontiers to Common Market competition, the French industrial planning problem underwent a fundamental change.[11] The utility of planning physical coherence of inputs and outputs declined very sharply—virtually to the vanishing point. So long as the overall payments position was in balance, French industry could buy whatever it chose not to make. For example, if more steel was required to produce more tractors or boxcars, it was no longer essential to build French steel capacity to fill this need. French companies could avail themselves of steelmaking capacity in Belgium, Luxembourg, Germany, or Japan. These imports could be paid for through exports of French products. In place of bottlenecks, French industry had an increasingly wide choice of suppliers, both in France and outside. Most, although not all, French productive units could reasonably expect to buy from a market somewhere and sell to a market somewhere (at home or abroad) and could, therefore, aspire to survive without being part of an integrated sequence of operations.

With this change to market relationships, the basic problem for French companies, industries, and the state was to decide which products to produce and which to buy: which areas of activity to develop and which to close down in favor of purchasing from lower-cost sources. Far from aiming for near self-sufficiency via coherence among sectors, the new problem was to aim for selective employment of resources in the industries and products where investment had the highest potential return. Selectivity rather than coherence had become the basic problem at the industry sector and company levels. Since the state was active in shaping industrial strategies, this fundamental change posed a problem for the state as its agencies went about their task of influencing the formulation of industrial strategy.

The change can be depicted in two diagrams. The immediate postwar situation can be represented as a closed system with internal rationing as well as foreign-exchange rationing, as suggested in Figure 3-1.

Given a quasi-closed economy of scarcity, the volume of goods

11. Ibid., p. 494 ff.

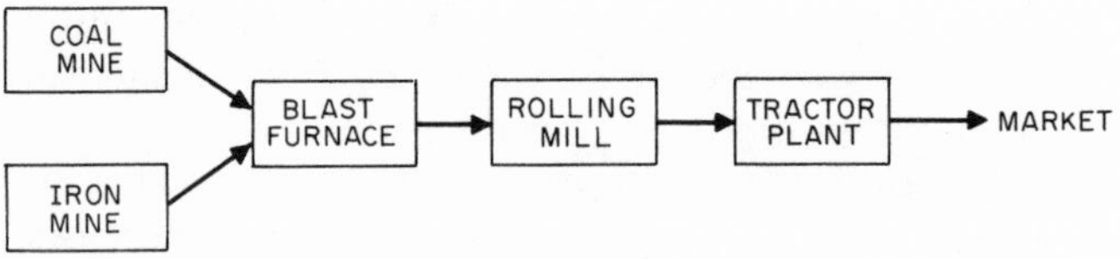

FIGURE 3-1 Closed Economy

reaching market was limited by bottlenecks along the way. Coherence planning was a means to distribute scarce investment capital and other scarce resources so as to develop the various activities in balance with one another, rather than having, for example, a surplus of blast-furnace capacity and a shortage of coal, ore, or rolling-mill capacity.

With the opening of the frontiers and the maintenance of a balance-of-payments equilibrium, the concept of physical coherence between sectoral inputs and outputs had lost much of its relevance. The new situation can be symbolized in Figure 3-2.

The essential difference between the closed and the open economy was that industry operations did not necessarily have to be integrated in order to protect the country from bottlenecks. It now became possible to judge most activities on the basis of their own economic performance rather than on the basis of their contribution to an integrated sequence of inputs and outputs.

To evaluate economic performance usually means sooner or later to evaluate return on investment. With the aid of return-on-investment analysis, one can decide to enlarge the most profitable activities and to diminish or eliminate the least attractive. For example, although the retirement of steelmaking capacity might create a break in the input-output chain, this gap could be closed by purchasing from more efficient plants abroad, such as those in Germany, Belgium, and Holland, not to mention others in Japan.

Not only did the planning problem change; there was also a crucial change in the types of information needed for planning. Three new types became essential: the expected level of imports and exports, the expected price levels, and the domestic cost structure. Forecasting physical demand with the aid of input-output analysis was only a beginning. Next, one had to estimate the share apt to be taken by imports, then the price at which imports might be sold (including the possibility that imports would drive down domestic prices), and finally, domestic costs and profit margins. In a market economy, expected prices and profits become the key determinants of investment decisions, and neither can be realistically assessed without evaluating prospective import quantities and prices.

As a result, the evaluation of foreign industries and foreign competition became a critical type of information for national planning. The continuation of coherence planning as though France were still a closed economy was a key reason why such planning lost relevance. When the

French planners failed to shift their planning concepts and information base to stay abreast of the new open economy and the Common Market in particular, their errors in forecasting imports became so large as to render their planning of little interest to anyone.

It is ironic that the influence of coherence planning declined just as the French planners enjoyed dramatic improvements in the information at their disposal and the techniques with which to manipulate it. Thus, national income accounting improved rapidly in the 1950s, and better and better input-output tables were developed during the 1960s. By the time they were formulating the Sixth Plan in 1969–1970, there was even a comprehensive physical and financial model of the economy. Nonetheless, coherence planning was dramatically downgraded in the Sixth Plan, and by the Seventh, it was abandoned for most sectors. In France, thirty years' experience suggests unmistakably that the open economy was more significant than the improvement in information or modeling techniques for supply-demand planning.

In assessing the implications of French experience for the United States, one is immediately tempted to note that imports account for only a small share of United States GNP, perhaps 7 percent, and that they therefore might be regarded as relatively unimportant. The United States is a relatively self-contained, if not exactly a closed, economy. France is much more dependent on foreign trade; hence its planning problems are different.

In practice, however, the planning problems for both countries are similar in one crucial respect: imports have an important influence on prices in the United States, just as they do in France and elsewhere. If the international prices of oil, steel, nonferrous metals, or foodstuffs rise, U.S. prices are affected by foreign trade, actual or potential. The U.S. economy is an open economy, tied by trade to the world economy. Coherence planning must be based on this worldwide perspective in most industries, or it will rapidly become irrelevant to both government and industry.

Some exceptions exist, of course, in that some important industries are truly domestic, and hence, the entire "supply" can be encompassed directly within the framework of a domestic plan. Such industries include ground transport, communications, and electric utilities. Hous-

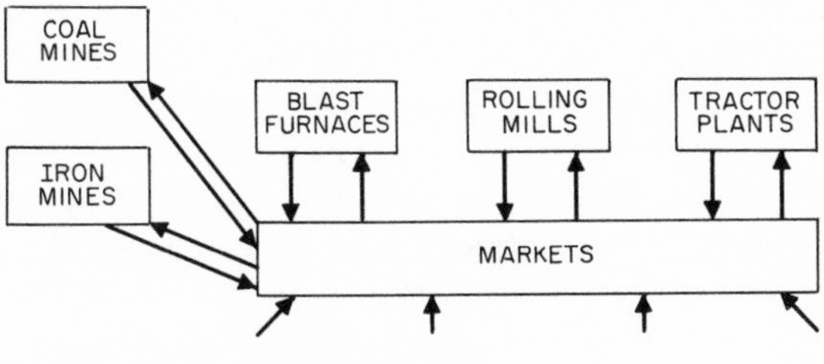

FIGURE 3-2 Open Economy

ing may be an intermediate case. Although largely domestic, it is strongly influenced by lumber imports and exports, notably exports to Japan. But most of our large industries are part of an open economy. Their prices, costs, and expected levels of imports and exports are essential data for coherence planning.

In terms of price, planning poses not only a very substantial technical or substantive challenge; it also poses a political problem when the planning process is democratic and quasi-public. Take the 1973 oil crisis as an illustration. What would have happened if a national planning agency had figured out in advance that the crunch was coming and that the price of oil might rise by a multiple of three to five? Could the planners have used such a forecast in building their balanced growth plan? Could they then have tried to define the impact on other sectors and the needed policy adjustments—such as a tax on automobile horsepower or weight, or a tax on gasoline? Unfortunately, experience to date suggests an emphatic negative answer to this question.

The oil-price forecast would have been considered politically sensitive information. A predicted price increase would have been likely to boost the aspirations of the producer nations. In addition, such a forecast would have been politically sensitive in the United States as well, raising questions about our foreign policy in the Middle East, about the future of the highway construction program, about the continued viability of the large, gas-guzzling Detroit models, and about the competitive position of the trucking industry vis-à-vis the railroads—just to mention a few of the most obvious and sensitive points. In such circumstances, experience suggests that the forecast would have been suppressed and that the planners would have been asked to go forward on the assumption that there would be little or no change in oil prices. In addition, it it unlikely that any preparations would have been made in secret to deal with the price increase.

If this seems a harsh or cynical view, it is well to ask what plans have been developed in the more than four years since the oil price increase. While proclaiming "operation independence," we have allowed domestic oil consumption to resume its growth while domestic production continues to decline, thereby permitting our dependence on foreigners to increase. The so-called independence program includes tapping naval oil reserves to gain short-term relief at the expense of having still less room for maneuver later. "Operation independence" is politics, not economics, and this is so even though the oil problem is a reality, not just a prediction.

Furthermore, late in 1971, at least one major international oil company made a detailed forecast or scenario for the oil industry which did predict a dramatic price increase by 1975, at the latest. This scenario was remarkably similar to what actually happened. The analysis noted most of the reasons which, as many economists now agree, made the problem an "obvious" one. This forecast was informally presented to high-level representatives of over half-a-dozen interested governments, including that of the United States, about eighteen months before the oil embargo and price increases actually came. According to company sources, none of the governments took significant actions on the basis of this forecast.[12]

If our government (along with others) would not act on the forecast of an energy crisis, and if (unlike the others) it will not even act to deal with the crisis once it has been with us for a period of years, what is the point of coherence planning in energy? It seems clear that the picture would be similar, if perhaps not quite so dramatic, in other key sectors. Forecasts of significant surpluses or shortages imply price changes and subsequent adjustments by sectors of the economy. As such, they have an inevitable political content, and they are likely to be treated first and foremost in political terms.

Given the need for a democratic government to plan in a quasi-public way, and given the likelihood of leaks as well as of political interference, there is little probability that a national planning agency could do as well as a private firm in the area of coherence planning. In all likelihood, the public agency would do worse, and on the average, probably much worse than the leading private firms in a given industry. Coherence planning is likely to be a failure in the United States as it has been in France, and for much the same reasons. The technical problems of planning in an open economy are formidable; the political problems of planning on the basis of "unwelcome" forecasts are overwhelming.

STRUCTURAL PLANNING

National planning could undertake to plan and promote structural changes as a means of promoting improved performance. It might, for example, attempt to promote greater specialization by firms within an industry, or consolidation to absorb marginal firms, or geographic relocation into areas with surplus labor. In most countries, planning and promoting structural change requires an especially active role for government in business affairs, with government promoting realignment of the firms within an industry and inducing business cooperation by substantial incentives, often in the form of low-cost loans. Since government has such a strong influence on most national capital markets, government support, if not initiative, is essential. It is appropriate to note that the United States is one of the few industrial countries with a very large, largely independent capital market capable of financing large-scale mergers. The history of the early railroad consolidations and the creation of United States Steel are eloquent testimony not only to the independence of the capital markets, but also to the vision and scope of the "structural planning" undertaken by some of our leading investment banking firms. The role of stock market booms in assisting

12. The company has asked that its name not be disclosed.

subsequent merger waves is also worth noting. The United States, Britain, and Switzerland are countries in which the banking communities have played a role often reserved to governments in other countries.

National planning appears to have had a significant influence on industry structure and performance in several foreign countries, of which Japan is probably the most dramatic example. In Japan, primary initiative for developing industrial policy has rested with the Ministry of International Trade and Industry (MITI) rather than with the Economic Planning Agency (EPA).[13] The EPA has taken the lead in macroeconomic planning, in a role similar to that of our Council of Economic Advisers. The Humphrey-Javits bill gives the United States planning board a mandate to consider structural issues as well as the macroeconomic, and so a brief review of the impact of MITI on Japanese industry is appropriate.

MITI has influenced industry structure in numerous ways, but particularly by excluding foreign firms from investing in Japan and hence by limiting participation in an industry to domestic firms. MITI has also controlled the purchase of foreign licenses, again limiting the number of firms that can participate. In some cases, such as the computer industry, MITI has actively promoted the development of a few selected firms through research contracts, preferential financing, and so on. MITI has also sponsored cartels to limit domestic competition in various industries, often serving as a counterbalance to Japan's Fair Trade Commission (FTC).

Among the results of MITI's influence, one must include a high degree of domestic control of Japanese industry, a relatively high degree of concentration within industries where scale is important, the achievement of this concentration with maximum speed and minimum shakeout of marginal firms, plus very aggressive development of those industries favored by MITI, thanks in part to their being given preferential access to funds by the banks. Thus, Japan was able to embark on a strategy in which key industries were rapidly developed, even where these industries were at a decided cost disadvantage in world markets, because protection in the domestic market gave them a safe home base in which to sell until such time as the leading firms had grown large enough to achieve a competitive cost structure. For example, the decisions to effect a dramatic expansion of steel bars and steel sheets were made in a period when costs in these industries were respectively 66 percent and 100 percent above United States levels.[14] Expansion helped to bring costs down and to allow both industries to become major exporters within a decade.

---

13. See, for example, Richard E. Caves and Masu Uekusa, *Industrial Organization in Japan*, The Brookings Institution, Washington, D.C., 1976, pp. 53–56.

14. Data for 1952 from Japanese Ministry of Finance as reproduced in *Japan (C): From Occupation to Independence*, Intercollegiate Case Clearing House, 1-375-032 (1975).

If Japan is a clear success story with respect to planned development of industries, it is not so obvious that this story contains many lessons for the United States. In large measure, MITI was able to base its decisions on which industries to promote on the experience of more developed nations, the United States in particular. Since the U.S. economy is the most advanced, we have no comparable model to follow.

MITI was not encumbered by serious government concern for enforcement of its antitrust laws. Antitrust was an alien concept, first imposed on Japan by the United States occupation. Enforcement was the province of the relatively weak Japanese FTC. Perhaps most important, MITI was influencing the development of Japanese industry at a time when it had enormous power to implement its plans. Although Japan had joined the Organization for Economic Cooperation and Development (OECD) in 1955, it was exempted from an obligation to observe the strict OECD rules on import restrictions and capital controls. Thus, MITI together with the Ministry of Finance had the power to control access to foreign capital and technology as well as to control the issuance of licenses to import raw materials. In the late 1960s, when the OECD nations successfully insisted that Japan adhere more closely to the rules, MITI's powers started to decline. The Japanese government's control of its frontiers had been an important source of power in implementing its industrial policy, and as those frontiers were progressively opened by OECD pressure, Japan's ability to implement its plans declined steadily. Recent experience increasingly reveals disagreement between business and government on structural change, and as often as not industry has the last word.[15]

France is another country that has used national planning to influence industry structure. Right after the war, the Planning Commission set out to encourage the construction of one or two hot-strip steel mills in France, mills with a capacity of a million tons. Since none of the French steel companies was big enough to build such a mill, the planners insisted on structural change, accepting a merger in one case and a joint venture in the other, in order to establish the new technology.

In 1965, after almost 15 years of inactivity in this area, the French planners returned to structural change as a major theme in the Fifth Plan. This time, their effort was primarily directed at promoting mergers among French firms that were increasingly exposed to the rigors of competition from other member-countries of the European Economic Community (EEC). The Fifth Plan did not so much plan or arrange the desired mergers as give official blessing to them, thereby providing government sponsorship despite traditional suspicions of big business as monopolistic and despite continuing threats from left-wing parties in the Parliament to nationalize such monopolies. Among the "results"

---

15. Nippon Electric Corporation, Intercollegiate Case Clearing House, 1-374-296 (1974).

of this change in climate were important mergers in chemicals and nonferrous metals.

In constrast to this hands-off approach, the Planning Commission was directly involved in securing an agreement between the government and the steel industry. Among its provisions was a production-sharing agreement between the two largest French steel companies, so that full utilization of their respective hot- and cold-rolling capacity would be achieved (by transshipment) before either could add capacity. Still more significant was the refusal by the Planning Commissioner, on behalf of the government, to give official support for low-cost loans to the steel industry until several nearly bankrupt firms had merged with other partners in a joint venture to form an integrated firm.

Like the Japanese, the French had a model to follow, namely that of the more advanced industrial economies. In addition, the French government was not seriously concerned about antitrust actions during these years. Despite provisions in the Rome Treaty prohibiting cartels, the government managed a cartel in electrical equipment, tolerated one covering much of the steel industry, and even insisted that the two leading French steel firms allocate output shares to their key production facilities.

In these circumstances, one must give the French planners credit for helping to change the climate of opinion in government, in business, and to some degree, among the public. Planning was but one force helping to alter the climate of opinion, but it was probably a significant one. This changing climate of opinion, moreover, helped business managers to move, in company with government or on their own, to restructure their firms.

On the other hand, some of the restructuring promoted by government may not have been all that constructive for the long run. The most frequently used model was that of the Galbraithian giant, the firm which dominates an industry and typically has a dominant share of its activity within that single industry.[16] The desired result in this case was to create French "national champions" of an international scale—capable of competing head on with foreign firms.[17] One of the inevitable consequences was to increase the number of "national champions" who could claim special favors in time of difficulty, alleging that part or all of the difficulty was caused by being a "French" company, without fear that another French competitor would have found a way to surmount the difficulty. This model opened the way to increasing the number of low-performing, state-aided companies. It carried substantial risks of economic costs as well as economic gains. An early example

---

16. John Kenneth Galbraith's *The New Industrial State* (Houghton Mifflin, Boston, 1967) was published subsequent to development of those ideas in France. However, the short-lived Industrial Reorganization Corporation in Britain explicitly used the Galbraithian model in the belief that it represented the archetype of the successful American firm.

17. *The Fifth Plan,* Commissariat General du Plan, 1966, English ed., p. 40.

was not hard to find, as the government was asked to bear the major burden of financing the next stage of development of the steel industry (at Fos) on behalf of financially weak companies in a grand-scale project of dubious economic merit.

Creating doubtful national champions in preference to multiindustry companies organized by divisions and geared to internal as well as external competition was a particularly significant weakness, given the French tendency to use government aid to support "losers" rather than "winners." Even a cursory familiarity with the pattern of state subsidies in France reveals an overwhelming balance in favor of aiding weak, noncompetitive firms rather than strong ones. The main reason is government sensitivity to jobs. A detailed study of this subject undertaken within the Ministry of Finance revealed a high correlation between net state aid and "losing" companies and industries, with the biggest losers—such as the coal company and the national rail system—being the biggest beneficiaries of state support.

In addition, the total impact of the French government seems rather modest in light of the problems facing French industry. These problems included not only small-scale production units and highly fragmented industries, but a whole syndrome of poor management practices which had persisted for a long time, thanks to the presence of cartels within France and to government protection from outside competition. For example, there had been so little pressure for performance that by the mid-1960s a leading electronics firm and a leading chemical firm, each making over three thousand products, were still organized into functional rather than product-line departments. In these companies, profit responsibility existed at no level below that of general manager of the firm. French firms were still all too often managed by technocrats who looked down on marketing and product development while emphasizing mainly high-technology machinery and equipment. Often, management had neither great interest nor ability in evaluating profitability by product-line or area.[18] In these circumstances, it was not just a few mergers that were needed, but a sweeping change in management practices and an internal restructuring, involving a switch to management by product divisions instead of management by functional specialty.

Changes in the organizational structure and management practices within French firms came rapidly in the late 1960s, not so much because of planning as because of the competitive pressures created by the Common Market. These pressures were evidenced by declining profitability and declining export performance in key sectors of manufacturing.[19] A first attempt to cut costs and improve efficiency via an implicit incomes policy which was designed to hold down wages and thus to

---

18. Bruce R. Scott, *Strengths and Weaknesses of French Industry*, Commissariat General du Plan, Paris, 1970. (Mimeographed.)

19. Ibid.

permit increases in profits and investment aborted in the "events of May" 1968, when France nearly suffered a general strike. Following this great upheaval, managerial attitudes and practices moved markedly toward a more competitive pattern, including widespread acceptance of the divisional form of organization.[20] As a result, management practices in France, as in Germany, England, and to a lesser degree in Italy, moved toward the pattern already established in the world's most competitive market, the United States.[21]

Planning was much less influential in restructuring French industry than was the increase in competitive pressures caused by the European Economic Community (EEC). Planning was not only more sporadic in its impact on particular sectors, it also was unable to achieve anything like so deep an impact on managerial practices within the firm. In addition, in a number of sectors, including chemicals, mechanical and electrical equipment, and machine tools in particular, France continued to lose ground in international markets (as measured by the ratio of French exports to imports for these sectors), despite the fact that planning had singled out these industries for special attention for approximately twenty years.[22] Planning and government intervention were significant in a limited number of key instances, but competitive pressures forced change throughout many industries—with the notable exception of industries in noncompetitive sectors, such as the national railroad. In short, the introduction of increased competition via the Rome Treaty had vastly more impact on the structure of French firms and industries than national planning did. The basic step in promoting structural change was the decision to join the EEC, so that outside competition could force change upon reluctant French firms. It is greatly to the credit of the French planners, and Jean Monnet in particular, that they recognized the need for and opportunity to harness the power of foreign competition to promote structural change within France.

What can be said at this point about the prospects for structural planning in the United States? As a first step, it seems important to distinguish between essentially domestic industries, such as electric power generation and distribution or ground transportation, and essentially international industries, such as shoes and electronics. This distinction between domestic and international industries is made first on simple economic grounds—the existence of foreign trade and, hence, of foreign competition, actual or potential. The U.S. market for electricity, rail service, or truck service is essentially a closed market; we do not import electricity, rail service, or truck service from Germany or Japan. We can and do import very limited amounts from Canada, but

20. Bruce R. Scott, "The Industrial State, Old Myths and New Realities," *Harvard Business Review*, vol. 51, no. 2, March–April 1973, p. 133 ff.

21. Ibid., p. 139.

22. *Yearbook of International Trade Statistics*, Publishing Service, United Nations, New York, 1974.

not enough to materially affect the national picture. By and large, if we did not maintain and develop these industries within the United States, we would have to do without. Not so with shoes or electronics. We could theoretically allow either or both these industries to close down and still be supplied from abroad.

The opportunity and the need for structural planning are quite different in the two cases. In electricity, for example, demand forecasts by area could be coupled with expansion of capacity in large units, coupled with shipment of electricity in regional networks to optimize service and to minimize cost in a nearly closed system. If planning went only this far, it would be traditional coherence planning, balancing growth in supply with growth in demand on a national scale. Planning on a national scale, however, would almost certainly increase regional imbalances in production and distribution, with some regions becoming net exporters and others net importers. Industry structure would be involved because many separate companies are involved, as well as various federal, state, and local regulatory authorities. National planning might bridge our fragmented, "investor-owned" utility system through joint venture plants located on the basis of cost and environmental advantages, without regard for the present territorial boundaries of the various power company franchises. At the same time, the regulatory framework would have to be modified to accommodate, if not to encourage, the breakdown of the present regional and local franchises.

Similar opportunities might exist in ground transportation and housing. In housing, for instance, national planning might provide a framework within which to work toward greater standardization of building codes, and thus toward greater possibilities for economies through standardization, mass production, and larger firms to take advantages of those economies. In each of these industries, it should be noted, structural change would almost surely involve multiple levels of the regulatory system as well as the business firms. And there is no reason at this point to think that state and local regulatory agencies are going to be more interested in a broad national interest than senators or congressmen. Effective planning would require reforming government as well as industry, and the former would almost surely be more difficult to achieve than the latter.

On the other hand, structural planning and intervention in the major competitive sector of the U.S. economy would seem to offer only slim prospects, at least in terms of achieving the objectives so far pursued by other advanced countries. Our firms may not all be international champions, but by and large American industry is the international model. To improve on what exists, the planners would either have to come up with a new, better model or tinker with the world leaders in the belief that bureaucrats are somehow more expert in the field than business managers.

Simply stated, the model of the leading firms in international business is that of a multi-industry firm organized by divisions, with the divisions usually representing industries but sometimes regions and sometimes both.[23] If we use the *Fortune* 500 as our sample population, we can say that a majority of these firms are sufficiently diversified that they no longer have a dominant business.[24] Furthermore, the model is one of a firm with manufacturing operations in numerous foreign countries, with transshipments from one country to another, and typically with a multicountry, if not worldwide, view of product sourcing for its sales network. A similar pattern is being adopted by foreign firms as they spread abroad, including into the United States. As a result, the international sector of the economy is characterized by firms which cross the national frontier and which, thus, have a different geographic base than that of the United States planning board.

The number of industries and of important firms, plus the complexity of the relationships within the United States and across the frontiers, are such as to make the notion of planning for this segment of the economy quite unrealistic. On the other hand, the question arises as to whether selective attention to some industries and their structural problems might be constructive.

A closer look at the *Fortune* 500 reveals significant differences in economic performance during the 1950s and 1960s, by degree of diversification, type of organization, and by industry. Thus, American firms which remained in a single industry, or still had a dominant share of sales (70 percent or more) in a single industry, experienced slower growth in sales and earnings than those firms which had diversified into related activities.[25] The Galbraithian firms, that is, those which had a dominant business based on vertically integrated operations, were particularly low performers not only in sales and earnings growth but also in average return on assets.[26] Thus, as I have argued elsewhere, Galbraith's identification of the large firm managed by the "technostructure" corresponds to a significant share (about 45 percent) of the *Fortune* 500 as of 1970, but the share is declining and the performance is the lowest of any major group identified on the basis of strategy and structure.[27] Galbraith's archetype of the modern industrial firm is out of date and, typically, a low performer in economic terms; yet, it is used as a model by economic planners in other countries, including France and England. This should give us some cause for concern about the comparative wisdom of business managers, economists, and government planners. For the United States, it suggests that the Galbraithian firms may

---

23. Scott, "The Industrial State," pp. 133 ff.

24. Ibid., pp. 138–139.

25. Richard P. Rumelt, *Strategy, Structure and Economic Performance,* Harvard Graduate School of Business Administration, Division of Research, Boston, 1974, p. 91.

26. Ibid., p. 92.

27. Scott, "The Industrial State," p. 142.

merit attention by the planners for their low performance, in addition to any concerns which exist over the military-industrial complex or excessive market power.

If we look at the low-performance firms and industries, we come face to face with another instance where economics and politics merge in the planning problem. The low-performing industries are typically based on raw materials, iron and steel, copper, wood, and petroleum. In economic terms, they are clearly international; indeed, they are likely to be particularly susceptible to foreign competition. And yet, it is possible to make a political decision that they will be treated as "essential" domestic industries. Voluntary steel import quotas for European and Japanese producers turn our steel industry into a quasi-domestic industry on the basis of politics, not economics. Politics dominates economics in the interests of preserving jobs for American voters.

Politically, it is possible to turn an international industry into a domestic industry by "closing" the frontiers to imports. Planning could then attempt to restructure the industry for "better performance." It is, however, certainly possible that better performance would be defined in social and political terms rather than economic, and that planning would become a guise in which to protect declining industries or weak firms, or both. Indeed, current research by a colleague suggests that just such a process may already be taking place in some of these industries, even though no formal regulatory or planning framework has yet developed.[28] In this segment of industry there is a clear possibility for formalized national planning, and likewise the possibility that the economic costs would outweigh the economic gains. Planning could lead to more government support for "losers," just as it has in France.

AN INCOMES POLICY

An incomes policy offers the possibility of reducing the wage-push element in inflation in a more equitable, longer-lasting way than across-the-board wage-and-price controls. An incomes policy might also establish more explicit guidelines for transfer payments or guaranteed incomes to the least fortunate segments of society. But, the principal opportunity is to find a reasonable or fair set of relationships among the incomes earned in various industry sectors, e.g., housing, auto manufacture, and public service. In effect, a planned incomes policy is a way to alleviate structural imperfections that give some unions much more bargaining power than others; the policy might also help to alleviate the broader problem of labor's bargaining power, which has led wages to rise more rapidly than productivity.

A successful incomes policy has yet to emerge in a major industrial country. The problems come in all sizes and shapes. They begin with

---

28. J. W. Rosenblum, *Negotiating the Business Environment: Business-Government Relationships in Basic but Unregulated Industries,* in preparation.

the question "What is income?" and include the question of how the comparability of required skills can be measured. Inevitably, they touch upon the "historic" relationship of wages in industry A versus industry B. Ultimately, they encounter the question of whether there is some standard for a fair income, other than that achieved through bargaining in the market place, and—if there is to be such a standard—of how is it to be established and by whom.

The potential significance of an incomes policy in the United States can be readily appreciated when one recalls that over the last decade wages have risen more rapidly in the service sector than in manufacturing.[29] This differential arises in part from increased unionization in the service sector, and in part from the fact that services have a purely domestic status and, hence, are not exposed to international competition. For example, housing and government service have no foreign competition; these sectors have little prospect of losing jobs to foreigners if wages get "too high." Steel and autos, on the other hand, face the prospect of continuing loss of jobs to foreigners; as a result, unions and management have some common interests in keeping wages in some reasonable relationship to productivity. It should be no surprise, therefore, that unionization has brought more rapid wage increases to domestic "monopoly" sectors than to the internationally competitive manufacturing sector. Given the rapid rise in productivity abroad, notably in Japan, Germany, and France, foreign pressures are likely to grow stronger in the manufacturing sector. Hence, the prospect of a growing disparity (even where strong manufacturing unions exist) in wage gains is present.

If the broad outlines of the problem, and, likewise, the advantages of a planned incomes policy to keep some balance between manufacturing and other sectors, are clear, it is not clear that this country is ready to accept such a discipline. The economics of the problem are not very complicated, but the politics are formidable. Who, for example, is going to wish to defend a policy which restrains the "rightful" demands of schoolteachers, firemen, and postal workers to much higher wages to "catch up" for decades of being underpaid? Surely an attempt to create an incomes policy is worthy of considerable effort, but at this stage it would seem premature to think that more sophisticated economic analysis and planning would play a significant role in influencing the outcome.

INFORMATION FOR NATIONAL PLANNING

If the foregoing analysis is sound, one of the prime requisites for effective national planning is that it be selective rather than comprehensive. Selectivity should be based on two basic criteria: (1) the priorities

---

29. U.S. Bureau of the Census, *Statistical Abstract of the United States, 1975,* table 596, p. 366; table 598, p. 368; table 603, p. 370.

in terms of opportunity for improvement in economic performance, and (2) the feasibility of national planning for the sector or industry. Those industries which we have defined as domestic qualify on both criteria, while those classified as international qualify on neither. Domestic industry can be planned; international industry cannot sensibly be planned by government. The distinction is pragmatic, not ideological. The key criteria are opportunity for improvement and feasibility. There is a third group of industries which are international in economic terms but might be defined as domestic in political terms. They merit special attention, both in terms of the opportunity and in terms of feasibility.

Domestic industries such as the railroads and electric utilities present obvious opportunities for improved performance. They, likewise, present feasible situations for planning industry capacity in relation to demand, for planning structural change on an industry basis, and, perhaps, for incomes planning as well. In each case, the data base seems readily available, if not already in the hands of existing regulatory authorities. Indeed, the principal obstacle to effective planning in these sectors will almost surely be existing regulatory agencies with their own "planning" and with political support relatively secure from pressures from the executive branch in Washington.

On the other hand, the international industries by and large show little promise that national planning would help, while the problems of adequate data collection and evaluation are so great as to make attempted national planning an almost certain failure. The critical information includes projected imports, exports, prices, and costs.

Evaluation of exports and imports sooner or later depends upon evaluation of foreign competition. Thirty years of experience in France suggests that a bureaucracy is much less suited to this type of analysis than are individual firms or private consulting companies. Which arm of the executive branch would undertake this task in the United States? Would it be the State Department, or Department of Commerce, or the planning board? Or would the bureaucrats depend upon industry and private consultants for such information? If industry were the primary source, how would the planners filter out the natural bias of self-interest in the information supplied? On the other hand, why would industry be interested in plans based on rapidly aging information that had been supplied by industry itself? Many big companies have their own methods for gathering data, and significant inputs come from branch-office personnel and from foreign travel by company employees. Major companies in international industries are likely to have much better sources of information than the national planners, and they are likely to share such information only when it would be in their own interest to do so.

For those industries which are international in economic terms but are politically defined as domestic, the situation is much less clear. The economic performance of some of these industries is low, has been for years, and seems likely to remain so (e.g., steel). However, it is not clear that there are big opportunities for improvement. As an old, relatively stable technology industry, it may be that steel should be thought of as a quasi-public utility which should earn a modest, steady return. Improvements might be made, but high performance in growth or earnings should not be expected.

However, it is not at all clear that planning would help achieve even modest improvements in performance. Regulation would probably relieve some of the market pressures for performance, and quite likely substitute political pressures for economic. A federal steel agency might well spring up alongside, for example, the FEA, ICC, and FPC, adding a new way for Congress and an "independent" regulatory agency to plan for an industry in light of a whole variety of concerns other than economic performance. The results might well include "overinvestment" in these industries, a slowing of the trend of the low performing firms to try to redeploy some of their resources into other industries, and new government agencies aiding losing companies and thereby helping preserve the status quo in the face of needed changes.

If an international industry were politically designated as "domestic," the information problems would be greatly simplified. Imports would be limited, perhaps by a quota; hence the impact of foreign competition would be limited. The essential data would be similar to that for the other domestic industries. The Humphrey-Javits bill provides for antitrust exemptions for furnishing such data, and there is little reason to doubt that the planners could soon establish a good working knowledge of several such industries. On the other hand, there is little reason to be concerned that collection of such information by government would harm competition. The industries concerned are ones where a great deal of information is made public either through trade associations or through public announcements by the firms.

In sum, it would seem that the industries where planning is most likely to be high priority, whether for economic or political reasons, are industries where access to essential information is not a critical problem. Only if planning were to blunder into an attempt to be comprehensive rather than selective would there be serious informational problems.

In addition, a selective approach to planning could minimize the technical and informational problems still more if the planners were to accept an indirect approach to influencing business as compared to direct planning for an industry. An indirect approach would attempt to influence firms by manipulating the economic environment in which they operate. The evidence is overwhelming, notwithstanding Galbraith, that most large firms are very sensitive to the market most of the time. It shows up in diversification into new growth industries as well as gradual abandonment of declining industries. Even our one-industry dinosaurs have been actively trying to improve their economic performance through diversification. Similarly, market sensitivity shows up in attempts to lobby for favorable treatment by government in matters such as taxes and tariffs.

Here, there is a useful analogy between managing the industrial sector of the economy and managing a large, highly diversified firm organized by product divisions. Our large, multi-industry, multidivisional firms manage their divisions in part through manipulation of an internal marketplace. Funds tend to be drawn away from low-profit, low-growth divisions in favor of higher performance divisions. In addition, managers in high-performance divisions may enjoy higher rewards. Management may also set minimum standards for performance, both for divisions and for individual managers. And a division which consistently fails to meet the minimum expected performance may be sold or closed down, even though it might be able to limp along as an independent company. It is not at all uncommon for the internal marketplace to generate higher pressure for economic performance than does the external.

The planners could use this approach to avoid becoming involved in unnecessary detail, and likewise, to utilize the sensitivity of existing corporate management to market incentives. Thus, instead of somehow trying to plan for the auto industry or the steel industry, the planners could attempt to devise incentives and penalties to bring about desired policy changes. Rather than getting bogged down in trying to plan for an increase in the output of small cars, the planners could recommend stiff taxes on large cars, leaving to industry the responsibility for planning in light of the new "market conditions." The more indirect and market-oriented the planning, the less significant the technical and informational problems would be.

I think it is obvious that the more indirect and market-oriented the planning, the more likely it is to be useful and effective in economic terms. However, the political feasibility is much less clear. New incentives and penalties would be subject to congressional scrutiny, if not always to prior congressional approval. There is nothing about national planning which would necessarily make the political aspect of managing the economy any more feasible or more rational than at present. The economics seem relatively simple, the politics seem formidable.

IMPROVING THE PROSPECTS FOR NATIONAL PLANNING

There appear to be at least four ways to improve the prospects for effective national planning in the United States: two involve modifications in the Humphrey-Javits bill and two involve changes in our regulatory practices.

The Humphrey-Javits bill enlists—although it does not require—commitment from the executive branch to act in accordance with the plan, as approved by Congress. The bill does not, however, enlist a similar commitment from the Congress. The text should be amended to require that all economic legislation contain an "impact statement" to show how, if at all, it relates to the national plan. Likewise, the planning board should have an opportunity to file its own impact statement with the appropriate congressional committee. The planning board should have the right to testify in such cases and, likewise, to make its testimony public. In addition, if prospective legislation failed to conform to the plan, perhaps a larger majority than the usual should be required to pass it. Requiring two-thirds for passage would seem a reasonable way to secure a measure of congressional commitment to the planning process.

Second, the planning board should probably be made as independent of Congress as possible. One essential element in such autonomy should be financial independence. The planning board should have its own source of revenues, just as the Federal Reserve system does.

Third, some of our regulatory laws and practices should be changed so as to increase the emphasis accorded to effective economic performance. Most of our regulatory legislation originated in response to abuses. Thus, most regulation has aimed at preventing wrongdoing, not at promoting efficiency. Developing a more performance-oriented set of regulatory criteria and a more performance-oriented attitude among our regulatory agencies would seem to be one of the fundamental questions to be addressed. National planning might well be a big help. But, by itself, it could hardly do the job.

For example, the regulatory practices of the Federal Reserve might be changed. At present, the Federal Reserve Board regulates the banking system in terms of its liabilities or sources of funds; it might shift to regulating in terms of banking assets or how the funds are used. Then, instead of slowing the economy through tight money across the board, which leads rapidly to a credit crunch in housing, the Federal Reserve Board could set guidelines for lending to business, for mortgages, for installment financing, and for loans to federal, state, and local government. The Fed could then squeeze by sector. Since business borrowers now get most-favored treatment by the banks, the Federal Reserve could then take aim and squeeze business lending more, thereby somewhat easing the pressure on mortgages and the housing industry.

This change implies an increase in Federal Reserve control of the banking system. It is similar in type to the increase in government control which is implicit in national planning for domestic industry. The present political independence of the Federal Reserve Board makes this agency seem a particularly good place to increase governmental control in the interest of improved economic performance. If the Fed guidelines for selective allocation of credit could then be tied into the national planning process, this would, of course, be still better.

A fourth possibility would be for the President and Congress to authorize national planning to be undertaken by several independent organizations. It would be preferable to have two or three such institutions, each with the same mission and each expected to develop one or more scenarios exploring problems and helping to educate the American public on the risks and opportunities facing the American economy. Government would provide legitimacy for such studies, and it would provide the funding for both the research and the dissemination of the results. Ideally, there would be a conservative institution, a liberal one, and perhaps a third to keep the first two from becoming too closely allied with particular political parties.

These institutions could be truly free to study basic economic problems, such as energy. They could publish their results and attempt to influence public opinion and, indirectly, public policy. To maintain this independent position, it would be essential that their scenarios *not* require approval either by the Congress or the President. The executive agencies could continue to do their own planning, using such ideas as they wished from the plans and scenarios of the independent planning institutions.

Development of authorized, yet independent, scenarios might help to build public pressure for a longer-range point of view in both Congress and the White House. These private institutions might do for planning what pressure groups, such as the Sierra Club, have done to promote concern for the environment. Since "all politics is ultimately local politics," it seems unlikely that national planning can be very effective until there is local interest in and pressure for more enlightened management of our economy.

The executive branch now has access to most, if not all, of the information needed for national planning in the domestic sectors of our economy. A skeleton structure is also available for this purpose in the Council of Economic Advisers. National planning could certainly have been developed within this framework, had any of our Presidents wanted to have it. The critical element that is missing is not the data but the sense of urgency to do a better job. Selfish local interests will continue to dominate United States economic policy until articulate competition comes from those with a broader view. Institutional legitimacy is what is needed most; better information and plans would follow close behind.

SUMMARY AND CONCLUSIONS

There can be little doubt about the need for better performance by our economy, including the productive sector. It seems equally obvious that we need better management of the economy if we are to achieve better performance. As a start, we need tools which are more precise and more selective than conventional monetary and fiscal policies. In addition, we need far more coodination among the government agencies that regulate or influence economic activity. National planning is a framework within which to develop and use more selective tools and through which to achieve better coordination of government programs.

National planning, as outlined in the Humphrey-Javits bill, could be a significant step forward in improving the institutional framework for managing the domestic sector of the economy. It could provide a framework for coherence planning, structural reform, and the development of an incomes policy in a limited segment of the economy. On the other hand, national planning offers little promise in those segments that face international competition. Thus, any notion of a comprehensive plan covering all industry is an illusion.

The major weakness of national planning lies in political control of the planning process. Politics dominates economics, even in the formulation of the options to be evaluated, let alone in the selection of one particular course to be followed. The Humphrey-Javits bill contains major weaknesses in this respect, because the planning board is left subject to just such dysfunctional political control. There is a strong possibility that the President would not allow the planners even to explore options which might be attractive for the long run if they would be impolitic in the short run. While close affiliation with the Chief Executive is a requisite for a relevant and useful planning agency, the requirements for a quasi-public planning process and published plan mean that the President is likely to turn the plan and the national planning process into a public-relations exercise.

The critical problems for consideration at this stage are not those of information or even planning methods. The critical problems are those of the structure of the planning institutions, their relation to the Congress, the regulatory agencies, and the executive branch, and the selection of the limited territory which can be effectively planned. Comprehensive planning of all sectors of the economy is doomed to failure from the start. It will be useless to all, and a threat to none. Selective planning of some sectors offers the promise of better management, not only for the selected sectors, but for the economy as a whole. Likewise, more concern for committing Congress to the planning process offers the hope of improving not only new legislation but also new initiatives in the executive branch. One of the most important challenges of national planning is to lift congressional politics away from local pressures toward national interests.

On balance, the most important test of the promise of national planning is *not* that of potential economic gains versus potential political costs. The real test is whether institutional arrangements can be devised and incorporated into the administrative structure of our government such that national planning yields net economic gains rather than net economic costs. The answer will not depend on data sources or economic models so much as on whether a broader, longer-range viewpoint is or is not good politics.

COMMENTARY

Wassily Leontief

I find myself somewhat in a quandary. I was invited about a year ago to prepare a paper on problems of privacy and confidentiality in governmental information gathering. These are very important problems. I then wrote a paper, and I permitted myself, not without previous consultation, a slightly wider perspective. I discussed the statistical organization of government.

But when I received Professor Scott's paper, I felt like a little pigeon that sees a gigantic missile whizzing toward him. In a sense, it is more comfortable than being in the position of an elephant, because I feel I can sit quietly and let the missile pass by. And I have a very great temptation to do so. I think, however, such a course might disappoint some of those present; so, after first dealing with information, I will try to meet Professor Scott's broader points.

The government now plays a very substantial role in the operation of our economic system. Whether we like it or not, this is true. Not only do about one-third of all goods and services produced in this country pass through government hands, but the government, for better or worse, does a terrific amount of economic regulation. As a matter of fact, policy decisions in the economic and social spheres are one of the principal businesses of federal, state, and local governments.

Policy decisions, I suppose, are intended to influence in some way the course of events. Consequently, a basic problem is how to decide what events you want to influence and how to design policies which bring about a desired result. And since, as Professor Scott properly emphasizes, our economic system is very complicated, both adequate information and analysis are needed.

At the present time, one of the principal problems we have in the government is that we design policies, pursue policies, which do not bring about the results that they are designed to achieve. In our government there is no internal consistency in designing different policies.

My feeling is that there is a very immediate, burning need to get better organized information. I think anybody who works in the government knows it. We now have essentially a troubleshooting approach, not only in making policy decisions, but even in collecting facts. I think our government should have a current information system, current analytical system, which will enable us to address key economic questions with the tools in hand. A sufficiently well-coordinated system would also allow us to coordinate the activities of the different departments of the government.

The word *coordination* is used very often now, but what it usually means in practice is that when policies of the Departments of Agriculture and Commerce, for example, come into conflict the two heads meet and simply agree to keep out of each other's hair. This is very bad because we often then have contradictory decisions that wash each other out.

Moreover, in terms of coordination of information, at the present time, such elementary things as information on employment and production are not coordinated. Even our export and import figures cannot, without a lot of gymnastics, be related to our production figures.

Most of the people in government dealing with these things—and I assure you I have watched government activities for 40 years—have simply tried to reconcile figures; reconciliation always means losing a lot of information. We speak of standardization of classifications, for example. We have some of it already. But everyone who works scientifically knows that a classification is only a first step to a theory.

Why not develop an analytical device, a modeling device, that essentially will store figures so that, for example, you could see the relationship between your energy requirements and an alternative solution to the energy problem? Environmental effects, agricultural impact, or export-import effects could also be calculated.

It is reasonable to try to improve the situation by organizing the government's statistics in a logical way. This would not mean taking away from the various departments their mandates for collecting statistics. Information in a given field is best collected by somebody who understands the field, and, obviously, the Department of Agriculture understands agriculture and so on. But somebody must see to it that the data collected fit into a wider informational picture. The need is not for centralized collection but for centralization of standards.

What we need is standardization and a statistical plan. The statistical plan must be based on a model, in other words, on an idea of how this information will be used. It must be a rather comprehensive model.

This essentially is what I had in mind in my paper. We need two things: first, a very strong organization—analytical body, statistical body, whatever you call it; second, an infusion of very large resources.

As to the second, my feeling is that we need $450 million or $500 million a year more than we spend now. To my surprise, I have very great support in this from industry and even from, for example, Herbert Stein, who is not exactly a planner.

Now, for Professor Scott's broader points. As I read his basic argument, he contends that planning has never been done successfully. I am afraid in human, economic, political, and social affairs we would never do anything if we abstained from trying just because it had never been done before. I am not prepared to reconcile myself—and I don't think the American people will be prepared to reconcile themselves—to the operation of an economy where half of the time a very high percentage of labor and capital are idle.

I think that it is quite possible to prepare not one but many alternative "plans"—in other words, scenarios—in considerable detail and then try (of course, in a democracy they must be public and not secret) to realize one thing or another. I am against stating national goals. My reply to the whole concept of a national goal is that I cannot describe my tastes when someone invites me to dinner and says: "Please, Wassily, describe your tastes so I can plan a menu." I say: "Never mind, show me a menu so I can choose."

If, however, I am given a choice among alternatives, I can make all the necessary compromises and choose the one that is preferable. My feeling is there is much to be done to develop real alternatives for the American people. And this is the direction in which we can change, if we change at all. For me, one thing is certain: there will be change.

Approximately two years ago, I had an exchange with my new Nobel colleague, Milton Friedman. At the end I said, "Now, Milton, who do you think will win?" And he said, "Wassily will win." There are still those who would like to liquidate the government. But, more realistically, if you have to live with a government, is it not wise to strive for as efficient a government as possible?

DIALOGUE

WILLIAM A. LOVETT: Professor Scott, your skepticism about, for example, the role of government in the energy field would seem to lead to this conclusion: Because of the substantial role of international markets, we should turn policy over to the multinational oil companies and cease all government supervision or influence. Would this be a fair characterization of your position?

SCOTT: No. My position is that I think the basics of the problem are pretty obvious: that having still another agency involved in national planning is not going to contribute very much to it; that the politics dominate the economics; and that the politics will dominate the economics no matter how many agencies we have involved or what we call them.

DAVID T. HULETT: I was interested in Professor Leontief's comments because I do interagency coordination all day, every day, in my work in the Statistical Policy Division at the Office of Management and Budget. We at OMB have developed the outlines of a statistical planning scheme. It is in draft form. It takes the approach of dealing with

The session was chaired by Dean Michael I. Sovern of the Columbia University School of Law. For further biographical information, see Appendix 1.

statistics in various functional (e.g., energy and health) areas.

It does not go about it from the standpoint of an overall macromodel, or input-output model, because I think there are too many other uses to put it into that single framework. Nonetheless, it is an attempt to coordinate across agency boundaries.

I should add that OMB does interagency coordination of statistics throughout the government and deals with fifty different agencies at one time or another during the day or year. We have some twenty-five professionals. I share Professor Leontief's view that, in fact, this is not nearly enough. If one-fifth of my time can be devoted to coordinating all of energy statistics, for instance, you have to know that it is a bad scene in general. And we have the same problem in other areas as well.

But we do have the authority to set standards. We do have the authority to review budgets—even though these are decentralized budgets. Perhaps, reorganization would help. We do have the authority to review questionnaire forms, at least for those agencies that are not excluded from your purview under the Federal Reports Act. All these tools, I believe, are efficient from the organizational standpoint.

LEONTIEF: First of all, of course, I am very gratified. This indicates a really responsible movement. But, in general, the government's policy is going in the other direction.

My feeling is that it is not enough to have coordinating activities here and there. This is a major problem; major steps must be taken to promote coordination. To organize statistics well within each field is not enough; it possibly encourages each field to work within itself, disregarding spillovers.

FREDERIC M. SCHERER: Professor Scott, in your paper, you are very critical of French planning related to the steel industry, and you note that the plant at Fos was of dubious economic merit. I have two questions. First, what does a nation do when it has a steel industry that is hopelessly out of date—i.e., with small and inefficient plants—and the steel producers show no inclination to solve the problem?

Second, Fos is probably the most modern, efficient plant in all of Europe. To be sure, demand at the moment is depressed, and Fos is probably not making money. But, in the long run, how does one make the transition from an outmoded steel industry to a modern, efficient steel industry other than by making such investments?

SCOTT: First, let me go back and comment upon one of Professor Leontief's observations; he suggested that planning has never been done successfully. I am aware of two instances of successful planning. The first involved the French steel industry right after the war for a period of six or seven years. The Marshall Plan financing was under the control of the Planning Commission, which said to industry: "You will have to regroup and build million-ton mills in order to obtain the money." At that stage, they were planning and implementing because they had access not only to the funds but to the foreign exchange to buy the equipment. The second instance involved strategic materials allocation in the United States during World War II.

Those instances have two things in common. Both governments were dealing essentially with a "shortage economy." France, after the war, had a shortage of almost everything. The United States had a shortage of strategic materials during the war. Both nations had basically closed economies, the United States because of the submarine threat during the war, France because of the shortage of foreign exchange and the inability to export competitively. In both instances, planning was essentially supply planning and it worked.

The planning in the French steel industry subsequent to the postwar period presents a complicated story. It is one of the few where somebody could allege national planning had some role.

In 1965, when French planners were putting together their plans, they asked the companies to come in and propose what kind of capacity they needed to build from 1965 to 1970. The planners quickly reached two conclusions. One was that industry was proposing to build substantially more than what was needed; and second, there wasn't enough potential profitability to justify building it.

Then, a new planning commissioner, who had been the Prime Minister's economic adviser, simply turned to the industry and said, "Steel is a very complicated business, and I am just a fellow who doesn't understand complicated businesses. The biggest complication is there are too many of you. If you'd simplify your situation, I'd be much more able to deal with the problem. The government is willing to back you with thirty-year loans at 3 percent in the beginning and 5 percent from then on, essentially free money. We are willing to finance you if a poor civil servant can understand the industry. If you don't merge, you go bankrupt." On that basis, we get consolidation of the industry down to two companies. That is not very sophisticated planning. In this country, we would have allowed some of the companies to die. The French, however, were concerned about communist unions and did not dare do so.

I suggest there is not much economics involved in this. You can raise the question, do we want to build the steel industry under the auspices of the public treasury, and under the auspices of people who do not have a very distinguished track record for managing it?

LEONTIEF: I would like to go back to the question about energy and Project Independence. If we had a sensible, coordinated model of the economy, the government never could have announced Project Independence, because it was such a ridiculous impossibility. This type of political thing would certainly be eliminated because accurate information would be published. And, here, you cannot limit yourself to one industry; you need a picture of the economy as a whole.

I had an opportunity to watch France develop, and I know France's statistical organization. It is terrible. The French are very elegant when theorizing, but their statistical organization is absolutely horrible. It is as bad as their income tax system. France is not a good model for judging what can be done in this country.

The same thing applies to England. They have a socialist government nationalizing industry. What has nationalization to do with running a good economy? Nothing.

FREDERICK ROWE: There have been a number of references to railroads and the ICC. I am wondering, as a domestic model rather than a foreign model, how would you interpret the history of transportation regulation since 1890 as a lesson for the success of planning on a broader scale?

LEONTIEF: I think what we are engaged in is regulation without planning and this, I think, is fatal. We really did not figure out what the consequences of various government actions would be. My feeling is that it would fare much better if we had a transportation plan, or alternative transportation plans, and could see how it all adds up—how railroads, highways, trucks, air transport relate and interact.

In the competitive system you can say, if you have a Darwinian approach, bankruptcy is a very important element of economic progress. That is how the system works. Some species don't survive. But when units are very large, it is a very expensive way of regulating a system.

SCOTT: I will not try to defend regulation. My sense is we are dealing essentially with a branch of government which has not been performance-oriented. The question is: Can we make it more performance-oriented? How do you make good economics into good politics? That is the difficult job to be attacked.

One way is to try to do it through the government. Professor Leontief is suggesting that a principled evaluation of "Project Independence" would have concluded that it could not work. I agree with that. I am not at all clear that such a governmental evaluation would ever surface. If somebody with a government job tried to publish it, I think he would have to be prepared to give up his job, if not his passport.

My feeling is that anybody proposing alternative scenarios has to be outside government and in a position of independence. If you are outside of government, you are not a government planning agency. From where does the legitimacy come for making this kind of scenario? From where does the funding come? I don't know. But if you want increased interest in good economic information and objective scenarios to evaluate the economic consequences of what we are doing, I think these must come from outside the government.

DONALD TURNER: The short answer to Professor Scott's "information won't surface" point is that if you have the kind of data-gathering organization that Professor Leontief recommends, and the data are public, then anybody is free to press for any of the alternatives that seem logical. You will not have a concealing of alternatives. New energy legislation would, for example, afford access to the model so that anybody, private or governmental, could evaluate alternatives.

CARL A. AUERBACH: Professor Scott, as I read your paper, I thought you were making a theoretical or conceptual distinction between the possibility of planning in what you call the domestic sector and the possibility of planning in what you call the international sector. In your answer to several questions, however, you seemed to indicate that you are not making a theoretical or conceptual objection to the possibility of planning in the international sector, but merely objecting to adding another agency, which is really a trivial point.

SCOTT: No, I intended to draw the distinction you suggest. A planner could, for example, have foreseen some of the major difficulties in oil in 1970 to 1972. Assume he said: "My goodness, our capacity has topped; we are headed downward; we are going to be much more dependent on foreign sources; you will have to be prepared for a dramatic increase in price because the bargaining power has shifted." I'm saying it is at that stage that planning done inside the government runs into substantial political obstacles; unpleasant projections are not going to be allowed to surface.

That does not have anything to do with whether or not there is going to be an energy agency to regulate the industry. There are limits to what government can do in an effort to forecast supply and demand and to develop a coherent energy supply for the country. And I think it just turns out to be extremely difficult to do much, for political reasons.

IRA M. MILLSTEIN: I can see a case for analysis being performed on a decentralized basis in various agencies of the government, but is there any case to be made for the continuation of the present process of data collection? Wouldn't it make sense to stop wasting time and effort and to put the data collection process in one place; you can let the analysis and goal-setting stay elsewhere. Is there any case to be made for decentralized data collection?

LEONTIEF: My feeling is that you want somebody in a consistent way to decide what data to collect, how to collect them, and I think, how to organize them. I think these go together. Which particular agency—who the people are who write the letters and get the questionnaires—is not a terribly important question. Given the way our government operates, it is possibly better to permit the data collection to be decentralized. I would not rush to put in a central statistical office.

WILLIAM K. JONES: I'd like to comment on two sides of the same coin. First, I'd like to associate myself with those who express some skepticism about the capacity of the United States to engage in planning. However great the need, we may simply be unable, because of our peculiar cultural characteristics, to do the job. And it is possible, therefore, that the patient may die for want of an operation simply because we happen not to have any surgeons available. I am very concerned about that in connection with matters like energy supply.

Second, I'd like to point out that this is not a universal phenomenon. The New York Public Service Commission, before the Arab oil embargo of 1973, was confronted with a number of serious problems in the field of energy supply, and it did not hesitate to think the unthinkable and tell people that Arab oil might not be available; it suggested options that might be available in such an instance.

All New York power plants were required to keep coal-burning capability on the line. No coal-burning capacity was permitted to be retired after 1970. All the oil-burning plants in the state were required to maintain forty-five-day and sixty-day inventories of oil to meet the possibilities of a curtailment.

So somebody was worrying. These materials were published. We knew there was going to be a gas shortage. We knew what the dimensions were. There was no problem of information. We had choices between unemployment in industries that use gas and depression in residential construction, which depended to some extent on gas supply. That is a hard choice to make. We made the choice in favor of maintaining employment at the expense of residential construction. It was made in the open, and it was a hard choice.

We did not have enough electric power to go around in the state of New York. Hearings were held on just who was going to be cut off. We did write scenarios on varying states of deterioration in power supply. And we did tell people, over obstreperous objections, that they were, indeed, going to be cut off, in favor of others with higher priority, when the power supply ran out.

I think that it is not inevitable that government should perform badly in this area. It is merely highly probable.

LEONTIEF: I'd like to make a comment. I think progress in the national scene is indicated by the fact that for two years there has been a budget organization in Congress which really, for the first time, induces Congress to take a more responsible stance in the budget-making process. That by itself indicates that some progress can be made.

Planning is the most difficult thing which society can do; there is no doubt about it. Ultimately, slowly, however, I think we will go on to do something.

RICHARD A. POSNER: I think this discussion has suffered a little from the fact that three completely different concepts are being discussed under the rubric of planning. This was brought home by Professor Jones's comment. The first and most innocuous concept, the one that it is very hard to get excited about, is improved data collection by the government. The second is forecasting future economic activities. The third is using government fiat to allocate goods and services.

It is the third version of planning which is emphasized in Professor Jones's comment and, I assume, was intended when Professor Scott talked about materials allocation in World War II.

For me, the first of these is relatively innocuous. The third is awful. Despite what Professor Jones says, it is unwise to use the government instead of the price system to determine who gets what.

The middle, the forecasting, is where I am most puzzled. I address this question to Professor Leontief. There are dozens of private consulting firms and thousands of companies engaged in forecasting. And since companies don't like to pay the price of bankruptcy for a mistake, they have a very strong self-interest in hiring the best forecasters to determine whatever economic trends are relevant to their business judgments. Now, why do you think that adding a government agency to make forecasts is going to improve the quality of economic forecasting in the country?

LEONTIEF: I am pleased you asked me the question. I think it is awful to leave the price system as it operates now to decide basic economic issues. The price system, after all, is not an invisible hand. It operates because ultimately there is information and analysis performed by people engaged in making market decisions.

I think that information which we have, to which we have access, is incredibly short of what information could be made available and used in order to see alternative possibilities.

You see, the price system is supposed to work automatically, but it makes errors and corrects them. At times it gives you a correct answer; sometimes it sends you on a wild goose chase.

POSNER: If I can follow that up, let's assume that your proposals, insofar as they relate to the gathering of information by the government, were implemented. Why would you think that the government would have any comparative advantage over Chase Econometric Associates, DRI, or any of those other private forecasters in constructing a model?

LEONTIEF: Look who is financing research in this country. I mean all research. Look at the research budget of this country. Something like 20 billion dollars. Most of the research in this country, certainly technical scientific research, is financed by the government.

A private corporation cannot justify to its stockholders the construction of a large model of the American economy. Rather than having twenty private corporations develop separate models of the American economy, it is much, much better to pool resources and then disclose the results to the public.

SCOTT: My sense is that DRI has, in fact, pooled the resources of hundreds of companies to make one gigantic model.

I agree, the fundamental question must be: What is the government's advantage in this field compared to those who can say what they think?

CHAPTER FOUR

The Limits of Numbers

EDITOR'S NOTE

Both Dr. Bock and Professor Weiss are eminent industrial organization economists who have spent most of their professional lives immersed in numbers. According to Professor Weiss, a major advantage of numbers is that they "can offer an objective test of hypotheses about what the world is like." Statistics has a powerful ability to sort out the effects of a variety of real world variables and speaks with more precision than English (e.g., compare the econometrician's 38.3 percent with the lawyer's word *substantial*).

But problems relating to assumption and classification, errors in data, "fishing," contamination, and a host of other concerns lead both principal researchers to warn against the uncritical acceptance of statistical studies. Both perceptively deal with the basic policy issue: In a world where policymakers are increasingly inundated with complex numerical formulations, how are they to judge the accuracy and reliability of what they receive? As Professor Arthur W. Murphy, who chaired the dialogue session on numbers, put it, "As a layman, I feel that I am too easily persuaded by statistical studies. Numbers seem tidier than words. When they do not wholly frighten me, they are very seductive."

In an important final section of his paper, Professor Weiss recommends a special "econometric witness" for judges and regulators who are not sufficiently trained to evaluate the statistical evidence presented to them. In Dr. Bock's paper, and in an extremely valuable dialogue, other significant suggestions are made. We are all coming to realize that the question of how to alleviate the strains imposed by controversies involving experts is among the paramount "legal-economic process" issues of our time. Possible solutions, it should be added, may have a profound impact on legal education.

THE LIMITS OF WORDS AND NUMBERS: BE CAREFUL WHEN WANDERING AT THE BRINK OF A PRECIPICE WITHOUT AN EXPERIENCED GUIDE

Betty Bock, *Director, Antitrust Research, The Conference Board*

To talk about the limits of numbers is like asking how close we can come to counting how many angels can dance on the point of a pin. For, regardless of how we formulate the meaning of the words *how many, angels, dance,* and *pinpoint,* we cannot answer the question unless we understand which of the words refer to real and which to imaginary entities and what operations will be performed by, and on, each. But because such understanding is often incomplete, this paper is designed to try to formulate some of the dimensions of our knowledge and our ignorance on these matters.

The subject of the limits of numbers has been regularly examined through the years in theoretical and in practical terms. But today, when numbers are increasingly available, we appear to have fewer and fewer qualms about what they mean. Let me present four deceptively simple propositions.

First, the act of enumeration implies a class of distinguishable members that are alike in the characteristics that make them members of the class.

Second, the words that accompany a count, or any set of numbers, should specify the characteristics of the class and, in the process, indicate how its members are alike.

Third, if differences among the members of a class make a difference to the uses to which the numbers concerning the class will be put, they must be specified.

Fourth, numbers that are part of a meaningful statement should be verifiable and should relate to external realities. When they do not, the probable dimensions of the shortfall should be stated.

These four propositions lead through the labyrinths of being and knowledge along a route marked by man's need to understand the meaning of word-number complexes, just as he needs to understand communication within a language and translation between languages. And, while the propositions sound obvious, failure to perceive and use them can result in nonsense.[1] These strictures are general in form. But from now on we will focus on the limits of numbers in understanding, assessing, and modifying competitive practices and competitive policy.

WORD-NUMBER COMPLEXES

A word is a label for a member, or set of members, of a class consisting of the real or imaginary or some blend of the two. Consider apples, unicorns, and beauty. By contrast, a number is not only a label for a member, or set of members, of a class consisting of the real or imaginary or some blend of the two, but also a signal of how many—or of more or fewer members—of a class or classes.

Generic words, as distinct from names of individuals, create an aura of sameness, as in one sense all apples are the same, but numbers are not similar to words in this respect. Indeed, "two" is two and "four" is four, but the terms are meaningless in the absence of related words or symbols: "four" what ("four apples" or "4*x*"). A word-number complex, therefore, takes on the "as-ifness" of the words themselves—even though the numbers retain an unchanging meaning.

This "as-ifness" stems from the fact that there are an infinite number of possible classes for products, space, and time and, therefore, an infinite number of ways of forming word-number complexes. Four elements are, however, critical to an understanding of such complexes: (1) we must understand what is distinct and what is not;[2] (2) we must understand the differences between what is comparable and not comparable;[3] (3) we must understand the degree to which words and numbers are congruent;[4] and (4) we must understand the relation of word-number complexes to the realities to which they refer.

If we say that Company X's profits fell by 20 percent last year, as compared with the year before, the sentence has one meaning if the company used the same materials and equipment, generated the same product-mix, distributed it in the same way, and followed the same

---

1. *Nonsense:* something written or said that is absurd or contrary to good sense; twaddle, drivel: a literary composition . . . marked by the use of words coined for the purpose that sometimes have an evocative character but no precise or generally accepted meaning (By permission. From *Webster's Third New International Dictionary* © 1976 by G. & C. Merriam Co., Publishers of the Merriam-Webster dictionaries.)

The fact is that a number is no better—and no worse—than the words in which it is embedded.

2. *Distinct:* characterized by qualities individualing. . . or not identical with another or others. *Id.*

3. *Comparable:* suitable for matching, coordinating, or contrasting. *Id.*

4. *Congruent:* coinciding, corresponding. *Id.*

accounting rules in each year; it means something different if there has been a significant change in any of these variables. And, the variables can contaminate the number.

Numbers as Translation

Let me note, however, that the limits of numbers in a word-number complex are equivalent to the limits of communication within a language and of translation from language to language. If, for example, I know what an apple is, I know what is not an apple. And if I know what an apple is, I know whether I have one apple or two. If I cannot make these distinctions, I have already reached the limits of numbers, communication, and translation.

To be able to count or measure, therefore, is to be able to find internal consistencies and boundaries and to have the ability to know the difference between them. But if the individuals, or institutions, that form a set have complex parts and the interrelations among the parts vary, there is no reason why a set of numbers appropriate for one purpose will be appropriate for another. What can happen to the meaning of numbers when the meaning of the words that specify them changes is elegantly illustrated by Professor Oskar Morgenstern in his book *On the Accuracy of Economic Observations.* Morgenstern relates that according to a census of January 1, 1910, Bulgaria had a total of 527,311 pigs; according to a census of January 1, 1920, the number was 1,089,699. But he who might conclude that the number of pigs in Bulgaria had more than doubled would be mistaken. The explanation is that in Bulgaria almost half the pigs are slaughtered before Christmas. After World War I, the country adopted the Gregorian calendar, abandoning the Julian calendar. It continued, however, to celebrate the religious holidays according to the older calendar, that is, with a delay of 13 days. Therefore, January 1, 1910, fell after Christmas, when the pigs were already slaughtered, and January 1, 1920, fell before Christmas, when the animals were still alive.[5]

The moral is clear. The number of pigs in Bulgaria on the same date in different years cannot be meaningfully compared if the calendar has changed. And the more possible meanings there are in the verbal framework for a set of numbers, the less sure one is of the meaning of the numbers.

These facts suggest that precise words, or due precautions and hesitations, or both, should be built into analyses of numbers. Our frequent failure to do this seems to be a function of our national positivism:[6] we want to be able to add—and we are more ready to teach

---

5. Oskar Morgenstern, *On the Accuracy of Economic Observations,* Princeton University Press, Princeton, N.J., 1973, pp. 46–47.

6. *Positivism:* a system of philosophy . . . which recognizes only positive facts and observable phenomena with the objective relations of these and the laws which determine them, abandoning all inquiry into causes or ultimate origins *(Webster's Third New International Dictionary).*

children how to add than to teach them to ask whether numbers can be added or what a particular sum means. We are a people who tend to believe that what appears quantifiable is factual—while that which can be described only in words is more uncertain and controversial!

Consider the following example of quantification, however. At a hearing of the Senate Subcommittee on Antitrust and Monopoly in 1959, the subcommittee's chief economist stated that the price druggists paid for Prednisolone was 1,118 times its cost: what he meant was that the price was over 1,000 times the bare production cost. Not included were general business expenses, such as selling and distribution costs, research, plant maintenance and depreciation, taxes, and so forth.[7]

What does this type of misfit between numbers, words, and the underlying fact matrix to which they refer mean when we consider competitive practices and competitive processes in a framework of law?

Internal and External Limits

A statute begins as a set of words that includes statements of purpose, prohibitions or mandates, procedures for determining whether violations have occurred, and the remedies and/or penalties. The words of a law, therefore, present a self-limiting framework within which charges, facts, and inferences are tested in particular cases. Economics knows no such limits.

In the early 1930s, we were taught that economics was a science dealing with the allocation of scarce resources to alternative ends—with a central focus on the economics of the firm operating in the private sector.[8] This is what is now called *microeconomics.* What is today called *macroeconomics* was just beginning.

Today, however, microeconomics deals not only with the firm, but with markets or industries as well as with acts of government. We have a microeconomics of health delivery, of education, of welfare, of urban problems, and of other crisscrossing systems in which government and private funding is mingled in an attempt to meet public needs.

The passage of the years has not, however, changed our desire to quantify ends and alternative means of attaining them. But the opportunity-costs of private, government, or combined functions are not necessarily quantifiable, because the alternatives given up in a regressive chain are themselves not fully identifiable and become quantifiable only by inference.

The problem here is typical of the limits of numbers. The greater the number of words required to explain a number, the more the words will blur the number. But the more a number requires words to explain it,

---

7. *Administered Prices in the Drug Industry (Corticosteroids),* Hearings before the Subcommittee on Antitrust and Monopoly of the Senate Committee on the Judiciary, 86th Cong., 1st Sess., Part 14, 1960, pp. 7856–7863.

8. Lionel Robbins, *An Essay on the Nature and Significance of Economic Science,* Macmillan, New York, 1952, p. 16.

the more meaningless it will be without the words. The question then arises as to whether it is possible to generalize the scope of, and constraints on, numbers representing corporate structure or conduct in a form that permits meaningful generalizations about the relations among companies, markets, and industries.

To begin to resolve this issue, it may be helpful to consider certain of the limits on the relations between naked numbers and their clothing. Some of the limits appear as internal and others as external to what is being enumerated. The internal limits appear in standard errors and language jumbles; the external limits, in word-oriented concepts surrounding numbers. These external limits include:

1. Word-number complexes which may be correct in themselves, but irrelevant to the purpose for which they are used
2. Word-number complexes which may be correct and relevant to the purpose for which they are designed, but are not valid when used in other ways
3. Word-number complexes where numbers are given more weight than their make-up warrants
4. Word-number complexes where there has been a failure to clarify how the data were compiled and how their meaning has been affected by the original questions asked and answered, as well as how the answers were treated for compilation purposes

How, for example, did each respondent identify and organize the data he reported? Were reporting inconsistencies checked with respondents? How were the reported figures aggregated? How were tabulation titles and designations of stubs and column heads selected—and were the words designed to apply literally to each item in a given tabulation? If not, do footnotes, or other appended materials, indicate the trustworthiness of each data item? Do they destroy the summary nature of the data?

Data and Information Problems

Data may be thought of as connected—or disconnected—words, numbers, or word-number complexes. Information, by contrast, is meaningful data. The distinction is not, however, always clear in research focusing on oligopoly, concentration, large companies, market structure, prices, profits, or capital expenditures. We have, however, already come far enough to suggest that there are a variety of reasons for reading statistical statements concerning companies or groups of companies (e.g., enterprise, product, or industry statistics) not as if they were statements of what "is," but as if they were statements whose accuracy depends on the degree to which problems such as the following have been solved.

CATEGORY HETEROGENEITY

Categories for which data are available are often not markets, but product-conglomerates. The Standard Industrial Classification (SIC) category 3272 (concrete products, except block and brick), for example, includes bathtubs, garbage boxes, manhole covers, Spanish floor tile, tombstones, and other objects whose only common denominator is that they are made of concrete.[9] A user of data for such a category will, of course, learn nothing about the bathtub, as distinct from the tombstone, business—and will have only the most general information for the compound category that includes all concrete products, except block and brick.

MEASURES

What does a unit of measurement add to—or subtract from—a word-number complex? A company's market share in dollars will normally differ from its share in units sold. If a company sells a higher-priced product than its competitors, its share of the market in dollars will be higher than in units; if it sells a lower-priced product than its competitors, its unit-share will be higher than its dollar-share. And related differences will occur if one compares capacity-shares with production-shares, sales-shares with shipments-plus-transfers-shares, manufacturers' sales-price-shares with retailers' sales-price-shares, and so on.

One commonly used measure of the combined shares of the first four companies in an SIC category is the *value of shipments* concentration ratio. Consider, however, how value of shipments figures are made up. Each year the Bureau of the Census asks manufacturing establishments to report dollar value of shipments, with shipments defined as value of shipments plus transfers. But what are transfers? They represent the value of goods transferred from one establishment of a company to another.[10]

A company could, for internal management purposes, derive such a figure in many ways: it might calculate transfers as direct—or indirect-plus-allocated—costs to the unit *from* which a product is transferred (with costs derived in a range of ways); or it might calculate transfers as a figure at which the transferred product might have sold on the market—if outside buyers were available; or it might calculate transfers as a figure that includes direct—or indirect-plus-allocated—costs plus a profit to the initiating unit.

The Bureau of the Census instructions ask that transfers be reported

---

9. Statistical Policy Division, *Standard Industrial Classification Manual 1972*, Office of Management and Budget, Statistical Policy Division, 1972.

10. U.S. Bureau of the Census, *1972 Census of Manufactures*, vol. VI, Subject and Special Report Series, Washington, D.C., p. 1–21.

at "full economic value,"[11] but what is "full economic value" if a product is not sold on the market, is sold only rarely, or is transferred on terms or at dates that have no relation to outside transactions?

Companies which must report transfers as part of their shipments will, therefore, find it necessary to make judgments that will, in the end, determine the aggregated value-of-shipments plus transfers figures the Bureau of the Census will publish, but no one reading the resulting product or industry value of shipments figures for a category will be able to tell what part of different shipments figures represent transfers or how the transfers were valued by different reporting establishments.

MULTICATEGORY REPORTING UNITS

Now, take the problem that occurs whenever an establishment or other reporting unit makes products classified in two or more categories. Suppose some establishments that make lead pencils, classified in census category SIC 3952 (lead pencils, crayons, and artists' materials), specialize, while others make other products as well. Some may make other products classified in the same SIC category. Others may make products substitutable for pencils, but not classified in the same category (e.g., ball-point pens). Others may make a range of products that include lead pencils, cuckoo clocks, or dollhouses.

If lead pencils account for the largest part of the value of shipments and transfers of an establishment, all products will be classified in the lead pencils, crayons, and artists' materials industry. The published data for this industry will, therefore, include differing proportions of data for ball-point pens, cuckoo clocks, and dollhouses. And, of course, the data for the categories to which these products belong will be understated. What we can learn from published figures on the value of shipments and transfers—or value added by manufacture, employment, or new capital expenditures—in the lead pencils, crayons, and artists' materials industry will, therefore, be blurred.

The Bureau of the Census publishes figures that show how much of the value of shipments-and-transfers figure for the lead pencils, crayons, and artists' materials industry represents shipments of other products and by how much the value of shipments figures for the ball-point pens, cuckoo clocks, and dollhouses categories are understated. But no such figures are available for other data that will be credited to the lead pencils, crayons, and artists' materials industry (e.g., value added by manufacture, employment, new capital expenditures, and so forth).

But unless the overstatement and understatement for value added, employment, new capital expenditures, and so forth in the pencils, crayons, and artists' materials industry are proportional to the overstatement and understatement for value of shipments and transfers, we

11. Ibid.

have no way of knowing what part of these other figures credited to the pencils, crayons, and artists' materials industry should not be—or the extent to which the value added, number of employees, and new capital expenditures for the dollhouses and cuckoo clocks categories are understated. These difficulties may not be serious if the relationships among the figures remain alike through the years, but this is one of the things we want to determine when we use the statistical data.[12]

RATIO CONSISTENCY

A ratio should not be read literally if the numerator does not match the denominator. A standard first-four-company concentration ratio is peculiarly vulnerable here. If, for example, the plants of the largest companies in an industry are more diversified than the average for all plants, the numerator of the concentration ratio will be overstated in comparison with the denominator, and concentration will appear to be higher than it is. Similar mirages occur if the largest companies sell products in higher price-lines than the average for an industry, or if the largest companies are more integrated or account for more exports than the average for the industry as a whole. These propositions are also true in reverse—but their likelihood is low.

GUILT-BY-ASSOCIATION

Another problem implicit in any ratio, but of serious significance in the case of the four-largest-company concentration ratio, is the assumption that the numerator represents like entities (e.g., that the four largest

---

12. Consider the following example: The *Census of Manufactures* shows that in 1972 the value of shipments of alkalies and chlorine (SIC 2812) amounted to $823 million. What users of the data might fail to note—although the Bureau of the Census publishes appropriate information—is that 35 percent of the $823 million figure represents shipments of products other than alkalies and chlorine, while 35 percent of all shipments of alkalies and chlorine ($806 million) are not accounted for in the $823 million figure.

Thus, $280 million worth of shipments of alkalies and chlorine are not accounted for in the $823 million figure, but are shipped by establishments classified in other industries: industrial inorganic chemicals, not elsewhere classified (SIC 2849) accounted for $31 million of shipments of alkalies and chlorine; industrial organic chemicals not elsewhere classified (SIC 2869), for $225 million of shipments; and the remaining $24 million of shipments of alkalies and chlorine were accounted for by other industries (U.S. Bureau of the Census, *1972 Census of Manufactures,* vol. II, pt. 2, Industry Statistics, pp. 28A-13, 28A-14).

Meanwhile, the Bureau of the Census also reported the number of companies in the alkalies and chlorine industry as 28 and the first-four-company concentration ratio as 72. But, these numbers should obviously be read as if companies in the alkalies and chlorine industry "might approximate" 28, and the first-four-company concentration ratio "might approximate" 72. In fact, more than 28 companies must be making alkalies and chlorine products and the four so-called first-four companies may not all be among the four companies who, in fact, account for the largest shipments of alkalies and chlorine; see *1972 Census of Manufactures,* Special Report Series, Concentration Ratios in Manufacturing, MC72 (SR)-2, table 5.

companies in an industry or product group have mutual interests that reduce or suppress competition). But this will not be the case unless all four companies are in a similar competitive position. The assumption will not normally hold, for example, if the first company has, let us say, four times the market share or reserves of the second; nor is it likely to hold if different companies among the first four perceive their interests differently.

"LARGE-NUMBERS" AND INDEPENDENT VARIABLES

Whenever relatively small samples of industries are examined and different series of data correlated, the observer is making the assumption that the data represent a large number of observations; that the variables are independent; and that the data are representative of those for other industries that are not examined. But a concentration ratio is in most cases based on a relatively limited number of observations, as are comparisons of ratios for different industries.[13] Furthermore, when one is viewing high concentration, one may well also be viewing not an independent variable, but high productivity—or the share of the top companies in a small, or a new, or a dying industry. One must find out.

Problems such as these underlie the fact that the limits of numbers are equivalent to the limits of the words in which they are embedded—these limits are, in turn, a function of the fit of the concepts and the operations which produce the numbers. Beyond these limits lies jargon. And number jargon is no less jargon than word jargon.[14]

Grammatical Continuity and Number Nonsense

What these problems mean is that tabulations, or other summaries of quantified data, and the inferences to be drawn from them can be no more accurate or meaningful than the language that specifies the raw data and the methods by which they are put together. A set of numbers scattered over a page may make an interesting exercise in nonobjective art. But that is all. Indeed, naked numbers have no more explicit meaning than a Rorschach.

It is, unfortunately, all too easy to produce grammatical word-number sentences that are ambiguous or meaningless. Three common rigidities in understanding contribute to this autistic mode of expression:[15] (1) frozen gestalts—or stereotyped and imprecise understanding of how data are made up; (2) lack of specific awareness—or belief that a whole

---

13. The median number of companies in any four-digit census category in 1972 (omitting the not elsewhere classified and miscellaneous categories) was 215.

14. *Jargon:* confused unintelligible language; gibberish. *(Webster's Third New International Dictionary.)*

15. *Autistic:* absorption in need-satisfying or wish-fulfilling fantasy as a mechanism of escape from reality. *Id.*

has no significant variations in its parts; and (3) misplaced conviction of concreteness—or belief that numbers have real counterparts when they do not.

Once we understand that word-number complexes can be misleading and/or wrong, we should review our economic canon under lenses that give appropriate perspective to the fact that the validity of a number begins with an observer. And, if one wants to form word-number complexes for a set of companies, markets, or industries, one should be examining whether the managements and organizations of the companies are sufficiently similar to make comparisons and aggregations appropriate.

Symmetrical comparisons among major companies are normally not possible within a simplified statistical framework, because similarities or differences are a function of corporate management, corporate organization, and corporate processes. At most, we can box up companies with respect to aspects of their similarities and differences—and try to determine the degree to which the boxes can be used to produce information we did not have before we went through the classification process.

Such problems are, however, not peculiar to enterprise analysis, but are indigenous to studies of nonhomogeneous individuals. This fact suggests that broad generalizations based on bare numbers about enterprises—or on ratios, correlations, or regressions derived from them—should be avoided, or formulated with perceptive restraint.

CONSISTENCY AND "NOISE" IN STANDARD COMPANY DATA

The forms of internal information developed within a company include what the company is required to report to the outside world, as well as its internal records and what its managers carry around in their heads. But internal information, whatever its detail, will not represent facets of an organization's processes that cannot be formulated in traditional word, or word-number, terms. Furthermore, data that may be set up by a company for its own purposes and labeled as costs, revenues, and profits for individual categories of activity are not necessarily definitive figures, but hypothetical numbers generated in terms of the company's management decisions.

If a government agency with appropriate powers wants such internal company information, its staff may forget that the material has gaps and idiosyncrasies stemming from specific corporate purposes and priorities. And there is no reason to believe that if an agency seeks to collect a consistent body of information from different companies the data will exist—or, if they do exist—that they will be meaningful and/or comparable from one company to another. Thus, before concluding that yet unreported data for a given company exists and will match verbally related data for other companies, an investigator should know whether it is possible for a company to keep elements of data about itself in such minuscule—and yet identifiable—form that they can be reoriented meaningfully in any required pattern.

The mere formulation of this constraint raises key issues concerning public information programs. First, what are the relations between a perceived "need" for information and the "feasibility" of gathering information that will meet the need within reasonable limits of accuracy, reliability, and relevance? Second, have corporate input problems been recognized and provided for? What are the distinctions between corporate information that can be quantified or verbalized and information that cannot? Third, have compilation and output problems been analyzed and provided for? Under what conditions will an aggregation of corporate data result in reliable information?

It is puzzling to realize that we understand that each human being is unique and differs from every other, no matter how carefully we classify him for specific purposes. We have, however, developed blind spots about the individuality of corporations and tend to see them solely as members of homogeneous classes—of big companies, of power hierarchies, of conglomerates, of oil companies, or of some other category. In the process, we tend to forget that information concerning a corporation begins with the corporation and its method of seeing itself.

This is not to say that corporations cannot be compared, but rather, that if the individual aspects of different corporate entities are not taken into account, the observer may well be perceiving "noise," and if he acts on the basis of such noise, he may destroy what he intends to accomplish.

A high concentration ratio is, for example, often thought of as an automatic indicator of a lack of competition and an excess of market power. Such data, however, tell little about the actual "power" of the different companies operating in a given industry or market. This is so because the theory and the basic statistics have been developed for different purposes. The theory has grown up through economic model building, industry studies, and a series of judicial decisions in specific antitrust cases. Meanwhile, various sets of statistics have been built up in terms of categories and numbers developed for a general range of purposes—and not specifically designed to reflect competition as such. Two sets of data—one on aggregate concentration and one on industry concentration—illustrate what questions such data can answer and the varying ways in which the answers can be read.

Aggregate Concentration Examples

Aggregate concentration is a label for a ratio representing the combined share of the economic activity of a major segment of the economy accounted for by a limited, but relatively substantial, number of companies. The ratio can be put together in several ways. One way is exemplified by data on the share of value added by manufacture accounted for by the 50, 100, or 200 largest manufacturing companies. Another appears in data on the share of the assets of all industrial, or in some cases, all manufacturing corporations accounted for by the total assets of the 50, 100, or 200 largest such corporations. What do such figures show?

VALUE ADDED BY MANUFACTURE

The 50 largest manufacturing companies in terms of value added by manufacture increased their share of all value added by manufacture by 8 percentage points between 1947 and 1963—and not at all between 1963 and 1972. A similar pattern holds for the 100 largest manufacturing companies, with no change in shares between 1963 and 1972. By contrast, the 200 largest companies increased their combined share of value added by manufacture by 2 percentage points between 1963 and 1972. This 2-percentage-point gain in the share of the 200 largest is, however, accounted for by the companies ranking from 101 to 200—not by the 50 or the 100 largest companies. Nor are the "largest" companies identical year in and year out. Indeed, of the 50 companies that were the largest in value added in 1972, only 25 were in that size class in 1947—for a turnover of 50 percent in the quarter-of-a-century period.[16]

ASSETS

Meanwhile, the 50 largest manufacturing corporations in terms of assets increased their share of the total assets of all manufacturing corporations by 6 percentage points between 1947 and 1963—and not at all between 1963 and 1972. The 100 largest increased their share of all manufacturing assets by 8 percentage points between 1947 and 1963—and by 2 percentage points between 1963 and 1972. The 200 largest increased their share of all manufacturing assets by 11 percentage points between 1947 and 1963—and by 4 percentage points between 1963 and 1972.[17] However, these figures do not mean what they appear to mean. The fact is that between 1947 and 1972, there was a turnover of one-third in the corporations making up the 200 largest in terms of assets. And, if one focuses separately on the 128 corporations that were among the 200 largest both in 1947 and 1972 and on the remaining 72 corporations, one finds that after 1963 the older corporations increased their share of the assets of all manufacturing corporations by only 0.01 percentage point, while the entrant corporations increased their share by 0.74 percentage points.[18]

---

16. Betty Bock, "New Numbers on Concentration: Fears and Facts," *The Conference Board Record,* vol. 13, no. 3, March 1976, p. 19.

17. Betty Bock, "Is Concentration Rising? Penetrating the Mazes of Numbers," *The Conference Board Record,* vol. 13, no. 9, Sept. 1976, p. 47.

18. Ibid.

Industry Concentration Examples

Now, let us ask a series of related questions about industry concentration—meaning, for present purposes, the share of the first four companies in various SIC industries in terms of value of shipments and transfers. If one focuses on the 146 manufacturing industries that were definitionally comparable in 1947 and 1972, one finds that 30 percent had concentration ratios of 50 percent or more in 1947, while 32 percent had ratios in this range in 1972. Looked at in this way, industry concentration rose over the 25-year period. But, if one focuses on all 439 manufacturing industry categories for which concentration data exist both for 1947 and for 1972, 33 percent had concentration ratios of 50 percent or more in 1947, while 27 percent had ratios in this range in 1972. Looked at in this way, industry concentration fell over the 25-year period.[19]

For additional insight into the nature of concentration at the top end of the range, the 20 industries with the highest value of shipments concentration ratios in 1972 were examined. Only seven of these industries were among the top 20 in terms of concentration in 1947—for a turnover of 65 percent in the industries in this highest concentration bracket. And, conversely, if one examines the 20 industries ranking highest in value of shipments concentration ratios in 1947, one finds that only seven were still among the top 20 in 1972; six ranked below the top 20; and seven had undergone major changes in definition so that comparisons for these industries for the period from 1947 to 1972 are not possible.[20]

CONSISTENCY AND "NOISE" IN COMPETITIVE ANALYSIS

With so many changes, what then is an industry or a market? This issue has been critical to major antitrust cases ever since the *Alcoa* decision of 1945. In that case, the Court of Appeal's specifications for how the market should be defined became the framework for its finding that Alcoa accounted for 90 percent of aluminum sales, and through its dominant market position, its pricing, its holdings of bauxite, and its advance expansions had monopolized the primary aluminum market.[21]

Although the court's purpose in *Alcoa*—as well as the government's purpose in later monopoly and merger cases—appears to have been to formulate a concept that would avoid a "bigness-as-such" attack on major corporations, later arguments under section 2 of the Sherman Act (and section 7 of the Clayton Act) have tended to revolve around market-boundary issues that sound not unlike arguments about how many angels can dance on the point of a pin. What has happened?

---

19. Betty Bock, "New Numbers on Concentration," p. 20.

20. Betty Bock, "Is Concentration Rising?" p. 50.

21. United States v. Aluminum Company of America, 148 F.2d 416 (2d Cir. 1945).

Two Case Examples

Rather than go back over the older and well-anointed cases, I propose to look at two recent ones to see how consideration of market definitions and competitive strategies have been interacting.

READY-TO-EAT CEREAL

In April 1972, the Federal Trade Commission brought a novel complaint, charging that four major companies—Kellogg Co., General Mills, Inc., General Foods Corp., and the Quaker Oats Co.—together accounted for some 90 percent of sales of ready-to-eat (RTE) cereals and that they had engaged in practices designed to retain a "shared monopoly" at the expense of existing and potential competitors.[22] Since this case is still before the FTC Administrative Law Judge, we will not examine the issues in depth. It is not too soon, however, to note in simplified form two pillars of the FTC complaint counsel's position. In a brief presented to the Administrative Law Judge, counsel supporting the complaint argued that all RTE cereals are part of a single market—marked by positive cross-elasticity of demand and price-sensitivity among RTE cereal products. Then, at a later point, he argued that the mutual price-sensitivity of RTE cereals is equivalent to single-company-monopoly pricing.[23]

Consider what FTC counsel said: first, the relevant market is defined as ready-to-eat cereals, because there is high price-sensitivity among such cereals; and, second, a failure of competition among the cereal companies is found because there is high price-sensitivity among cereals. This would mean, if correct, that the indicia of a market are the indicia of a lack of competition.

TIRES

By contrast to the position taken by the FTC complaint counsel in the RTE cereal case, the limits of numbers representing market shares are nowhere acknowledged more clearly than in the stipulation filed by the Antitrust Division of the Department of Justice in March 1976 dismissing the tire cases.[24]

In August 1973, the Department had filed complaints charging that Goodyear Tire and Rubber Co. and Firestone Tire and Rubber Co. had

22. *In the matter of Kellogg Co., et al.* (complaint, Dkt. 8883, April 26, 1972) 3 C.C.H. Trade Reg. Rep. (Transfer Binder 1970–73) ¶ 19,898.

23. *In the matter of Kellogg, et al.*, FTC Dkt. 8883, FTC Complaint Counsel's Trial Brief presented to the Administrative Law Judge, Feb. 1976.

24. United States v. Goodyear Tire and Rubber Co., United States v. Firestone Tire and Rubber Co. (ND Ohio March 2, 1976) 5 C.C.H. Trade Reg. Rep. ¶ 50,259. *Tire Company Cases—U.S. Information Memorandum.*

violated section 2 of the Sherman Act because they were in a monopolistic position and had been cutting the price of replacement tires in order to drive smaller tire manufacturers out of business. Impetus for the complaints appears to have come from the oligopolistic structure of the industry and the Antitrust Division's belief that it could show that Goodyear and Firestone had used their market power to consolidate and tighten their dominance in the industry.

Upon examination of the evidence, however, the Antitrust Division found that the price cuts were commercially justified. Although natural rubber prices and labor costs had been rising, the complaint had failed to take account of increases in the manufacturing productivity of the two companies or of the significance of the industry's distribution structure as a check on the market power that the Antitrust Division had associated with high levels of concentration.

The major oil companies—and chain stores, such as Sears and Montgomery Ward—significantly limited the market power of the major tire manufacturers and had tended to keep tire prices nearer competitive levels than might have been expected. Furthermore, there was great diversity in retail channels of distribution which had generated a discount structure that facilitated price cutting. Meanwhile, although tire sales had been strong in the aggregate during the late 1950s, there had been a change in purchasing mix as buyers tended to buy fewer premium and first-line tires for replacement purposes. Both Goodyear and Firestone were also facing strong competition from Michelin. And, finally, at no time were Goodyear's or Firestone's prices below cost.

The Antitrust Division, therefore, acknowledged that the companies' price cuts had been designed as a defense against losing markets. And, although the lower prices had contributed to the demise of some smaller tire manufacturers, this was not, said Assistant Attorney General Kauper, sufficient ground for establishing monopolization under section 2 of the Sherman Act.

This position suggests that a bare concentration or market-share figure tells nothing, since to have called for divestiture on those facts alone would, said the Assistant Attorney General, have discouraged price competition, and if such enforcement rules were to become precedents, they would be likely to reduce competition in precisely the industries where competition was most strongly needed.

A Fundamental Conundrum

Regardless of the future outcome in RTE cereals or the actual outcome in tires, a fundamental problem remains unchanged. We fear what we perceive as power. We want to be able to identify power automatically. We want a template for identifying anticompetitive situations. But use of a template assumes that significant and remediable losses of competition come in recognizable patterns and that the major corporations operating in such patterns can be classified, measured, and eventually cut into new, neat, viable, and more competitive parts. In the face of so drastic an assumption, it may be worthwhile to reexamine a basic conundrum that has generated major competitive paradoxes.

Take, for example, the problem of an oligopolistic market, or a market in which there are few sellers. Obviously, a determination of whether there are few sellers depends on the definition of the market. But the definition of the market depends on what companies are considered sellers. We have here a merry-go-round that is not a form of recreation for children. Many of us were brought up to believe that an oligopoly is anticompetitive; that the major companies operating in an oligopolistic market have market power; and that individual oligopolists do not engage in independent and competitive action for fear they will lose their gains to competitors (otherwise called *implicit collaborators*).

Heads or Tails?

As one looks at the fundamental oligopoly theorem, one cannot escape asking whether it may not often operate to support the less competitive, while eroding the capabilities of the more competitive—in the name of competition. The opportunity for such a reversal is implicit both in the theory of oligopoly and in the double-meaning word-number concepts that have become a part of industrial organization and antitrust case analysis. And, in consequence of these dualities, we are beginning to see proposals for a public policy designed to scale down major companies on the basis of relatively simple numbers.

No such policy would be responsible, however, if it did not also focus on the consequences of such rescaling. But understanding of consequences requires study of costs and intermediate and final needs. Such studies cannot be turned out automatically, but must take account of specific product-service processes—while avoiding word-number concepts with conflicting internal meanings.

If we do not seek to realign such concepts, we are in danger of substituting "due faith" for "due process"—by forgetting that word-number concepts can have opposite meanings suggesting opposite applications, depending on the fact-complexes to which the words and numbers refer. For example:

1. A high market share can mean that a company has engaged in monopolistic practices; or it can mean that the market has been defined artificially and that a company with an apparently high share has no power to control entry or prices. Or, it can mean that a company has grown to its present position through high efficiency, responsiveness to customer needs, and perceptive planning and innovation in a changing world.

2. A high concentration ratio can mean that an industry or market is being controlled by its members in ways that permit them to avoid

price competition and keep potential entrants out. Or, it can mean that an industry or a market is small compared to the capital and/or the technology required to produce the products that define it. Or, it can mean that one of the top companies has a high market share, while all others are dwarfs.

3. Fewness of companies in a market can be an indicator that these companies are engaged in collusion and/or predatory acts that prevent other companies from growing or entering the market. Or, it can indicate that the market is "small" in the sense that relatively few suppliers can support total demand; or that capital costs are so high and/or technology demands so stringent that few companies are able and willing to risk them.
4. Now, consider price cutting. If a seller reduces his prices, is he competing or attempting to drive competitors out of business? If he cuts in one market or for one set of customers only, is he meeting competition or seeking anticompetitive advantages? If he cuts below average, but not below marginal, cost, is he engaging in sophisticated or excessive competition—in the short or in the long run?
5. What of markets where exit rates are high? Has excess competition nullified the competitive future of weaker members of such markets? Or, are companies going out of these markets because they can invest their money in more productive ways? Or, are companies disappearing because demand has fallen? Or, has modernization by competitors outstripped the ability of some companies to compete?
6. Consider markets with low entrance rates. Does this mean that the companies already in the market are behaving in an anticompetitive fashion, or is it simply that essential resources are scarce, capital and/or technology requirements high, foreign competition severe, or demand so narrow that a few companies can supply the market?
7. What are we to say of the age of an industry or a market? Suppose that a market is new because a product has just been invented. Is fewness of companies per se anticompetitive? Suppose a market is so old and battered (e.g., handkerchiefs) that it does not pay many companies to stay in it. Are the companies who continue to make handkerchiefs automatically behaving in an anticompetitive fashion because other companies stop making handkerchiefs?
8. What of advertising? There is a large literature suggesting that advertising is used by major producers of consumer products to prevent competitors from growing or from coming into a market. Others assert that advertising is a method through which a company obtains markets large enough to produce and sell at lower unit costs and prices than it otherwise could.
9. What of R&D? Are large expenditures which may or may not pay off over unforseeable periods competitive or anticompetitive?
10. Finally, what of profits? For classical economics, where no firm is any bigger than any other, where each firm produces only homogeneous products, where each product is made by many firms, where there is

instant knowledge by all firms concerning the costs and prices of transactions, and where capital and workers drain immediately from areas of low to areas of high return, profits will tend toward zero. But, in the real world, where companies produce complex and highly differentiated products, capital is fixed and employees do not move easily, and there is no instantaneous communication of costs or prices, there is no reason to conclude that profits should always tend toward zero or that there should not be a differential return to differential-risk, differential-uncertainty, or differential-efficiency.

NINE QUESTIONS AND NINE ANSWERS

We are now ready to formulate experimental answers to the nine questions that were posed as the starting point of our observations on the limits of numbers. Although the answers are phrased in positive tones, their more tentative overtones appear in the references to word-number complexes and fact matrixes which some will read as sober correlates of the worlds of concepts and realities—and others will read as childlike nonsense. There is far more to be said here than is said—and yet, too much is said. Paradoxes lie everywhere—and two grow up for each one cut down. But, for what they may be worth, here are the nine questions with nine answers:

1. What standard should be used to judge the accuracy and reliability of numbers? The accuracy and reliability of a word-number complex is a direct function of the specificity with which the fact matrix to which the numbers refer is detailed, the degree to which the numbers relate consistently to the fact matrix, the methods by which changes in the matrix can be traced and formulated, and the verifiability of the word-number complex in the framework in which it is used.

2. What are the distinctions between corporate information that can be quantified and information that cannot? The complexity of an economic institution, like that of a human being, cannot be fully represented in a word-number complex. Similar facets of different institutions may be quantifiable, depending on the extent to which each facet is separate from, or intricately related to, other facets of the same institution. The more complex the interrelations within the same institution, the less definitive will be comparisons among the facets of different institutions.

3. What tends to be lost in numerical formulations? Individual items pertaining to individual institutions are, by definition, lost when individual elements are classified and enumerated.

4. Can constraints on the use of numbers to explain ongoing processes be generalized? The answer here is yes—and no. Numbers should correspond to specific items or to identifiable elements of an ongoing operation, and it must be possible to specify when and how categories and operations change. If this is not possible, we may find ourselves wandering at the brink of a precipice, but we will never know it.

5. Should standards vary with the purposes for which information is sought? Yes.

6. What alternatives are available when numbers do not reflect corporate processes? One should be prepared to use words to describe corporate operations and corporate decision making and should be willing to face the problem of translation and comparability squarely. One should recognize and make clear that value judgments are implicit in all qualitative statements.

7. What are the limits of verbal formulations? A verbal formulation can be objective only if there is a clear and distinguishable referent for each word. Such situations are not so common as is often supposed, and this is why different observers tend to use different statements in describing—and come to different conclusions in evaluating—corporate governance and operations and government policy. In the end, the limits of verbal formulation are set by the fact that one cannot be assured that different observers will form the same images—let alone come to the same conclusions. This is the human condition.

8. What strains are imposed on the judicial and administrative process by controversies concerning quantified information or verbal formulations? Ultimately, judges and administrators must decide among conflicting perceptions, inferences, and recommendations. But, since the scope of their responsibilities cannot be fully specified, they must try to foresee not only the direct and intended, but also the indirect—and unintended—effects of given decisions. The strains imposed by these needs on the judicial and administrative process are severe, are not always understood, and can, if not handled perceptively, erode our system of freedom under law. In the end, however, we must reach conclusions—in spite of and in the midst of—known and unknown uncertainty.

9. What are the problems in alleviating these strains? I believe that these strains cannot be reduced toward zero. They can only be faced and described—situation by situation. The measure of numbers in an economic setting is man. Smallness and bigness, good and bad, freedom and control are functions of what one is and what one is studying. They do not have definable meanings, in and of themselves.

WORKING WITH NUMBERS: THE GREAT ADVANTAGES AND THE PROBLEMS TO BE CURED

Leonard W. Weiss *Chief Economist, Senate Government Operations Committee, Professor of Economics, University of Wisconsin*

The topic assigned me is the limits of numbers. Limitations certainly exist. Still, numbers have very great advantages, and I propose to cite those before pointing out the difficulties.

THE ADVANTAGES OF NUMBERS

An Objective Standard

A major advantage of numbers, when they are available, is that they can offer an objective test of hypotheses about what the world is like. The statistician can take available data, compute the average relationships shown in them, and ask the concrete question, "Could this relationship occur by pure chance as often as one time in twenty if there were no such underlying relationship in the world as a whole?" This criterion is an objective one and can offer convincing evidence to observers of every stripe.

This standard is not the only one. A statistically significant estimated relationship can still be unimportant, but statistics can also answer the question of importance. It is the easiest thing to find the range of observation of the independent variable and compute the difference it can make for the dependent variable.[1] The result is a number that a judge with little statistical sophistication can evaluate.

The alternatives highlight the advantages of the statistical approach. The main alternative today is theory. You make some assumptions—always simplifications of real-world conditions—and then try to derive

1. A dependent variable is one that is being explained. An independent variable is one that is used to partially explain a dependent variable.

from those assumptions their logical implications about the question at hand. The theories can be checked for internal consistency, but this is only occasionally a problem. The more realistic difficulty is that a wide range of initial assumptions can be made, and the implications of them are bound to differ. It is not always clear which set of assumptions and, therefore, which conclusions are most appropriate. What follows if firms are assumed to maximize profits in a certain and static world (by far the most common assumptions) may not follow if the assumptions are that firms make decisions to maximize the utility of managers (where size or growth, managerial income, leisure, reputation, and safety count along with profits), or where the firm faces uncertainty, or where the firm anticipates and continually adjusts, or all three. Given a set of alternative theoretical systems with correspondingly diverse predictions, theory leads us directly back to numbers. In fact, that is where theory ought to lead us generally, even if there is no conflict and the theory has no internal inconsistencies or contradicting predictions. Pure theory yields only hypotheses to be tested.

Real-world experience is subject to a wide range of influences, and the effect predicted by theory may be swamped by the others or may even be completely wrong. A nice example is the much-studied Averch Johnson effect. There must be a hundred theoretical articles written about it, but so far the empirical evidence has been meager—not in the same ball park with the empirical evidence supporting some positive effect for concentration on profits. If I were a regulator, I would *not* let the Averch Johnson hypothesis much influence my decisions about utility rates (*certainly* not the prediction that tighter regulation leads to greater distortions); I would, however, base merger policy on a belief that greater concentration is associated with more market power—even though I cannot say for sure which of many competing theories in that area is most nearly correct.

Another problem with theory is that it almost always offers predictions based on the assumption that all other things are constant. An increase in price leads unequivocally to a decrease in quantity consumed *if* incomes, tastes, and prices of other goods do not change. But in real life, incomes, tastes, and the prices of other goods always change, and so the prediction about the real world is not a bit "unequivocal." The correct statement is that quantity will change at a certain rate with price and a certain other rate with income and yet another rate with other prices and will change in other ways with temperature, age distribution of the population, and so forth. That leads back to numbers again. There is no way that theory will separate those many effects. In the real world, there is almost always more than one important influence at work on the variables we want to know about, and that means that an accurate application of even an unquestioned theoretical framework *must* rely on the numbers thrown up by experience.

An alternative approach is the old verbal-historical one. You immersed yourself in the data for a couple of years, went into a trance, and came up with an interpretation. You "proved" points with multiple examples. If you did a thorough job with the data and were an articulate writer, you had a good chance of carrying the day, though it was very likely that in another generation an equally articulate scholar who bathed in the same data would produce an equally convincing but different interpretation. We still do some of this and are subject to risks accordingly.

At its best, this approach amounts to a crude way of doing statistical studies in your head, but for all but the smartest of us, they are simply two variable studies, since few are wise enough to perceive clearly the effects of more than one or two simultaneous influences intuitively. E. S. Mason started the field of industrial organization in this direction in the late thirties, when he induced the profession to undertake 20 years of painstaking industry studies. The result was lots of rich detail and, happily, one valuable generalization due to the brilliant ability of Joe Bain to synthesize. I feel we accomplished far more in terms of useful generalizations in the subsequent 15 years, since abandoning the case study for the computer.

The much more common result of the verbal approach has been not-so-general "generalizations" which are "proven" by examples. These almost never hold up very long, because in the real world statements of the sort "X is always true" are never correct except for definitional relationships. It is wrong to say "college graduates always earn more than high school graduates," but it is as wrong to say they do not. The correct statement is that "on the average, college graduates earn X percent more than high school graduates." This is a result that few people, if any, can come up with using only the "data immersal" technique. That statement brings you back to numbers again.

Multiple Causes and Multiple Regressions

A second advantage of statistics, to which I have already alluded, is their powerful ability to sort out the effects of the variety of different influences bearing on any real world variable. The best of theories or verbal interpretations (e.g., Bain again) are stumped by more than two or three simultaneous independent variables. Our minds often have to struggle with even one variable.

Multiple regression[2] is a very powerful tool nevertheless. With it, we can get clear readings of not only the direction but also the quantitative importance of each of many independent influences on a variable, and

2. A multiple regression is one in which two or more independent variables are used to explain a dependent variable. It will yield estimates of the significance and quantitative effect of each independent variable separately, and of the overall proportion of the variability of the dependent variable that can be accounted for by variations in the independent variables used when taken as a group.

we can make a reasonable judgment as to whether what we see is likely to be merely a matter of chance.

A particularly difficult relationship to derive by theory or by the empirical bath approach is the interaction variable. It may well be that some independent variable has little effect when another is small but a great deal of effect when the other variable is large. For instance, education may increase income little when a person is twenty-five but quite a lot when he is fifty. Regression models can deal with such problems quite easily. A regression where both education and age past eighteen are independent variables will not catch this interaction. But one which includes an interaction term—education times age—will do it. If either education or age is low, the interaction term will be small, but where both are high, it will be large. The computer can tell you whether such an interaction term is important compared with education and age taken as separate variables, something that large amounts of theory or empirical bathings are unlikely to do.

These tools are accessible to persons of only average intelligence, and the results can be tested by others of the same ilk who have other data or models, or both.

Precision

Finally, numbers are much more precise than words. From my limited observation, the English language is one of the richer and more exact of the languages spoken by men. We can distinguish between "I had done" and "I have done," which the Japanese cannot do, and English has a much larger vocabulary than most languages. But mathematics is much more exact than English. There is a large difference between "substantial" and 43.7 percent or even 43.7 percent ± 5.2 percent. Statistical studies seldom yield precisely correct statements, but they do say how fuzzy the statements are, which is more than English does.

The average mind presented with a problem to be solved in verbal terms will produce a statement that is vague and easily misunderstood, even by the owner of the mind itself. The same mind seeking to run a multiple regression will, if it is honest, formulate a particular functional form[3] and a prediction with respect to the expected signs of the coefficients.

A mere formulation of the problem, in terms precise enough for the computer to accept, serves often to provide a clarity that most of us can seldom achieve in verbal terms. And the relationship that appears when the regression is complete puts a sharp limit on the interpretation we can give to the data—much more so than the results of a verbal-historical bath.

---

3. A functional form is the expected form of a relationship. For instance, y may be expected to increase with x or with the log of x or increase with x at first but decrease with x when x is large (in which case the relationship would involve x and x^2).

PROBLEMS WITH NUMBERS

After all this, it must be acknowledged that numbers can be garbled, that there are things that statistics do not measure well, that not all statisticians are perfectly honest or competent, and that econometric methods can be maddeningly complex at times.

Errors in the Data

If statements that are always true in the real world are very scarce, so is measurement without error. All numbers describing the economic world are somewhat innaccurate. Contrary to common opinion, this is *not* an insurmountable problem. Even if there are serious, but random, errors in a dependent variable, the regression technique will still yield the most likely underlying relationship. The errors will result in reduced correlation, so that if the errors are large enough or the relationship is weak enough, it may seem that a true relationship could easily be the result of pure chance.

But statistical techniques can survive some very serious errors. Galileo, by dropping iron balls through open air and using very crude measurements of time, was able to derive the law of falling bodies with such accuracy of the coefficient of acceleration that we have only slightly changed it over the 3½ centuries since. Crime statistics are notoriously bad, so bad that criminologists long resisted analyzing them using standard techniques. And yet in recent years we have been able to demonstrate plausible, consistent, and statistically significant effects on crime of differences in the probability of arrest and conviction among jurisdictions or over time.

If there are random errors in a single independent variable, statistical techniques do introduce a bias, but at least we know its direction. In general, such errors bias statistical effects toward zero. This implies that if we see an effect for an independent variable, we can expect that it exists in fact and that it is understated.

If the errors are not random, the standard treatment of errors in variables does not apply, but all is not lost. If the errors are positively correlated with the independent variable, we can estimate an upper limit in the relationship between it and the dependent variable. Or, if the bias is in the other direction, we can estimate the lower limit.

An example of the latter bias is profit rates. There is strong reason to believe that accounting procedures tend to understate high rates of return and overstate low ones. This arises because properties that yield high returns tend to change hands at prices that reflect those high returns and are, therefore, revalued upward until the reported rate of return is only an average one. Unprofitable properties are revalued downward by a similar process. In addition, rapidly growing firms, which are generally the more profitable ones, have a large proportion of new plant and equipment which is relatively costly after a period of inflation. Slowly growing, generally less profitable firms have more equipment that is old and cheap. As a result, the rapidly growing firms tend to understate their true economic profit rates relative to slowly growing firms, thus biasing recorded rates of return toward equality once more. A third bias working in the same direction is the tendency for the more profitable firms to pay relatively high wages and salaries, presumably resulting in some transfer of economic profits to employees. A fourth bias arises because of the treatment of advertising and R&D as current expenses. The direction of bias is complex, depending on the intensity and rate of growth of advertising and R&D, but the most likely error is to overstate profit rates for slowly growing consumer goods industries of moderate concentration. Finally, various accounting conventions adopted by the firm will also introduce error. This has not been carefully studied, but one would expect the more profitable firms to adopt conventions that understate their profit rates and the less profitable firms to adopt those that overstate theirs for both public relations and stockholder relations purposes. Altogether, all these biases, except perhaps the expensing of intangibles, tend to bias profit rates toward equality. As a result, one would expect statistical studies of the determinants of profitability to understate the effects of the variables that tend to increase profits.

One of the most thoroughly studied variables affecting profitability is industrial concentration. That variable is itself measured with a good deal of error. As a result, I would surely expect the estimated relationship between it and profitability to be understated in the studies. There have been more than fifty studies of the effect of concentration on profit rates. They cover several countries and periods, various industries, and a large variety of measures and models. The vast majority of them show a significant positive effect of concentration on profitability, except perhaps in periods of rapid inflation. In view of the biases in the data, I feel we can say that profits do increase with concentration and that our many statistical studies systematically understate the amount by which they increase.

In general, bad data weaken statistical estimates, but they do not make statisticians helpless by any means.

Nonquantifiable Data

Even if the numbers used by a statistician were perfect, he could still make serious mistakes if he ignored the nonquantitative data available to him. A nice example is, once more, education and earnings. Many smart people go to college. Many less smart people do not, or if they do, they often do not stay the four years. If we stick to the easily quantified years-of-school variable, we are likely to exaggerate the effect of education on earnings. Part of the effect of education is probably the effect of greater intelligence on earnings. The relatively smart people would probably earn more than the not so smart, even without college.

Actually, intelligence is at least approximately quantified in IQ test scores, but those scores are hard to come by.

There are many relevant nonquantitative variables. The fact that a person is black, or a woman, or a black woman living in the South are all important in determining his or her income.

Actually, these variables *can* be incorporated in statistical studies. They can be introduced as *dummy* variables—that is, variables with a value of one—if the observation has a particular attribute—e.g., black—and zero if it does not. The coefficient of such a variable will tell you what, on average, is the effect of being black after taking account of age, education, and the like. Or better yet, if there are enough observations, you can run separate regressions for blacks and whites, or males and females, or all four. This permits you to see how the effects of age and education vary among the races and sexes.

However, that leaves some characteristics that just do not lend themselves to quantitative analysis. Beauty, sobriety, willingness to work, and good health are all characteristics that undoubtedly affect earning ability. Conceptually, they could all be measured, or at least people could be classified by these characteristics. In fact, they almost never are. When these characteristics are ignored, at least a large part of observed variation in the dependent variable will go unexplained. That, by itself, may not be serious, unless we are directly interested in the effects of beauty, sobriety, or what have you. If they are correlated with measured variables, however, omitting them will bias the results once more. What looks to the statistician like the effect of education may, in fact, be the effect of a propensity to work hard or an aversion to alcohol.

It is hard to say a priori how serious the omission of nonquantifiable and nonclassifiable variables may be. Certainly, the statistician and his audience should keep their eyes open for such omissions. I will have more to say about excluded variables later.

Choosing Your Cases

Some of the limits of numbers lie with the people who use them.

A fairly transparent fault occurs when the statistician chooses his cases. He simply throws out, for reasons that sound plausible, observations that do not fit his preconceived ideas as to the result. After that, it is easy for him to demonstrate that the desired results hold. No amount of sophisticated statistical technique will make up for his exclusions.

Still, this approach may be hard to detect or correct. Some of the data really are faulty and should be excluded. Often, some data are more faulty than other data. There is unquestionably a large element of judgment permissible in throwing out cases. The obvious answer to the dishonest statistician is to put the cases back in and see what difference they make, but some of the rescued cases probably really do not belong there. The end of all this is that suspicions are raised about both results.

An alternative approach is to try to correct the faulty data, but this also involves judgment and can quite rightly raise suspicions once more. My own solution in the cases where errors in the data are most severe is for a committee of widely representative experts to review the data and come up with a consensus about the most appropriate corrections. A good case might be our industrial concentration data. My impression is that we could reach consensus on where concentration might best be measured at the five-, four-, or three-digit levels and where local or regional concentration figures would be more appropriate than national figures. With such a consensus, the Bureau of the Census might be prevailed upon to calculate and report concentration at the appropriate levels as well as the four-digit national figures it turns out now. The result could be a real improvement in our knowledge.

"Fishing"

Another, more subtle, form of statistical dishonesty occurs when someone runs 100 regressions on a body of data and then reports those results that turned out "well." This can be very misleading. A result will be "statistically significant" one time in twenty by pure chance. Such "fishing expeditions" are likely to yield quite a lot of "knowledge" that would not hold when applied elsewhere.

The same result can be obtained if a large number of quite honest statisticians work with the same set of data, each testing different hypotheses. Among them, it is very likely that 100 regressions will be tried. If the five that "work" are published, we can reach the same result as with a single "fisherman." This problem seems especially serious in macroeconomics, where everyone works with the same 30 postwar years.

The usual reaction of statisticians is to be skeptical about statistical results that do not have good theoretical underpinnings. Presumably, the right thing to do is to work out theoretical predictions as to what variables to include and what signs to expect their coefficients to bear. Then, one tests these predictions against the statistics.

This is not a foolproof procedure by any means. It is usually possible for a person who is fishing to think up some theoretical justification after the fact for anything turned up. How is the outsider to tell when the thinking was done? In the case of the macroeconomists, the scholars whose studies "worked" really did do their thinking first.

Moreover, the theory-first-and-statistical-tests-later approach may throw away some information. There undoubtedly is some knowledge lurking out there that no existing theory would suggest. Physical scientists often run hundreds of experiments in places where logic does not lead them to see what the world is like. They have the advantage that they can run the experiments that "work" over and over to see if the result that they found really was part of nature or just a random event. The physical scientists can generate their own data. The economy is less generous with ours.

In areas where we have a lot of observations, we could do the same sort of thing. We could take a random sample of our data and "fish" it for unexpected results. Then, we could test such things as we found on the remaining data to see if there was anything to them.

Then, there is the statistical fact for which there is no theory. I am quite sure that there is a tendency for concentrated industries to use more capital per dollar of sale than the unconcentrated industries. I have derived this result in a number of studies using different data, models, and periods. I have no idea at all why it occurs. Should I simply ignore it, or should I treat it as an unexplained fact of life? I am inclined to do the latter, but I am uncomfortable about it.

In view of all these considerations, my own approach is to be skeptical about any single study, even where the theory came first. But, I am inclined to accept a result that has held up after many independent tests, even if the theory involved is equivocal.

Omitted Variables

If an important independent variable is omitted, the estimated relationship among the variables that are included may be distorted. Of course, it is realistically impossible to include all the independent influences on some dependent variables in a statistical study. Indeed, when I find a study where most of the variability is "explained," I become suspicious that either the relationship is really just a matter of definition (assets are bound to be perfectly correlated with liabilities and equity) or that all the variables are correlated with something else (a common situation in time series studies). In the more usual case, a large part of the variability in the dependent variable is left "unexplained." Many influences are left out. This does *not* necessarily mean that the statistically estimated relationship is misleading. If the omitted variables are independent of (uncorrelated with) the included independent variables, the estimated relationship is the same as would be found with that variable included. Indeed, correlation and regression models were designed to deal precisely with such a situation.

There *will* be bias in the results, however, if the omitted variable *is* correlated with an included independent variable or variables. It is up to the statistician to search out and include any important variables that are so correlated. An advantage of "publish or perish" on the academic scene or adversary proceedings in court is that rivals will introduce such additional variables if the original study did not.

In many cases, we are not equally interested in the effects of all the independent variables in a regression. Many are introduced in order to capture extraneous effects that are likely to be correlated with the independent variable on which the study focuses. For instance, this is true of the variable that controls for "trend" in time series studies or for growth in cross-sectional studies of industries. The fact that these variables may be correlated with a number of excluded variables is an advantage, not a disadvantage, unless we are actually interested in the effects of trend or growth themselves, which is seldom the case. Ordinarily, these variables can be expected to pick up much of the effect of the related omitted variables (for instance, the effect of inflation in distorting profit rates) and can yield more accurate estimates of the effects of variables in which we are actually interested.

Collinearity

Closely related to the last point is the fact that when two independent variables are closely correlated, their independent effects are apt to be indistinguishable by statistical studies. The computer tries to answer for each independent variable the following question: "What does this variable add to the explanation, holding everything else constant?" When the "everything else" includes a variable that is very close to the one being examined, the answer is apt to be "not much."

This may be very misleading. It is quite possible, using a so-called F-test, to test what difference the two highly correlated variables make together. The result often is that the two together have a very significant effect, although the researcher cannot actually distinguish between them.

An example is the pair of variables, concentration and minimum efficient scale, as a percentage of industry shipments. There is good reason to expect both variables to increase profit rates. In statistical studies where both variables are used, the correlation between them usually results in weak apparent relationships. Sometimes concentration wins, sometimes the scale variable wins, and sometimes neither has a significant effect. However, in all such cases that I have investigated, the combined effects of the two variables are always significant and positive. The correct statement is that either or both affect profitability and that we cannot distinguish among these possibilities.

An alternative which is not helpful is to run the same regression with one of the two related variables excluded. If this is done, the result is apt to be that the included variable assumes the role of both and that the effect of the included variable is overstated. It is entirely a matter of taste which of the two is included, as both are partly wrong.

A good case is the macromodels which have often been used to try to distinguish between the effects of monetary and fiscal policy actions. Most of the time, these point in the same direction, so that an attempt to distinguish between them will depend on a few aberrant periods. Many other things are going on in the same periods, and so it is quite bold to assume that those few special cases can give much information about what is really happening. By now, however, there cannot be much doubt that the combined effects of monetary and fiscal policy are very strong. If they both push in the same direction, the economy will go in that direction.

What has happened in the last few years in macromodels is that we have shifted from trying to distinguish among the effects of particular variables toward attempts to predict the overall performance of the economy. The results are certainly not perfect, but they seem to be good enough (at least in terms of real output and employment, if not prices) for a lot of hardheaded businessmen and businesswomen to buy the macromodel predictions at prices that make some economists quite wealthy.

If we really do want to distinguish between the effects of two closely related variables, the best approach is to get more data, but the data may not be helpful. Getting more data for macromodels means either going to earlier years or working with quarterly or monthly data. The longer time period may mean ignoring fundamental changes that have occurred in the structure of the economy, and the use of quarterly or monthly data may result in problems of seasonal adjustment and, perhaps, more correlation between events of successive periods. Similarly, for cross-sectional studies, more data are apt to mean using firms rather than industries. We are apt to exaggerate how many independent observations we have if the experiences of the firms in an industry are similar. There is a way of dealing with such problems of *serial correlation,* but we may wind up without much more data for all our efforts. There is a good chance that we will simply be unable to distinguish between the effects of two closely correlated variables.

Simultaneous Equations

Another place where statistics can go awry is where the true relationship involves interaction of two or more groups of influences. A simple case is supply and demand. Most economists believe that the lower the price, the more consumers will buy. At the same time, on the supply side, producers will sell more, the *higher* the price. What we actually see is a series of observations where both demand and supply are satisfied. If someone runs a single regression of quantity on price, he would not see either the demand or the supply relationship, but some amalgam of both. If more are sold at lower prices, he may interpret what he sees as demand, but he will be wrong. The same applies to "supply," if more are sold at higher prices. The true demand and supply are likely to be more responsive to prices than the observations suggest.

Such relationships may be more subtle than this story suggests. For instance, many economists have tried to estimate single-equation models relating advertising and concentration, but the true relationship is probably one where concentration and margins, along with other variables, determine advertising; advertising and minimum efficient scale determine concentration; and concentration, advertising, and several other variables determine margins. Any single-equation model is apt to confuse these multiple influences.

Econometrics has a variety of ways around these problems. A common one is to estimate values of the *endogenous variables*[4] by regressing them on all the *exogenous variables* (things like incomes and weather in the demand and supply model, or the proportion sold to ultimate consumers, minimum efficient scale, industry growth, and capital intensity in the second example). Then, the estimated values are substituted for observed values in estimating the actual regressions of interest. This can eliminate simultaneous equations bias, involved when a single equation of a simultaneous system is estimated.

This will not always work. If there are no exogenous variables that importantly affect a particular endogenous variable, other than those in the equation where that endogenous variable appears, then the estimated value of the endogenous variable will be highly correlated with the exogenous variables in that equation, and it will be impossible to evaluate its independent effect. This need not be caused by errors on the part of the researcher. There just may not be any exogenous variables outside the estimated equation that make any difference to the endogenous variable. If so, we are back with the problem of collinearity that cannot be unraveled, and the best we can do is estimate the joint effect of the related variables again.

WHAT IS A POOR JUDGE TO DO?

These stories are not meant to be memorized. There are much better places to read them if you are interested. The main point I want to make is that econometrics is not easy, and what is easy is not always right.

Statistics has a lot to offer in the way of generalizations relevant to many economic, legal, and regulatory cases, but judges and regulators are usually not sufficiently trained to evaluate the statistical evidence presented to them. What can they do with such materials?

One possibility that I am afraid is often followed is simply to ignore them. As might be guessed, this does not seem to be an adequate solution to me. It means throwing out the baby with the bath. I think the baby is quite valuable.

Adversary Proceedings

Presumably, the genius of adversary proceedings is that the parties to a case will introduce any relevant criticisms of their opponent's evidence. This is surely often true, but there are difficulties with statistical evidence.

First, if the judge is not sophisticated with respect to statistics, the

4. An endogenous variable is one whose value is determined by the simultaneous system of equations. Ordinarily, it is a dependent variable in one of the equations and, at the same time, an independent variable in one or more equations. An exogenous variable is one whose value is determined outside the model. For instance, in a demand and supply model, price and quantity are endogenous, while weather and consumer incomes are exogenous.

result may be merely confusion. He may not be able to evaluate the statements made by the two sides, and the result may be an incorrect decision.

Or, consider the case where one of the adversaries is not really interested in having statistical evidence in the case, perhaps suspecting that it will work against him. The result will be a great deal of sophisticated criticism of the statistical evidence, leaving the impression that it is not really reliable, regardless of how good it is. I am afraid that often the more sophisticated the study, the easier it will be to leave that impression. In particular, random errors in data or some range of uncertainty in the results may be unimportant but can be made to appear damning.

Or both parties to a case may be partly wrong. I once had the experience of actually cross-examining witnesses in a regulatory case. I asked witnesses on both sides what the effect of errors in an independent variable was and, especially, if the errors would introduce a bias in the results. The answer I received from witnesses from both sides was that such errors would reduce the apparent correlation but that they would not cause any bias. Both witnesses were wrong. Such errors would bias the apparent relationships toward zero. I knew this, but I suspect the typical judge would not, and the record would, therefore, go uncorrected. It went uncorrected in my case, too. I did not know how to put it straight, short of arguing with the witnesses, which I understood to be poor practice. I later talked to some lawyers about it and found out what should have been done. I will save the solution for later, since it seems much more general and useful than merely dealing with this special case.

More important, suppose that both sides have statistical studies that support their cases and that both are imperfect. The judge will be back in the position of being presented with a series of criticisms of the two studies with no real basis for choosing between them. Indeed, he probably should not, if both are partly wrong. He needs a third opinion that avoids the errors of both.

The Econometric Clerk

One way around this is for the judge to appoint an econometrician as a clerk to help him in evaluating the contending claims and, if necessary, to develop alternative statistical studies. The problem here is obvious. The clerk himself may be biased and may produce results as wrong as those of the two sides with no opportunity for cross-examination.

Another problem is finding a truly expert econometrician who is willing to take the time to do the job thoroughly. My impression is that law clerks are generally young men who are gaining experience that can stand them in good stead in their future lives as attorneys. Econometric clerks are apt to have much less incentive. Few of them would be likely to look to a future made up primarily of consulting in lawsuits. I suspect the judges would be unlikely to get the best young econometricians as clerks.

The Econometric Witness

My own solution to the problem is for the judge, faced with econometric evidence, to call as his own witness a well-established econometrician to critique the statistical evidence presented in the case and to draw conclusions from it. Conceivably, this specialist might have to do his own statistical study, if he felt that both sides' work was lacking. More commonly, I would expect him to evaluate the various points presented in the prepared statements and the cross-examinations. He would be subject to cross-examination just as expert witnesses called by the adversaries were. And the full impact of the statistical evidence would be enhanced rather than ignored.

The quality of witnesses, both those called by the adversaries and by the judge, might be enhanced. Adversaries faced with the prospect that an independent expert would evaluate their work might take greater care to avoid econometric legerdemain. And well-established experts might find the position of objective, judge-chosen witness attractive because they would not be beholden to either side, because the time involved would usually be brief (just enough to analyze both sides' econometric evidence and arguments), and because the pay would normally be good compared with that of a clerk. Even if his evidence involved rerunning regressions, the cost to him would ordinarily be less than for the adversaries because he could use the data they had put together. In many cases, the witness could do a better job by reviewing a large body of evidence from the academic press which bears on the case and which may not correspond very closely to that presented by the adversaries.

This approach undoubtedly has its failings. An obvious problem is how the judge is to select an outside expert in the first place. I suspect it would not be very difficult. The profession can probably agree fairly well on who the leading men in the field of econometrics are, and they would probably self-select on their ability to present points in simple but accurate language. I may be wrong, but I would like to see it tried.

DIALOGUE

FREDERIC M. SCHERER: I would like to make two comments, the first philosophical and the second detailed and narrow. I believe in numbers and their use in industrial organization. Betty Bock is obviously much more skeptical and so is George Benston. Why do I believe? There is a very simple explanation, and it comes out of my experience.

My most recent quantitative research has involved plant sizes and market structure in six different nations. I constructed a theoretical model. I then went out and collected data, and I found that there were, in fact, the kinds of relationships between market structure and plant size that economic theory would lead one to expect.

Well, the data were quite imperfect. George Benston has pointed to some of the imperfections. And yet, I broke down my sample of data into three groups: the United States, Canada, and the Western European countries. I reran the principal analyses for these different groups, and in

The session was chaired by Arthur W. Murphy, Professor of Law, Columbia University School of Law. For further biographical information, see Appendix 1.

almost every case all the relationships were identical.

The point is that across quite diverse national jurisdictions you find the same kinds of structural relationships appearing in the data, despite different census bureaus, different assumptions about the way the data are collected, and inherent errors in the data themselves. Independent economic studies in various nations have supported my conclusions.

We all know there are difficulties in the data; we all know there are errors. I firmly believe, however, that there are also strong elements of order in the economic universe, and that these elements of order are sufficiently robust that they outweigh in statistical analyses the elements of disorder that we know are there. This is my philosophical point.

Now, the detailed point. Betty Bock talked about the problem of contamination in data, and I have heard this point made time and again. Betty concocted an example, and George Benston uses it in his paper, about the milk industry and the cottage cheese industry. You can find all sorts of horror stories, but I think this story is typical of the true problem. Unfortunately, George must be a city boy and Betty a city girl. Neither had the advantage of having a deputy director who grew up on a Georgia farm. When Betty's analysis came out, my deputy explained to me how you make cottage cheese. Cottage cheese is what you do with the milk that is too sour to market. Therefore, cottage cheese is a natural product to include in the activities of a milk industry. It is a natural by-product of running a dairy. To call that contamination, it seems to me, is simply to shun looking at real-world facts. I suggest that many examples of what Betty alleges to be contamination are of a similar character.

GEORGE J. BENSTON: As it happens, I can milk cows. I grew up on a farm. Professor Scherer is right. Cottage cheese is contaminated milk and that is where the contamination comes from.

Let me say that I think everybody here is saying sensible things. We know we have to look at the data carefully. I cannot say too much for Betty's paper. It points to basic issues that we all should be thinking about.

I say to the lawyers, if you have an economist who has some data against you, hire another one. It is not hard to tear apart statistical studies, especially those with small data sets. You can remove something with a good rationale and get different results. This is the world we live in.

BOCK: Professor Scherer has said many times that I have been exaggerating the contamination problem. I don't think that being a city girl or a country girl has anything to do with the issue. To the best of my knowledge, the FTC invented the word *contamination* to refer to situations where a reported value of shipments and transfers figure for a line of business (LB) category is larger than the actual shipments and transfers of products classified in the category—because category and noncategory products are made in the same company reporting segment.

The FTC has said that such distortions would be 9 percent or less. But I doubt this. Let me explain.

The FTC's 9 percent figure refers to only one of six possible forms of contamination: overstatement due to the mixing of figures for secondary products with primary products for an LB category. Left out are the related understatements in other categories due to the same cause. Omitted also are the overstatements and understatements in LB category figures which will result from the use of the forward and the backward vertical integration reporting options. Furthermore, all six forms of contamination will have different levels for value of shipments and transfers, and for each cost, asset, and profit figure.

Coming back now to the FTC's estimate of 9 percent for contamination, we should note that this figure seems to have been derived by adding up census figures on overstatements due to primary-secondary product reporting in each reporting category—and dividing by the number of categories. But there are three fallacies in this method of determining the level of contamination: first, it covers only one aspect of the problems, not six; second, it measures only overstatement in value of shipments and transfers and takes no account of the different distortions associated with other reportable figures; and third, the 9 percent figure is obtained by assuming that high overstatement in some LB categories should be averaged out against low overstatement in others. But this assumption implies that LB data will be aggregated to all manufacturing totals when, in fact, the purpose of the program is the opposite.

CHARLES E. WYZANSKI, JR.: As the only trial judge, and speaking subject to the correction of the three circuit judges present, I would like to address myself to the last problem which Professor Weiss raised. My reference is to the problem of how one handles economic data in a trial court. I suppose I am the most notorious offender because of my use of Carl Kaysen in *United States v. United Shoe Machinery Corp*. [110 F. Supp. 295, *affirmed per curiam,* 347 U.S. 521 (1954)], a use which was, in my judgment, correctly criticized by Bethuel Webster in a speech he made at a meeting of the ABA's Section on Antitrust Law.

I quite agree with the adverse comments made by Professor Weiss about the use of an economist as a law clerk for a judge—

not necessarily for the reasons he gave, but in part for the reasons he gave. It certainly is true that an economist who is operating within the judicial system is supplying a judge with a form of knowledge about which the judge himself is likely not to be an expert. He is giving it to the judge under circumstances where it is not subject to cross-examination and has all the dangers which are involved in that kind of presentation, including the danger that the information is not available for review by an appellate court.

The suggestion which was made as to how to circumvent this is sensible but difficult to accomplish. Professor Weiss said that the economist should be a court witness subject to cross-examination. And to show that I do agree with this as a possible alternative, let me say that I have, in effect, done the same thing, although in a rather different field. I had to determine the validity of radar patents, and the physics I learned at the Phillips Exeter Academy stopped with Isaac Newton. I was faced with a problem I could not possibly have handled without the assistance of an expert physicist. And I did in that case ask the president of MIT to recommend an expert. He gave me the name of Professor Chu. I asked the plaintiff and the defendant each to give me the names of the five persons they thought most expert. And, fortunately, Professor Chu was on the list furnished by both.

So I named Professor Chu. I authorized him to listen to anything that either party wished to give him, either orally or in writing or by way of experiment, always on the condition that the other party was present. At the end he was to write a report, submit it to the parties, submit it to me, take the stand as a court witness, and subject himself to cross-examination.

It worked out even better than one could have anticipated because he wrote the report and the parties settled on the basis of it. I do not promise equally good results from this system every time. But, in general, the approach was correct.

The trouble, however, is that our federal system and I daresay most states do not contemplate the courts appointing such a witness. Unless the Supreme Court of the United States decides differently from some lower federal courts, and from the Administrative Office of the United States Courts, it is very doubtful that there are any funds to pay for such an expert.

And so it may be necessary, as it was in the radar case, to get an agreement of the parties that they would be willing to divide the costs of such an expert. Otherwise, one may be blocked by the financial difficulties of the situation.

Furthermore, I think one ought to recognize that in connection with at least economic information, the moment you have chosen the economist, you may have decided the case. It is by no means easy to find, if indeed it is possible to find, somebody who is a neutral in the eyes of both parties with respect to economic questions. Thus, you may be blocked at the very outset by that great difficulty if you are trying to get agreement by the parties in connection with the matter.

So, I am not sure that the present structure of payment and appointment permits the solution Professor Weiss suggests. Although if it does permit it, I certainly favor it.

There is a further problem which is rarely faced. The beginning of the consideration of social and economic information in the federal courts is usually traced to the brief filed by the then, as he was, Mr. Brandeis in *Muller v. Oregon* [208 U.S. 412 (1908)]. What is generally forgotten, however, is that Mr. Brandeis furnished the economic and like information in order to support the reasonableness of a legislative act. It was offered, therefore, merely to show the rationality, not necessarily the correctness, of the legislative conclusion.

Since the time of *Muller v. Oregon,* the Supreme Court, lower courts, and lawyers generally have assumed that it is perfectly proper to use social and economic information for a totally different purpose, to prove which of two or more contending positions is correct. Now, this runs into a number of difficulties. The most obvious is that it is the use of hearsay evidence. Now, I do not think that is a very serious, even though it is a very obvious, objection. I am not aware of any case in which the Supreme Court, or any other federal appellate court, has reversed a trial judge for admitting this kind of evidence on the ground that it is hearsay. And we all know that this kind of information is regularly taken into account by the federal agencies, and that there never has been any problem in connection with the admission of such evidence.

What is much more important than what I have said so far is the general problem of how far it is appropriate for either a trial court or an appellate court to take into account anything which is not clearly laid out before the parties at the time that the case is being tried. Quite correctly, I was criticized because, in a trademark case, I relied upon some research which I myself engaged in at the library of the Harvard Business School. My critic properly noted that anything which I took into account ought to have first been laid before the parties for their comment and, if necessary, for rebuttal or qualification.

No doubt the method of proceeding by way of a court witness is one way of handling the problem. But it may very well be that there are other ways which could more easily be used, including, for example, the preparation of memoranda submitted to the parties in advance of the judge writing his opinion. It may very well be that the working out of this kind of procedural technique is quite as important as the substance itself.

CARL A. AUERBACH: I should like to point out an instance in which a judge of a federal court of appeals used an expert to help him evaluate the record on appeal. The case involved a merger between the holding company of Du Pont and Du Pont itself. At issue was the price to be paid for securities. The judge felt it necessary to get some help in evaluating the record. He employed an expert in securities evaluation and was able, after some minor difficulty, to get the Administrative Office of the United States Courts to pay the bill. The expert drafted a memorandum which was made available to the parties, who commented on it; the judge then decided the case.

WARREN F. SCHWARTZ: Why are you statisticians being so modest in trying to explain your results in words and suggesting that we get experts? If you really believe that the world is a certain way and that the way to capture it is through these techniques, why don't you say to us: "Your ignorance is no longer forgivable, and if you are too old to learn, don't pass on your ignorance. What we are really good at is what you need to know, and for God's sake, improve your legal education. We cannot turn those equations into words because the words are not as good."

I have a rough idea what a dependent variable is, but once you said "dependent variable and independent variable," you lost most of the crowd. You cannot speak our language, and the reason is fundamental. Your language is much better for the kind of reality that the legal system is about. So why not tell us, "Stop being so smug and learn this stuff. If you can't learn it anymore, recognize its importance."

I don't know why you apologize. If you really believe it is the best way to describe reality—not because you like it but because it is the best way—tell us that plain out.

WILFRED FEINBERG: I was a trial judge for a while and acquired some of the wisdom that Judge Wyzanski displays. Mine has been tainted by some ten years as an appellate judge. But I still recall some of the feelings I had as a trial judge with experts, and I do know my feelings when I see records come up with conflicting testimony of experts.

And I generally join with Judge Wyzanski in saying that the suggestion of Professor Weiss can be a useful one, but I hasten to add that I do not think we should downplay the benefits of the adversary system or throw it aside too quickly. I would like to give you a few examples.

It seems to me that the problems with experts fall into a number of categories. First, are the experts bending their answers to give the kind of testimony that the party presenting the expert wants? Usually the adversary system will take care of this in the sense that the judge will hear testimony from both sides.

In the typical medical case, where somebody says the plaintiff has a very bad back, the plaintiff will present an expert who will so testify and give his reasons. The railroad, or whoever it was who allegedly injured the plaintiff, will present an expert who will say the plaintiff's back was really objectively in fine shape, all the symptoms are subjective, and it must be psychosomatic.

The judge has a "feel," based on numbers of cases, that experts on back injuries tend to bend their testimony a bit; the problem is corrected by the adversary system.

Another problem—and I think this is the kind economists worry about most—is that the judge will not realize the answers are being bent because he does not understand the question or the answer. I think that kind of problem is not the sort of thing that you, Professor Weiss, were talking about in your paper.

The real problem is when the expert's answer and the field are so technical that the judge does not realize what is being left out or what is not being said. And there, I think, having an independent expert could be useful if you assume that the independent expert will educate the judge as to what he does not know when someone bends his answer. But I do not see how you can know that ahead of time.

It may very well be that Professor Schwartz is most on target; that is, it is up to judges, and the legal profession generally, to try to educate themselves to the language with which they are not familiar.

WEISS: I think the case that led me to this suggestion was one where both parties gave the wrong answer. I should think the approach would also be useful in instances where the problem is interpretation or "bending."

In big antitrust cases, for example, it seems to be conventional to include two or three economic witnesses on each side; the economic witnesses come in almost as advocates. Under such circumstances, at least conceivably, it would be possible to find a reputable economist who was not hostage to either side, and who could interpret their comments.

So long as verbal economics is being presented, I suspect that the judge is capable of learning, as you say, the materials that are necessary to evaluate the testimony of witnesses. When it is econometric material that is being introduced, the problem is much more difficult. The questions are technical; the analogy is to Judge Wyzanski's physicist. I certainly would not be a candidate for the position of econometric witness who can evaluate two studies. But I think you could probably get agreement on who are some leading econometricians. They would be answering technical questions.

I do not think that this is something the judge should be expected to learn. It is a very large and complex field. As I said, I do not feel competent to act as such a witness. I think, however, I could name some people who would be appropriate.

CHAPTER FIVE

Government-Mandated Business Disclosure Addressed to Consumers

EDITOR'S NOTE

Over the past decade, Congress and federal agencies have promulgated affirmative-disclosure programs with increasing frequency. Although such programs may trace their roots to the Securities Act of 1933 and various pieces of labeling legislation, the present trend requires a new evaluation of the theoretical underpinnings and real-world effects of these programs.

At issue are questions such as the following: What needs are served by legislation or administrative regulations mandating disclosure of various matters to consumers? Is government-mandated disclosure administratively practicable? What are its costs? Are viable alternatives available? What impact, if any, does mandatory disclosure have on consumer or producer behavior?

On a theoretical level, Professors Pitofsky and Posner share much common ground. Miles W. Kirkpatrick, who chaired this session, summarized some of their areas of agreement:

> Both agree that the consumer should not have to play a game of blindman's buff in the marketplace, and that market forces will usually generate sufficient information. Both seem to agree that there are limited areas to be explored—for example, where there is a so-called "hidden characteristic" that would not be revealed on inspection. Finally, both agree the whole area deserves further objective study to determine, for example, how various programs are working and under what circumstances mandated information is likely to influence the consumer.

Pitofsky and Posner, however, part ways dramatically when evaluating the effectiveness of specific disclosure programs. Pitofsky, acknowledging disappointing experiences (e.g., truth-in-lending and unit-price marketing), sees a "legitimate government role in mandating the disclosure of information to consumers as a supplement to ordinary market forces. At their best, these programs put consumers in a position to protect their own interests in the marketplace."

Posner, on the other hand, sees much cost and little benefit in these programs. As to the FTC's program, he expresses "profound skepticism concerning both [its] wisdom and legality."

MANDATED DISCLOSURE IN THE ADVERTISING OF CONSUMER PRODUCTS

Robert Pitofsky *Professor of Law, Georgetown University Law Center*

Government requirements that advertisers disclose information to consumers in labeling and advertising have increased sharply in recent years. Mandated disclosure has certain obvious appeals. It is consistent with free market notions of consumer sovereignty and usually is imposed against all similarly situated sellers in a product category (thereby tending to muffle cries of anguish from individually regulated companies); the costs of any such regulation tend to be modest and widely distributed and therefore can be made to appear insignificant.

This paper will argue that government-mandated information disclosure to consumers in appropriate circumstances can be a sensible supplement to ordinary market forces that give sellers incentives to provide accurate and relevant product information. I urge that view, even though I accept that existing empirical data indicate that several disclosure systems in the consumer field—most notably, consumer credit cost data required by the Truth-in-Lending Act[1] and unit-price marketing—have failed for the most part to achieve desired results.[2] Part of the explanation for these failures may be that the disclosure

1. See Consumer Credit Protection Act, 15 U.S.C. §§ 1601 *et seq.* (1970).

2. A review of studies of the impact of truth-in-lending is found in William C. Whitford, "The Function of Disclosure Regulation in Consumer Transactions," *Wisconsin Law Review*, vol. 1973, no. 2, 1973, pp. 405–420. Experience with unit pricing is discussed in Hans R. Isakson and Alex R. Maurizi, "The Consumer Economics of Unit Pricing,' *Journal of Marketing Research*, vol. 10, no. 3, August 1973, pp. 277–285, and in Kent B. Monroe and Peter J. LaPlaca, "What are the Benefits of Unit Pricing?" *Journal of Marketing*, vol. 36, no. 3, July 1972, pp. 17–19.

The author expresses his gratitude to Michael E. Kipling for his exceptionally able research work and to his colleague Tom Krattenmaker for his thoughtful suggestions in the preparation of this paper.

systems exhaustively studied are not characteristic of most of the recent disclosure programs. For example, it could be contended that truth-in-lending was certain to have only a modest impact on consumer lending practices because the comparative credit data disclosed were too complicated to be widely understood. Nevertheless, I doubt such arguments can explain all the adverse returns that have come in on the effect of disclosure systems. And, given that disappointing experience, those advocating mandatory information disclosure should have the burden of demonstrating that government intervention is necessary.

INTRODUCTION: LOCATION OF THE CENTRAL ISSUES

I will begin this discussion with a brief review of some basic principles and the statement of some premises about which, to my way of thinking, we can probably agree. My goal is to narrow the area of differences to a few central questions and focus discussion on those questions.

Common Ground

Accurate, relevant, and informative product descriptions contained in advertising[3] are socially useful in that they substitute for search costs that otherwise would have to be undertaken by consumers. Since sellers can measure and describe product characteristics for their products more efficiently than consumers, who would have to conduct tests and analyze product characterisitcs for thousands of different purchased items each year, it makes sense, with respect to the sale of most products, that sellers discharge the principal burdens of the information task.

Accurate and relevant product information in advertising is procompetitive and proconsumer. When buyers are informed, markets tend to be more competitive (i.e., products are improved and profits driven down toward marginal cost) because informed buyers are in a position to compare a range of substitutable products and select those with relative price/characteristic advantages. Informed purchasers naturally prefer relatively low-cost/high-quality products, and that preference in turn places pressure on competing sellers to equal or exceed advantageous product characteristic combinations.

A supplemental procompetitive aspect of advertising has to do with entry. The ability of a company to obtain or expand market share through product innovations—e.g., ball-point pens, instant cameras, frozen pizza—is enormously augmented by its ability to inform a wide

---

3. For purposes of discussing mandatory-disclosure programs, I will not distinguish in the remainder of this paper between advertising and labeling, nor among different types of advertising.

range of consumers promptly of the availability and characteristics of the new product.[4]

Most information contained in contemporary advertising is accurate and relevant. Sellers with superior products have a natural incentive to disclose the price and characteristics of their products; sellers who exaggerate or deceive with respect to qualities that are ascertainable in the course of purchase or use will diminish their opportunity for repeat sales.

Occasionally, market incentives are inadequate to prevent sellers from exaggerating or being deceitful about their products. False information disseminated to consumers through advertising and acted upon by consumers is anticompetitive and anticonsumer. It leads to a misallocation of economic resources (purchase of products of relatively low quality or high cost compared to other similar commodities; possibly purchase of certain commodities which would not otherwise occur), and because of widespread consumer skepticism it tends to undermine the entire operation of competitive markets. Of this, a good deal more later. At least regarding express false claims in advertising, most commentators agree that as a matter of law and policy the government should intervene by developing a system of detection and penalty adequate to deprive false advertisers of the incentive to deceive.

Differences of View

Views begin to diverge when the question is raised of what to do about noninformative advertising. Specifically, what is government's role in market situations where key product information is not available to consumers to make sensible choices among competing products? Unavailability of information occurs principally in two situations: *first* (and more commonly), where all sellers are silent as to important product characteristics, and *second,* where disclosure occurs in noncomparable terms.[5] There is a formidable body of opinion to the effect that, under either of these circumstances, government intervention is unnecessary and misguided. I detect three related arguments supporting that view:

---

4. It may be that at some point massive noninformative advertising has an adverse effect on entry, though that continues to be a hotly debated point. Compare Yale Brozen, "Entry Barriers: Advertising and Product Differentiation," with H. Michael Mann, "Advertising, Concentration and Profitability: The State of Knowledge and Directions for Public Policy," in Harvey J. Goldschmid, H. Michael Mann, and J. Fred Weston (eds.), *Industrial Concentration: The New Learning,* Little, Brown, Boston, 1974, pp. 115–155. Even those who believe advertising in some markets can raise entry barriers and profits would accept that in other markets, nonmassive informational advertising ordinarily will facilitate entry.

5. Mandated disclosure can also be a remedial device to dissipate prior fraud, as in the "corrective advertising" remedy proposed against Listerine for false claims concerning its therapeutic effects (see *In re Warner-Lambert,* FTC Dkt. No. 8891 [Dec. 1975]). The propriety of such remedies raises special problems beyond the scope of this paper.

1. It is occasionally suggested that natural market incentives are adequate to induce disclosure, and that if disclosure has not occurred, the reason must be that the information would not influence purchasing decisions or that the influence would be so slight as not to justify the costs of accumulation and dissemination of the data.[6]

2. A variation on the first argument is that even if market incentives are inadequate to induce sellers to provide key product information through advertising, it does not follow that consumers are unprotected or the competitive process is defective unless the government intervenes. When the market fails to perform directly through stimulation of informational advertising, there is a variety of alternatives to which consumers can turn. Consumers can resort to "advisers" (e.g., magazines like *Consumer Reports,* brokers to assist in the purchase of insurance, word-of-mouth reports from other consumers), outlet reputation or brand names, guarantees or warranties assuring some level of performance of products that consumers are not in a position to evaluate, or they can turn to specialized dealers who select and offer only products with advantageous/characteristic combinations. Arguably, premature or unnecessary government intervention may abort development of these alternative consumer protection devices.

3. A third argument challenges the presumption that conspicuous information disclosure in advertising will lead a significant number of consumers to modify their commercial behavior. The contention here is that consumer purchasing motivation is complex and that almost any information disclosure system is unlikely to be fully understood to the point where it can significantly influence conduct.[7]

Many who oppose government intervention through mandated disclosure will assert some combination of these three arguments. They will, for example, contend that particular information-disclosure systems will not be learned or understood by consumers, and that if the systems were more easily capable of comprehension, sellers would have resorted without coercion to the disclosure system as part of a competitive strategy. However, I think there is some value in isolating, for purposes of discussion, the three different approaches.

The first—which seems the more doctrinaire view—in effect asserts that the market automatically produces optimal levels of information. This paper will argue that such views are wrong. I find more formidable the argument that the market generally produces adequate consumer information, and that in those rare situations where it does not, the cost and disadvantages of government intervention will outweigh any pro-

---

6. See Whitford, op. cit., p. 400, and FTC, Office of Policy Planning and Evaluation, *Mid-Year Budget Review,* pp. 1–2, reprinted in BNA, *Antitrust and Trade Regulation Reporter,* no. 758, April 1976, p. H-1. There are suggestions of a similar view in Richard A. Posner, *Dissenting Statement to the ABA Commission to Study the FTC,* pp. 108–114 (1969), but also a recognition that market incentives are not necessarily universally effective, so that situations can arise where key product data will not be available.

7. See Whitford, op. cit., pp. 403–440, and discussion at pp. 325–329 in this paper.

consumer and procompetitive effect. This paper will argue, however, that there are instances where only government intervention is likely to alleviate, in an acceptably brief period of time, information gaps resulting from market failure.

Before turning to analysis of these arguments, the next section will summarize recent developments with respect to mandated-disclosure programs to determine how pervasive this approach is at present, and whether there are trends toward expansion.

RECENT DEVELOPMENTS

Mandated disclosure at the federal level designed to increase consumer protection appears to be on the increase in the last decade or so.[8] In several statutes, Congress has chosen affirmative disclosure as a technique of regulation. Thus, the truth-in-lending statute mandated a comprehensive scheme of disclosure with respect to consumer credit;[9] the Fair Packaging and Labeling Act required label disclosure of contents of foods and other products;[10] the Interstate Land Sales Disclosure Act of 1968 required disclosure of key information relating to sale of interests in land subdivisions; [11] the recently enacted federal warranty statute appears to rely largely on disclosure of warranty terms (e.g., the limited scope of coverage) as a basic form of consumer protection;[12] and the Energy Policy and Conservation Act will require label disclosures of the energy efficiency of thirteen categories of appliances.

Government regulatory agencies, particularly the FTC, have been far more aggressive and innovative in recent years in using mandatory disclosure approaches to alleviate consumer problems. The Federal Energy Administration has required disclosure of miles-per-gallon capabilities of new cars.[13] At the FTC, there are rules currently in effect which require disclosure of the average durability of light bulbs,[14] octane ratings for gasoline,[15] and care labeling instructions on textile wearing apparel.[16] In addition, public indications of governmental

---

8. See Whitford, op. cit., pp. 400, 401. This piece contains an extensive catalogue of federal and state enactments and proposals for disclosure regulation in consumer transactions.

9. Consumer Credit Protection Act, 15 U.S.C. § 1601 *et seq.* (1970).

10. Fair Packaging and Labeling Act, 15 U.S.C. §§ 1451–1461 (1970).

11. Interstate Land Sales Disclosure Act, 15 U.S.C. § 1701–1720 (1968).

12. Magnuson-Moss Federal Trade Commission Improvements Act, 15 U.S.C. § 2301 (1975).

13. Federal Energy Administration, *Guide Concerning Fuel Economy Advertising for New Automobiles,* 16 C.F.R. § 259, 40 Fed. Reg. 42,004 (1975).

14. FTC, *Incandescent Lamp (Light Bulb) Industry,* 16 C.F.R. § 409, 35 Fed. Reg. 11,784 (1970).

15. FTC, *Posting of Minimum Octane Numbers on Gasoline Dispensing Pumps,* 16 C.F.R. § 422, 36 Fed. Reg. 23, 871 (1971).

16. FTC, *Care Labeling of Textile Wearing Apparel,* 16 C.F.R. § 423, 36 Fed. Reg. 23,883, as amended at 37 Fed. Reg. 24,815 (1972).

concern and the threat of rule-making action have led to voluntary industry arrangements for disclosure of phosphate content on the labels of soaps and detergents, and tar and nicotine content in print advertisements for cigarettes. The FTC also has proposed disclosure of a variety of information with respect to nutritional qualities of foods,[17] and has proposed a rule permitting disclosure of prescription drug price information by preempting state regulations declaring such disclosures illegal.[18] Another proposed rule would require those offering business opportunities through franchising to disclose to potential franchisees broad categories of information relating to likely profitability of the franchise ventures.[19]

The Commission also has resorted to mandated disclosure as a remedy in some of its consumer protection case work. For example, the Commission, in a dozen or so cases, has challenged vocational school advertising on grounds that failure to disclose the percentage of enrollees who do not complete the course and do not obtain employment on graduation is unfair.[20] Similarly, in complaints challenging alleged fraudulent land sales schemes, separate violations have been charged for failure to disclose specifics about future land development programs and failure to state that the purchase price of lots was not all-inclusive (e.g., paved roads and sewer systems were not available, and telephone service and electricity were available but at unreasonable prices).[21] While affirmative disclosure in case-by-case enforcement is hardly a novel remedial approach,[22] recent cases do seem more demanding in the kinds of information required to be disclosed.

---

17. See Commission Notice of Proceeding with Respect to Food Advertising, 16 C.F.R. Part 437 (1974).

18. See Disclosure Regulations Concerning Retail Prices for Prescription Drugs, 16 C.F.R. Part 447 (1975).

19. See Disclosure Requirements and Prohibitions Concerning Franchising, 36 C.F.R. 21607 (1971).

20. See, e.g., *Lear-Sigler*, 3 C.C.H. Trade Reg. Rep. (Transfer Binder 1970–73) 19,980 (1973); *Lafayette United Corp.*, 3 C.C.H. Trade Reg. Rep. (Transfer Binder 1973–76), ¶20,499 (1974).

21. See, e.g., *Horizon Corp.*, 3 C.C.H. Trade Reg. Rep. (Transfer Binder 1973–76), ¶20,845 (1975); *AmRep Corp.*, 3 C.C.H. Trade Reg. Rep. (Transfer Binder 1973–76), ¶20,846 (1975).

22. For example, disclosure requirements in the remedy context were imposed in J.B. Williams Co. v. FTC, 381 F.2d 884 (6th Cir. 1967), involving failure to disclose in connection with advertisements of the iron tonic Geritol that most fatigue has nothing to do with iron deficiency anemia, and Keele Hair & Scalp Specialists, Inc. v. FTC, 275 F.2d 18 (5th Cir. 1960), involving failure to disclose that most baldness cures will not work because baldness is hereditary. Indeed, some classic examples of what now appears to be wrongheaded, nitpicking, and anticompetitive advertising regulation at the Commission involved affirmative disclosure approaches—for example, forced disclosure of foreign origin or of the "reprocessed" qualities of low-priced substitute oil; see Posner, op. cit. pp. 109–110.

PROS AND CONS OF AFFIRMATIVE DISCLOSURE PROGRAMS

The remainder of this paper will be devoted to an analysis of arguments supporting and opposing government programs mandating information disclosure. In an effort to avoid a totally theoretical discussion of what should properly be regarded as a practical question of policy, two specific information disclosure programs will be examined—octane content in gasoline and tar and nicotine content in cigarettes.

Required Disclosure Programs and the Consequences of Buyer Ignorance

In evaluating information disclosure programs, it is important to specify how consumer ignorance tends to undermine effective competitive conditions in a market and leads, eventually, to impaired competition and consumer abuse. It was noted earlier that markets tend to be more competitive when buyers are informed, because those buyers are in a position to compare a range of substitute products and select those with price/characteristic advantages. Where buyers are ignorant, two principal competitive consequences occur.[23]

First, accurate product comparisons are impossible; therefore, the incentive for sellers to improve products or lower prices is sharply diminished. For example, if consumers are in no position to evaluate the claimed therapeutic efficacy of a mouthwash[24] or assertions that a particular gasoline will reduce air pollution,[25] there can be no effective check in the marketplace on spurious product claims. If consumers can be confused or misled by massive false advertising so as to lose the ability to compare similar products—as the FTC has alleged has occurred with respect to analgesics[26]—sellers can segregate markets and successfully extract higher prices for products substantially identical to lower-priced brands (in the analgesics example, over low-priced private label substitutes). Indeed, one would expect to find the heaviest advertising expenditures and the most aggressive efforts at product differentiation in connection with product categories where consumers are completely incapable of evaluating product claims.

Second, if consumer ignorance is sufficiently widespread, its presence can ultimately undermine competitive forces in broad market

---

23. For an elaboration of these arguments, see Tibor Scitovsky, "Ignorance as a Source of Oligopoly Power," *American Economic Review,* vol. 40, no. 2, May 1950, pp. 48–53.

24. See *In re Warner-Lambert Co.,* N. 5 *supra,* where the claim by Listerine that it was effective to prevent or ameliorate colds and flu was found to be deceptive.

25. *In re Standard Oil of California,* 80 FTC 1030 (1974).

26. For example, see *In re Bristol-Myers Co.,* FTC Dkt. No. 3287 (1972).

areas. Without the direct or indirect ability to judge for themselves the intrinsic merit of products, consumers often will turn to price as an indicator of quality or to brand name reputation as a substitute for direct product evaluation. Once high price becomes an indicator of quality for the majority of purchasers—for example, in the markets for wines, costume jewelry, and perfumes—it becomes self-defeating for sellers to lower price in order to attract customers.[27] It also follows that newcomers in markets characterized by consumer ignorance are virtually forced to follow a strategy of penetration by heavy noninformational (i.e., image) advertising, since consumers are unlikely to be influenced by informational claims, with the result that entry or the threat of entry are unlikely to result in a lowering of above-competitive prices. It has been suggested that the low price elasticity in such markets may be comparable to the patterns that emerge when collusion suspends price competition,[28] though consumer ignorance probably is never so complete as to duplicate the effects of a well-policed cartel.

If these arguments are correct, it follows that conditions of buyer ignorance undermine in a major way the operations of effectively competitive markets. The question remains what efforts may reasonably be undertaken to remedy those conditions.

Challenges to Government-Mandated Disclosure Programs

As noted, there appear to be three related challenges to the wisdom of government programs requiring disclosure of product information to consumers.

MARKET FAILURE AND THE ROLE OF GOVERNMENT-MANDATED INFORMATION PROGRAMS

Market incentives are generally adequate to produce most key product information through advertising, and when private sources make accurate information available, there is no reason for government intrusion. The question worth addressing is why situations would ever occur in which a seller with the superior product or lower price would not use its access to advertising channels to make the qualities of its product and the defects in competitive products known to consumers, and in so

---

27. I recognize that consumers in extreme ignorance can turn to indirect indicators of value other than price—for example, brand names of the manufacturers or reputation of the outlet. The point here is simply that they often do use price as an indicator of quality, and when they do, the competitive system becomes unworkable.

28. Scitovsky, op. cit. p. 50.

doing, inform consumers about essential features of the product category.

Causes of Information Failure. There are several obvious general situations in which sellers cannot be relied upon to supply key product information about their products. The first involves situations in which serious hazards attend purchase and use of the product and apply relatively equally to all competing brands in the line. An obvious example involves the failure of cigarette manufacturers to supply detailed information about health hazards of smoking. These situations are relatively rare, but I assume that most would agree that at least until safer substitute products begin to emerge (with an incentive to discuss health hazards), the government has a legitimate role in warning consumers about latent adverse effects.

Even when safer substitute products exist, free-market pressures may also be inadequate to produce acceptable levels of information if immediate and serious health and safety hazards attend uninformed use of the product. This general category is probably the least controversial instance of government-mandated disclosure, and would include such generally accepted programs as label disclosures of adverse side effects for drugs or dangerous consequences that accompany improper use of pesticides. Even if it were assumed that competitive conditions will eventually lead manufacturers of superior products to inform consumers of their less dangerous characteristics, that market mechanism would not afford adequate protection if consumers, during the educational process, could suffer serious injury or even death.

Another general situation in which sellers cannot be relied upon to advertise informatively relates to those instances where fraud pays; for example, furnishing of products or services that are generally once-in-a-lifetime purchases, such as tourist accommodations in a foreign country, encyclopedias, and hearing aids. Again, I assume most people would agree that government has a special obligation to protect consumers—particularly where there is a track record of extensive prior fraud in connection with the product or service category. That protection need not necessarily take the form of required disclosure. For example, a brief mandated trial period for hearing aids might serve far more effectively than disclosure of complicated technological information. Affirmative disclosure, however, could be one form of useful regulation in those areas of sale where the market cannot be relied upon to generate adequate inducements for sellers to supply key product information.

Firms with inferior products may be able to avoid effective comparisons by complicating comparison shopping. The proliferation of odd-sized "economy," "giant," and "super" packages in contempory retailing seems to have made comparison shopping in supermarkets an almost impossible task. The problem could not be easily remedied through advertising by the single most efficient seller.

There are a number of additional specific reasons why market incentives will be inadequate to ensure the availability to consumers of essential product information. Absence of data may reflect imperfections in market organization. For example, a monopolist may concentrate on public image advertising—confident that aggressive informational approaches by sellers of imperfect substitutes will make no serious inroads in the monopolist's sales volume. In highly concentrated markets, sellers may avoid specific product claims in order not to trigger mutually disadvantageous technological competition. Tar and nicotine disclosure in cigarettes—a form of mandated information disclosure that will be discussed more extensively below—is an interesting example of the possibilities of oligopoly interdependence. Once any company emphasizes the low tar/low nicotine qualities of its product, it is subject to retaliatory advertising claims for cigarettes with even lower tar and nicotine content. All the major American cigarette companies (accounting for 99 percent of domestic sales) offer a wide range of brands, including some high in tar and nicotine, and therefore are certain to suffer from aggressive marketing tied to tar and nicotine content in at least part of their product line. In other market situations, companies will find themselves making expenditures for research into new products which could diminish total profits. Finally, an informed consumer group may generate the kind of pressure against brands with less attractive product characteristics that eventually leads to a price war. At least where no one company believes itself to have a decisive competitive advantage over others, all may reach the conclusion that avoidance of certain kinds of product claims is mutually advantageous.

Finally, individual companies may forgo ad campaigns keyed to product information disclosure because unilateral disclosure is competitively useless. Unless all companies offering competing products make information available about their own product, consumers may not be in a position to select between rival brands. A related but similar problem arises when the form of disclosure is complicated and there is no obvious similar form of measurement upon which all sellers can base disclosed data. In that situation, one virtue of government intervention may be to supply a neutral outsider to measure or establish the standards of measurement for a disclosure system.

Obviously, it does not follow that mandated disclosure is justified where any one or several of these described conditions apply. Whether the disclosure of particular categories of product information should be required will depend on cost-benefit considerations in specific circumstances. Rather, the point here is that there are market situations in which standard market incentives are likely to be inadequate to stimulate competitors to make certain categories of product information available, and that some supplement to market forces—possibly government intervention—will be necessary if consumers are to have access to that information.

DISCLOSURE FAILURES APPLIED[29]

Octane. Prior to 1971, when the FTC issued its rule requiring disclosure of octane ratings on gasoline pumps,[30] only one integrated oil company (Sun)[31] and a few of the independents consistently disclosed specific octane levels (i.e., antiknock properties) of gasoline for sale. Instead, octane levels were indicated in a rough fashion under such vague labels as *high test* or *premium* (for example, 97 octane and more), *regular* (ranging from perhaps 93 octane up to 95 or 96), and *subregular* (which might range down to 91 or 92 octane).

Required octane levels for particular gasolines were often included in operational booklets distributed to motorists at the time of purchase of their car. Cars will not perform properly on gasoline with less than adequate octane, but once an adequate level of octane is reached, additional octane content is useless. Also, excess octane content is imperceptible during use, so that consumers, lacking precise data, could approach a minimum level of octane purchase only by a laborious process of trial and error. Since higher octane levels usually meant higher prices, many motorists were overpaying for octane that they could not possibly use for their cars.

One reason integrated major petroleum companies may have avoided octane disclosure, and attendant product-quality competition, is that disclosure would have spotlighted the fact that higher-priced advertised brands and low-priced unadvertised brands had substantially equivalent octane ratings. Obviously, the low-priced marketers could have made much of octane equivalence. Some did incorporate octane references in advertising, but since the market survival of those cut-rate marketers depended upon their maintaining a cost advantage by saving on advertising and other marketing expenses, they could not easily undertake an expensive advertising campaign to educate consumers about octane ratings in comparable gasolines.

In addition, comparable data from all sources are necessary if consumers are to make an informed choice about octane content. One problem the independents faced was that there was a variety of tests to measure octane and, therefore, the possibility of a confusing array of

---

29. Discussion here is limited to reasons why market forces were inadequate to generate these categories of product data. The further questions of whether required disclosure was advisable in light of possible alternatives and whether consumers would be likely to understand and use the disclosed data will be taken up below.

30. The FTC rule was challenged in the courts and never implemented (National Petroleum Refiners Ass'n. v. FTC, 482 F. 2d 672 [D.C. Cir. 1973], *cert. denied,* 415 U.S. 951 [1974]), but octane disclosure was later required by the Federal Energy Commission.

31. The numbering method used in Sun's disclosure system was unique, and therefore of limited value even to conscientious motorists who were interested in octane and knew the octane needs of their cars.

data in the market. Beyond that, octane content for particular brands will vary in different parts of the country and even at different outlets, so that accurate octane comparisons necessarily would have to be made on a pump-versus-pump basis. While octane content obviously is not the only relevant characteristic one would care to know about competing brands of gasoline and gasoline sellers (additives, credit arrangements, and outlet service are other factors which come to mind), it was an important indicator of product quality and was not available in the market before government intervention.

Tar and Nicotine Content. Even before recent scientific data had more clearly substantiated the likely connection between high-tar and high-nicotine content in cigarettes and serious health hazards, there was some suspicion that tar and nicotine elements would eventually be proven to be the chief causes of disease. As a result, there were references to tar and nicotine content in cigarette advertising prior to any government intervention. Partly because the standard of measurement of such content was uncertain, that advertising occasionally involved exaggeration or outright deception with respect to product quality.[32] Moreover, occasional bursts of advertising activity with respect to tar and nicotine invariably subsided, and for long periods there were no data on these characteristics available to consumers through advertising.

The reasons why tar and nicotine advertising was irregular and tended to be unreliable are not hard to understand.[33] Intensive and constant advertising campaigns by any of the six major cigarette manufacturers stressing low tar and nicotine content as a way of diminishing health hazards involved in smoking would result in underscoring health problems and diminishing total cigarette sales. Since each of the major companies offered popular brands with high tar and nicotine content, aggressive advertising programs could rebound, at least in part, to the disadvantage of the advertiser. Finally, the measurement of tar and nicotine content is a classic example of an area in which information disclosure is hampered unless there is a neutral outside source which ensures a uniform standard of measurement and guarantees the accuracy of the measurements. For all these reasons, there was little reliable tar and nicotine information available to consumers before the cigarette manufacturers, responding to the prospect of government

---

32. For example, see *American Brands, Inc.* (American Tobacco Co.), FTC Dkt. No. 8799 (August 1971).

33. The reason for one decline in tar and nicotine disclosure was that the FTC—in one of its more misguided campaigns—obtained the agreement of the cigarette manufacturers to discontinue all such references: *TRR for the Prevention of Unfair or Deceptive Advertising and Labeling of Cigarettes in Relation to the Health Hazard of Smoking* (issued on June 22, 1964,)p. 1. The Commission believed all cigarette smoking was dangerous, and decided that *any* reference to low tar and nicotine, however accurate, would give the erroneous impression that some smoking was relatively safe. The Commission reversed its position in 1967 and supported legislation requiring tar and nicotine disclosure.

action, elected voluntarily to report government test results in their advertising.[34]

ADEQUACY OF ALTERNATIVE CHANNELS OF INFORMATION

Consumers who are ignorant about actual product quality and left uninformed by the advertising process can protect their interests or be protected in alternative ways. If the rewards are substantial, consumers can assume the role usually discharged by sellers and search out otherwise unavailable product information. The market itself often produces neutral information sources through such publications as *Consumer Reports,* and consumers can purchase protection in the form of guarantees and warranties from those sellers offering such services. As a practical matter, many consumers depend on word-of-mouth reports from other consumers. Also, consumers in virtually all situations have some indication of quality through reliance on brand names or outlet reputation. Obviously, there is no reason for the government to intervene and commit its limited resources to mandatory disclosure programs and policing of enforcement if the market works adequately and consumers are protected as a result of alternative information sources. The question is whether these substitute information sources, some with inherent limitations, are an adequate substitute for the admittedly imperfect consumer protection achieved through mandated disclosure programs.

Take, as an example, reliance on brand names as an indicator of product quality. Certainly, it is not irrational in many situations for consumers to select among competing products on the basis of brand names, which in turn reflect confidence and satisfaction derived from prior experience. Consumers frequently rely on brand reputation as a kind of "information shorthand" where search costs are high or information about product quality unusually complex. Studies also indicate an interesting positive correlation between high perceived risk (i.e., situations where a "wrong choice" will produce serious adverse consequences) and durable brand loyalty.[35]

On the other hand, brand name reliance—particularly when accompanied by considerable consumer ignorance of product quality—has some disadvantages from the point of view of both consumers and the competitive system. All things being equal, consumer reliance on brand names tends to result in a preference for large companies that engage in substantial and protracted advertising programs. This is a preference usually unrelated to product quality or industrial efficiency.

---

34. Government pressure leading to a voluntary agreement is reported in BNA, *Antitrust and Trade Regulation Report,* no. 482, Oct. 6, 1970, p. A-22 and no. 487, Nov. 10, 1970, p. A-8.

35. Scott M. Cunningham, "Perceived Risk and Brand Loyalty," in Donald F. Cox (ed.), *Risk Taking and Information Handling in Consumer Behavior,* Harvard Graduate School of Business Administration, Division of Research, Boston, 1967, p. 523.

More important, brand reputation, again assuming substantially complete consumer ignorance, may itself depend upon false advertising or repetitive-image advertising devoid of product information. Finally, widespread consumer reliance on brand names has the defects of much noninformational advertising competition in that it encourages strategies of countercompetition through noninformational advertising and reduces incentives for product improvement or price reductions.

Perhaps the most useful conclusions about the role of information alternatives are that they constitute some outside limit on seller ability to exploit consumer ignorance; their adequacy will vary from case to case; and it is difficult to generalize about their adequacy.

Again, it is instructive to consider government-mandated information disclosure systems relating to gasoline and cigarette competition. As to required disclosure of octane levels, octane content was obviously not a product quality that could be determined by consumers on their own through training or education, though it could be deduced by conscientious and sophisticated motorists by a routine of trial and error. As noted previously, octane content varies within brands by region and even by station, so that dissemination of octane information by some specialized advisory service would have been virtually impossible. Moreover, since gasoline sales at retail are almost invariably through outlets selling a single brand, outlet reputation for careful selection of products would be irrelevant. The fact is that there was little accurate octane information in the market at the time the octane disclosure rule was proposed, nor any indication that additional octane information would become available in the near future.

Similarly, there was no comprehensive system of tar and nicotine disclosure prior to government involvement that led to a voluntary industry arrangement. Of course, it has been only recently that the Surgeon General and other authoritative sources have begun to indicate, with a fair degree of certainty, a connection between tar and nicotine content and dangers to the health of smokers. Given the seriousness of the consequences of smoking more dangerous brands of cigarettes, it may be that eventually the market would have generated independent and private measures of tar and nicotine levels and that individual competitors would then have turned to advertising featuring information about these elements. Government intervention may have aborted that development. On the other hand, it seems likely that government participation would have been necessary to develop a system of accurate measurement, if not mandatory disclosure. Finally, it is hard to imagine that any private system of disclosure would have been more accurate, less costly, and less intrusive than the current arrangement whereby tar and nicotine numbers—derived from a government-financed and operated testing program—are reported in small print on the face of cigarette ads.

In sum, octane and tar and nicotine disclosures appear to be situations where the market was not directly producing important product information, and where there was little prospect of consumers being accurately informed in the absence of some government action.

CAPACITY AND WILLINGNESS OF CONSUMERS TO USE INFORMATION SYSTEMS

I suggest that the main reason several mandated disclosure systems directed to consumers have been unsuccessful has less to do with theoretical misperceptions about the operation of market forces and more to do with the failure of program designers to judge accurately the capacity and willingness of consumers to use complicated data. If disclosure programs currently being considered are to have any chance of success, it is essential to begin to understand why these miscalculations have occurred.

An assumption of many government-mandated disclosure programs appears to be that consumers are highly rational in their purchasing behavior, that they are maximizers of their own interests, and that their purchasing decisions occur at a specific point in time in response to all available and relevant data. These premises are almost certainly not valid in the context of most consumer decisions.[36] On the contrary, there is, of course, a highly significant, irrational element in many purchasing decisions; information is taken from a variety of sources with a final purchasing decision reflecting a series of sequential reactions to perceptions of products and services;[37] and many consumers may opt to satisfy (e.g., by setting a reserve price and making a purchase whenever bids are submitted at that price) rather than to maximize their interests.[38]

Some critics of mandated-disclosure programs have suggested that a central problem with the design of those programs relates to the failure of those supporting disclosure to develop a clear model of the type of consumer on whose needs and capacity disclosure requirements will be based,[39] and generally to overestimate the capacity and willingness of consumers to integrate new information themes into ingrained patterns

---

6. Purchasing decisions which turn entirely or substantially on considerations of price may reflect more accurately this model of assumed consumer behavior. This is true in part because, unlike product characteristic claims, price information is almost perfectly quantifiable (with little subjective distortion), is unidimensional in the sense that a low price is almost always regarded by consumers as better than a high price, and is easily and uniformly understood by almost every consumer.

7. See John A. Howard and James Hulbert, *Advertising and the Public Interest* (a staff report to the FTC), Crain Communications, Chicago, 1973, pp. 34–45.

8. See John T. Lanzetta and Vera T. Kanareff, "Information Cost, Amount of Payoff, and Level of Aspiration as Determinants of Information Seeking in Decision Making," *Behavioral Science,* vol. 7, no. 4, October 1962, p. 459, and Dorothy Cohen, "The FTC and the Regulation of Advertising in the Consumer Interest," *Journal of Marketing,* vol. 33, no. 1, Jan. 1969, pp. 40–44.

9. John A. Howard and Lyman E. Ostlund (eds), *Buyer Behavior: Theoretical and Empirical Foundations,* Knopf, New York, 1973, p. 571.

of purchasing behavior. Ironically, government regulation of deceptive advertising often has been criticized on grounds that its effort to protect "the ignorant, the unthinking and the credulous"[40] resulted in a low-sophistication model of the average consumer that was unreasonable and unrealistic.[41] Past disclosure regulations (the obvious example is truth-in-lending) may have had little impact on consumer purchasing patterns because the disclosure system assumed a higher level of buyer sophistication, which was equally removed from reality.

Consumer behavior research has demonstrated convincingly that consumer reaction to disclosed data is highly complex and difficult to predict. At the same time, many government disclosure programs have not analyzed in advance what reaction would be likely to follow mandated disclosure. The most significant limitation on consumer capacity to assimilate information relates to the complexity of the data disclosed. Information disclosure programs obviously will not work where a substantial majority of consumers cannot conveniently assimilate or apply the disclosed information. Also, consumers in high-income categories may conclude that their time is more valuable than would justify its expenditure in efforts to understand and use new information systems. Therefore, they may accept the risks of making less than optimal purchases or rely on brand names rather than commit the time necessary to be influenced by mandated disclosure. This seems a valid theoretical point, but one unlikely to undermine the validity of most disclosure requirements. Assuming the disclosed data are fairly simple (e.g., average durability of light bulbs, efficiency of energy-using appliances, miles-per-gallon of automobiles) and the rewards of informed shopping substantial in terms of higher-quality or lower-priced products, it seems self-evident (given the premise of a market system) that most shoppers would take the information into account in their purchasing decisions.

Several other limitations on consumer capacity to use disclosed data are worth noting. The very poor may have few outlets for products or credit available to them, so that they have little incentive to put themselves in a position to be thoughtful comparison shoppers. And, consumers at all economic levels will not bother with information disclosure systems if the savings from comparison shopping are not sufficient to justify its costs.

Another important limitation on the feasibility of required disclosure has to do with *information overload*. Studies indicate that at some point—extremely difficult to identify in advance—most consumers will already possess all the information they are capable of using with respect to purchasing decisions. In those circumstances, newly dis-

---

40. Aronberg v. FTC, 132 F.2d 165, 167 (7th Cir. 1942).

41. Decisions which have gone to astonishing lengths to protect unwary and unsophisticated consumers are collected in Ira M. Millstein, "The Federal Trade Commission and False Advertising," *Columbia Law Review*, vol. 64, no. 3, March 1964, pp. 458–461.

closed data will do no more than drive out of consumers' minds other relevant and useful information.[42] A related problem has to do with *consumer selectivity* in acceptance of new information. For example, consumer behavior investigations suggest that information which contrasts with consumers' preconceived ideas about a brand or product may be "tuned out" and become irrelevant to purchasing decisions.[43]

These observations are not intended as an argument against all required disclosure. While predictions of likely consumer reactions to product information are difficult and complex, they certainly are not impossible to make. Indeed, they are the type of predictions that sellers constantly make when considering new marketing approaches. In some situations—e.g., disclosure of the price of eyeglasses or funeral services—it should be virtually self-evident that disclosure will have proconsumer and procompetitive effects.[44] Required disclosure of important product characteristics—where that can be achieved at a modest cost and in easy-to-understand terms—also should have beneficial effects. Moreover, as far as benefits to the competitive system are concerned, it is important to recognize that it is not necessary for all or substantially all consumers to be influenced by the disclosed data in order to produce procompetitive effects. If a substantial class of consumers becomes more selective in its purchasing decisions, sellers are likely to respond through lower prices or product improvements to the demands of this informed segment of the market. And, unless sellers can somehow isolate these informed purchasers (by introducing special custom items for their separate satisfaction), all consumers are likely to profit from competitive pressures generated by the more demanding minority. Thus the most benighted status seeker among automobile purchasers has probably "profited" by the demands of a large segment of the purchasing public for cars that give better miles-per-gallon performance. Nevertheless, information about miles-per-gallon was necessary before customers could make their collective will felt in local showrooms, and eventually in design planning in Detroit.

What can we learn from consumer reaction to disclosure of tar and nicotine content and octane levels in terms of capacity and willingness to use disclosed data? Unfortunately, not a great deal, since neither disclosure system was preceded by any careful study of likely consumer response or (to my knowledge) followed by published studies of consumer reaction. The disclosed facts—milligrams of nicotine and tar, and levels of octane—are relatively simple and easy to compare among

---

42. For example, see George A. Miller, "The Magical Number Seven, Plus or Minus Two: Limits on Our Capacity for Processing Information," *Psychological Review*, vol. 63, no. 2, March 1956, p. 81.

43. Cohen, op.cit., p. 40.

44. Persuasive studies document those results. For example, see Lee Benham, "Study of the Effect of Advertising on the Price of Eyeglasses," *Journal of Law and Economics*, vol. 15, no. 2, Oct. 1972, p. 342.

brands. Moreover, the advantages of informed purchasing—reducing serious health risks in connection with smoking and substantial economies in gasoline purchase—would seem sufficient to induce many consumers to take account of the data. There is certainly a plausible case that consumer purchasing patterns would be influenced by these kinds of data, but no clear documentation of that effect exists.

Seller reaction, since disclosure was mandated, is ambiguous. In recent years, American cigarette manufacturers have introduced highly advertised brands emphasizing low tar and nicotine content and have increased their advertising budgets for preexisting low tar and nicotine brands; there appears to be a sharp swing among purchasers toward these "safer" cigarettes.[45] The market is witnessing the "tar-and-nicotine derby" that was predicted when mandatory disclosure was first proposed. Of course, this change in consumer preference may have occurred primarily because of increased recent perception by smokers that high tar and nicotine cigarettes are more dangerous. Nevertheless, it seems likely that the introduction of these new products and the change in consumer preferences were assisted, to some considerable extent, by the disclosure of simple and comparable tar and nicotine data.

By contrast, there is little or no emphasis on octane levels in current marketing of gasoline. The oil boycott and subsequent operations of the OPEC cartel for a time virtually drove cut-rate independents out of the market, and these were the sellers most likely to emphasize octane content in their sales efforts. Also, since the oil boycott all gasoline advertising has avoided any price or product quality claims; thus, there is no occasion to discuss in advertising the comparative qualities of gasolines. Whether consumers will react to octane information when full retail competition in the oil industry is restored remains an open question.

Limiting Factors: Preconditions to Effective Mandatory-Disclosure Programs

If the analysis of the preceding sections is correct, mandatory disclosure of information to consumers is hardly a panacea for consumer complaints. Nevertheless, carefully selected disclosure programs should result in higher levels of consumer welfare. While each proposed program must be considered in the context of its special market significance, a few general suggestions indicating programs likely to be effective can be offered.

For reasons spelled out previously, a precondition for any govern-

---

45. *Hearings on Cigarette Smoking and Disease, 1976,* Subcommittee on Health of Senate Committee on Labor and Public Welfare, 94th Cong., 2d Sess., May 27, 1976, pp. 3–5 (testimony of Curtis H. Judge).

ment program ought to be a finding that market incentives are inadequate and are likely to continue to be inadequate to encourage sellers to provide the information voluntarily as part of the competitive process. Similarly, such programs should be based on findings—difficult in many circumstances because of the complexity of the issue involved—that consumers are likely to understand and use the disclosed information in connection with their purchasing decisions.[46]

One way of ensuring that disclosure programs will be effective is to limit them to simple key elements of product information. No disclosure program will be successful if it requires publication of a broad range of relevant information about product categories. In this context, octane numbers on the side of a pump and tar and nicotine figures seem to constitute a far more sensible form of mandated disclosure than, for example, extensive and complicated nutritional information about foods or complicated pharmacological data describing the formula of various drug products.

Another factor that should be taken into account relates to the expense of companies measuring, accumulating, and disseminating information, and the expense to the government of policing enforcement. At some point, mandated disclosure will simply be too expensive to justify the results it is intended to produce. This, of course, may be the reason the information was not available in the first place. A related point has to do with entry barriers. Expensive disclosure systems could raise entry barriers or prefer large over small firms because of the ability of large firms to finance testing and disclosure systems. Disclosure systems also could make product differentiation more difficult, and thereby impede the ability of new entrants to launch new brands. On the other hand, the disadvantages of preventing artificial product differentiation should be more than offset by the ability of new entrants to market low-priced private brands against entrenched brand-name rivals. In either event, if disclosure programs do lead to adverse competitive effects on industry structure, those considerations must also be taken into account.

CONCLUSION

Subject to the various constraints discussed here, there does appear to be a legitimate government role in mandatory disclosure of information

46. Past failures may have induced useful reforms in this area. In connection with its statutory responsibility to devise labels disclosing comparative annual operating costs and energy efficiency of 13 classes of appliances, the FTC recently put out an invitation for bids to consumer behavior research groups for a study designed to measure (1) current consumer understanding of energy efficiency data, and (2) consumer capacity to understand different forms of additional data that could be disclosed. Request for Proposal FTC 11-76, *Study to Evaluate Methods of Communicating Energy Cost Information on Consumer Product Labels* (June 1, 1976).

to consumers as a supplement to ordinary market forces. At their best, these programs put consumers in a position to protect their own interests in the marketplace. They provide a sensible substitute for case-by-case enforcement programs against alleged fraud, which entail inevitable problems of delay, expense, and unfairness to those individual advertisers sued for practices which are no different from those engaged in by their competitors.

THE FEDERAL TRADE COMMISSION'S MANDATED-DISCLOSURE PROGRAM: A CRITICAL ANALYSIS

Richard A. Posner, *Professor of Law, University of Chicago*

Section 5 of the Federal Trade Commission Act forbids "unfair or deceptive acts or practices in commerce."[1] The thrust of the FTC's activity in enforcing this provision has been to prevent false claims in advertising and labeling. Occasionally, the Commission has deemed an omission misleading and ordered the advertiser to rectify it—requiring, for example, that a seller of reprocessed oil disclose the fact that it is reprocessed, since otherwise the consumer would assume it was new.[2] More recently, the Commission, as part of the remedy for misrepresentations, has sometimes required an advertiser to include in future advertising affirmative statements (*corrective advertising*) designed to eliminate any confusion that might have been created in the public's mind by the advertiser's misrepresentations.[3]

Recently too, the Commission, also acting under the authority granted to it by the prohibition in section 5 of unfair or deceptive acts or practices, has required the disclosure of information about a product where the advertiser was not guilty of previous false claims or misleading omissions. An example is the trade regulation rule requiring producers of gasoline to post the octane rating of their gasoline brands.[4]

---

1. Federal Trade Commission Act, 15 U.S.C. § 46 (1914).
2. See, e.g., Mohawk Refining Co. v. FTC, 263 F.2d 818 (3d Cir. 1959).
3. For my views on "corrective advertising," see Richard A. Posner, "Truth in Advertising: The Role of Government," in Yale Brozen (ed.), *Advertising and Society*, New York University Press, New York, 1974, pp. 111, 119–120.
4. FTC, *Posting of Minimum Octane Numbers on Gasoline Dispensing Pumps*, 16 C.F.R. § 422, 36 Fed. Reg. 23, 871 (1972).

George J. Benston, David Bickert, Edmund W. Kitch, William M. Landes, George L. Priest, and George J. Stigler made helpful comments on an earlier draft of this paper, and Garry Cohen rendered valuable research assistance.

The premise of this rule is not that the gasoline companies must be punished for previous false claims regarding the octane or other characteristics of their gasoline; nor is it that silence conveys a false impression to the consumer. The premise is, simply, that the gasoline consumer needs the numerical octane rating to make sensible purchases.[5]

The rule-making and related activities of the Commission so premised have been called by the editor of this volume a program of "mandated disclosure," and I shall adopt his terminology. Of course, mandated disclosure in this sense is not a new concept. The Securities Act of 1933 requires new issuers of securities to make elaborate disclosures of financial and related information to the purchasers of the securities, regardless of any antecedent fraud by the issuer or anyone else. The Truth-in-Lending Act requires lenders to disclose detailed information concerning the terms of credit, again regardless of any history of fraud or misleading omissions. Professor Pitofsky, in his paper, mentions other statutes embodying the principle of mandated disclosure.[6] In this paper, however, I shall refer only incidentally to other experiences with mandated disclosure; my focus is on the FTC's program.

That program raises important economic and legal questions. The basic economic question is whether mandated disclosure is justified, either generally or in the specific instances in which the FTC has thus far required it. The legal question is whether the Commission has the authority, as it believes, under section 5 of the Federal Trade Commission Act to require mandated disclosure, whether by trade regulation rule or otherwise. I shall discuss both the economic and legal issues (the economic first), not attempting to conceal my profound skepticism concerning both the wisdom and the legality of the Commission's program.

THE ECONOMIC NEED FOR MANDATED DISCLOSURE

General Need

The question discussed in this section is whether the marketplace can be relied upon to provide consumers with enough accurate product information to enable rational product choices. Of course, even if the answer is no, it does not follow that the FTC's program of mandated disclosure is warranted (its legality aside). The ultimate policy question is whether the program is likely to improve the situation. It may not,

---

5. FTC, *Trade Regulation Rule Including a Statement of its Basis and Purpose: The Failure to Post Minimum Research Octane Ratings on Gasoline Dispensing Pumps Constitutes an Unfair Trade Practice and an Unfair Method of Competition* (1971) (found in 36 Fed. Reg. 23,871 [1971]).

6. See Pitofsky, above, pp. 315–316.

even if the situation is bad. History suggests that every FTC program carries a presumption of failure.[7]

I have written elsewhere on the subject of the circumstances in which the private market is unlikely to provide adequate product information,[8] and I shall repeat only the highlights of that discussion here. There are relatively few firms that sell information as such (though stock market newsletters, for example, illustrate the private sales of information); this is probably because of the difficulty of establishing property rights in information. Nonetheless, a good deal of information about products is generated in the private sector—by producers, by consumers, and by middlemen of all sorts. In an era of paternalism, the consumer's role in the production of product information tends to be ignored. Yet, to the extent that the relevant characteristics of a product can be ascertained on casual inspection or handling, it is probably the consumer who can produce the requisite information about the product at the least cost, simply by combining a modest expenditure of his time with his accumulated experience as a consumer. Even where the characteristics of the product are hidden from casual inspection, if they become revealed in the use of the product *and* if the product is one purchased repeatedly by the same consumers, the consumer is in a good position to learn the relevant product characteristics at low cost. The cost is the cost of the first purchase, and is normally low because products purchased repeatedly tend to be low cost (automobiles are an exception). Many consumers will avoid even this cost, learning of the product characteristics by word of mouth from other consumers.

In short, the dangers of consumer misrepresentation seem slight in cases where the consumer himself is able to ascertain at low cost the characteristics of the product in question, either by (1) casual inspection or handling prior to purchase or by (2) first use of a low-cost product that he purchases repeatedly. That leaves two areas of potential concern. These are (1) the costly or infrequently purchased product that has an important characteristic which is not apparent on casual inspection (the accuracy of an expensive watch would be an example); and (2) the product, whether cheap or expensive and whether frequently or infrequently purchased, that has an important characteristic which may remain hidden to the consumer throughout a long period of use. A food product containing a carcinogenic additive would be an illustration of the second problem.

The problem of standardizing industry product information is different, however. The consumer is aided by an industry's adoption of a standard of performance that enables comparisons to be made among

---

7. See, e.g., Richard A. Posner, "Regulation of Advertising by the FTC," American Enterprise Institute for Public Policy Research, Evaluative Studies, no. 11, Washington, D.C., 1973.

8. See, e.g., ibid., pp. 3–9.

competing brands. A traditional function of trade associations is to develop such standards. Perhaps there is some governmental role to be played in facilitating the voluntary adoption by an industry of the necessary standards, for, especially where the members of the industry are numerous, cooperative action to establish standards may encounter free-rider problems. However, there is no justification for imposing standards over the objections of most industry members or for compelling adherence to whatever standards are adopted. Once a standard is set, nonadherence by a member of the industry will be penalized by the consumer, or, if misrepresentations are involved, will present a standard case for invoking the legal remedies against fraudulent advertising. A trade regulation rule that imposes a standard not desired by the industry and that punishes deviations, whether fraudulent or not, is an inappropriate response to the problem of standardization.

The general problem area with which we should be concerned thus involves what, for want of a better term, I shall call the *well-hidden characteristic*. The characteristic may be either positive or negative—a health benefit as well as a health hazard (the cholesterol content of margarine, and of butter). Although it will be convenient to discuss the positive and negative characteristics separately, I emphasize that they are, in principle, of equal importance to the consumer.

With the consumer as policeman by assumption out of the picture—the characteristic is well hidden—and the possibility of an explicit market in the sale of product information also ruled out (because of the difficulty of establishing property rights in information), the critical question becomes whether producers (or other sellers, including intermediate sellers) have an incentive to disclose the well-hidden characteristic. This answer depends on the ability of the producer to profit from the disclosure.

Let us begin with the positive characteristic, using as our example the cholesterol content of a low-cholesterol margarine. There is medical opinion that people would improve their health prospects by substituting such a margarine for butter. It would seem obvious, therefore, that the producers of margarine have an incentive to advertise the cholesterol content of margarine and its significance for health. However, the margarine producer who so advertised would be conferring an uncompensated benefit on competing producers of margarine, for unless the first producer's margarine had even less cholesterol than his competitors' margarine, his advertisement of the benefits of using margarine would benefit all margarine producers (proportionately) equally. The advertiser would derive no greater benefit from his advertisement than his competitors, but only he would have paid for the advertisement, which would put him at a competitive disadvantage. The prospect that other producers would take a "free ride" on the advertisement operates to discourage advertising of this character.

The problem would disappear with monopoly. A margarine monopolist would reap all the benefits from the increased demand for margarine stimulated by the advertisement. Monopoly (and to a lesser extent presumably oligopoly) is a positive feature in informing the consumer about the genuinely good qualities of a product. Yet, even without monopoly, one observes that producers of margarine do advertise its low-cholesterol qualities, despite the free-rider problem discussed above; the problem is serious, but evidently not wholly insurmountable. Trade association advertising may also provide a solution to the free-rider problem, though in one sense it merely shifts the problem to a different level: why should a producer join a trade association and thereby help pay for a share in advertising that will benefit the non-member producer just as much?

The obverse problem is that of the well-hidden negative characteristic. The health hazards of smoking provide a now-classic example. No producer of cigarettes has any incentive to disclose those hazards, save perhaps to establish the factual predicate of a defense of assumption of risk in a tort case. The competitors of the cigarette companies would like the dangers of smoking to be widely trumpeted—but who are the competitors of the cigarette industry? While a reduction in the demand for cigarettes would lead to an increase in the demand for other products, the increase would be diffused across many industries and firms. Producers of pipes and cigars, soft drinks and chewing gum, candies and weight-reducing agents, and of alcohol and tranquilizers would be among those benefitting from a decline in cigarette consumption. The benefits would be so widely distributed among products and producers that no single producer would have an incentive to bear the expense of an advertising campaign designed to acquaint the consuming public with the hazards of smoking.

The problem in both cases I have discussed (the positive and the negative well-hidden characteristic) is that the characteristic is common to all the producers in the market—that is, to all producers of close substitutes. The margarine producer is reluctant to advertise the beneficial qualities of his product because other producers make essentially the same product and will therefore benefit as much as he will from the advertisement. No producer will advertise that cigarettes are harmful, because no producer makes a product that is a close substitute for cigarettes—unless he is another cigarette producer.

Conversely, where the characteristic in question is specific to one or some, but not all, producers of a product and its close substitutes, the problem I have been discussing does not arise. The producer of a cigarette that was not harmful to health would have every incentive to advertise the fact (unless, perhaps, the product could be very quickly duplicated by competitors or new entrants). The only producer of a low-cholesterol margarine would have a strong incentive to advertise the beneficial qualities of low-cholesterol margarine. Pitofsky suggests that the producer of *both* a high- and a low-nicotine cigarette would be reluctant to advertise the nicotine content of his low-nicotine cigarette because the disclosure would implicitly disparage, and hence reduce the sales of, the other cigarette.[9] But this is not a problem of advertising at all. The real question presented by Professor Pitofsky's example is why a manufacturer would bring out a product (here, a low-nicotine cigarette) that competes with the product he already makes. Once he decides to produce the new product, surely he will advertise its novel characteristics; otherwise, the product will not sell. If he does not want it to sell, why did he produce it in the first place? I do not think that suppression of new products is a serious economic problem, but if it is, it will not be solved by mandated disclosure.

An analytically difficult case is that of the *relative* claim of being free from some hazard or defect that may not be well known. Today, everyone knows that cigarette smoking is (almost certainly) hazardous, but it was not always known. At a time when most people were unaware of the hazard, the manufacturer of a safer cigarette would have had to balance the gain in sales that he could anticipate from advertising the safety characteristics of his cigarette against the loss in sales that would result from his having alerted the consumer to hazards that his brand shared with other brands of cigarettes. An advertisement that one brand is less likely than others to cause lung cancer contains an implicit acknowledgment that the advertised brand, though less hazardous than other cigarette brands, is more hazardous than other products (e.g., chewing gum). Some consumers, instead of substituting the advertised brand for other brands of cigarettes, will substitute other products altogether.

To illustrate the nature of the trade-off faced by the producer, assume that brand A, the safer one, now has 10 percent of the market, and if the producer advertised its superior safety, that market share would increase to 15 percent; but the implicit acknowledgment of hazard in the advertisement would also cause total sales of cigarettes to decline by 50 percent. Sales of brand A would decline. As this example suggests, however, a quite drastic effect on overall sales is required to offset a seller's gains from successfully differentiating his brand in the public eye (and I have ignored the possibility that a decline in total sales might be offset by the premium price that the safer brand might command, over and above any additional costs of producing it). Moreover, the nondisclosure strategy may be inhibited by competitive considerations. The producer of brand A may be confident that it is not in *his* interest to advertise its superior safety characteristics, but he may be unsure how other producers, existing or potential, of safer cigarettes reckon their self-interest in this regard. His uncertainty may lead him to go ahead and advertise brand A's superior safety, fearing that if he does not, he will lose the sales advantage of being first in the market with a safer cigarette, with no corresponding gain from having withheld from the public information concerning the hazardousness of cigarettes generally.

---

9. See Pitofsky, above, p. 322.

The foregoing analysis suggests that, even in the case of the well-hidden characteristic, there can be no presumption that sellers will lack substantial incentives to disclose it unless there is no variance in the characteristic across sellers—a strong assumption, though one satisfied, for example, in the case of the cholesterol content of eggs. Still another consideration is that there are other sources of product information in our society besides sellers and buyers. Product hazards are often newsworthy, and information about them can become rapidly (sometimes prematurely) disseminated by the news media to the consuming public. This fact, in turn, suggests a doubt about the likely efficacy of mandated disclosure. A responsible government agency would not compel the disclosure of a product characteristic until the existence of that characteristic had been convincingly demonstrated. Once a characteristic is well known, however, it is unlikely to be well hidden. If it is a characteristic, like the hazards of smoking or of high-cholesterol foods, in which large numbers of consumers are interested, its existence will have been communicated to the public through the news media. Mandated disclosure will, at best, increase rather than first create public awareness of important product characteristics.

To summarize, there may be some case for public intervention to compel disclosure of a well-hidden characteristic that is common to an entire industry, but only if—a vital qualification—the intervention is not so costly as to swallow up the benefits, which may well be slight, of the additional information generated.

Mandated Disclosure in Practice

It is time to take a closer look at the actual operation of the FTC's program of mandated disclosure. I want first to distinguish the question of the program's substantive merits from the procedural question of the Commission's power to issue substantive rules under the Federal Trade Commission Act. The primary vehicle for mandated disclosure has been the *trade regulation rule,* the name the Commission has given to its substantive rules. Most trade regulation rules do not involve mandated disclosure, although the case in which the legality of the trade regulation rule procedure was established happened to involve a mandated-disclosure rule (the octane-posting rule mentioned earlier).[10] In principle, the Commission could have implemented a program of mandated disclosure through conventional cease-and-desist-order proceedings. Programs of affirmative disclosure that, while distinguishable from mandated disclosure, have at least a family relationship to it—like requiring disclosure of the foreign origin of imported products—were developed and implemented long before the Commission's assertion of its dormant rule-making powers.

---

10. National Petroleum Refiners Ass'n v. FTC, 482 F.2d 672 (D.C. Cir. 1973), *cert. denied,* 415 U.S. 951 (1974).

The starting place for a discussion of the mandated-disclosure program is the Commission's 1964 trade regulation rule proceeding involving the health hazards of cigarette smoking. The upshot of the proceeding was a rule (later preempted by Congress) requiring the cigarette manufacturers to disclose, in both labeling and advertising, that smoking had been found to be hazardous to health. The rule cannot easily be defended by reference either to previous representations by the cigarette manufacturers that smoking was nonhazardous or to a well-founded consumer expectation that, in the absence of some statement to the contrary, smoking must be safe. It is not like a case where the Commission might require an importer, who had falsely represented that his product was made in France, to disclose that it was actually made in Hong Kong; or a manufacturer of reprocessed oil to disclose that it was reprocessed, since otherwise the consumer would naturally assume (though the manufacturer had never affirmatively represented the oil to be new) that it was new. The cigarette case is more like one where, for the reasons mentioned in the previous section, market incentives for the development of highly material product information simply were lacking.

To be sure, the Commission, in true common-law fashion, tried to fit the cigarette rule into the pattern of the earlier affirmative-disclosure cases. It pointed out that the industry's advertising, while not containing explicit representations that cigarette smoking was nonhazardous, had by its choice of themes seemingly sought to allay possible public concern over the hazards of smoking.[11] And it argued, by analogy to cases of the reprocessed-oil type, that given the extensive government regulation of hazardous products, people would assume, in the absence of a warning, that any product so widely advertised as cigarettes was safe for human consumption.[12] But alternatively, and perhaps persuasively, the cigarette rule could have been defended by reference to the theoretical case for mandated disclosure presented in the previous section of this article—were it not for well-founded doubts (see pages 344–345) as to the Commission's authority to implement a program of "pure" mandated disclosure, that is, where there is no history of misrepresentations or misleading omissions.

As will become clear from my discussion of the Commission's subsequent initiatives in the area of mandated disclosure, I regard the 1964 cigarette rule as the high-water mark of the Commission's program. Even so, it is subject to the criticism suggested earlier that once a well-hidden characteristic has become sufficiently demonstrated to justify governmental action to compel producers to disclose it, the characteristic is likely no longer to be well hidden. The Commission did not act to require disclosure of the health hazards of smoking until those hazards

---

11. FTC, *Unfair or Deceptive Advertising and Labeling of Cigarettes in Relation to the Health Hazards of Smoking,* 16 C.F.R. § 408, *Statement of Basis and Purpose of TRR,* 29 Fed. Reg. 8325, 8341–8348, 8356–8357 (1964).

12. Ibid., pp. 8356, 8361.

had been documented in a long series of scientific studies, culminating in the Surgeon General's report on which the Commission relied in finding that there was a consensus of medical opinion on the hazards of smoking.[13] The Commission could hardly have acted much earlier, and yet the scientific studies on the basis of which it took action were widely publicized, especially the Surgeon General's report. The trade regulation rule, had it been allowed to go into effect, would have provided, at best, an incremental addition to public awareness of the hazards of smoking. This may be an additional reason why the Commission stressed, as the basis for the rule, the alleged efforts of the cigarette companies to offset, through massive and tendentious advertising campaigns, the public impact of the publicity about the hazards of smoking.

Since 1964, the Commission has issued a number of trade regulation rules requiring disclosure of product information. However, most of these do not require mandated disclosure in the sense in which I am using that term. For example, the trade regulation rule requiring the disclosure of the odds and other characteristics of games of chance in food and gasoline retailing was expressly based on a history of affirmative misrepresentations in the industries involved.[14] I have found only four relatively pure examples of mandated disclosure: three trade regulation rules, involving light bulb wattage and related characteristics,[15] care labeling of textile products,[16] and gasoline octane ratings,[17] respectively, plus two informal agreements between the FTC and (1) the cigarette manufacturers, requiring them to disclose the tar and nicotine content of their cigarettes, (2) the detergent manufacturers, requiring them to disclose the phosphate content of their detergents.[18] I shall follow Professor Pitofsky's lead and concentrate on the rules regarding octane and tar and nicotine.

Octane is a characteristic of gasoline related to the problem of "knocking," a malfunction familiar to all automobile owners which can cause engine damage as well as the unpleasant sound that gives it its name.[19] If the owner uses a gasoline with an octane rating too low for

---

13. Ibid., pp. 8327–8332; *Smoking and Health*, Report of the Advisory Committee to the Surgeon General of the Public Health Service, Jan. 11, 1964.

14. FTC, *Games of Chance in the Food Retailing and Gasoline Industries*, 16 C.F.R. § 419, 34 Fed. Reg. 13,302 (1969). See FTC Staff Report to the Federal Trade Commission, *Economic Report on the Use of Games of Chance in Food and Gasoline Retailing*, 1968, pp. 459–467.

15. FTC, *Incandescent Lamp (Light Bulb) Industry*, 16 C.F.R. § 409, 35 Fed. Reg. 11,784 (1970).

16. FTC, *Care Labeling of Textile Wearing Apparel*, 16 C.F.R. § 423, 36 Fed. Reg. 23,883 as amended at 37 Fed. Reg. 24,815 (1972).

17. *Posting of Minimum Octane Numbers*, N. 4 *supra*.

18. There are also, at this writing, various proposed trade regulation rules for mandated disclosure on which the Commission has not yet finally acted. See Pitofsky, above, p. 316.

19. All the facts about the octane-rating problem recited here are drawn from the Commission's statement of the basis and purpose of the rule. See *Trade Regulation Rule, N. 5 supra*.

the car's type of engine, knocking will ensue. But, since increasing a gasoline's octane rating increases its cost, one does not want to buy a gasoline whose octane rating is higher than is needed to avoid causing knocking.

The method of octane rating traditionally used by the industry was very simple. The automobile owner had a choice between *premium* (high-octane) and *regular* (low-octane) gasoline; the owner's manual for the car provided the octane requirements of the engine. With the advent of compact cars that did not require even the octane rating of regular gasoline, some refiners began offering *subregular* gasoline having a lower octane rating.

Although numerical octane ratings were generally not communicated to the consumer either in the owner's manual or at the pump, it is unclear that the consumer was disserved. The members of the highly competitive petroleum industry had an incentive to produce the minimum octane rating that would avoid knocking, for a higher octane rating would not improve engine performance but simply increase the cost of the gasoline (and hence, price). Nor were members of the industry likely to cheat the consumer by reducing the octane rating of their gasoline below the level required to avoid knocking, since knocking is a perfectly obvious malfunction to the driver. As an example of the workings of competition in this area, I point out that when the gasoline refiners discovered that in warm climates a lower octane rating would still avoid knocking, they reduced the octane rating of their regular gasoline or offered subregular. The consumer did not know the octane rating had been changed—but what value would the information have had for him?

The Commission's trade regulation rule requires numerical octane postings at the pump. The goal is a better-informed consuming public. If this means providing the consumer with more information than he wants or can use, it is a foolish goal. It is far from obvious what value the numerical octane posting would have to drivers. To the extent that there is a public demand for a finer gradation of octane ratings than the traditional distinction between premium and regular (and now subregular), we can expect the refiners to supply it. Indeed, as increases in the price of gasoline have made consumers more sensitive to factors (such as octane rating) affecting that price, refiners *have* introduced new gradations (e.g., *subpremium*), specifying the auto makes in which the new gasoline can be used without causing knocking. If gradations were to become too numerous for convenient verbal descriptions, no doubt the refiners would begin to use numerical ratings voluntarily.

A case for *requiring* numerical ratings would be presented if the verbal categories (premium, regular, etc.) concealed significant variations in octane rating. Such variations would be unlikely. A refiner would hardly increase the octane rating of his gasoline above the level necessary to avoid knocking, since that would do nothing for performance and would increase the cost of the gasoline; nor would he be likely to reduce the octane rating below that level, for the consumer would experience knocking and know that he had been cheated. In any event, the Commission conceded that octane ratings vary insignificantly within the verbal categories; so this is not a problem.

The Commission's reasons for nonetheless requiring numerical postings are unconvincing. It expressed a general hope that the requirement would lead to a better-informed public, a finer matching of engine octane requirements to gasoline octane ratings, and a reduction in the purchase of unnecessarily high octane gasoline; but the why and how were left out. The Commission expressed itself as greatly concerned with the consumer who buys premium gasoline unnecessarily; but it is unclear how numerical ratings will help this foolish consumer's plight. If he is buying premium, even though his owner's manual tells him he does not need it, why does the FTC expect that he will purchase gasoline with an octane rating of 92 rather than 101 just because the owner's manual tells him that 92 is enough? Is "101" more informative than "premium"? All this assumes, moreover, that auto manufacturers will play the Commission's game by revising the owner's manuals to specify the minimum octane rating of the gasoline required by the engine, rather than just specifying premium, regular, or subregular.

Information that is valueless is not, however, costless. It was pointed out in the hearings before the Commission that the methods for computing numerical octane ratings suffered from various infirmities, that the choice of one yardstick might cause misleading results, etc. These objections were brushed aside as outweighed by the clear public need for the information; no such need was demonstrated or seems plausible in the circumstances. Thus, I disagree with Professor Pitofsky's statement that "absent accurate information with respect to gasoline octane levels, most consumers cannot judge whether a purchase of gasoline constitutes a useless extravagance in the sense that the consumer is purchasing unnecessary octane qualities for a particular car."[20]

I turn now to the informal agreement with the Commission whereby the cigarette manufacturers agreed to disclose the tar and nicotine content of their cigarettes. For reasons explained earlier, I think there would be market disincentives to generating information about the relative safety of cigarettes—if the hazards of smoking were not by now widely known. There can be few if any smokers in this country who are unaware that the weight of expert opinion is strongly against the safety of smoking. In these circumstances, a cigarette manufacturer who developed and advertised a safer cigarette (if there is such a thing) could not be seriously concerned that his advertising would awaken consumers to the existence of hazards to which they would otherwise have remained oblivious. Since there are no longer market disincentives to the advertising of low-tar and/or low-nicotine cigarettes, there

---

20. Robert Pitofsky, "Changing Focus in the Regulation of Advertising," in Brozen (ed.), *Advertising and Society*, p. 143.

is no rationale for requiring disclosure of tar and nicotine content, save in cases where the manufacturer's advertising may have created a misleading impression of the tar and nicotine content of his cigarettes.

I have not, of course, "proved" that the gasoline octane and tar and nicotine disclosure requirements have been of no significant value to consumers. My argument, like the Commission's, has been conjectural rather than theoretical, though surely the burden of persuasion rests on the proponent of government action. I invite a rigorous empirical examination of the question. That examination would take the form of studying consumer behavior in the markets in question before and after the introduction of the requirement, holding constant (to the extent possible) other factors (e.g., changes in income and price) that might have simultaneously affected consumer behavior. If the relative market shares of gasoline brands having different octane ratings and cigarette brands having different levels of tar and/or nicotine did not change as a result of the Commission's disclosure requirements,[21] that would be strong evidence that mandated disclosure did not provide the consumer with valuable information—information that he would act upon by altering his buying. Comparable studies of other mandated-disclosure programs, such as the disclosure requirements of the Securities Act of 1933, have indicated that they do not, in fact, alter consumer behavior.[22] These studies establish a presumption of futility (apparently conceded by Pitofsky) for such programs, which could be confirmed or refuted as to the FTC's program by conducting studies of the sort just described.

I would go further and urge the Commission to adopt (or Congress to impose on the Commission) a policy of studying the effects of each of its mandated-disclosure requirements. The Commission should *want* to know whether the flimsy conjectures on the basis of which it requires sweeping changes in the advertising and marketing of products have a factual foundation. It can find out by conducting follow-up studies, along the lines suggested, of its mandated-disclosure rules. The appendix to this paper contains some very preliminary results of an attempt to study the effects of the tar and nicotine rule.

I want to make clear that I am not arguing that there is no conceivable place for mandated disclosure in the arsenal of public policy. For reasons indicated earlier, one can imagine situations in which an unregulated market would fail to provide an optimum amount of product information. These situations may be, but probably are not, com-

21. The octane-posting rule was never implemented, but a similar rule, promulgated by the Federal Energy Administration, went into effect in 1975.

22. On the effect of the Securities Act, see George J. Benston, *Corporate Financial Disclosure in the UK and USA,* Lexington Books, Heath, Lexington, Mass., 1976; George J. Stigler, "Public Regulation of the Securities Market," in Sitgler (ed.), *The Citizen and the State: Essays on Regulation,* University of Chicago Press, Chicago, 1975, p. 78. For generally similar conclusions regarding truth-in-lending, see William C. Whitford, "The Functions of Disclosure Regulations in Consumer Transactions," *Wisconsin Law Review,* vol. 1973, no. 2, 1973, p. 420 (surveying the empirical literature).

mon. They appear to be limited to cases in which the product in question has a well-hidden characteristic common to all producers of the product and its close substitutes. In such cases, if the Commission could act before the well-hidden characteristic became well known, it might be able to promote the public welfare. But the two examples of mandated disclosure that I have discussed—octane and tar and nicotine—do not involve situations where the market cannot be expected to generate appropriate incentives for the production and dissemination of product information. No more do the Commission's other forays into mandated disclosure. If consumers wish to purchase low-phosphate detergents, detergent manufacturers will produce and advertise low-phosphate detergents without prodding from government. Manufacturers and retailers of wearing apparel have every incentive to provide accurate instructions for laundering their products. As for requiring producers of light bulbs to disclose facts concerning the light output, life, etc. of their bulbs, the producer who increases the life of his bulb relative to that of other brands has every incentive to advertise this fact; and so with the producer who trades long life for greater light output. So long as false advertising of light bulb characteristics is prevented, I can see no persuasive case for public intervention.

Now some industries may not behave, in fact, as economic theory predicts they will. This is surely a possibility, although the sorts of hearsay and anecdotes that the Commission in its rule-making proceedings accepts as proof of "market failure" are not convincing evidence that this has happened in the industries in which disclosure has been mandated. The question is, should government focus its regulatory efforts on activities where the self-interest of producers coincides with the public interest, on the ground that producers may misconceive their self-interest, or on activities where there is reason to believe that the goals of profit maximization and of consumer welfare maximization may diverge?

At the least, where mandated disclosure lacks any theoretical basis in the analysis of competition and information, as in the examples I have discussed, the Commission should be required to present a convincing factual basis for mandated disclosure in advance of requiring it. This the Commission has signally failed to do. With the exception of the statement of basis and purpose in the 1964 cigarette proceeding, the statements accompanying the Commission's mandated-disclosure rules are unimpressive collations of rumor, anecdote, and assertion. The Commission has used the freedom of rule-making procedure from the rules of evidence to adopt standards of fact-finding on a par with those of the sloppier congressional committees; anyone who doubts me should read the statement accompanying the octane-posting rule in its entirety.[23] This makes it all the more important that the Commission

---

23. See *Trade Regulation Rule, N. 5 supra.*

should undertake responsible studies of the impact of each mandated-disclosure rule along the lines suggested earlier.

THE LEGAL BASIS OF MANDATED DISCLOSURE

I want to examine now the question of the Commission's statutory power to order disclosure in the absence of antecedent misrepresentations (including omissions that would be actionable under conventional theories of misrepresentation). Again, I stress that I am interested in the substantive merits of mandated disclosure rather than in the propriety of rule making as a method of implementing it.

Oddly, there appears to be no adjudicated case dealing with the Commission's power to mandate disclosure. The challenge to the octane-posting rule was based solely on the Commission's alleged lack of power to issue substantive rules.[24]

The statutory basis of mandated disclosure is the prohibition in section 5 of the Federal Trade Commission Act of "unfair or deceptive acts or practices." The failure of the gasoline producers to post numerical octane ratings cannot be deemed a deceptive practice. The terms *premium, regular,* and so on, were not deceptive, and the failure to translate these terms into numbers for the consumer was not an attempt to "exploit the normal expectations of consumers in order to deceive," which is how the Commission has defined a deceptive omission.[25] Neither was the cigarette companies' nondisclosure of tar and nicotine content.[26]

Inevitably, the Commission has emphasized the concept of the unfair practice as an independent basis for regulating sales practices, distinct from deception.[27] The origin of this approach is a series of cases in which the Commission forbade the use of lotteries to sell merchandise as contrary to a national public policy against gambling.[28] But, in the context of mandated disclosure, the Commission has defined an "unfair" practice not as something contrary to settled public policy but as anything that is oppressive to consumers.[29] This usage gives the Commission carte blanche to condemn sales practices, for a term like *oppressive* has no obvious limitations.

The legislative histories of the various statutes defining the Commis-

---

24. National Petroleum Refiners Ass'n v. FTC, N. 10 *supra.*

25. In the cigarette proceeding, see Posner, "Regulation of Advertising by the FTC," and 29 Fed. Reg. 8352.

26. See pp. 335–337 in this paper.

27. The seed was planted in the cigarette statement, FTC, *Unfair or Deceptive Advertising and Labeling of Cigarettes,* pp. 8354–8355.

28. See, e.g., FTC v. R. F. Keppel & Bros., Inc., 291 U.S. 304 (1934).

29. See cigarette statement, FTC, *Unfair or Deceptive Advertising and Labeling of Cigarettes,* p. 8355.

sion's powers do not reveal a congressional intent to endow the Commission with a wholly undefined discretion to regulate sales practices neither deceptive nor contrary to any established public policy of the United States. It is one thing to forbid deceptive advertising, building upon a long common-law policy against misrepresentation, and another to mandate informative advertising, not as a remedy for previous misrepresentations, express or implied, but to correct nonculpable "market failures" or, even more dubiously, to implement a vague goal of a better-informed public without any economic guidelines. So significant a redefinition of the Commission's role should be made by Congress rather than by the Commission.

Another relevant consideration in interpreting the Commission's statutory power is the possible significance of the Supreme Court's recent decision that the First Amendment protects commercial speech from (undue?) government regulation.[30] The decision held that the Commonwealth of Virginia could not forbid price advertising of prescription drugs. The constitutionality of a myriad of other public regulations of commercial speech was left open, though there are strong indications in the Court's opinion that the conventional legal remedies for deceptive advertising will survive any constitutional challenge to them. But the constitutionality of mandated disclosure remains, to my mind, open to doubt. To return to the octane case, oil companies have chosen to disclose octane ratings in verbal rather than numerical form—premium, regular, etc. The Commission has not found that the verbal description is misleading. Nonetheless, it is requiring the oil companies to adopt a different description. This would seem to place a heavy burden on the exercise of commercial speech.[31] But, whether in the end mandated disclosure is or is not held to be unconstitutional, that it raises a serious constitutional question affords a traditional reason for interpreting the Federal Trade Commission Act in a way that prevents the question from arising. The act should not be construed to authorize the Commission to require disclosure of product information in the absence of antecedent deceptive acts or omissions.

---

30. Virginia State Board of Pharmacy v. Virginia Citizens Consumer Council, 425 U.S. 748 (1976).

31. Cf. Miami Herald Publishing Co. v. Tornillo, 418 U.S. 241 (1974).

APPENDIX—AN EMPIRICAL STUDY OF THE TAR AND NICOTINE DISCLOSURE RULE

This appendix contains the highly tentative and preliminary results of an attempt (or rather two attempts using different methods) to study empirically the effects of the Federal Trade Commission's tar and nicotine disclosure requirement.[32] The study cannot be considered either complete or definitive, but the results to date are reported here for what they may be worth.

The initial methodology I employed involved dividing cigarette brands into four categories depending on the tar and nicotine content of each brand and tracing changes over time in the market share of each category. This procedure assumes that the tar and nicotine content of each brand remained at least approximately constant during the period covered by the study. If it did not, then, for example, the tar and nicotine content for the entire category of high tar and nicotine brands might be falling, even if the market share of the category was rising. In that event, the rise in the market share of high tar and nicotine brands might be concealing an actual reduction in the average tar and nicotine content of the cigarettes that people were smoking.

A random sampling of brands indicates that the changes in tar and nicotine levels over the period from 1968 to 1975 were small,[33] although they generally involved a decline in those levels rather than a rise; no data are available for earlier years. Thus, my initial empirical procedure, which, as I have said, assumed constant tar and nicotine levels over the entire period (from 1965 to 1974) covered by the study, proba-

---

32. See pp. 338–339 in this paper.

33. Data on tar and nicotine levels by brand were supplied by the FTC.

bly understates, though slightly, the trend toward lower tar and nicotine levels. Whether it affects the observed impact of the disclosure requirement is another question, the answer to which is unknown.

Figures 5-1 to 5-6 reveal the results of this first empirical procedure. The informal agreement between the Commission and the industry requiring disclosure of tar and nicotine content was adopted in December 1970 and took effect in February 1971, and so its effects, if any, should have been felt in 1971 and subsequent years. Figure 5-1 shows the changes in the market shares of low, low-middle, high-middle, and high tar and nicotine brands between 1965 and 1975. Casual inspection reveals no apparent effect from tar and nicotine disclosure. To be sure, the market share of the lowest tar and nicotine brands rose sharply in 1971 after several flat years, but the market share of the next lowest

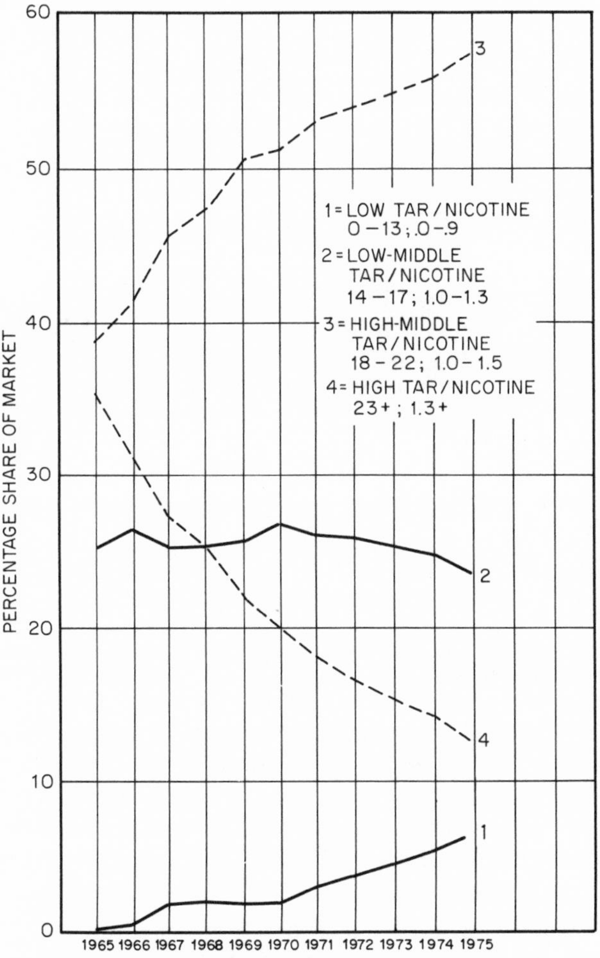

FIGURE 5-1 Percentage Share of Market

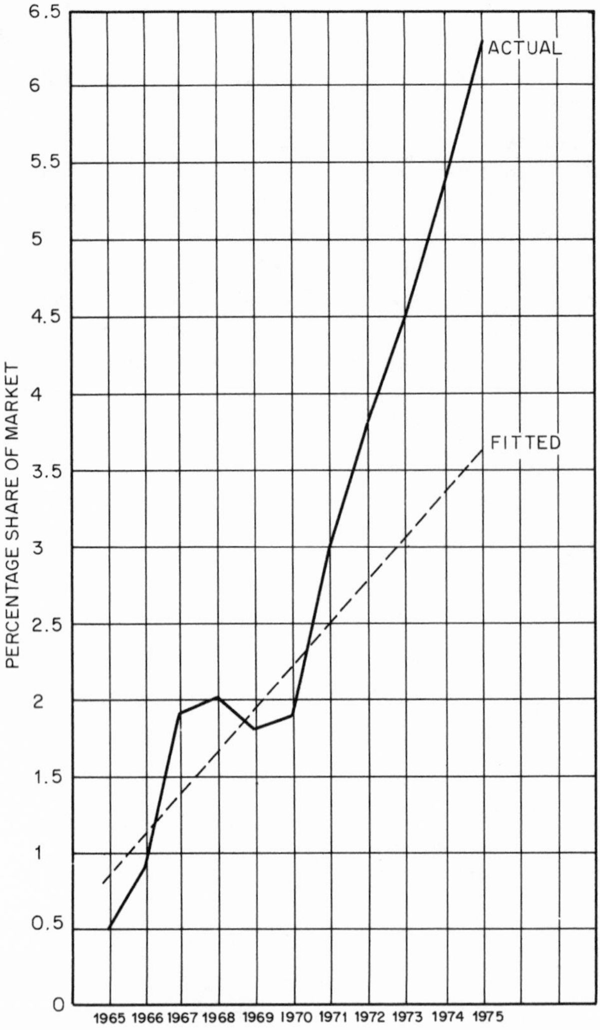

FIGURE 5-2 Category No. 1

category fell, and the rate of decline of the highest tar and nicotine brands slowed.

Figures 5-2 to 5-5 use regression analysis to enable a more precise assessment of the effect of the disclosure requirement.[34] The trend line marked *fitted* is a projection based on the actual market-share data for 1965 through 1970, i.e., the period before the disclosure. The fitted line indicates how the market shares of the various brand categories might

---

34. The form of the regression equation was $M = \alpha + \beta T$, where M = market share and T = time.

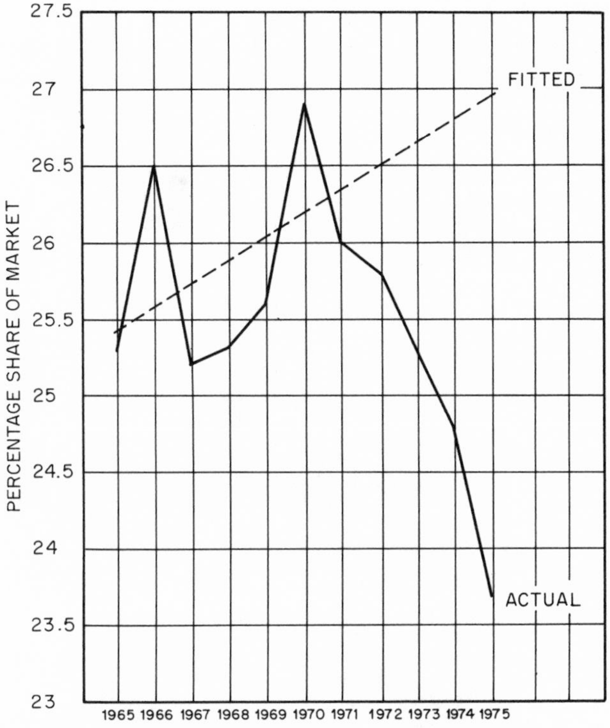

FIGURE 5-3 Category No. 2

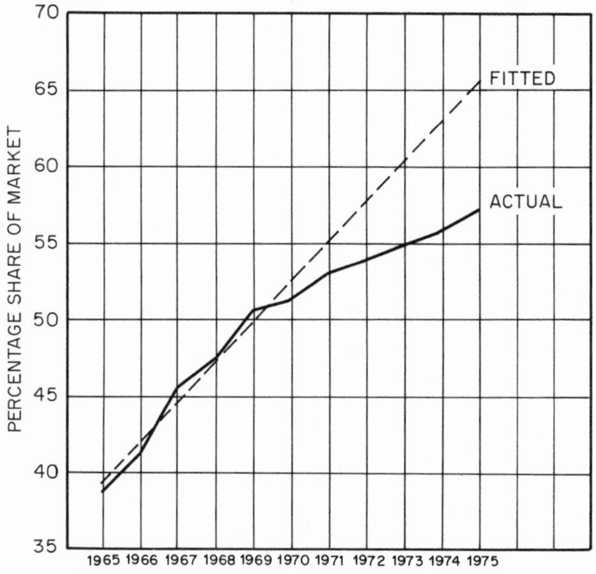

FIGURE 5-4 Category No. 3

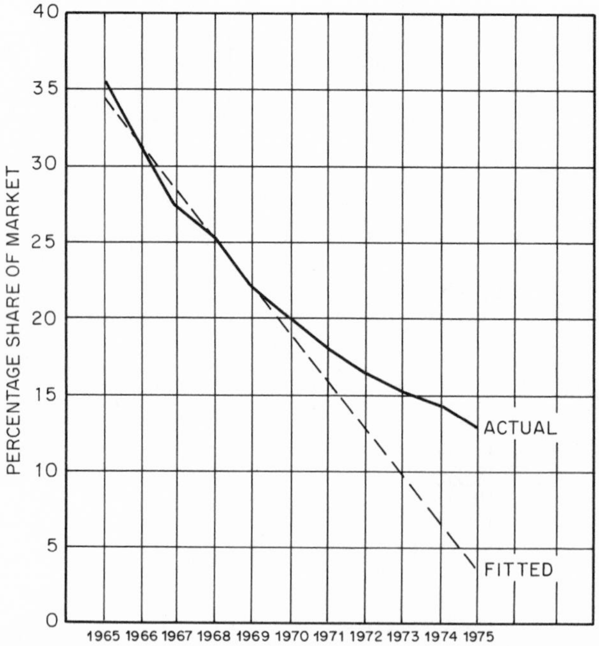

FIGURE 5-5 Category No. 4

have been expected to change had there been no change in the environment subsequent to 1970, the period in which disclosure was in effect. If the actual trend lines lay above the fitted lines for low tar and nicotine brands beginning in 1971, and below them for high tar and nicotine brands, that would be some evidence that the disclosure requirement had altered consumer behavior. This hypothesis is not supported by the data shown in Figures 5-2 to 5-5. True, the actual trend line for the lowest tar and nicotine brands lies above the fitted line beginning in 1971, but in the next lowest tar and nicotine category, the actual trend line lies *below* the fitted line after 1970. In the high-middle category (Figure 5-4), the actual trend line is below the fitted line, but it went below it in 1970—before the disclosure requirement went into effect. Also, beginning in 1970, and seemingly unaffected by the disclosure requirement, the market share of the highest tar and nicotine brands has declined *less* than one would have predicted on the basis of the 1965 to 1970 experience.

Figures 5-6 and 5-7 collapse the two largest tar and nicotine categories and the two highest, forming two new categories—higher and lower tar and nicotine content. Figure 5-6 indicates that in 1970 the market share of the lower tar and nicotine brands began to grow faster than one would have predicted on the basis of 1965-to-1970 data, and actually declined in 1975; no effect is apparent from a disclosure requirement the impact of which first should have been felt in 1971. Figure 5-7 tells a similar story for the higher tar and nicotine brands. Their market share declined below the predicted level beginning in 1970 and rose above it in 1974 and 1975; again, no effect from the disclosure requirement is discernible.

These results are highly tentative. Even disregarding the problem discussed earlier of changes over time in the tar and nicotine content of particular brands,[35] the procedure may conceal an effect of disclosure that was offset by other factors—price, or whatever—affecting the

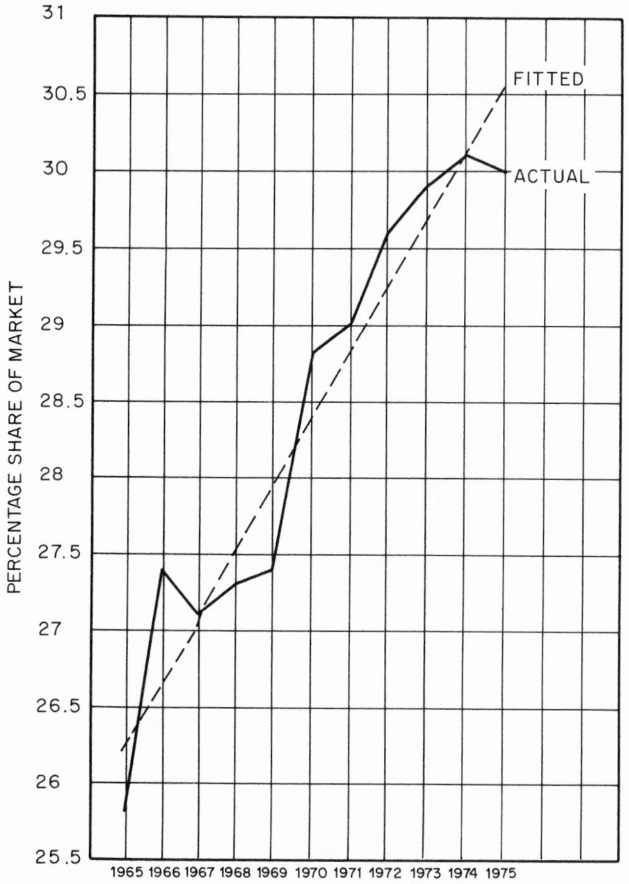

FIGURE 5-6 Category No. 5 (1 & 2 combined)

. There is also a technical objection to our procedure: the sum of the projected market shares is not constrained to equal 100 percent, though in fact it does not exceed it. A slightly more complicated regression procedure would eliminate this anomaly but not alter the results significantly.

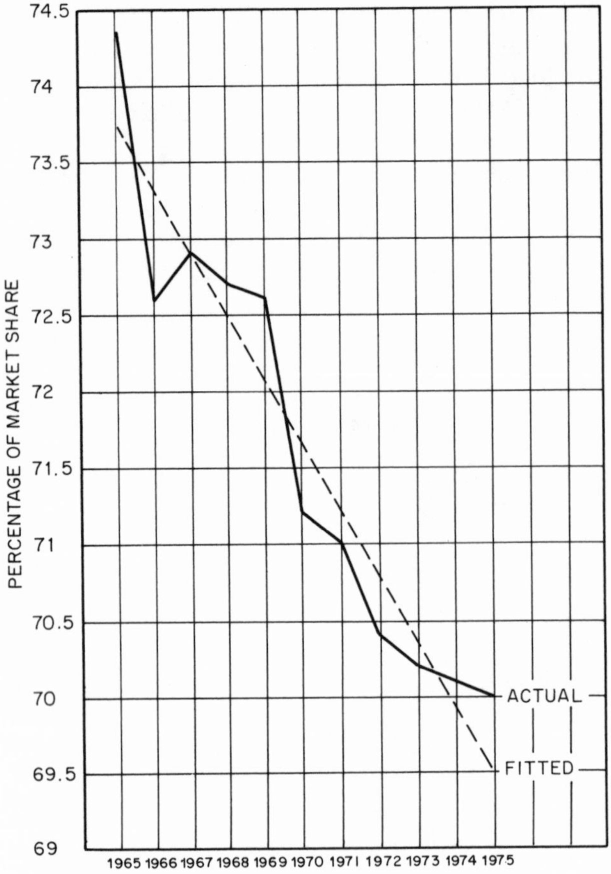

FIGURE 5-7 Category No. 6 (3 & 4 combined)

relative market shares of low and high tar and nicotine brands. A more complete study would attempt to control for such other factors.

The second procedure I used traces, over the period (1968–1975) for which the necessary data are available, changes in the average tar and nicotine content of cigarettes to see whether the required disclosure of that content beginning early in 1971 might have altered the underlying trend in regard to that content. The average used here is a weighted average, the weighting factor being the market share of the brands of a given tar or nicotine level. An immediate problem is presented by the fact that there is no obvious method of combining tar and nicotine levels into a single index of smoking hazard. A possible solution which I have adopted, is to add together the number of milligrams of tar and *ten times* the number of milligrams of nicotine. The rationale is that since cigarettes contain, on the average, ten times as much tar as nicotine, to multiply nicotine content by ten is in effect to weight the tar and nicotine content of a brand equally in determining its overall hazardousness. Obviously, this procedure is arbitrary, and a more complete study would consider alternative weighting methods.

Figures 5-8 to 5-10 trace changes in the average tar and nicotine content of cigarettes sold in the United States each year from 1968 to 1975.[36] The results are puzzling—especially to those who believe that a disclosure requirement that took effect in 1971 affected the tar and

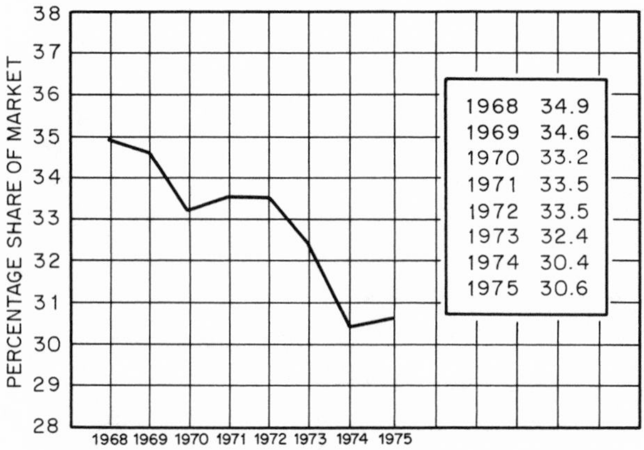

FIGURE 5-8 Average Tar+ (10 × nicotine) Content

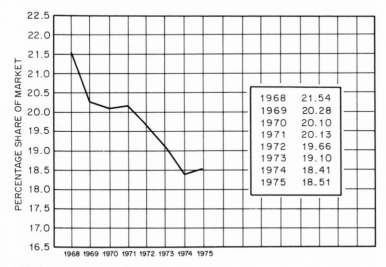

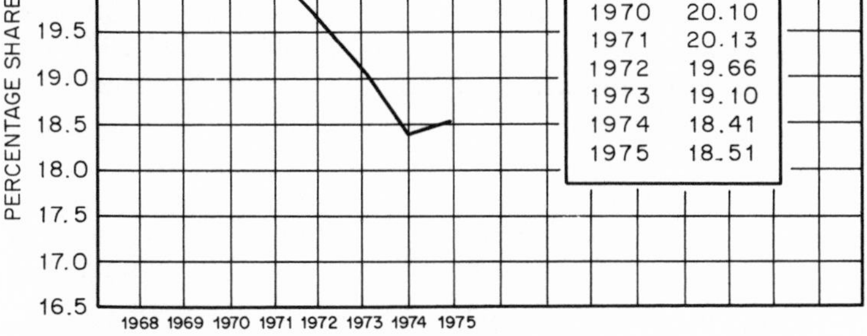

FIGURE 5-9 Tar Only

---

36. Figures 5-9 and 5-10 show tar and nicotine separately.

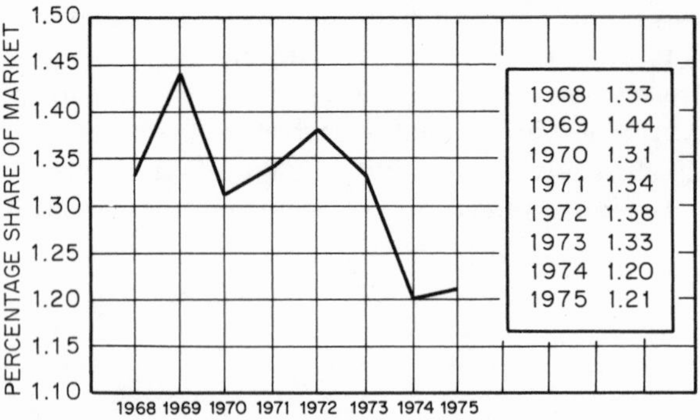

FIGURE 5-10 Nicotine Only

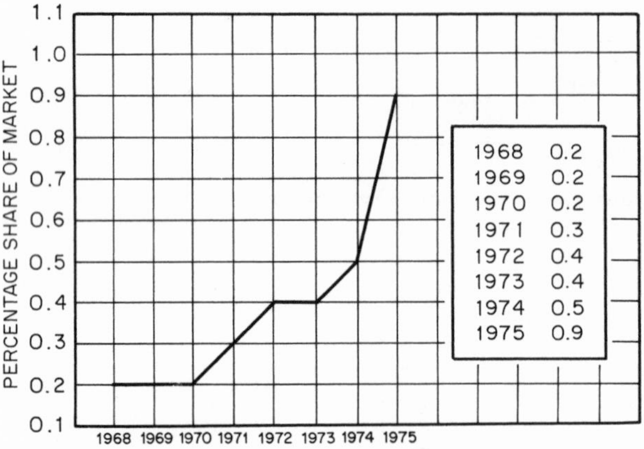

FIGURE 5-11 Category 6–10 mg

nicotine content of cigarettes, weighted by market share. A distinct downward trend in tar and nicotine content was reversed in 1971 and 1972—*after* the disclosure requirement took effect—and resumed only in 1973.

Figures 5-11 to 5-18 use the method of combining tar and nicotine described above to recompute market shares of the various categories of brands defined by their tar and nicotine content (omitted categories are ones where there were too few brands to permit meaningful year-to-year comparisons). The results shown in these figures do not seem to bear out the contention that the disclosure requirement affected consumer preferences for low versus high tar and nicotine brands. To be sure, the contention is supported by the experience of the lowest tar and nicotine category (6–10 milligrams); the market share of this group of brands was flat through 1970 but began to rise in 1971. Too, the next lowest category (for which adequate data are available)—16–20 milligrams—flattened out in 1971 and then began rising steeply; and the next category—21–25 milligrams—shows roughly the same movement.

A comparison of the next two categories, however, reveals anomalies. The 26–30 milligram category does not begin to rise, or the 31–35 milligram to fall, until 1973; the disclosure requirement (effective 1971) appears to have had no effect on these categories.

Even more surprising is the behavior of the "dirtiest" categories, shown in Figures 5-16 to 5-18. The 36–40 milligram category fell dramatically in 1971 and 1972 but recovered some of the lost ground in the following years. The 41–45 milligram category plunged in 1971 but more than recovered the lost ground the next year, while the fortunes of the very dirtiest category seem wholly symmetrical with regard to the introduction in 1971 of the disclosure requirement. In sum, it would seem hard to ascribe a consistent or pronounced effect on smoking

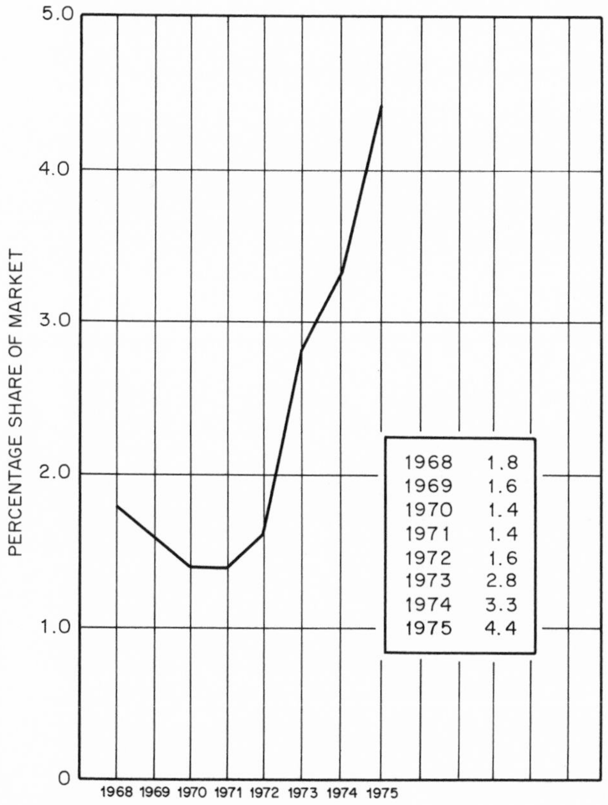

FIGURE 5-12 Category 16–20 mg

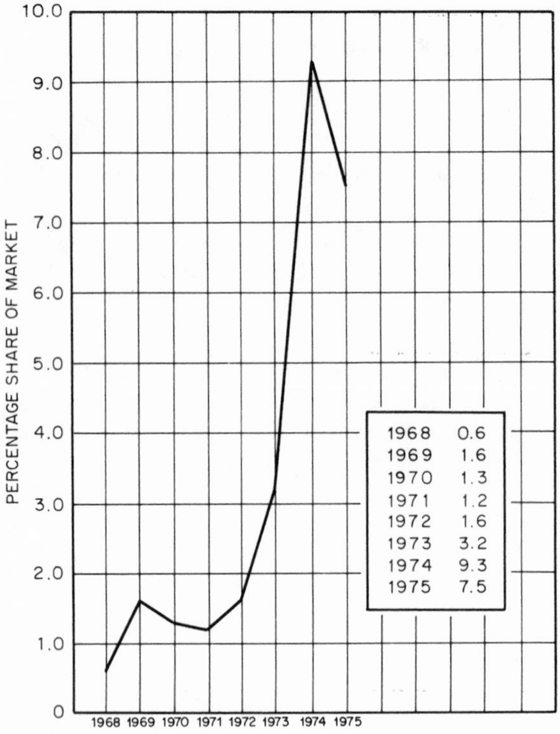

FIGURE 5-13 Category 21–25 mg

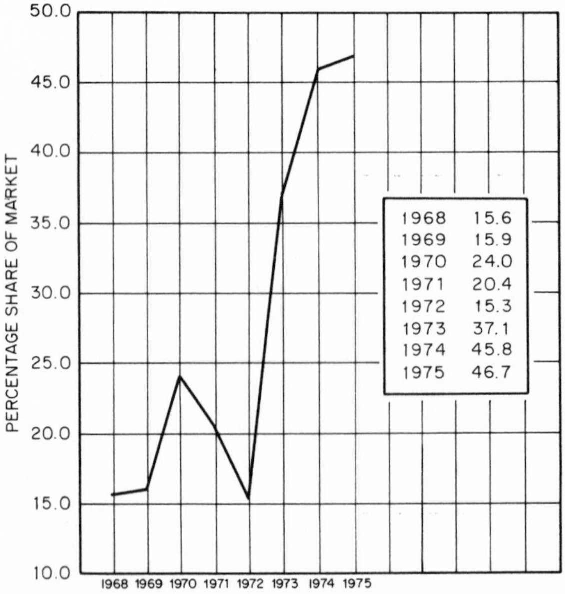

FIGURE 5-14 Category 26–30 mg

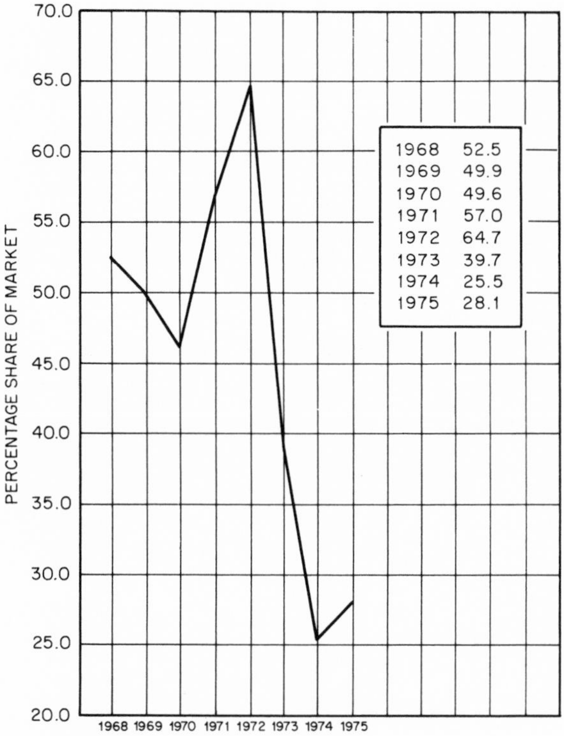

FIGURE 5-15 Category 31–35 mg

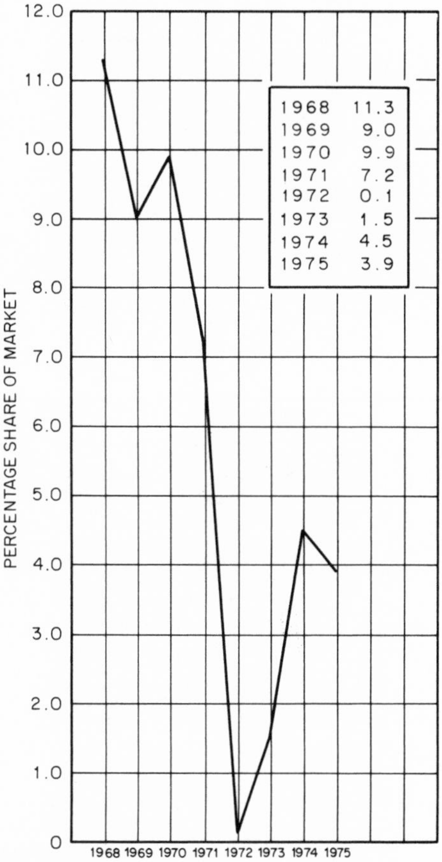

FIGURE 5-16 Category 36–40 mg

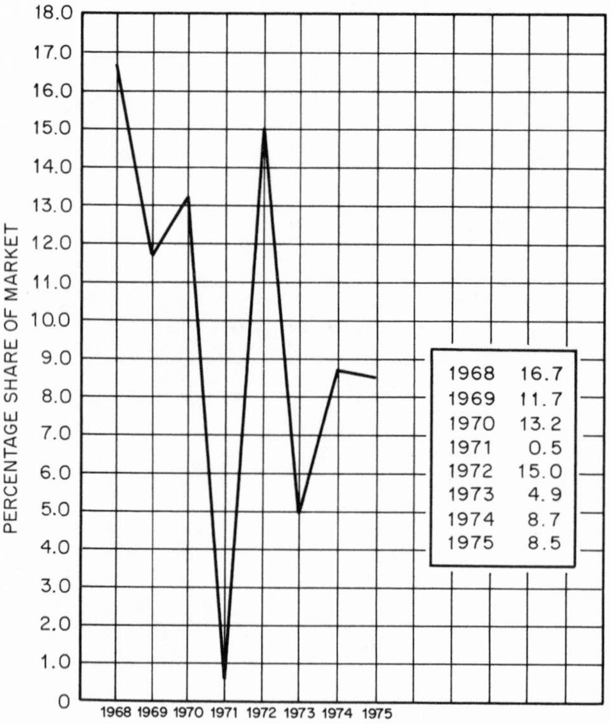

FIGURE 5-17 Category 41–45 mg

behavior to the disclosure requirement.[37] However, I wish once again to emphasize the highly tentative and preliminary character of this result, as of the others obtained in my study to date.[38]

---

37. Compare the dramatic results obtained by Ross in his study of the effects of introducing the "breathalyzer" in automobile accidents in Great Britain. See H. Laurence Ross, "Law, Science and Accidents: The British Road Safety Act of 1967," *Journal of Legal Studies,* vol. 2, 1973, p. 1.

38. Regression analysis was not used in my second empirical procedure (Figures 5-8 to 5-18) because of the small number (three) of predisclosure observations.

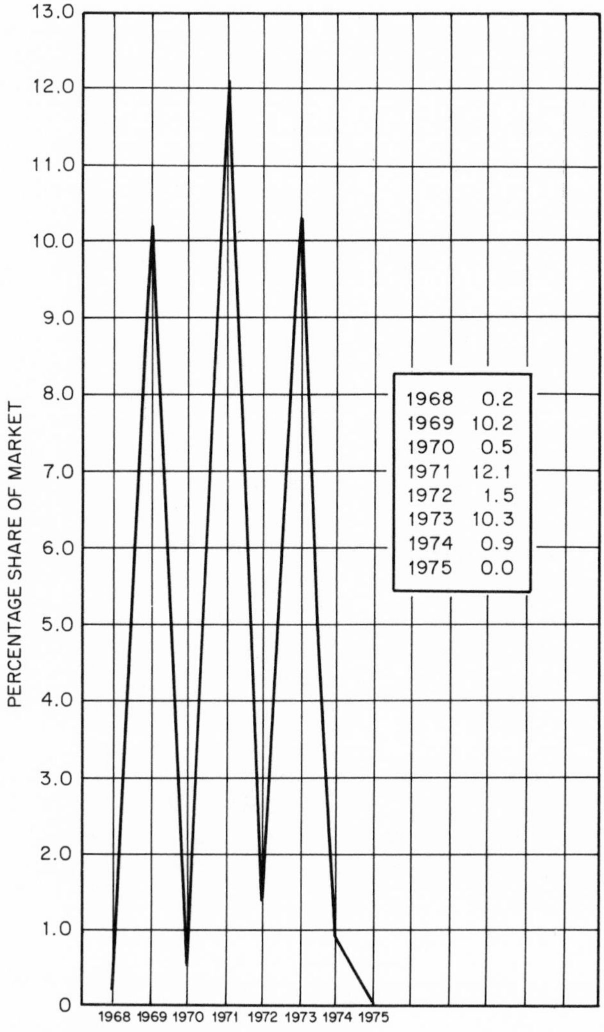

FIGURE 5-18 Category 46–50 mg

COMMENTARY

Robert Pitofsky

At a theoretical level, there is little difference between Posner and me. We both believe that in most instances relevant product information is made available to consumers through advertising. Even where it is not, there is usually no justification for government intervention if consumers can discern for themselves product characteristics prior to purchase, or if product characteristics are easily discoverable in the course of use with respect to a low-cost, repeat-purchase item. In effect, that means mandatory-disclosure programs are rarely necessary. We also agree, with respect to several programs now in effect, particularly those initiated by the FTC, that they were introduced with little careful prior study and, worse, that they have been followed by virtually no careful analysis of effects or costs.

When it comes to the advisability of specific disclosure programs, however, Posner and I often part company. As to FTC programs, he raises questions about whether the agency has any legal authority to require disclosure, in the absence of evidence that disclosure is necessary to dissipate prior fraud. As to the advisability of particular programs, he appears invariably to discover that sellers would have provided the information anyway, if only it were apparent that consumers wanted or would use such data in their purchasing decisions. While Posner firmly disavows any intention to argue that mandatory disclosure is *never* justified, readers might feel some pessimism about ever finding a market situation that will satisfy his demanding standards.

MANDATORY DISCLOSURE AT THE FTC—THE QUESTION OF LEGAL AUTHORITY

Posner argues that mandated disclosure programs at the FTC are unprecedented and that such radical departures from prior regulatory approaches should not be undertaken without specific authorization from Congress.[1] He suggests that a cautious view of Commission authority in this area is particularly appropriate in light of recent Supreme Court cases indicating that "commercial speech" enjoys some First Amendment protection.

"Pure" mandatory disclosure requirements—not operating against any background of deception or fraud, but based on the notion that consumers are "entitled" to important product information necessary to make informed purchasing decisions—does, indeed, go beyond traditional Commission regulatory efforts.[2] I do not, however, regard mandatory disclosure as a radical break with the past. For example, the Commission in *In re Pfizer*,[3] required that nonfraudulent advertising might nevertheless be "unfair" if the advertiser lacked objective substantiation prior to publication of the ad. The substantiation requirement would apply even though the ad was truthful. The Commission's decision turned on findings that it was impractical for consumers to run tests to evaluate product characteristics of a wide range of products, that it would be much more efficient for sellers to incur the expense of substantiation, and that there was a need for reliable information in the marketplace in order for consumers to protect themselves from economic or other injury and to make a free-market system operate efficiently. These are largely the same sort of considerations that would support any mandatory-disclosure program. Posner is correct, however, that no court in an adjudicated case has confirmed Commission authority to mandate disclosure in the absence of a background of fraud.

As to possible constitutional challenges to mandatory-disclosure programs, it seems doubtful to me that recent Supreme Court decisions expanding the scope of First Amendment protection of advertising would create serious constitutional problems. The Supreme Court, in the past several years, has renounced the view stated in *Valentine v. Chrestensen*,[4] that commercial advertising is entitled to no constitutional

---

1. The issue of legal authority would not arise if Congress specifically authorized a disclosure program. Moreover, the theory that "pure" mandatory disclosure might be a sensible legislative scheme is not alien to congressional thinking. In the statement of policy issued in connection with promulgation of the Fair Packaging and Labeling Act of 1966, 15 U.S.C. § 1451 (1966), the following policy position was stated:

> Informed consumers are essential to the fair and efficient functioning of a free market economy. Packages and their labels should enable consumers to obtain accurate information as to the quantity of their contents and should facilitate value comparison. Therefore, it is declared to be the policy of the Congress to assist consumers and manufacturers in reaching these goals in the marketing of consumer goods.

2. For a more extended discussion of development in this area, see Robert Pitofsky, "Beyond Nader: Consumer Protection and the Regulation of Advertising," *Harvard Law Review*, vol. 90, no. 4, Feb. 1977, pp. 661–701.

3. 81 FTC 23 (1972).

4. Valentine v. Chrestensen, 316 U.S. 52 (1942).

protection. It is important to appreciate, however, the context in which this expanded concept of constitutional protection for advertising occurred. The two most recent Supreme Court cases involved constitutional challenges to state statutes suppressing disclosure of product or service information—in *Bigelow*, striking down a state statute making it a misdemeanor to advertise the availability of an abortion,[5] and in *Virginia Board of Pharmacies*, striking down a state statute making it illegal to advertise terms of sale of prescription drugs.[6] The Supreme Court's reasoning in these cases was stated in *Virginia Board of Pharmacies*, dealing with the question of why prescription drug price information ought to be available to consumers: "It is a matter of public interest that [purchasing] decisions, in the aggregate, be intelligent and well-informed. To this end, the free flow of commercial information is indispensable. . . ."

If mandatory disclosure could be shown to be so expensive or otherwise burdensome as to interfere with the free flow of commercial information—e.g., by deterring sellers from resorting to advertising at all—a First Amendment argument might be offered that the disclosure program is an undue limitation or unreasonable burden. But, typically, mandatory disclosure simply adds to information in a seller's message. In that respect, I disagree with Posner's assertion that the octane rule requires "the oil companies to adopt a different description . . ." of octane ratings. Those companies are free under the octane rule to continue to describe octane content with such terms as premium, regular, etc., and to make those disclosures in any form they see fit. All the octane rule requires is that sellers disclose, on the pump, octane content measured by number in a uniform manner. Mandated disclosure has the effect of adding to information otherwise available in the market, but suppressing no message that sellers choose to disclose. Accordingly, recent constitutional decisions aimed at protecting the free flow of commercial information seem no threat to mandatory disclosure programs.

GOVERNMENT STANDARDIZATION PROGRAMS

Posner argues that it is never appropriate for the government to impose uniform standards of measurement against the wishes of a majority of sellers in a particular market category. Why not? If problems of standardization of measurement are precisely the reason why information is not available to consumers, and if all the other preconditions of sensible mandatory-disclosure programs are present, a government program in those circumstances seems justifiable. Experience shows

---

5. Bigelow v. Virginia, 421 U.S. 809 (1975).

6. Virginia Board of Pharmacies v. Virginia Citizens Consumer Counsel, Inc., 425 U.S. 748 (1976).

that voluntary trade association solutions are subject to problems of the "weakest link"—that is, many sellers will go along with a disclosure program only if substantially all competitors agree. Trade association efforts to adopt voluntary programs of disclosure of care labeling information on garments apparently broke down several times for such reasons. Since the FTC mandated disclosure, there has been better than 99 percent compliance and considerable praise for the program from industry and consumer groups.

DISCLOSURE IN PRACTICE

Octane Ratings

Posner says he cannot understand why consumers would want or need "finer" octane ratings than those communicated through traditional categories of premium, regular, etc., and, if there were a public demand for finer gradations, "we can expect the refiners to supply it." That seems to me to reflect what I have described as the doctrinaire view, that the market automatically produces optimal levels of information.

As to why consumers need finer gradations of information, I thought the point was made in the statement of basis and purpose supporting the octane rule and in my paper, but perhaps the request for a more specific elaboration is justified. Consider the following two situations:

1. Assume a consumer buys regular gasoline and his car knocks. Regular gasoline of the brand he is purchasing may be 93 or 94 octane, but his car needs 96—and 96 is available in the regular of another seller at a comparable price. Without more precise information about octane levels, the consumer may shift to premium gasoline and pay 3 cents to 5 cents more per gallon for the life of his car.

2. Assume an automobile manual for a particular make indicates that the car will not operate efficiently with gasoline of less than 91 octane. The consumer has no idea what the labels *regular* or *subregular* represent; he buys regular and his car performs adequately. With more precise disclosure, the consumer would realize he could shift to subregular and save several cents per gallon on every purchase.

In fact, specific octane information was not available in the marketplace when the government intervened and, given the steadfast and vigorous opposition by major elements of the oil industry to the Commission's octane proposal, there seems little likelihood that the information would have been forthcoming voluntarily. Also, added costs as a result of mandated disclosure do not seem a problem since the companies had to measure octane anyway to be able to advertise accurately whether gasoline was regular or premium. If there is a problem with octane disclosure, I continue to believe it relates to the willingness and capacity of consumers to use octane information in purchasing decisions. I agree with Posner's call for follow-up studies at the earliest feasible time.

Tar and Nicotine

Again, Posner's essential point is that there is no apparent reason why sellers with a superior product would not advertise aggressively. Thus, if a significant segment of consumers wanted cigarettes with low tar and nicotine content, the makers of relatively "safe" cigarettes would make information about tar and nicotine content available. This is clearly the case, he argues, because virtually all smokers already know that the weight of scientific opinion opposes cigarette smoking, so that messages about "safe" cigarettes generate no backlash. Posner does not directly address several of the points I made: (1) that tar and nicotine data were not present in the market after those elements were implicated in health dangers associated with cigarette smoking but before the government stepped in; and (2) absent government intervention to provide a standardized and reliable technique for measurement, effective comparative advertisement would be difficult.

I suggested an explanation for this absence of data that Posner rejects—that is, that the six major cigarette manufacturers (accounting for about 99 percent of United States sales) had an interest in not advertising tar and nicotine numbers in a way that would injure existing and then-popular brands. Posner cannot understand why a manufacturer might introduce a product and yet not advertise its novel characteristics. I suspect a difference between us relates to the either/or nature of an unexpressed premise in Posner's reasoning—that the choice is between no advertising of tar and nicotine numbers, or maximum advertising of novel product characteristics and the health hazards of smoking high-tar and high-nicotine cigarettes. In fact, Madison Avenue is adept at varying volume, intensity, and emphasis in advertising messages so as to "position" products to serve different market segments without unnecessarily undermining existing market shares of other products. In the context of tar and nicotine advertising, positioning took the form of ads talking about a safer cigarette with disclosure of low-tar and low-nicotine numbers, but no disclosure of high numbers in ads for the unsafe cigarette and few explicit comparative ads on behalf of the low-number brands. One result of government-mandated disclosure was to permit consumer comparisons of tar and nicotine content across the whole range of cigarettes available for sale.

The most interesting section of Posner's paper on the tar and nicotine question purports to show that the tar and nicotine disclosure program did not "cause" any change in consumer purchasing habits, relying on comparative market share data before and after inauguration of the program. Specifically, his charts show that while the lowest category of tar and nicotine brands increased market share substantially above what would have been expected after the program was introduced, the second-lowest category performed below expectations, and the two highest categories did not decline more sharply than would have been expected after the program went into effect.

I question a premise of the Posner study. By looking at market-share data before and after tar and nicotine data were disclosed, there is an assumption that the disclosed numbers themselves were the major influence on purchasing behavior. It may be that there are some disclosure programs which are themselves the principal cause of consumer behavior changes, but given what we know about consumer motivation and reaction, it is doubtful that smokers would be much influenced by a tiny logo in print ads with some tar and nicotine numbers. It is far more likely that outside information about health hazards in smoking (Surgeon General's reports, magazine articles, doctors' advice), plus advertising itself, have influenced purchasing conduct; the role of the disclosure system was to make it possible, or at least more feasible, for those forces to take effect. Hence, a simple comparison of market-share data before and after December 1970 probably would not be completely reliable as an indicator of the influence of the tar and nicotine disclosure rule. Posner, of course, recognizes the possibility that the kind of point I am raising could be influential. Certainly, his study is a more serious attempt at reasonable evaluation of the Commission program than anything the Commission has done, and it deserves the most thoughtful consideration.

In connection with that consideration, however, several other points should be made about his conclusion that the tar and nicotine disclosure system had no effect:

(1) Regression analysis and other complicated statistical techniques can sometimes overlook more obvious points. As I read Posner's data, sales of low tar and nicotine cigarettes were virtually level during the period from 1967 to 1970, and then increased about 300 percent during the period from 1970 to 1975. If people influenced by tar and nicotine numbers would not simply shift from a high-medium to a low-medium tar and nicotine cigarette but, rather, would switch to the advertised "safer" cigarettes like Vantage and True, then this is the principal category that should be considered. The market-share data for that category are significant.

(2) Posner's findings, that sales volume in the second-lowest category did not increase as much as might have been expected over performance before disclosure and that sales in the third-lowest category increased more than might have been expected over previous performance, are troublesome for those defending tar and nicotine disclosure and need to be explained. One possible explanation has to do with which brands are in each category. Category no. 2, where sales growth was disappointing, included Alpine, Belair, Doral, Pall Mall, Parliament, Raleigh, Silva Thins, Viceroy, and Virginia Slims. Category

no. 3, which did much better, included Benson & Hedges, Camel, Chesterfield, Lark, Newport, Old Gold, Salem, Tareyton, and Winston.[7] It is possible that advertising expenditures for the third category of cigarettes may have increased considerably in the period from 1970 to 1975 over expenditures in the previous five years, and over comparable expenditures in category no. 2—a plausible explanation of category performance. Certainly, Posner's study approach should be qualified with some weighting system that takes into account advertising expenditures.

(3) Finally, the cutoff date in the study may coincidentally cloak the most pronounced effect resulting from the tar and nicotine disclosure program. There is reason to believe from industry sources that low tar and nicotine cigarettes have begun to make enormous inroads in the market. By late 1976, Vantage was up sharply, ranking twelfth among brands in the market, while True ranked sixteenth. Meanwhile, in December 1975, Philip Morris introduced Merit, and Reynolds introduced Now, to the accompaniment of massive advertising campaigns, and American Brands cut the tar and nicotine content for Carlton at about the same time and began advertising that brand aggressively. The low-tar, low-nicotine segment of the market increased 5 percent during 1976 (from 10 percent to 15 percent of total sales), and the cigarette companies were estimated to be spending nearly one-half their total advertising budgets on these brands.[8]

A plausible scenario here is that the government's tar and nicotine disclosure program helped to create an increasingly significant and substantial segment of consumers who sought products with a special set of characteristics. Private advertising and product innovation increasingly responded to that demand. Market-share changes are likely to accelerate accordingly.

I have no doubt that the most pronounced changes in consumer behavior do occur when private advertising spotlights a particular set of characteristics—automobile mileage, energy-efficient appliances, low-phosphate detergents, and so on. But if the government's disclosure program triggers or facilitates those market changes, that is a measure of the success of the program. With 1976 data included, I believe Posner's study would show that result has been achieved. But that is conjecture and may not be right. The Commission would do well to follow the lead of one of its severest critics and conduct a survey along the lines Posner suggests.

---

7. Several brands appear to have been in both categories, depending on lengths and filters: Belair, Kent, Kool, L&M, Marlboro, Pall Mall, and Parliament.

8. *The New York Times,* Oct. 30, 1976, p. 8; "Puff Piece," *Barron's,* Nov. 8, 1976, p. 11.

DIALOGUE

ERNEST GELLHORN: I have two questions. First, Professor Pitofsky, by what measure would you determine what and how much information should be required to be disclosed once you make the decision the market is inadequate?

Second, would you extend the disclosure requirement to those situations where the products are identical rather than different? Take, for example, the products involved in two Supreme Court cases. In *Procter & Gamble,* the Supreme Court indicated that chemical bleaches were all identical. Would you extend the disclosure requirement to require companies with branded bleaches to explain that their product is no different from the nonbranded items? A similar issue may be raised with respect to the *Borden* case, as to evaporated milk and canned goods.

PITOFSKY: Let me address the second question first. I would not require disclosure, where there are identical products, of the fact of identity. Some people thought the FTC was doing that in the *Wonder Bread* case but, in fact, it was not. There are many reasons for rejecting such a program. Perhaps the simplest one to state is that it could not be effective; if there were an "identity disclosure" rule,

---

This session was chaired by Miles W. Kirkpatrick, of Morgan, Lewis & Bockius, a former chairman of the FTC. For further biographical information, see Appendix 1.

companies would simply throw useless additives into products in order to have something to talk about.

Also, there is the problem of defining what constitutes an identical product. I do not think there are that many identical products in the economy. So, do not think of this as a serious problem; I don't think the kind of rule suggested could be enforced.

As to the standards for deciding what information ought to be disclosed, that, of course, presents the hardest question. I do not think I can offer an across-the-board general response. I use the phrase in my paper "key product information." I mean information that goes centrally to the competitive merits of the product. I do not, for example, mean leg room for automobiles, and I do mean miles per gallon. I do not mean credit arrangements for oil companies, and I do mean octane. Some sensible line would have to be drawn to be sure that it is information that consumers want and that it would make a considerable difference in influencing their purchases.

IRA M. MILLSTEIN: I think the problem is defining what is central to the purchasing decision. I think Dick Posner's point that the market is probably the best determinant of what is central is buttressed by our truth-in-lending experience. Certainly, when this all began about ten years ago everybody assumed that the number of percentage points per month which the consumer would pay for the extension of credit was the most central item in the purchasing decision. When the industry marched in and said it was not so and claimed that the key factor was how many dollars a month a consumer had to pay to get a particular item, we all rejected industry's position. Now, after ten years and how many millions of dollars' worth of litigation, it turns out the industry was right. The consumer does not seem to care. It turns out that the rate of interest is not central at all.

Who is going to make the decision as to what is central? And assuming someone in government makes it, can we go to court to have it overturned? By what standard are we going to review the determination that it is central? Suppose the FTC decides that octane is central, can we go to court and fight about the issue of whether it is central or can we fight only about whether or not the Commission has the right to mandate some kind of disclosure? And how does the court review that?

PITOFSKY: I suppose the most important issue raised by Mr. Millstein is the question of whether or not we are to assume that the market will always operate adequately. Because, obviously, there are going to be circumstances in which outsiders think they know better than the market, and they are going to be wrong. But, I believe, there are also situations in which the market will not perform adequately. A product with a hidden characteristic will, for example, be involved, and in such circumstances outsiders may perform a service by requiring disclosure. One problem in the area is that the more successful a mandatory-disclosure program is, the more it appears you did not need it in the first place; when it works, the industry responds to it by going over to aggressive voluntary advertising.

As to a court review, I see no problem with overturning a mandatory-disclosure program either on the ground that the information was not essential or, if it was, that people did not want it and would not use it. And as to who is to make that decision, I think the reviewing courts would. I see no problem with judicial review in this area.

PETER STRAUSS: I am struck again, as I have been at other points, by the extent to which I think our understanding may have been diverted somewhat by a tendency to focus on the FTC and its concerns. In this session, our focus has been almost exclusively on the repetitive theme that what we are talking about is information that is necessarily central to consumer decisions.

Information may often be useful to consumer decisions without being central to it. Also, one may require that information be provided in the hope that consumers will make it central to their decisions, without necessary regard to whether or not they do so (for example, food labeling).

Professor Posner, would you address the theoretical differences you see, if you do, between cigarette labeling and the regulations of the Pennsylvania Department of Agriculture as to the labeling of baked foodstuffs.

POSNER: I agree with you, the general question of required disclosure of consumer information ought to be addressed more broadly. I think the result of doing so is to underscore one's skepticism about the program.

I am not familiar with every consumer-disclosure program. The largest example of consumer-protection disclosure before truth-in-lending and the FTC's program was, of course, the requirements of the Securities Act of 1933. My impression of the literature is that most economists believe that the registration and prospectus requirements of the 1933 act have not had a beneficial effect. Specifically, purchasers of new issues of securities do no better today than they did before 1933.

STRAUSS: We are again back to talking about economics. If I could go back to the Pennsylvania Department of Agriculture, which to some extent has a larger effect than the FTC in terms of consumer disclosure, there are hundreds, if not thousands, of people in the country with allergies to eggs. I am sure you will agree that knowing the content of baked goods is of interest to them and, indeed, provides an adequate basis for requiring the information to be presented. Similarly, I would not think that much justification is required for denominating the tar and nicotine in a cigarette.

POSNER: Those seem to me to be completely different cases. I do not understand how you go from the allergy to tar and nicotine. I think a lot depends on how many people are allergic to eggs and what the severity of the allergy is. If there are a number of people allergic to eggs and the consequences to the allergy are serious, I would expect producers to market products for that group.

The real problem, I think, would occur if there were so few egg-allergic people that their aggregate purchasing power was not sufficient to induce this sort of special tailoring of food products to their needs, and then you would have a serious, largely noneconomic problem. The issue then would be, what kind of cost do you want to impose on the rest of society in order to protect people with this vulnerability which the market will not take into account? In general, I would like to see a study of food and drug and/or food content labeling to see whether, in fact, such programs are, on balance, a good thing.

CARL A. AUERBACH: I wonder why, in answer to Dean Gellhorn's question, Professor Pitofsky yielded so quickly on the disclosure of the sameness among products. As I recall, the original studies of monopolistic competition showed that advertising had as one of its primary purposes product differentiation, that is, to create in the consumer's mind differences among products that did not exist. From the consumer point of view, the indication or disclosure of sameness may be one of the most important things. One of the examples that comes to mind is, of course, the famous recent action of the FDA with regard to disclosing the generic names of drugs which were sold under trade names; this disclosure has resulted in the savings of great amounts of money for the consumer and it helps competition.

PITOFSKY: Well, you understand that if a company manufactures a product that is identical to rival products and claims otherwise, then there is no problem. That is straight fraud. So the "sameness" issue arises only if the company is silent.

Suppose, in fact, all simple analgesics are chemically identical, and all Bayer ever says is, "Bayer works wonders." By definition all other products are the same and they probably work wonders too. The question is whether there is sense in trying to devise a remedy.

My answer remains the same as before. I really do not think there are many instances in which chemically identical products are involved. I think it would be difficult to enforce a "sameness disclosure" rule. You would get into all sorts of bizarre situations. As somebody once pointed out, if the Chamber of Commerce in Miami advertises, "Come to sunny Miami," do they also have to say, "The sun also shines in San Juan, Freeport, and so on?" It just gets you into a morass. I would rely on regulation of fraud in this area and, at most, consumer education through other channels to make people aware of the similarity of products.

POSNER: I'd like to comment briefly on Dean Auerbach's question, which I think is kind of a nice example of the sort of fallacy that abounds in this area. It is not irrational to prefer Bayer aspirin to aspirin X. After all, the important thing in the aspirin is not the chemical identification of the formula for making aspirin, but the contents of the aspirin that goes into your stomach. The consumer would like to avoid aspirin that contains something other than aspirin, such as rat droppings. It is true, of course, that the government has elaborate programs for the inspection and control of the manufacture of drugs. If you trust the government a great deal, you may not consider there is a significant incremental benefit to purchasing from a reputable firm that has been around a long time and is answerable in damages should there be some misfortune. The physical characteristics of the product are only one dimension; the price is only one dimension. And the fact that products often are based on the same formula is not decisive.

It is not enough to invoke programs which sound as if they are good because they are protecting consumers against a palpable evil; you have to ask how the programs actually work. And most of the studies I know show that these programs work very poorly.

AUERBACH: Are you opposed to the requirement that the generic name of the drug be indicated when its trade name is used? And, if so, on what conceivable theoretical basis if you are interested in competition?

POSNER: You are talking about prescription drugs?

AUERBACH: Yes.

POSNER: It seems to me if the drug is prescribed, it is the doctor who is the consumer's proxy. The doctor who writes a prescription can, of course, specify a trade name if he has some preference for the trade name, or he can write it in terms of a generic name. And I assume if the patient goes to the pharmacist and asks for a generic name, and then asks for the cheapest brand of whatever is written on the prescription, he will get that. As long as the doctor is making the essential decision, it seems to me that if there is a problem, the problem is whether doctors are reputable agents of consumers in looking out for their best interests and minimizing the costs of drugs to them.

DONALD SCHWARTZ: Reputable or informed?

POSNER: Certainly the doctor is informed. He knows what Terramycin is and knows that it is identical to Achromycin.

DAVID T. HULETT: Who says that?

POSNER: Carl Auerbach says as a kind of truism, as a self-evident proposition, which only some sort of market bigot would deny, that the generic name should be disclosed. I say if the doctor is acting as the agent for the patient and the doctor is making the decision as to what drug to buy, there is no need for generic disclosure. Then all of a sudden I have to prove that doctors are true agents of patients, rather than maximizing their own utility. Why do I have that burden of proof?

MARK GREEN: On a far less controversial note, I do not think Dick Posner answered a point raised by Bob Pitofsky earlier. Bob acknowledged that prior to the FTC requirement that tar and nicotine be listed in advertisements, True and Vantage did so because it was to their advantage. Cigarettes with higher tar and nicotine content, like Chesterfield and Winston, did not. So a consumer who wanted the most satisfactory cigarette, if such a thing exists, could buy True or Vantage, but there was no comparability up and down the scale. You could not compare Chesterfield and True.

What about consumers who may have wanted to buy the best-tasting cigarette that had the least tar and nicotine? They would have wanted to know the content of the ten worst tar and nicotine cigarettes but could not have found out prior to the rule. I assume the market failed to encourage or compel Chesterfield to disclose. This is an area where it is not terribly expensive for manufacturers to provide information in an advertisement. So, why not require disclosure?

POSNER: Your logic is defective. Suppose I went into a store and said, "I cannot find in this toy store a pink rubber dolphin." And you would say, "Aha, a market failure, because there must be consumers who want this."

You say there must be consumers who did not want a low-nicotine cigarette but a moderate-nicotine cigarette that would still taste good. If there were a lot of those people, why didn't the manufacturers who had such a brand cater to those people?

GREEN: Two points. The trivialization of the point is important. We are not talking about disclosure about wine, cheese, or toy dolphins. We are talking about a product sold by the billions to millions of people which has been documented to cause hundreds of thousands of cases of death and disease each year. So the potential benefit—I cannot prove this—seems enormous, given small margins of increased information.

Second, HEW produced a survey showing that 23 percent of all consumers are functionally illiterate—not illiterate but functionally illiterate. I presume over time, if information is provided in advertisements, perhaps not five years later but six years later, as Bob hypothesized, consumers will be educated. It is a process that takes time.

The potential benefit could be enormous. What I am saying is I cannot see any reason to argue against the FTC rule, which would encourage comparisons between Chesterfield and True.

POSNER: You have a funny definition of illiteracy. An illiterate is someone who will be helped by government-mandated disclosure in the form of a written statement on a cigarette package. You are just cutting the cloth to fit the particular body you want to drape it around.

PITOFSKY: It seems to me that Mark Green is making a very sound point. One has to be practical about the capacity of consumers to engage on their own in extensive investigations and to find information in the marketplace when it is not easily available.

The fact is that well after the Surgeon General's report was published, and well after there was a large segment of consumers who indicated they wanted a low-tar, low-nicotine cigarette, there was hardly any advertising in the market and little room to make comparisons. It seems to me that government should at times facilitate the consumer's ability to make choices.

GREEN: It seems eminently reasonable to provide information to consumers who are functionally illiterate, which means that the government should encourage the dissemination of information that will have an impact over time.

DONALD TURNER: I think buried in what Mark Green and Carl Auerbach are saying is a real issue. In assessing what kind of evidence you would think appropriate to require disclosure, it seems to me—and I think, Professor Posner, you would agree—that you must consider the cost that is imposed by requiring the disclosure.

It appears to me that to require the drug companies to list the generic name as well as the trade name is virtually costless. And it would not take much in the way of evidence—that this would promote a more competitive system of distribution of drugs and lead more doctors to prescribe generic drugs—to come to the conclusion that it would be a sensible thing to do. And the amount of money involved is enormous in terms of the price difference.

POSNER: I disagree only for this reason. I think in evaluating the full cost of a government program, it is a mistake to focus on just the out-of-pocket costs of compliance. If you are going to have a government program of mandatory information disclosure, on the basis of history, I think you have to assume an error rate of something like 95 percent. And the cost of the failures must be recognized as well as the cost of success. It is like the dry holes in oil drilling.

I grant you that there must be cases where mandatory disclosure would be in the public interest, or where the cost of the particular disclosure would be so small that it would probably be cost-justified. But the real question is: Do we want to have an FDA, an SEC, or an FTC? If you evaluate not the individual program but the institution, I think a cost-benefit analysis points toward a negative answer.

WESLEY J. LIEBELER: I think it is an encouraging sign that both Pitofsky and Posner agree on the utility of "market failure" analysis when considering the question of when there should be government mandated disclosure. But I think it is mostly a semantic commitment to the notion.

I want to point out what happened in the exchange between Auerbach and Turner. Carl Auerbach asked a question, "Would you require the disclosure of the generic name?" And Don Turner talked about the costs involved in the fact that the generic name is not always disclosed, and concluded that because of these costs there ought to be mandatory disclosure. It seems to me we should ask ourselves why it is that the information about the generic equivalent of the brand-name drug is not available. We should think about it in terms of the market-failure concept. That way we can aim our remedy at the market failure.

The fact is that pharmaceutical manufacturers have gotten legislation in most states to prohibit substitution of a generic drug for a brand-name drug by the pharmacist. The pharmacists have gotten legislation that prohibits pharmacists from advertising prices of brand-name drugs.

These are the reasons for an absence of information. I put it to you that if a pharmacist could substitute, and if pharmacists could advertise price, the competition among pharmacists for consumers' patronage would both lower prices of all drugs and induce substitution. They would advertise the fact that they could substitute and advertise that lower prices are available. You could, therefore, cure your market failure without requiring mandatory disclosure by getting rid of the factors that caused the market to fail. If you think about the problem in this way, you will find many cases where mandatory disclosure is not required.

CHAPTER SIX

Confidentiality Claims: Glittering Illusions or Legitimate Concerns?

EDITOR'S NOTE

A vast legal literature deals with individual claims to privacy. A barren landscape faces the researcher on parallel business claims. The Greenawalt-Noam paper is a pathbreaking attempt to systematically analyze claims by business organizations that information sought by government—either for internal planning and enforcement purposes or for public dissemination—may be withheld on confidentiality grounds. This is a subject of enormous economic importance.

At issue are questions such as the following: How closely related are the confidentiality concerns of business organizations and individuals? How should a company's claim of confidentiality be weighed against the government's need to know? What confidentiality considerations, if any, might limit interagency access to information or the dissemination of information to the public at large? When is the publishing of only aggregate company data appropriate? What impact, if any, would disclosure of heretofore confidential information (either to federal agencies or the public) have on company behavior? On competition?

Greenawalt and Noam see two basic rationales for affording privacy protection to individuals. The first is cast in terms of ultimate values and suggests that privacy is essential for the intimate personal relationships that are valued in a liberal democratic society. The second is utilitarian in nature and may be measured in terms of the functioning of larger institutions. The claims of business organizations, Greenawalt and Noam conclude, fall almost exclusively in the second category; their legitimacy rests on whether or not they will lead to more long-term economic efficiency.

This chapter does not provide definitive answers; the subject is simply too large and the issues too complex. But Greenawalt (a law professor) and Noam (a professor of economics) do offer an interdisciplinary perspective containing a more thorough—and thoughtful—analysis than I have ever seen before. Careful reading of their paper will be richly rewarded.

CONFIDENTIALITY CLAIMS OF BUSINESS ORGANIZATIONS

Kent Greenawalt, *Professor of Law, Columbia University*
Eli Noam, *Assistant Professor of Business and Lecturer in Law, Columbia University*

This paper concerns claims by business organizations that information sought by an agency of the government for its own purposes or for dissemination to the public should be withheld from that agency on grounds of confidentiality. We begin by outlining the sorts of information that various government agencies might seek from businesses and their reasons for seeking it. We then compare the bases for business claims of confidentiality to the bases for individual claims of privacy. We next examine general legal supports to claims of individual privacy and business confidentiality, considering how far these general legal doctrines actually protect business information and how far, when not providing actual protection, they at least reflect implicit values that should carry weight in the context of acquisition of business information. We then turn to an analysis of the effects of a required disclosure to the government and consider its impact on policy formulation and regulatory enforcement. We next broaden the discussion to include government-mandated disclosure to the public. An important question is whether there is a need for a governmental role in the provision of such information. Finally, we investigate the effects of public disclosure on economic efficiency, competition, and innovation.

THE PURPOSES FOR WHICH THE GOVERNMENT SEEKS INFORMATION

The government may seek information from businesses for a variety of overlapping purposes. First, businesses are subject to a vast number of legal requirements, and many businesses are closely regulated by

The authors would like to thank John Belferman and Douglas Berman for their helpful research assistance.

administrative bodies. Acquiring information is the way in which the government ascertains if "the rules" are being followed. In their enforcement capacities, government agencies seek much routine information that establishes routine compliance with pervasive legal norms; for example, druggists and liquor dealers must keep detailed records of purchase and sale so that government officials can assure themselves that illegal dispositions are not being made in these closely regulated industries. Virtually all businesses pay taxes and must submit relevant records to appropriate authorities. When wrongdoing is seriously suspected, agencies of enforcement typically go beyond routine information and attempt to compile a more detailed account of what has transpired.

Second, the government needs information in order to decide how to regulate businesses intelligently. Congress does a great deal of investigating to help it determine what laws to pass and whether laws it has passed are effective. Regulating agencies rely on information about the businesses they regulate in establishing general rules, fixing rates, or setting safety standards.

Third, the government wants general information about how segments of the economy are working. Such information may eventually be put to use in decisions about regulation, but the government may not have any such specific purpose in mind when it asks for the information. In part, it may proceed on the assumption that the fullest possible picture of the economy is desirable for a multiplicity of government decisions in a complex economy. How businesses are operating may be important for peripheral decisions such as what tariff to impose on a particular product, whether to aid a country with a possibly valuable raw material, or whether to expand the money supply.

Fourth, the government may want information about industries or specific businesses to be made available to the public and deem its own acquisition of the information the most effective way to accomplish that purpose, either because it can most easily distribute the information to the relevant public or because the information requires further processing that can be done by the government agency. The relevant public may be consumers, other actual or potential competitors of the businesses concerned, or those touched in some way by the businesses' activities, for example, persons breathing smoke emitted by a local factory. The present dispute over whether the FTC should be able to require major corporations to report sales, profits, research, and advertising for particular lines of business, such as refrigerators, illustrates the point about government processing. It is apparently conceded that an individual company need not make public its line of business (LB) information. But, aggregated data about lines of business may be valuable for investors trying to decide where new funds should flow as well as for other purposes. The FTC would, therefore, receive information that it would not make public, but would aggregate the information in a form appropriate for public use. The Bureau of the Census similarly makes public a substantial amount of aggregated information based on information about individuals and businesses that it keeps confidential.

Fifth, the government may be interested in information that will permit it to protect political processes from undue influence. Some information may relate to enforcement of an existing law, as when investigators try to determine if illegal contributions have been made to candidates. Other information may simply indicate the source of influences so that those on whom the influences operate will be more fully aware of the sources and, therefore, will perhaps be better able to respond wisely. Registration of lobbyists, for example, serves this function as well as providing a degree of possible scrutiny by the general public that may help curb excesses and potential improper collusion.

Sixth, in vast areas, the government deals with businesses on a business level. Information about those businesses may help the government negotiate contracts that are better from its point of view and to oversee whether those contracts are properly carried out.

Seventh, the government may seek information from businesses because the businesses hold information about individuals in which the government is interested for such reasons as employment decisions and law enforcement. Most businesses hold considerable information about their employees, and some businesses, for example banks and insurance companies, have detailed information about consumers.

Eighth, and finally, the government is ultimately responsible for resolving private legal disputes. When private parties in a civil case seek information from other private parties under discovery procedures or judicial subpoenas, in a sense it is the government which is seeking, or at least supporting, the search for information in order that the private dispute may be fairly resolved.

Of these types of information, the first four are important for our purposes. These categories reflect the government's role as an economic policymaker in the broad sense and will be analyzed more closely in the following sections.

BUSINESS CLAIMS TO CONFIDENTIALITY AND INDIVIDUAL CLAIMS TO PRIVACY

Loose comparisons are sometimes drawn between individual claims to privacy and organizational claims to confidentiality. It is important to analyze with some care the extent to which arguments that individuals should be able to withhold information about themselves do and do not apply to similar claims of business organizations.

Individuals need to be able to keep private some facts about themselves if they are to develop individual viewpoints and lifestyles; in a society in which everything is exposed, the pressure for conformity would be extraordinarily great. A low level of informational privacy would strike extraordinarily hard at persons who, because of previous antisocial behavior, an unpleasant family situation, or some other kind of social obloquy, need a "second chance" in life; and those who in some sense are misfits, for example, those who wish to keep major aspects of their private lives secret from their working associates, as would a homosexual who believes he must appear "straight" at his job. Relationships of love and friendship depend largely on selective disclosure of information; unless much about our thoughts and feelings that is communicated to loved ones and friends can be withheld from a more general public, genuinely intimate relationships would be difficult or impossible. Individuals may function more effectively at work and in other social activities if they enjoy a degree of privacy. Privacy may be important for emotional stability and may contribute to effective work performance. A person would be less likely to think and work creatively if he could not choose when to discuss matters with colleagues and when to disclose his thoughts to his superiors, for example.

The arguments for individual privacy are complex, and not only because privacy itself is a complex and amorphous concept.[1] Some of the arguments rest on the premise that privacy is essential for the kinds of individuals and personal relationships that are valued in a liberal democratic society. Other arguments rest on the premise that privacy contributes to the effective functioning of economic and political institutions.

The first kind of argument may be cast in terms of an ultimate value for privacy. It might be urged that whatever other characteristics were present, individuals or intimate relationships would be diminished in value if individuals had no power of selective disclosure. More typically, the argument is cast in terms of a close linkage between privacy and valued attributes. It is asserted, for example, that selective disclosure is necessarily linked with qualities like independence of mind and strong emotional attachments. In this form, the argument is at least open to the counterargument that the valued attribute could exist in spite of a diminution of informational privacy. The relevant data for settling such an argument would be largely psychological. This argument for privacy still would not depend on the effective functioning of larger social institutions, and it could not be rebutted effectively by economic and sociological studies.

The second kind of argument, cast in terms of the functioning of larger social institutions, is more obviously utilitarian and lends itself more clearly to sociological and economic study. If an effective measure of performance is agreed upon for a particular job, actual performance can be related to levels of privacy. It can be tested, for example, whether workers perform less effectively if they are searched every day for stolen items, and whether more able workers will refuse to work in that

---

1. See generally, R. Kent Greenawalt, *Legal Protections of Privacy: Final Report to the Office of Telecommunications Policy*, Washington, D.C., 1976.

setting. In an important First Amendment case, *Shelton v. Tucker,*[2] the Supreme Court held that public school teachers could not be required to disclose all their associational memberships, reasoning in part that individuals would be discouraged from participating in controversial organizations if their memberships were known. Though it might be difficult to set up the experiment, the question of whether disclosure of membership would exert a "chilling effect" on organizational participation is a fairly straightforward empirical one.

With certain exceptions, arguments for confidentiality by business organizations must be cast in terms of the functioning of social institutions, and most of the arguments rest on assumptions about economic efficiency. The exceptions can arise when a business organization is asked to disclose information about stockholders, managers, employees, or customers; then it may assert claims to confidentiality that rest ultimately on the claims of privacy of the individuals concerned. For example, a bank resisting disclosure of financial records may assert that an intolerable invasion of the customer's privacy will occur. The bank is not a disinterested spectator—disclosure may impose administrative burdens on it, and customers may eschew United States banks for more favorable environments if compelled disclosure is too extensive—but the bank's confidentiality claim is essentially a claim on behalf of the customer.

When a business is asked to disclose its internal processes or the political involvements of its leaders, claims on behalf of individuals might also be made. It is conceivable that business operations could be so exposed that individuals working in the organization would have to sacrifice their personal privacy in substantial degree. This might occur, for example, if all conversations were recorded or all memoranda examined. But this sort of sacrifice is rarely demanded; even fairly extensive disclosure of internal operations does not usually touch the genuinely personal privacy of employees in a significant way. There is a good argument that too much disclosure of internal operations will produce timidity in assessing options and will discourage the able from seeking positions in which their recommendations will be exposed to public view. It is precisely such an argument that has been used to support doctrines of executive and legislative privilege; this argument is, however, put in utilitarian terms, subject in theory at least to validation without deep psychological assessments of individual personalities. The assertion that corporate leaders have a fundamental claim to confidentiality about their political beliefs and associations is more appealing, and in this area, as in respect to other individual facts about employees and customers, a business resisting compelled disclosure might be standing in the shoes of an ultimate individual interest in privacy.

Such claims, however, cannot be made about the economic information that government agencies typically seek. The interest in confiden-

2. Shelton v. Tucker, 364 U.S. 479 (1960).

tiality, if it exists, rests on utilitarian hypotheses that are, at least in theory, testable by empirical study. If information is made public or given to the government, will an industry be made less or more competitive? Will the burden of producing the information outweigh the likely benefits of its being produced? If the overall "economic" effect of disclosure of the information is likely to be negative, does some other justification, such as assuring the public that nuclear power plants are safe, support its being revealed? These are the sorts of questions which should be asked by the government agency before it seeks the information. They may also sometimes be relevant to judicial decisions when companies resist disclosing information that the government seeks, though in this area courts are rarely involved in a simple balancing of costs and benefits.

There may be another kind of argument for confidentiality that rests on assumptions about larger social institutions but is neither economic nor conveniently subject to empirical analysis. It can be argued that a liberal democratic society can exist only if important pockets of power exist besides the government. If the government has too extensive information about other organizations, it may manipulate these organizations and ultimately deprive them of their independence. Whether the production of particular information will have any such effect may conceptually be an empirical question, but the variables are so complex that one's answer in practice is likely to turn on political ideology rather than sociological or economic fact.

The concept of a power balance can also be applied in a different way to distinguish personal claims to privacy from those of business corporations. One reason for the desirability of personal privacy is the need to afford the individual some extra help in his dealings with society. The concept of privacy is a recognition of the relative weakness of the individual with respect to not only the government but also other social institutions. Guarantees of privacy are an attempt at redressing the balance. This theory cannot be applied equally to large corporations, since it may be feared that society at large is subject to corporations' pervasive power, and that power needs to be scrutinized and controlled.

In any event, broad arguments about proper balances of independent institutional power are likely to be only a marginal counter in actual conflicts over the acquisition of information. Most arguments advanced by businesses for keeping particular business information confidential are based on economic premises. After providing a summary of relevant legal rules, we examine some of those arguments in more detail.

LEGAL RULES AND VALUES REFLECTED IN LAW

For an understanding of business claims to confidentiality, a summary examination of important legal protections of informational privacy serves two purposes. It reveals the extent to which existing legal norms do and do not preclude the government from acquiring information, and it provides one source for the value judgments that may be necessary when decisions are made whether to demand disclosure of information.

Constitutional Restraints

The most important constitutional protections of informational privacy are in the Fourth and Fifth Amendments, made applicable against the states by the Fourteenth Amendment. The Fifth Amendment privilege against self-incrimination bars any person from being "compelled in any criminal case to be a witness against himself." The Fourth Amendment forbids unreasonable searches and seizures and requires that searches be based on warrants supported by probable cause.

Although the Fifth Amendment privilege against self-incrimination refers to "any person" and it is clear that a corporation is a person for purposes of other Fifth Amendment rights (e.g., the right not to be deprived of property without due process of law), the Supreme Court has consistently held that the privilege does not apply to corporations.[3] In *Hale v. Henkel,*[4] the Court reasoned that since the corporation is a creature of the state and receives privileges and franchises from the state, it holds those privileges subject to any limitations the state may set. One reserved power, termed the "visitorial power" was that of investigating all a corporation's books and records regardless of any claim of incrimination. At the time *Hale* was decided, it was generally supposed that if the government could withhold certain benefits altogether, it could condition those benefits on any bases it chose. Since that time, the Supreme Court has held that the government may not impose unconstitutional conditions in granting benefits; clearly, for example, corporate status could not be granted on the condition that all officers refrain from personal political activity. Nevertheless, the holding of *Hale* remains firmly entrenched. The underlying rationale for the privilege rests on an idea of individual dignity and the unpalatability of requiring people to participate actively in the process by which they are sent to jail; and this rationale has no obvious applicability to corporate criminality. The notion that compulsory production of corporate records may help make out the case of corporate criminality is simply not offensive in the way that compelling a man to convict himself may be offensive; and the historical development of the privilege against self-incrimination concerned individual humans. As Justice Marshall wrote for the Court in *Bellis v. United States,*[5] the inapplicability of the

---

3. Hale v. Henkel, 201 U.S. 43 (1906); Wilson v. United States, 221 U.S. 361 (1911); United States v. White, 322 U.S. 694 (1944).

4. Ibid.

5. Bellis v. United States, 417 U.S. 85 (1974).

privilege for corporate books and papers "can easily be understood as a recognition that corporate records do not contain the requisite element of privacy or confidentiality essential for the privilege to attach."

In *United States v. White,*[6] the Supreme Court declined to apply the privilege against self-incrimination to an unincorporated labor union, holding that the Fifth Amendment privilege exists only for natural persons. In that case, the Court confirmed its earlier judgment in *Wilson v. United States,*[7] that if an organization does not have a right to withhold records, neither does an individual officer acting in a "representative capacity." An officer must produce subpoenaed documents of a business enterprise even if the documents incriminate him personally. In *Bellis,* this principle was extended to the records of a very small law firm, the Court deciding that one of the three partners held the partnership's financial records in a representative capacity and that he could be required by a grand jury to produce those records despite his claim that they might incriminate him.

The Court in *White* offered a pragmatic reason for its narrow reading of the privilege. It said, "the greater portion of the evidence of wrongdoing by an organization or its representatives is usually to be found in the official records and documents of that organization. Were the cloak of the privilege to be thrown around these impersonal records and documents, effective enforcement of many federal and state laws would be impossible." The present Court repeated these words in *Bellis,* but it also emphasized the modern interpretation of the privilege as protecting a "private enclave," a "private inner sanctum of individual feeling and thought." It concluded that the rationale for the privilege had little applicability to organizational records, for "a substantial claim of privacy or confidentiality cannot often be maintained with respect to the financial records of an organized collective entity."

Another related principle that limits the scope of the privilege against self-incrimination as it applies to business records is the "required records" doctrine. In *Wilson,* the Court wrote that the privilege was inapplicable "to records required by law to be kept in order that there may be suitable information of transactions which are the appropriate subjects of governmental regulation and the enforcement of restrictions validly established." The theory that required records were quasi-public documents open to inspection was accepted again in *Shapiro v. United States,*[8] a case involving records required to be kept by the Office of Price Administration.

Subsequently, the doctrine has been narrowed somewhat. In *Albertson v. Subversive Activities Control Board,*[9] the Supreme Court held that

---

6. See N. 3 *supra.*

7. See N. 3 *supra.*

8. Shapiro v. United States, 335 U.S. 1 (1948).

9. Albertson v. Subversive Activities Control Board, 382 U.S. 70 (1965).

required registration of members of Communist organizations violated the privilege against self-incrimination. Three years later, it sustained constitutional attacks on convictions for failure to register under the federal wagering tax statute and the National Firearms Act, holding that when its purpose was essentially one of criminal enforcement, the government could not require individuals to supply evidence of their crimes.[10] In *Grosso v. United States,*[11] it indicated the circumstances in which the "required records" doctrine would apply: "first the purposes of the United States' inquiry must be essentially regulatory; second, information is to be obtained by requiring the preservation of records of a kind which the regulated party has customarily kept; and third, the records themselves must have assumed 'public aspects' which render them at least analogous to public documents."

Since the "required records" doctrine applies to individual business records as well as those of organizations, it does apparently make vulnerable to public inspection some documents which would otherwise be protected, although a recent Supreme Court decision, *Fisher v. United States,*[12] casts some doubt on whether the Fifth Amendment will now be held to immunize any ordinary business records from subpoena. As far as the records of business organizations are concerned, the situation is clearer. Since none of them are reached by the privilege against self-incrimination, the "required records" doctrine merely provides an independent reason why some records are not protected.

In contrast to the Fifth Amendment, the Fourth Amendment does apply to corporations and other businesses, but the degree of its protection is significantly limited. The rules governing ordinary criminal searches are the same for corporate and individual premises; the police must have a warrant based on probable cause, but ordinary criminal searches are rarely the technique for uncovering corporate wrongdoing. When in 1967 the Supreme Court extended the warrant requirement to administrative inspections, it did so with respect to commercial premises as well as homes.[13] However, the warrants for such inspections need not be based on the probability of any violations existing on the particular premises searched. Even this watered-down warrant standard does not apply to certain closely regulated enterprises, such as liquor and gun dealers, whose premises may be searched by authorized officers without warrants.[14]

Application of the Fourth Amendment to grand jury subpoenas and

---

10. Marchetti v. United States, 390 U.S. 39 (1968); Grosso v. United States, 390 U.S. 62 (1968); Haynes v. United States, 390 U.S. 85 (1968).

11. See *Grosso* in ibid.

12. Fisher v. United States, 425 U.S. 391 (1976).

13. See v. City of Seattle, 387 U.S. 541 (1967).

14. Colonnade Catering Corp. v. United States, 397 U.S. 72 (1970); United States v. Biswell, 406 U.S. 311 (1972).

questioning, administrative subpoenas, discovery, and general disclosure requirements is very circumscribed; and it is these techniques which would commonly be used to ascertain corporate crimes. The warrant requirement is not relevant, and no showing need be made that the documents or other information demanded will probably establish guilt. The Fourth Amendment bar on "unreasonable" searches is, however, of some relevance for subpoenas. Information sought must be relevant to the inquiry, documents must be adequately specified, and the subpoena must not be too broad in what it demands.[15] The government is not supposed to go on "fishing expeditions,"[16] sifting through a great deal of material in the bare hope of coming up with evidence of wrongdoing. But for some years, the bar on "fishing expeditions" has not been a very strenuous limitation. In *United States v. Morton Salt*,[17] the Supreme Court said: "Even if one were to regard the request for information in this case as caused by nothing more than official curiosity, nevertheless law-enforcing agencies have a legitimate right to satisfy themselves that corporate behavior is consistent with the law and the public interest. . . . It is sufficient if the inquiry is within the authority of the agency, the demand is not too indefinite, and the information sought is relevant." Subsequent cases indicate that very broad subpoenas are often accepted, with considerable deference being given to the judgment of investigators as to what breadth is necessary.[18]

Whether a government agency is seeking information in an investigation of a particular company or for more general purposes, the Fourth Amendment may impose some outside limit on how burdensome demands may be in light of the likely utility of information sought. In a 1922 case, *Federal Trade Commission v. Baltimore Grain Co.*,[19] the court declared that companies could be required to disclose information only when "there is some reasonable proportion between the public value of the information likely to be obtained and the private annoyance and irritation it will occasion." Although the argument of undue burdensomeness has been raised against the FTC's demand for line of business reporting, there is some doubt whether courts will now involve themselves in the sort of balancing envisioned by *Baltimore Grain* so long as the material sought is of possible utility.[20] Certainly, a court would now give great weight to an administrative judgment of need, and it would

---

15. See Oklahoma Press Publishing Co. v. Walling, 327 U.S. 186 (1946).

16. United States v. Morton Salt Co., 338 U.S. 632, 642 (1950).

17. Ibid.

18. Federal Trade Commission v. Crafts, 355 U.S. 9 (1957); Civil Aeronautics Board v. Hermann, 353 U.S. 322 (1957).

19. Federal Trade Commission v. Baltimore Grain Co., 284 F. 886 (D.Md. 1922), *aff'd per curiam*, 267 U.S. 586 (1925).

20. See A. O. Smith Corp. v. Federal Trade Commission, 396 F.Supp. 1108 (D.Del. 1975), *rev'd in part*, 530 F.2d 515 (3rd Cir. 1976).

be a rare case in which the Fourth Amendment argument would succeed.

Despite the very scanty protections the bans on unreasonable searches and compelled self-incrimination give to business organizations, these constitutional provisions contain the seed of a principle that may have relevance to relations between the government and private businesses. It is that in a liberal democratic society the government should not act on the assumption that any particular individual or enterprise is disobeying the law unless it has some basis for such a belief, and, except in the instance of very tightly regulated industries, the initial basis for that belief should be something other than the ordinary records of the individual or business. In connection with business, extensive acquisition of information by law enforcement officials does not pose the same threat to personal privacy as the acquisition of information about private persons, but the dangers of arbitrary treatment and government suppression of private centers of power may be present for businesses as well as individuals if law enforcers "know everything." It is perhaps this concern that underlies the belief that even when businesses routinely disclose economic information to a research agency of government, such information should not be routinely turned over to law enforcement agencies.

In some First Amendment cases, the Supreme Court has accepted organizational claims that demands for disclosure were unconstitutional. Most notably, it has declared that neither executive officials nor legislative committees can compel production of the membership lists of civil rights organizations without a specific and strong showing of public need.[21] These First Amendment holdings, however, have little to do with the kind of information typically sought from businesses. The Supreme Court's approval of registration requirements of the Federal Regulation of Lobbying Act[22] demonstrates that even when a fairly strong argument can be made that required disclosure of information touches the political rights of businesses and other organizations, the requirements will be upheld so long as they further a substantial public interest. Ingenious arguments for confidentiality might be framed in terms of the Ninth Amendment's reservation of rights to the people, the Fifth Amendment's requirement of due process, or penumbras of specific guarantees,[23] but such arguments would not be likely to add anything of substance to those already discussed. "Due process" contentions may have more force when the complaint is that decisions to acquire information have been reached by unfair procedures.

---

21. NAACP v. Alabama, 357 U.S. 449 (1958); Bates v. Little Rock, 361 U.S. 516 (1960); Gibson v. Florida Legislative Investigation Committee, 372 U.S. 539 (1963).

22. United States v. Harriss, 347 U.S. 612 (1954).

23. See Griswold v. Connecticut, 381 U.S. 479 (1965).

Nonconstitutional Restraints

Government demands for information are often resisted on other than constitutional grounds. The most obvious contention, though not typically a successful one, is that whatever government agency is seeking information is without authority to do so. If an agency demands information that is simply none of its concern, then it has no power to compel disclosure. The courts, however, interpret generously both the powers of legislative committees and administrative agencies; any plausible connection between information sought and one of the many functions of the agency seeking it is likely to suffice. In the *A. O. Smith* case[24] the district court found quite unpersuasive the contention that the FTC's gathering of information had to be closely linked to enforcement proceedings.

There is a procedural version of the absence of authority argument that courts often take more seriously. The Administrative Procedure Act, among other legislation, requires agencies to follow particular procedures for particular kinds of decisions. The authority of the agency to act rests on its following the prescribed procedures; and if it fails to do so, its demands may not be valid. One of the issues in line of business litigation is whether the FTC's demand for reporting in those terms constitutes an exercise in rule making subject to the requirements of section 4 of the Administrative Procedure Act.[25] It was the argument that the agency had disregarded applicable procedural rules that led the district court to grant a preliminary injunction in *A. O. Smith.* Since the court of appeals held that plaintiff had not shown irreparable injury, it reversed the district court's decision without passing on the procedural claim.

The argument that a demand for information is unduly burdensome need not be solely a constitutional contention. In cases in which a general requirement for information is challenged, as in the line of business litigation, a court might decide that the likely value of the information is so slight in comparison with the cost of producing it that the agency has abused its discretion, and therefore acted ultra vires, in demanding the information. Such a determination could still leave open whether the information might constitutionally be required if, say, Congress explicitly authorized a demand for it. In cases in which information is sought by subpoena, the courts have even greater latitude to control the scope of disclosure. As in ordinary civil litigation, courts may assure that their processes are fairly used, and judges can tailor the demands of subpoenas to comport with their ideas of what is reasonable.[26] Although complete denial of what an agency seeks may be

---

24. See N. 20 *supra.*

25. Administrative Procedure Act, 5 U.S.C. § 553 (1976).

26. See, e.g., Federal Trade Commission v. Texaco, Inc., 517 F.2d 137, 149–150 (D.C. Cir. 1975).

rare, judges more commonly narrow requests and adjust them to information businesses can more conveniently produce. Often, the final boundaries of what is demanded will result from negotiation between the parties that has been strongly encouraged by the judge. Indeed, the courts have sometimes functioned as organs of adjustment even when businesses have challenged general reporting requirements, pushing the affected businesses and relevant agencies to arrive at some mutually acceptable resolution. Of course, a similar process of negotiation often takes place directly between an agency and affected businesses without judicial intervention, but the insistence of a court that concessions be made may sometimes bring about accommodations that would not otherwise be reached.

Strong arguments of undue burden may, therefore, be more important in practice than is indicated by the opinions in reported cases. It may also be that they will take on increasing significance as the government asks more frequently for information that is not already available to businesses. Although the cost of producing already existing information can occasionally be considerable, the cost of compiling new information and producing it will usually be greater. The courts, therefore, may look more closely at undue burden contentions when corporations claim, as they have with respect to line of business demands, that they do not now have information in the form required. Despite the somewhat greater possibilities for "undue burden" arguments than may be reflected in reported cases, it is true nevertheless that on crucial questions concerning the need for information, deference will be given to agency judgment. Substantial costs for businesses will be accepted if the agency makes a plausible argument that they are necessary.

Some statutes restrict the flow of information from one government agency to another. The best known and most stringent limitations of this sort apply to the Bureau of the Census.[27] When information is supplied to the Bureau for statistical purposes, it is severely restricted in the form it can distribute the information; and the information may not "be used to the detriment of the persons" to whom it relates. Census officials are not allowed to permit anyone outside the Commerce Department to examine individual census reports. It has never been in doubt that the Census Act forbids regulatory agencies from acquiring the reports of individual companies from the Bureau of the Census, but initially it was not clear whether agencies might seek file copies of those reports from the companies themselves. In *St. Regis Paper Co. v. United States*,[28] the Supreme Court held that the FTC could direct a company to submit a file copy of its report to the Bureau. The dissenters urged that this result undermined the assurance of confidentiality offered by the Bureau and intended by the statute; Congress

---

27. 13 U.S.C. §§ 8–9(a) (1976).

28. St. Regis Paper Co. v. United States, 368 U.S. 208 (1961).

apparently agreed, because shortly thereafter it amended the statute to protect file copies. More recently, the issue of census confidentiality has been posed in somewhat different form when the FTC, without seeking copies of reports submitted to the Bureau of the Census, has attempted to obtain data it knows is provided by businesses to the Bureau. The FTC has demanded that the country's 1,000 largest manufacturing corporations submit corporate pattern reports giving value of shipment data in terms of Bureau product class codes. It has said it may make individual data for 1972 publicly available in 1978, an assurance of confidentiality that compares unfavorably from the point of view of the corporations with the perpetual guarantee of the Bureau of the Census. Corporations have urged that required submission of the data would violate the guarantee. Resolution of this problem is difficult. Certainly, if information would be easily available to the companies concerned regardless of a Census request, submission to the Bureau of the Census should not insulate the information from other government agencies with a legitimate interest in it. However, if information has been specially compiled for the Census agency and could not reasonably have been demanded by the other agency but for the fact that it had already been compiled for the Census, then forced disclosure arguably does interfere with Bureau of the Census guarantees of confidentiality and might discourage complete cooperation with future Bureau requests.

In contrast to the Census Act, the Federal Reports Act is intended to encourage the flow of information from one government agency to another, but it is meant to restrict to some degree the acquisition of information from nongovernment sources. Clearly, the main purpose of the act, which requires approval for information gathering by the Office of Management and Budget (OMB) for executive departments and by the General Accounting Office (GAO) for independent agencies, is to discourage duplicative waste among government agencies. Corporations subject to FTC demands for corporate pattern and line of business reports have urged that in clearing the agency programs, the GAO has committed procedural errors and has acted inconsistently with the statutory purpose[29] in approving requests for information that is already available to the Bureau of the Census. It is highly doubtful that the act is intended to create rights for individual litigants, and implausible to suppose that it was meant to bar an agency's request for information that is held by another government agency but cannot be obtained from it. It is arguable that GAO could probably give weight to considerations of confidentiality in refusing to clear a request for information, but since the protection of confidentiality is hardly an obvious purpose of the act, it would be plainly inappropriate for a court to invalidate an agency's demand because of GAO's failure to protect supposedly confidential information.

---

29. See 44 U.S.C. § 3512(c) (1970 ed. Supp. V 1975).

Federal and state statutes, as well as common-law doctrines, protect businesses against the forced public disclosure of certain kinds of information, such as "trade secrets." Thus far, the courts have not accepted the argument that because information can be withheld from the public, it can also be withheld from the government.[30] Typically, the special reasons for protecting information from competitors or those with whom a company does business do not apply to the government. Needless to say, courts are hesitant to assume that information will be leaked to outsiders despite guarantees of confidentiality by the agency seeking the information; and a business would have to carry a heavy burden to establish that an agency or congressional committee is unable to carry out its own stated policies, even though this may be the fact. Nevertheless, in deciding whether to compel the submission of sensitive information, and in deciding how to handle the information if it does compel submission, a government agency should weigh in the balance the possibility that the information may be obtained by those whose acquisition of it would conflict with the legitimate interests of the company supplying the information.

In other cases, the problem of public disclosure is more sharply posed. The agency may refuse to guarantee that it will keep information confidential or it may have an announced policy to disclose arguably confidential data, as in the case of the FTC's plan to publish in 1978 individual company data for 1972 obtained in the corporate pattern reports. Or, the agency may plan to disclose data that is not apparently confidential but from which perceptive observers will arguably be able to ascertain confidential facts; companies assert that published aggregated information drawn from line of business inquiries will be "disaggregated," yielding conclusions about particular companies. Or, the agency may actually be resisting or plan to resist disclosure against claims by third parties that disclosure is mandatory.

The issue of public disclosure may arise over the handling of information already in the government's possession. It may also arise before a company submits information to the government. Although some Supreme Court language suggests that courts should not easily impose judicial orders of confidentiality before it is clear precisely what sort of information is involved and what an agency plans to do with it,[31] litigants have sometimes acquired judicial guarantees of confidentiality even when they have not successfully resisted disclosure. In *Federal*

---

30. E.g., Federal Trade Commission v. Tuttle, 244 F.2d 605 (2d Cir. 1957), *cert. denied*, 354 U.S. 925 (1957); Federal Trade Commission v. Manager, Retail Credit Co., Miami Branch, 515 F.2d 988 (D.C. Cir. 1975); Federal Trade Commission v. Waltham Watch Co., 169 F. Supp. 614 (S.D.N.Y. 1959).

31. Federal Communications Commission v. Schreiber, 381 U.S. 279 (1965); see Ernest Gellhorn, "The Treatment of Confidential Information by the Federal Trade Commission: Pretrial Practices," *University of Chicago Law Review*, vol. 36, no. 1, Fall 1968, p. 126.

Trade Commission v. Texaco, Inc.,[32] for example, a case involving subpoenas for information about natural gas reserves, the court of appeals approved the district court's ruling, made before Texaco had produced relevant documents, that access to the documents within the FTC would be restricted to those assigned to the immediate investigation, that removal of the documents from their place of deposit would be allowed only with court approval, and that at the end of the investigation the documents would be returned to Texaco.

In some instances, statutes explicitly preclude disclosure to the public of certain kinds of facts. The Federal Trade Commission Act,[33] for example, grants the agency power to make public information it has collected "except trade secrets and names of customers." Companies resisting demands to submit corporate pattern reports have contended that information about individual company sales, profits, costs and operations are "trade secrets"; the agency insists, on the basis of legislative history, the purposes of the FTC Act, and the meaning of the phrase in other statutes, that "trade secrets" has a much narrower meaning and does not embrace all confidential business data.

In some cases, the argument is not that disclosure directly violates the language of a particular statute, but that it is inconsistent with basic policies underlying a statute. In *Federal Trade Commission v. Continental Can Co.*,[34] the agency sought sales data from Continental that was relevant to its complaint against one of Continental's competitors. Continental resisted the subpoena on the ground that the information was highly confidential and that the agency had not guaranteed against its being revealed to Continental's competitor. The district court decided that Continental should have such a guarantee before having to submit the information; and it directed the parties to work out some procedure whereby the competitor-defendant would receive information relevant to the litigation but in a form that would not reveal confidential facts about individual companies like Continental.

Another possible conflict between the policies of the antitrust laws and the interest in disclosure was posed in *Alabama Power Co. v. Federal Power Commission*.[35] The FPC issued a regulation requiring electric utility companies to supply information about their monthly purchases of fuel, with this information to be promptly disclosed to the public. The utilities argued that the Commission should reconsider the regulation because the knowledge of suppliers of what prices had recently been paid to other suppliers would have anticompetitive effects. The court treated the problem not only as whether the FPC action itself

---

32. Federal Trade Commission v. Texaco, Inc., 517 F.2d 137, 150–151 (D.C. Cir. 1975).

33. Federal Trade Commission Act, 15 U.S.C. § 46(f) (1976).

34. Federal Trade Commission v. Continental Can Co., 267 F. Supp. 713 (S.D.N.Y. 1967).

35. Alabama Power Co. v. Federal Power Commission, 511 F.2d 383 (D.C. Cir. 1974).

violated the antitrust laws, which it clearly did not, nor only as whether disclosure would be likely to cause actual antitrust violations by suppliers, but also as whether disclosure violated a vague but pervasive antitrust policy of competition. All three judges seemed to assume that a sufficiently strong showing that the regulation conflicted with this policy and did not result in countervailing benefits would be a basis for judicial invalidation of the regulation. All three judges also agreed that the record did not show that the Commission had dealt with or answered the utilities' argument as carefully as it might have. The majority, nevertheless, giving considerable deference to agency judgment and finding that the utilities had not established substantial risks of anticompetitive effects, upheld the Commission's refusal to reconsider the regulation. In the corporate pattern reports and line of business controversies, we can assume, given judicial deference to agency judgment, that it would take an extraordinarily strong showing that Federal Trade Commission plans to publish individual or aggregated data would have anticompetitive effects for the court to sustain company claims to withhold data or bar planned publication.

Although *Continental Can* and *Alabama Power* reflect the hesitancy of the courts to interfere significantly with the acquisition and disclosure of relevant information by administrative agencies, they also reflect both the duty that agencies have not to breach rights of confidentiality or to encourage anticompetitive behavior and the ultimate willingness of the courts to intervene if the breaches are clear enough and serious enough.

Recently, the issue of public disclosure has often been posed in the context of the Freedom of Information Act.[36] In *National Parks and Conservation Ass'n v. Morton*,[37] for example, the association sought to obtain from the Department of the Interior financial records of companies operating concessions in the national parks. The Freedom of Information Act requires that ordinary government records be disclosed to members of the public upon request, but it exempts, among other things, "trade secrets and commercial or financial information obtained from a person and privileged or confidential. . . ." The court quite properly concluded that this exemption is meant to protect not only the government's interest in being able to continue to gather such information but also the interest of those who produce such information. It said, "section 552(b)(4) may be applicable even though the Government itself has no interest in keeping the information secret. The exemption may be invoked for the benefit of the person who has provided commercial or financial information if it can be shown that public disclosure is likely to cause substantial harm to his competitive

---

36. Freedom of Information Act, 5 U.S.C. § 552 (1976).

37. National Parks and Conservation Ass'n v. Morton, 498 F.2d 765 (D.C. Cir. 1974).

position." The court concluded that the concessionaires should have an opportunity to demonstrate damage to their competitive positions. More generally, the spirit of the case suggests that when agencies are asked to produce information that may be regarded as confidential by the business that supplied it, the agencies should involve the business in the process of reaching a decision whether disclosure should be made.

In *National Parks,* the government agency was at least formally resisting disclosure, but a number of cases have arisen in which private enterprises have claimed that the Freedom of Information Act bars disclosure of exempted material, even if the relevant agency wishes to disclose. Most courts have taken the position that the exemption does not give a right to the subject of information against an agency that wants to disclose the information.[38] But some have taken a contrary position. In *Continental Oil Co. v. Federal Power Commission,*[39] for example, the court reviewed a FPC order that required natural gas companies to disclose detailed information about intrastate sales, which the Commission was to make public. The court sustained the Commission's right to collect the information, but it barred public disclosure, reasoning that disclosure would have harmful anticompetitive effects and was within the exemption of the Freedom of Information Act. The court's reliance on the act seems ill-founded. The act compels government disclosure, and the exemption removes compulsion with respect to some information. Unlike the Privacy Act of 1974,[40] the Freedom of Information Act does not appear to bear directly on information a government agency wishes to make public. Perhaps, however, the court in *Continental Oil* could have reached a similar result on the basis of the general policy of competition that underlies the antitrust laws. If it is determined that agencies, either pursuant to Freedom of Information Act claims or on their own initiative, are with some frequency unjustifiably disclosing confidential business information that is not adequately protected by specific legal safeguards, then possibly some general protection explicitly giving individual companies a right to sue may be warranted.

The cases overall suggest a somewhat greater judicial willingness to prevent unwarranted disclosures outside the government than to scrutinize decisions by government agencies that they need commercial information themselves. Even when judicial review is not likely, agencies should pay careful attention to the possible anticompetitive effects of some kinds of disclosures.

---

38. See, e.g., Charles River Park "A", Inc. v. Department of Housing and Urban Development, 519 F.2d 935 (D.C. Cir. 1975); Pennzoil Co. v. Federal Power Commission, 534 F.2d 627 (5th Cir. 1976).

39. Continental Oil Co. v. Federal Power Commission, 519 F.2d 31 (5th Cir. 1975).

40. Privacy Act of 1974, 5 U.S.C. § 552a (1976).

THE EFFECT OF DISCLOSURE TO THE GOVERNMENT ON REGULATORY POLICY AND ENFORCEMENT

One important function of disclosure is to make law enforcement easier. With information available through disclosure, it will be less difficult to identify and prosecute violators of regulations.[41]

The impact of eased access to information will tend to decrease the cost and increase the quantity of the information that is potentially available to an agency. The availability is "potential" because the agency may well adjust to the easier access to information by cutting down on its own fact-finding efforts. Let us assume for analytical purposes that success in law enforcement is determined by two factors, efforts of fact-finding and efforts of prosecution, and that the agency allocates part of its budget to each of these activities. Disclosure requirements will lead to an increase in facts available for each level of prosecutory effort. This will tend to raise the marginal productivity of the prosecutory effort. Hence, it will make sense to increase the budget of the prosecutorial branch, because its productivity per budget dollar has risen. And, if we have a given total budget, an increase in prosecution resources means a reduction in the resources used for fact-finding. In addition, the impact of disclosure requirements on fact-finding efforts will be very uneven. Since the disclosure has made information on some companies more easily available, there will be more information than before about these companies. But those firms or activities that are not governed by disclosure requirements may now very well receive less fact-finding attention than before, because, first, it is cheaper to concentrate on the prosecution of disclosing firms whose data are available, and, second, the agency's investigatory budget may have been reduced, as explained above. This point is worth emphasizing: with a given agency budget, an increase of control over companies of type A may well reduce the control over other firms, because the relative attractiveness of investigating type B cases is reduced and because more of the agency's budget may be shifted into prosecution rather than investigation.

There are other reasons why disclosures help the enforcement process. First, by stating a disclosure requirement, the government has in effect created a new offense—false disclosure. It may often be easier to prosecute for this offense than for the underlying reason for the false disclosure, such as conspiracies or unfair methods of competition.

---

41. This may also be true for aggregate data. Such information which does not identify individual companies can still give important clues for enforcement purposes. For example, one of the admitted justifications for the FTC's line of business reporting requirements is the desire to find industries with unusually high profit patterns. Even if information about individual companies could not be extracted from aggregate data—which many companies resisting the program dispute—it is still possible that industry-wide high profits would trigger an investigation which will eventually produce such specific information.

Second, if the information is available to the public, law enforcement by private parties through civil suits will be made easier. This, in turn, will reduce the willingness of companies to violate regulatory laws. Being in public view, moreover, may reduce borderline activities that would otherwise be undertaken. Sunshine, it is said, is the best disinfectant. Thirdly, the disclosure of information may lead to a faster realization of an existing problem by the agency, and a faster initiation of action may be the result. It is conceivable that a company will fight back with less tenacity at an early stage of a project, when it has invested only little in a venture. And, where there is less resistance, enforcement may prove cheaper to the agency.

While it is likely that disclosure requirements will aid agency enforcement, it is important to note that there may be benefits for the affected companies as well. Some of the inflexibilities of strict regulations and per se rules can be traced to the severe resource constraints under which agencies operate, and which prevent a closer look at the merits of special cases. Flexibility requires time, and more time may be available if fewer basic fact-finding efforts are necessary. There is also a second way in which an agency's easier access to information may have some benefits for an offending firm. This point relates to the agency's strategy of deterring violations. An agency that can bring only very few cases because of the difficulty in obtaining information is likely to seek a relatively severe penalty to the offender in order to deter others. It relies on the *severity* effect of punishment. An agency that can prosecute relatively many cases, on the other hand, may rely on the higher *probability* of punishment to deter offenders, and in its prosecution can therefore seek less harsh penalties. Thus, an increase in the resources of prosecution may well reduce the average punishment for offenders.

Disclosure requirements will be important for the formulation of regulatory policy. In a hypothetical world of unlimited fact-finding resources, a government agency would have produced all the necessary facts by its own efforts. The impact of disclosure requirements would then not be to produce more information, but rather the same quantity of necessary information at a lower cost. Since ours is not a world of unlimited investigative resources, however, a disclosure requirement will affect the quantity of information available. If we believe that increments in knowledge have a positive impact, we may expect that policymaking will benefit from a larger fact base. There may also be more resources available for policy formulation if an agency has to spend less on fact-finding. In addition, information may be more quickly available as feedback, making corrections in policy possible.

On the other hand, it is possible that the additional information will be used not only for improving existing policies but also to formulate additional ones. If means determine ends and if Parkinson is right, new regulations will be added, presumably up to the point where they are barely supportable by facts. Thus, overall regulation policy may not be more rational than before. "Old" policies could be based on more facts;

"new" policies on the other hand could be based on more "marginal" knowledge; and the overall effect would be uncertain. Some critics of disclosure requirements do not object primarily to the release of information, as such, but rather to what they believe is yet another step on the road to comprehensive economic planning.

THE EFFECTS OF PUBLIC DISCLOSURE OF INFORMATION ON PRIVATE DECISION MAKING

Are Government-Imposed Disclosures of Information Necessary?

Disclosure requirements are government interventions into the exchange of information. The question may be asked why it is necessary to have the government play an active role in this exchange. The fact that information is useful and valuable is not in itself a sufficient justification for governmental action. There are many other useful goods and services whose distribution is governed by market forces rather than by government rules. Why, then, is information treated differently? Advocates of a reduction of the government's role in the economy have argued that there is no need for required disclosure of information. Their basic claim is that if the information is useful to some people, they will pay for it, either outright or indirectly, by choosing the products or shares of a firm that provides them with the desired information. Hence, information will end up in the hands of those who need it, without requiring heavy-handed governmental intervention.

It is interesting to analyze this claim. Our conclusion is that free transactions in information will not occur in many cases without government intervention.

Much of the issue of disclosure can be seen as a problem of property rights. One party holds an asset of value to itself and to some others—information. It is useful to distinguish between types of information. One is *positive* information, whose distribution to the public is of greater value to the firm than the direct and indirect costs of its distribution. There is presumably no role for the government in this area except to assure its integrity. A second class of information may be called *neutral;* its value would be neither diminished nor increased if others shared in it. The third type of information is *exclusive;* its distribution is detrimental to the firm's interest, and its exclusivity is an asset. Information of this latter kind will not be disclosed voluntarily and is the subject of most of the government-mandated disclosure requirements.

To protect against loss of the value of exclusive information, its holder will try to secure exclusivity of control. Several peculiarities of information as property then become apparent. The first is that one may not exclude others from using one's exclusive information in the same way that one can exclude them from using other property. Unlike other forms of property, information is normally not protected by property rights. The knowledge of a firm's investment strategy is not protected in a way that a machine is, although the value of the information may be greater. Another peculiarity of information as quasi-property is that it can be used by others "jointly," that is, without depriving the original holder of its use (although possibly at lower profitability). Thus, the unauthorized use of information by another becomes more difficult to detect and control. Finally, it is a characteristic of information that its exclusivity, once lost, can only rarely be restored.

The consequence of these peculiarities can lead to several strategies of protection. First, the holder will attempt to maintain the exclusivity of information by secrecy, since it has no property rights protection. Because the private maintenance of secrecy is expensive and inefficient, there is some justification in terms of economic efficiency for the government's protection of this secrecy. One kind of such protection is contained in various rights of privacy. The protection does not cover the exclusive information itself, but rather restricts certain methods of obtaining it. It is not prohibited to own information against the will of its original producer, but some methods of acquisition are forbidden. In this sense, we may consider rights of privacy as barriers around otherwise unprotected items of value. An analogy would be a fence around a private forest with wild animals. One may not trespass, but the animals themselves are not protected.

One other strategy is to seek the status of property for information, by patents or copyrights. These rights do not protect against the appropriation of the information as knowledge by others—indeed one of their rationales is to foster its dispersion—but they restrict the *use* of information in a gainful manner against the wishes of its creator.

After this discussion of the nature of information, it is now possible to analyze the claim that it would be disseminated even without a governmental requirement.

An important contribution to property rights analysis is the so-called Coase Theorem.[42] This theorem states that a property right, under certain conditions, will end up with the same party, regardless of its initial assignment. Applied to information, this means that whether A has the right to keep information exclusive or whether B has the right to receive the information (as shareholders may), the outcome (i.e., dissemination or nondissemination) will be the same. Party B will be able to buy the information from A if its gain to him or her is higher than is A's loss from giving it up. And, if B's benefit is smaller than A's loss, the information will stay with A. Whether the property right is initially assigned to B or to A makes no difference to the outcome, since the relative costs and benefits will yield the same final result. Since this will

---

42. R. H. Coase, "The Problem of Social Cost," *Journal of Law and Economics*, vol. 3, Oct. 1960, p. 1.

assure an efficient allocation of the productive resource "information," there is no need for governmental action, since the market will get the information by itself.

The problem with this analysis is that it disregards the peculiarities of information that were mentioned before. Unlike most other types of property that are private in nature, information has some of the characteristics of a "public" good: it can be used by more than one person at the same time, and it may not be possible to exclude third parties. If free riders cannot be excluded from benefiting from the information, no one would ordinarily pay enough for it to make its dissemination or even production worthwhile to the original holder, and no trading in information would occur. This is a relatively simple point. Much less obvious is why it is not practicable, by secrecy and selective selling of the information, to maintain its "private" character and make trading in it possible. If nonexcludability prevents trades, why not pass on the information in a protected way that benefits only the purchaser (i.e., expand the circle of participants in the secret information but keep it secret)? The answer to that objection may be stated in the following principle of gossip:

> Information of value, once released to one person (or very few persons at most) will spread—in the absence of collusion—to all participants.[43]

The principle is readily explained. Suppose the exclusive control of a piece of information yields its holder a special profit *P*; and suppose for the moment that the size of the benefit, if shared by several people, will still remain the same but that it will be divided among all of the holders. For example, the individual share for two owners will be $P/2$, for three owners $P/3$, and so on. These assumptions can be relaxed later. Thus, the individual profit from the information will diminish and approach zero as the number of holders becomes large. Now assume that the original holder A has sold the information to B, and A and B do not coordinate their actions. Both will confront a similar situation with a potential additional buyer C. The sale of the information to C will reduce B's profit share from $P/2$ to $P/3$, a reduction of $P/6$. On the other hand, the benefit share going to C will be $P/3$, so that C may offer B up to that sum for obtaining the information. Since the price $P/3$ that may be obtained by B is larger than his profit reduction $P/6$, it will pay B to sell the information to C. B will receive a private benefit for selling, but he can "socialize" its cost by spreading it to A as well. B will also consider the effects of inaction. Suppose he does not sell the information, but A does. In that case, he receives no benefit at all, but must share the cost of having a new participant to the information. Given a gain for selling and a potential loss for not selling, B will sell. Since A

---

43. This is so if the incremental losses associated with additional participants are constant or diminishing.

has the same incentives, the information price may end up being lower than $P/3$; but whatever it is, it is still a private gain, whereas its cost is spread to the other beneficiary of information.

Once C is also a holder, the same mechanism applies with respect to new potential buyers D, E, etc. The system thus will generate more and more sales, until the number of participants in the previously secret information becomes so large as to make it virtually worthless. That is what is meant by the principle of gossip. It will pay to be the one who passes information on when the cost of doing it is shared by all participants. Mathematically, we have as the individual profit-share $F = P/x$, where x is the number of participants. P/x is the maximum price offered by the xth participant for obtaining the information. The cost to each of the earlier participants of an additional member is the reduction in F due to an increase in x, which is the absolute value of the first derivative $F' = |-P/x^2|$. It can be seen that $P/x > P/x^2$ for all values of $x > 1$. In other words, the benefit that may be obtained by a sale is larger than the share of the cost as soon as the number of participants exceeds $x = 1$, i.e., the original holder.

What is the consequence of this analysis? The original holder of information, when approached by B for the information, will realize that in the absence of effective collusion the cost to him will not be just sharing his profits with one additional partner but quite possibly the entire profit, because the information will spread and eliminate *all* the benefits he had from his exclusive holding. Thus, he will ask for a price of at least P. On the other hand, B will not be foolish to pay that much for information, both because B's profit would be only $P/2$ in the absence of further dissemination and because the information could be easily passed on by A to others, too, reducing B's profits to zero. Hence, there will be no sale of the information.

The principle can easily be generalized further. We have assumed a zero-sum game, i.e., that total benefit P remains the same as the number of participants rises. Suppose, however, that total P diminishes with more participants. This could be described by an exponential formula of the profit share

$$F = \frac{P}{x^{\alpha}}$$

where α is a positive constant $\alpha \geqslant 1$. The previous example is the case where $\alpha = 1$. The rapid reduction in profit share as the number of participants rises is shown in Figure 6-1. The reduction in profit share is the derivative,

$$F'' = \left| -\frac{\alpha P}{x^{\alpha+1}} \right|$$

F' will be larger than F (i.e., it will not pay to sell information to another participant) when $x < \alpha$. And so $x = \alpha$ may be called the

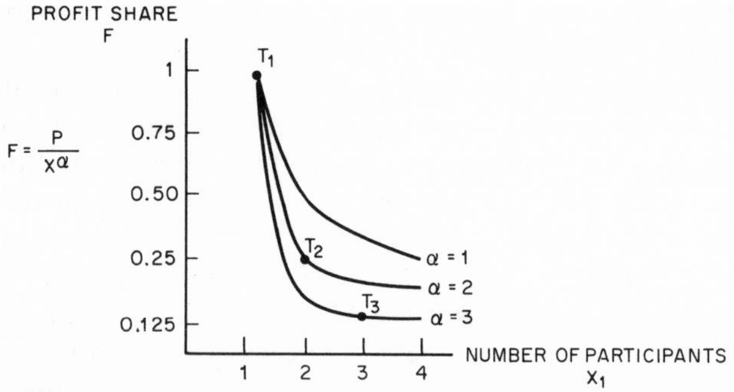

FIGURE 6-1 Profit Share as a Function of Participants in Valuable Information

"gossip tipping point." When x reaches that magnitude, the spreading mechanism described earlier will begin. For values of $x < \alpha$, there will be no trading of information, since the reduction in the individual profit share is larger than the gain to the additional purchaser, and no trade will occur. However, if for some reason the information should be shared, it would not spread as long as the number of participants is less than α. In our graph, the tipping points are labeled T_1, T_2, etc. It may be noted that the number of participants in such a situation will be extremely small. Suppose that $\alpha = 3$, leading to a reduction in the profit share of the original owner of 87.5 percent as he shares the information with only one other person. The maximum number of people who could share that information without the spreading mechanism starting to operate would be only two people. Including a third person would start the dissemination process.

It is also possible to assume that not all participants in the information would lose equally from its dissemination to yet another party, or that they do not have an identical profit-share. Such assumptions only increase the incentives of the low-loss parties to pass the information, and it accelerates the gossip mechanism.

The question may be raised of whether it is not reasonable to expect some potential purchasers of information to be so interested in it that they would buy the information, even if they knew that it would reach others for free. This can only be explained by a market imperfection. Under circumstances of rapid dissemination of information, it will pay to wait to be the free rider. If the spread of information is slow, however, one may not be able or willing to wait; at the same time, the information will ret in its exclusive value longer. Under these circumstances, there may be willing buyers. It is also possible that the value of information is time-dependent, so that it will depreciate over time, even if it remains exclusive. We can define a rate of devaluation δ and a speed of information-spread α, both functions of time t. There is no problem in incorporating these two concepts into the basic analysis.

The gossip tipping point, beyond which no trading will take place, will be reached somewhat later, but still quite rapidly. There may be trading for a short time, but the market will fail very soon.

One form in which the holder of information will try to control its further dissemination is by selling it with the provision that it may not be resold to third parties. To be attractive to a buyer, such a restriction must usually apply to the seller, too. It is possible to conceive such contracts, but more difficult to see how they would be enforced. It would be profitable to break the restriction, risky not to do so when the others might, hard to detect a breach, and difficult to rectify its impact. It would involve a social cost of enforcement that will be high and often ineffective, and it is hard to conceive much support for it. Beyond these more practical objections to the enforcement of such contracts is the problem raised by the *uncertainty* of enforcement. As soon as there is a chance of successful breach of contract, the price demanded for the sale of information will rise and the price offered will fall, resulting again in market failure, unless the uncertainty is quite small.

The result of all this is that one should not expect trading in information to occur (unless the dissemination of information is imperfect). Because of the spreading mechanism, it will normally be impossible to prevent information from achieving a quasi "public good" status. But if this is true, then the argument that the government should leave disclosure to market forces loses considerable force. If there is a built-in market failure in the trading of information, it may be necessary to have a governmental action simply to provide the information that would otherwise not be bought or sold. This argument goes beyond the more traditional defenses of government-mandated disclosures.[44]

The fact that there is no smoothly working market in information does not prove the need for governmental action if a reasonable alternative exists. It is possible, for example, for information not to be bought by its seekers, but to be produced anew.[45] The problem with renewed production—besides the inefficiencies of recreating the same commodity—is that, for the same reason as before, there is no real incentive to invest in the production of information when its worth depends on the

---

44. These typically include an efficiency argument, i.e., that the transaction costs of buying and selling information in a "retail" fashion are far greater than they are for general disclosure. A related argument is that it takes governmental action to ensure the accuracy of the information. While these points have some merit, it is still possible to conceive market arrangements, such as information services, overcoming the efficiency problem, and normal criminal and civil law provisions preventing the sale of false information. Another objection is that the seeker of information may act in an economically inefficient way and may not purchase the "right" information, because the investment in information is a function of the expected payoff to that information; but the expected payoff is itself uncertain. To seek information in the most efficient way, one needs information. See John P. Gould, "Risk, Stochastic Preference, and the Value of Information," *Journal of Economic Theory*, vol. 8, no. 1, May 1974, p. 64.

45. See also Harold Demsetz, "The Private Production of Public Goods," *Journal of Law and Economics*, vol. 13, no. 2, Oct. 1970, p. 293.

actions of other parties, all of whom have an incentive to be the winners rather than the losers from further dissemination. The replication of information makes sense only if there is coordination with the previous holders of the same information about its resale. But if such collusion exists anyway, it is hard to conceive reasons for recreating the information in the first place.

A similar rationale applies to attempts to organize information buyers in such a way that they could either share the price demanded by the original information holder or produce it for all buyers. Theoretically, this may sometimes be possible, but the incentive to be a free rider will be strong, and with free riders, the group effort will be undermined. Many governmental functions exist precisely because of the inability of groups to make the beneficiaries of its services pay.

A third possibility is shareholder and investor action. By preferring disclosing companies to nondisclosing ones, the argument goes, economic pressure is put on management to disclose. There is a good deal of literature on the effects of SEC disclosure requirements on share prices. The issue is worth a special paper, and only a few observations will be made here. First, it is not obvious that potential investors will prefer more information to less, even at no cost to themselves. Those who are risk preferrers may find the riskiness of the gamble reduced, and with it the potential payoff. Secondly, shareholders may not necessarily feel inclined toward subsidizing others' information gathering. Some information, if released, would only reduce the profitability or image of the firm and, hence, the value of their shares. To be sure, they want the company to spread some good news, but why should they be interested in having to pay for the publication of market-depressing bad news? One possible reason could be that they may want to have the information also for themselves. This is true for some information, but it does not follow that they want everyone to share in that information just because they would like to have it. It is a fallacy of composition to believe that everyone is necessarily better off if everyone receives the information he wants. If it will damage the competitive position of the firm or its access to capital markets to have some information disclosed to the world, a shareholder with basic confidence in management may prefer not to receive the information. This attitude must be particularly developed among large shareholders. Because of their greater proximity to the center of the company or their greater attention to its operation, they may have a reasonable half-knowledge of the firm. Outsiders and small shareholders, on the other hand, may have no knowledge at all. In such a situation, it is by no means clear if large shareholders would prefer a general full knowledge to their exclusive half-knowledge. One should note that most of the arguments for stock market disclosure are framed in terms of protecting the "little" investor.

A fourth contention is that consumer demand will force companies to supply relevant product information. This may be possible for certain consumer-type information, but it is important to note that it will not always happen. A firm faced with competitive pressure may respond by providing information as an added service. But, this action is not cost-free. The information, if it is unfavorable to the firm, will reduce its sales. The firm will have to compare losses of disclosing with losses of not disclosing. It is not obvious why such a comparison would always result in disclosure. Where the information is beneficial to the firm, because it is unfavorable to its competitors, it may not be cost-free. First, it must be obtained and disseminated at some cost; secondly, it may invite retaliatory comparisons by competitors; and thirdly, as a result of negative comparisons, there may be a reduced market for all competitors in the field.[46]

Even where the cost of nondisclosure would be higher than that of disclosure, disclosure need not occur. The reason is that the firm may decide that rather than offering information as an extra service to maintain its market share, it will reduce the price of its product. The firm will provide information, or alternatively lower its price, depending on the profit reductions associated with each strategy. These losses will depend on the relative elasticities of demand for the product with respect to price and with respect to information. If the price elasticity is high but the information elasticity is low, there will be no disclosure.

Figure 6-2 may illustrate this point in a simplified form. Note that the example is purely hypothetical. A firm faces two different demand schedules, one when it discloses unfavorable information about its product, and one when it does not disclose and where consumers are aware of the nondisclosure. Both curves are lower in quantity demanded at each given price than the original demand curve that existed when the disclosure issue was not on consumers' minds. At the higher prices, nondisclosure may reduce demand more than disclosure, i.e., the harm of suspicion and the loss of goodwill is greater than the harm of the disclosed negative information itself. This may be explained by the type of people who buy the good at a high price. At a low price, however, consumers react more to the actual disclosure than to the refusal to provide it. At price P_1 the firm will not disclose, because its revenue with nondisclosure P_1Q_1 is larger than that for

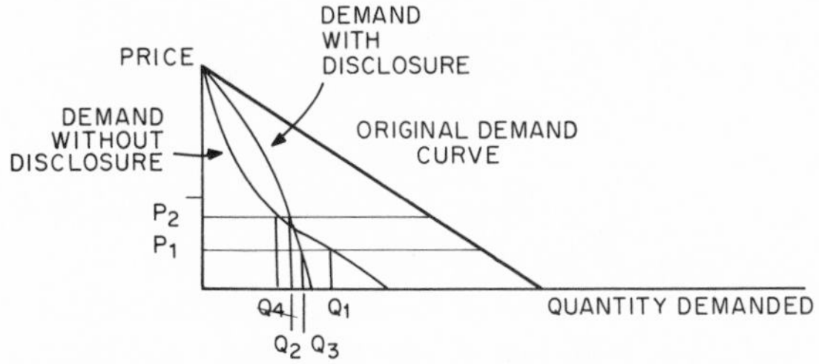

FIGURE 6-2 Demand Curves under Disclosure and Nondisclosure

46. See the paper by Richard A. Posner in Chapter 5.

disclosure, where it is P_1Q_3. At a higher price, P_2, the firm may consider disclosing, because its total revenue P_2Q_2 under disclosure will be larger than the revenue without disclosure P_2Q_4. But, this is not the end of the analysis. Even where the nondisclosure may have a stronger impact than disclosure, such as at P_2, it does not follow necessarily that disclosure will occur. It may be better for the firm to refuse to disclose and, instead, to lower its price to P_1, if the area P_1Q_1, representing total revenue under nondisclosure, is larger than P_2Q_2, under disclosure.

It is, therefore, far from certain how in theory or in practice indirect private actions could take the place of a direct market in information; and the market for information, as we have shown, is subject to market failure. The result is an imperfect or nonexistent market in information. There will be an underutilization of existing information because it will not be bought, and an underproduction because it cannot be sold.

Because of the central role of information in the economic system, such market failure is a particularly serious problem. Microeconomic theory of the economy assumes the availability of information as a condition for economic efficiency. Distortions in the information market mean distortions in the entire economy. If a competitive economy is desired, the supply of the vital input "information" is essential. Where free market cannot accomplish this dissemination, there may be a role for governmental action.

After discussing the reason for a governmental role in the provision of information, we now turn to the effects of such information on resource allocation, market structure, and competition.

The Effects of Public Disclosure on Resource Allocation

An efficient allocation of resources is based on the knowledge of investors and managers about alternative investment possibilities. An increase in information will tend to improve the fact base of allocative decisions. With information available, resources will be withdrawn from low-profit industries and put to more profitable use. One consequence of this shift in resources is that new entrants will increase competition in high-profit industries and reduce prices and profits. At the same time, management of existing firms may be subject to a closer scrutiny by shareholders if its own performance can be compared with that of the rest of the industry. But, it is also possible that the disclosed information will actually reduce the quality of investor decision making. This will happen if the disclosed data do not, in fact, increase knowledge. In the case of SEC disclosure requirements, for example, it has been charged that the stress on investor protection has resulted in very conservative accounting practices that may obscure rather than illuminate a company's true position. This results mainly from the attempt to accomplish two tasks, information and protection, with only one variable. A paternalistic disclosure policy contradicts the primary rationale of disclosure, which is to provide information to the public. Paternalistic disclosure guidelines attempt to limit the distribution of some relevant information because the unsophisticated investor may be misled.

A special aspect of allocation due to disclosure exists in industries and types of transactions whose major product is confidentiality. Swiss banks are one example. The removal of confidentiality protection will make them less attractive for their depositors and, hence, for investors. There may be some perfectly legitimate transactions which, for some reason, require confidentiality. The elimination of such confidentiality then may have two results: some of those transactions will be foregone and less profitable, but nonconfidential alternatives will be chosen instead; or else some other form of confidentiality will be purchased, presumably at a higher cost. Those with an inelastic demand for confidentiality will obtain it in some form. The alternative to confidentiality may then be cash transactions or money under the mattress, hardly indicators of efficient allocation. On the positive side, however, illegitimate deals will become more costly and some may be abandoned.

The Impact of Disclosure on Competition

There are several effects of disclosure on competition. As mentioned before, increased information may lead to better market signals, and new firms will enter high-profit industries, improving competition in the process. On the other hand, the same signals may lead firms to withdraw from an industry or to cancel their planned entry. They will do so if they see that their rivals earn high profits while they cannot. The same information that may lead some firms to withdraw voluntarily may also encourage strong firms to push small or inefficient competitors out of the industry. With knowledge of a competitor's costs and profits, a firm may be encouraged to engage in predatory conduct and drive a competitor out of business. While this action may lead to reduced profits in the short run, it makes sense in the long run if there is enough cost advantage over the victim. A better knowledge of this cost advantage facilitates predation and subsequent concentration in an industry. But the marginal operator may now have a better warning about his rivals' advantages. Such knowledge may result in abandonment, but it may also lead to increased stress on efficiency by the weaker firm.

Besides the impact on market structure, there may be an effect of disclosure on competitive conduct. Does increased information increase or reduce competitive behavior? This is an important question. In a highly concentrated industry, the decisions of each firm will tend to be influenced by its rivals' moves. A policy of collusion would result in maximizing the industry's profits. Since this is not legally possible, the next best alternative is tacit coordination. The problem of such an arrangement is its enforcement. There will always be an incentive for some firm to cheat on the collusive agreement in order to get additional orders, and the arrangement will tend to break down. One important way to reduce such cheating is to make company information available to the partners in collusion. Thus, no sooner had price fixing and market divisions been held illegal by the courts than trade associations came to life whose main purpose was to distribute information on sales and cost. Many, but not all, of these "open price associations" were eventually curbed by court decisions. It would be ironic if the government itself would provide firms with information it had prevented them earlier from exchanging privately. One cannot ignore this problem; on the other hand, it exists only for some kinds of information and for some methods of its dissemination. Frequent and up-to-date reports will facilitate collusion, as will disclosures that identify buyers or sellers in individual transactions. Disclosure requirements and publication policies can be tailored in such a way as to reduce this problem.

Knowledge of rivals' cost may have an anticompetitive impact. Cost figures can provide information for tacit collusion if there is a general understanding on markups. On the other hand, cost figures may also undermine a price-fixing agreement. The realization by A that a fixed price is more advantageous to his partner, B, whose costs in that range of production are lower, will encourage A to depart from the fixed price. He may want to produce, for example, at a quantity where his profitability is higher. It is, of course, still possible to collude, but when the number of variables to consider increases, it may turn out to be more difficult to maintain a collusive agreement.

Facilitating retaliation seems to be a frequent danger of a disclosure program. Interdependent firms will keep one another in check if they know more about one another's actions, and disclosure helps them to know. It is, of course, probable that their knowledge of one another is already large. But there will still be incremental information that disclosure makes available. In consequence, for oligopolistic industries disclosure rules should be designed to, at best, facilitate the formulation of long-range planning by firms and avoid being a tool for their day-to-day operations.

Disclosure also affects the cost of production. Since information is a costly input, its free supply by the government will reduce the costs of production for a company. More information will also tend to reduce managerial miscalculations and will thus reduce costs further. These benefits to producers and consumers can be large. For example, the social benefits of an agricultural data collection system were found to exceed $600 for each dollar of government expenditure.[47] Of course, farmers have few managerial secrets to protect, and so they do not give up much by disclosure. It may be different with other firms, where disclosure will reduce the value of their exclusive information and

---

47. Yujiro Hayami and Willis Peterson, "Social Returns to Public Information Service, Statistical Reporting of U.S. Farm Commodities," *American Economic Review*, vol. 62, no. 1, March 1972, pp. 119–131.

where the administrative cost of complying with the requirements is high. This loss explains the resistance by many companies against disclosure. However, the benefits should not be forgotten. The same companies will also receive information of value, the importance of which is admitted by their own resistance to disclose it. With disclosure, companies have a better knowledge of their competitors, suppliers, customers, new processes, etc. Will they be better off? This question is hard to answer. Some will be winners, some losers. Within an industry, the entire transfer of information value may be zero where one company's loss of information value is another firm's gain. But, since the information is also available to the public and to regulatory agencies, it may have a somewhat negative impact for most firms.

The Impact of Disclosure on the Production of Information and Innovation

Because of the inadequate functioning of markets in information, there will be an underutilization of existing information in the absence of disclosure. There may also be an impact of disclosure on the production of *new* information. One effect may be a reduction in the effort to create valuable information. Investment in R&D, for example, may decline if its results must be shared with the public and with competitors. There is no reason to assume that disclosure will reduce the creation of information whose usefulness to the creator is independent of others' use of it. On the other hand, there will be information whose value depends on its exclusivity. The returns on investment in such information will become smaller if others can share in its benefits. Will that reduce its production? For some types of exclusive information, disclosure should make no difference, for example, if the information is an indispensable element or a by-product of operations (e.g., cost figures for raw materials, inventory figures), or if the profitability of the information is high for some time until others can make use of it. In each case, the producers of the information would prefer to keep it from their competitors, but if that proves impossible, they should still produce it in the same quantity. There are, however, types of information whose production will be reduced if others can share in the benefits.

The problem of production and distribution of information is interdependent. It would be most efficient, in economic terms, to distribute information for free or at dissemination cost. But then less of it would be produced. Kenneth Arrow contends:

> Any information obtained . . . should, from the welfare point of view, be available free of charge (apart from the cost of transmitting information). This insures optimal utilization of the information but of course provides no incentive for investment in research. In an ideal socialist economy, the reward for invention would be completely separated from any charge to the users of information. In a free enterprise economy, inventive activity is

supported by using the invention to create property rights; precisely to the extent that it is successful, there is an underutilization of the information.[48]

Harold Demsetz, on the other hand, points to the problem that one cannot separate the act of producing new information from the act of disseminating existing information:

> It is hardly useful to say that there is "underutilization" of information if the method recommended to avoid "underutilization" discourages the research required to produce the information. These two activities simply cannot be judged independently. . . . If somehow, we knew how much and what types of information it would be desirable to produce, then we could administer production independently of the distribution of any stock of information. But we do not know these things.[49]

One imperfect incentive for the creation of innovative information is the granting of patents or copyrights. This method could theoretically be extended. Disclosure makes other valuable information more easily accessible to competitors. If a significant social importance is attached to ensuring the incentives for its undiminished creation, one may consider some limited patent-type protection for some other information for which the enforcement of such protection is practicable.

Alternatively, one may do nothing and accept some reduced production of information. How large its effect will be is hard to say. It should be noted that even the need for patents is disputed. For example, the natural advantage of being the first to introduce an innovative process will usually last for several years, even in the absence of patents. It will take some time until competitors receive and digest the new information, and even more until they can act upon it. Thus, the new information may well have enough time of exclusivity to make its production worthwhile. For some types of information, one could institute as an added protection a time-delayed disclosure. The government agency would receive information from the disclosing firm and would release it only after a few months or years. Such delayed publication of data by the government seems to be the normal procedure anyway, evoking the description of the Middle Ages as a system whose rigid policies were softened by the inability to carry them out.

Oligopolistic markets present special problems. Where each competitor watches closely the others' behavior, dissemination of data will have a special impact. For the case of R&D, it has been found that

---

48. K. J. Arrow, "Economic Welfare and the Allocation for Invention," in Universities—National Bureau Commission for Economic Research, *The Rate and Direction of Inventive Activity: Economic and Social Factors,* Princeton University Press, Princeton, N.J., 1962, p. 615.

49. Harold Demsetz, "Information and Efficiency: Another Viewpoint," *Journal of Law and Economics,* vol. 22, no. 1, April 1969, p. 11.

companies' efforts are related to their rivals' expenditures in the area.[50] Hence, the publication of R&D data will lead to a more rapid matching by competitors. Whether this will increase or diminish R&D depends, then, on the trend, which will probably show a cyclical pattern. It is possible, however, that a company embarking on an innovation will not be matched by innovation, but by some other form of retaliation that will reduce the profitability of the innovation and, hence, its production.

It is important to put this reduction of new information in its proper perspective. Most information must be produced in any case, because a company's operations require it. (Some, of course, may not be available in the *form* the government asks for it, but that is a different question.) And, there is no reason to believe that detailed "innovative" information would be a high priority of disclosure requirements, nor that its eventual disclosure would have major effects. In the cases where it might, it is not difficult to conceive of methods that will reduce the harm, at least partly. Thus, in most circumstances, the price in reduced innovation that one has to pay for increased disclosure does not seem to be intolerable.

A related question is the impact of required disclosure on the quality of information. It is alleged that a company fearing prosecution or a leak will make its data as meaningless as legally possible. This argument is used in support of voluntary disclosures, or disclosures to "neutral" agencies, such as the Bureau of the Census. A voluntary request for information sometimes elicits cooperative behavior, but that does not negate the need for mandatory disclosure. It is highly questionable whether a confidential voluntary disclosure program would work. There is no particular incentive for firms to participate, and there is presumably no legal compulsion for high standards of accuracy. The main benefit for a firm would be to have a more favorable regulatory policy if the agency knows better what is going on. In such an arrangement, the incentives to be a free rider rather than to pay in kind by providing information can become too strong for the voluntary reporting system to survive.

CONCLUSION

Our conclusions are that claims of confidentiality for business information occupy a different place on the scale of values in this society from claims of individual privacy. Legal restraints on the government acquisition of such information are very circumscribed; forced disclosure to

---

50. Henry G. Grabowski and Nevins D. Baxter, "Rivalry in Industrial Research and Development: An Empirical Study," *Journal of Industrial Economics,* vol. 21, no. 3, July 1973, pp. 209–235.

the public is subject to somewhat greater limits, but government agencies retain considerable discretion in this area as well.

There are sound economic reasons for the government to acquire information for itself. The formulation and enforcement of regulatory policy will tend to be improved, although the effectiveness of regulating nondisclosing companies may be reduced. There is a strong reason for a governmental role in ensuring the flow of information to the public, since, as we find, the exchange of many kinds of information is subject to market failure. The economic effects of public disclosure will depend on particular circumstances. Resource allocation and managerial efficiency will tend to improve and the costs of production to decrease. Competition will, in many cases, be invigorated, but the chances for predatory, collusive, or retaliatory actions in oligopolistic industries will increase. While there will be an improved utilization of existing information, the production of new information may decrease.

DIALOGUE

DAVID SIVE: Should we draw a distinction between disclosure in litigation and other types of informational demands?

GELLHORN: That is a worthwhile comment. I have noticed increasingly that courts do differentiate, though I could not quantify the differentiation. Courts distinguish between litigation, where the object is to discover all the facts necessary to do justice, whether or not it involves invasion of an area that someone would like to protect, and the mere gathering of information, which may or may not be utilized in some fashion for governmental purposes.

RUSSELL B. STEVENSON: Kent Greenawalt asked whether there is a value in preserving independent centers of power in corporations. It seems to me there is an alternative hypothesis—that is, that private corporations often have more power than we would like them to have in the economic, political, and social fields. And there are some of us here, I believe, who feel that more access to corporation information, whether it is by mandated disclosure or access through a cor-

This session was chaired by Walter Gellhorn, Professor of Law, Columbia University School of Law. For further biographical information, see Appendix 1.

porate Freedom of Information Act, would make that power more accountable.

Disclosure of corporate information affords an opportunity to put political pressure on corporations. The interesting question that raises in my mind is whether this departure from market regulation of corporate behavior, and greater emphasis on political regulation of corporate behavior, is desirable in light of the benefits that it might achieve.

GREENAWALT: I guess the question really comes down—I mean, putting it generally—to whether you are more worried about the government's dominating all private centers of power or whether you are more worried about big private centers of power suppressing or dominating small private centers of power. For any particular kind of information you may be seeking, you must look at the relationship among individuals, businesses, and government.

RICHARD A. POSNER: This notion of privacy is sort of a pretentious word for secrecy, and there are a lot of things people want to keep secret, either from the whole world or from people outside their immediate circle. It seems to me it is equally true of organizations. And I do not see a fundamental difference—maybe you do—between tape recording my dinner conversations and having them publicly disseminated, and tape recording meetings between corporate officials.

GREENAWALT: I was trying to suggest there is a distinction in terms of what the underlying values are that are arguably served by protecting privacy or secrecy. I do not know what you discuss at dinner, but we can think of more private situations than most people's dinner conversations. If such conversations were freely disclosed to the government, you would be striking at the heart of our notion of what it means to be an individual in a democratic society. Now, I do think the same thing is true to some extent, insofar as in any business there are friendships that go on and personal information is disclosed during business conversations.

But, if we think of things that are just business information, not including personal information that is disclosed, then it seems to me you have to make a kind of utilitarian argument that the business will function less effectively if this kind of information is disclosed. There are justifications for protecting individual privacy in the dinner table context that are really not applicable to the business setting.

POSNER: Suppose at dinner I say that my colleague X is really a jerk. Of course, I would never say that to him and to a lot of other people who might repeat it to him. Suppose that at a meeting of the board, the president says: "The labor representative of our workers is really a jerk." Now, in both cases, I think there is a strong interest in maintaining the secrecy of the conversation in order to permit people to speak freely.

GELLHORN: You do not disagree with that.

GREENAWALT: I do not disagree. That is not the kind of business information that we are talking about.

POSNER: Let's turn it around. The government requires me to provide intimate financial information which is, of course, necessary to collect taxes. Now, I do not see any serious objection to that. We could not have an income tax system without disclosure.

GREENAWALT: Wait a minute. First of all, when you say you have no serious objection, you are really saying that *on balance* it is desirable. I do think it is an impingement on people's privacy, at least to some degree, for government to get the information; and it would be a much greater impingement, and really quite frightening, if not only the Internal Revenue Service but a lot of other people could get that information.

So while I think on balance it is desirable that a lot of information is obtained in tax returns, some of the information that is submitted for tax returns may involve aspects of private life that people feel pretty strongly about, for example, medical matters.

JOSEPH SWIDLER: I might mention one category or one purpose for obtaining information that is not included in the eight that are listed in the paper; it applies particularly to regulated industries. That is to enable regulated companies to measure themselves against one another, and therefore the information serves in itself as a regulatory tool.

The filings with the Federal Power Commission, for example, are used by the utilities to line themselves up against other companies operating under similar circumstances so that they can see where their performance may be better or worse than that of other companies. The information serves as a substitute for competition.

VICTOR H. KRAMER: Have either of the two principal researchers done any comparative research on how other industrial countries handle the problems that they discussed in the paper?

NOAM: I have not.

GREENAWALT: No.

GEORGE J. BENSTON: I just completed a book comparing required financial disclosure in the United Kingdom and the United States. Britain's securities act requirements are much less extensive than ours, and by every measure that is available, its securities market works as well as ours does.

FREDERIC M. SCHERER: I might add a little bit of other information along the census of manufacturing lines. I have studied several European countries. In Sweden, the census makes available data on individual companies. As Professor Leontief pointed out earlier, the French statistical agency is rather inefficient, and although they have secrecy rules, they do not abide by them; so you can get data on individual companies.

On the other hand, the Germans and the British are quite strict. The British tend to be somewhat more strict in terms of disclosure than the United States, and the Germans perhaps even tougher, although it is difficult precisely to ascertain their policies.

IRA M. MILLSTEIN: I think to rely exclusively on decided cases is to ignore where most of the action takes place. Disclosure cases almost always get settled by the court mediating the dispute. Normally the court asks, "What do you need it for, and can you cut it down; can we compromise?" I find more and more that courts are questioning the degree and scope of what government agencies are asking for.

GELLHORN: I am glad to hear that comment; it confirms my own belief. Also, I stress the often considerable time gaps between the agency's expressed desire to have the information and the ultimate handing over of documents through mediation efforts of a court.

MILLSTEIN: I believe government would make more progress in getting information if it asked for just a little less. My experience is that the government lawyers, or whoever wants the information, will ask for the kitchen sink and fight for it vigorously. They might have gotten more if they had focused on what they really wanted.

Also, I have found that where the government comes in and says, "If you have pieces of paper which say the following, produce them," that is very hard to resist. But if the government comes in and says, "I don't care if you do not have the information; if you don't, generate it," it is much easier to resist. Professor Greenawalt, do you draw a distinction between these two types of requests? Should there be different standards?

GREENAWALT: I think your first comment is well taken. This is a new area to me, and I did limit myself to decided cases. I hope you will tell me more about what is happening in cases that are not reflected in reported decisions.

Obviously, it is more reasonable to ask for something that is not going to cost very much to produce than it is to ask for something that will cost a lot. You can make a better argument about undue burden if you have to produce the information. It seems to me the suggestions in decided cases are that if what the government is doing is basically reasonable, it is not going to be an undue burden. You are certainly right that there must be a lot of trimming that is not reflected in the decided cases and some that is even reflected in them. Now, when you ask what different standards should apply, I am a little unclear. Do you mean some different formulation?

MILLSTEIN: No. What I meant to suggest is that when you are asked to generate information, the ability to prove unreasonableness or burden goes up somewhat.

GREENAWALT: I think that may well be right.

PHILIP LOOMIS: Government requests for information have certainly been unduly broad on occasion, but part of the problem is that the government agency does not know exactly what information a private corporation has in its files. And so the agency initially makes its request broad enough so that nothing that it wants will be left out. Then a process of negotiation usually occurs. The company says, "Well, we don't have that," and the reply is, "Well, if you don't have it, you don't have to produce it." The request gets narrowed down in practice. So, what looks like an unduly broad request for information is in practice negotiated down.

Appendixes

APPENDIX 1—BIOGRAPHICAL INFORMATION ON CONFERENCE SPEAKERS AND CHAIRMEN

Angermueller, Hans H., *Senior Vice President and General Counsel, Citicorp and Citibank, N.A.*

LL.B., 1950; M.S., School of Engineering, 1947, B.A., 1946, Harvard

Partner, Shearman & Sterling (until 1970), specializing in international and domestic corporate finance. Chairman, Munich-American Reinsurance Corporation and Munich Management Corporation.

Benston, George J., *Professor of Finance and Accounting, Graduate School of Management, University of Rochester*

Ph.D., 1963, University of Chicago Graduate School of Business; M.B.A., 1953, New York University; B.A., 1952, Queens College; C.P.A., 1955, North Carolina

Director, Center for Study of Financial Institutions and Securities Markets, University of Rochester; currently consultant to the Federal Reserve Board; consultant to the General Accounting Office on its review of the FTC's line of business (LB) program (1975) and expert witness for several corporations in a lawsuit against the FTC's LB program. Recent publications include *Corporate Financial Disclosure in the U.K. and the U.S.A.* (1976).

Bock, Betty, *Director, Antitrust Research, The Conference Board*

Ph.D., 1942; M.A., 1937, B.A., 1936, Bryn Mawr

Adjunct Professor of Law, New York University Law School. Formerly Senior Economist, Federal Trade Commission; Economist, United States Department of Commerce. Retained occasionally as consultant to government agencies and to law firms on economic evidence in specific case settings (including one opposing the FTC's line of business program). Member Advisory Board, *Antitrust Bulletin*. Author of many monographs and articles.

Cary, William L., *Dwight Professor of Law, Columbia University School of Law*

LL.D., 1965, Amherst; M.B.A., 1938, Harvard; LL.B., 1934, B.A., 1931, Yale

After eight years at Northwestern University Law School, joined the Columbia Law Faculty in 1955. Formerly served as chairman of the Securities and Exchange Commission (1961–1964). Areas of special interest are corporations, corporate finance, business planning, the public corporation, and securities regulation. Recent publications include *Cases and Materials on Corporations* (1970), *Politics and the Regulatory Agencies* (1967).

Gellhorn, Walter, *University Professor Emeritus, Columbia University*

LL.B., 1931, Columbia; A.B., 1927, Amherst (and many honorary degrees)

Member of the Faculty of Law at Columbia (1933–1973); University Professor (1973–1974); University Professor Emeritus at Columbia since 1974. Recent publications include *When Americans Complain* (1966), *Ombudsmen and Others* (1966).

Goldschmid, Harvey J., *Professor of Law, Columbia University School of Law*

J.D., 1965, B.A., 1962, Columbia

Consultant to government agencies, "corporate responsibility" groups, and private firms; Chairman of the Section on Antitrust and Economic Regulation of the American Association of Law Schools; former chairman of the Committee on Trade Regulation of the Association of the Bar of the City of New York. Recent publications include *Cases and Materials on Trade Regulation* (with Handler, Blake, and Pitofsky, 1975), *Industrial Concentration: The New Learning* (with Mann and Weston, 1974).

Greenawalt, R. Kent, *Professor of Law, Columbia University School of Law*

LL.B., 1963, Columbia; B.Phil., 1960, Oxford; A.B., 1958, Swarthmore

Deputy Solicitor General, Department of Justice (1971–1972); Fellow, American Council of Learned Societies (to do research on law and privacy) (1972–1973); consultant, Office of Telecommunications Policy (1974–1975). Recent publications include *Legal Protections of Privacy* (1976), "Discretion and Judicial Decision: The Elusive Quest for the Fetters That Bind Judges," *Columbia Law Review* (1975).

Jones, William K., *Milton Handler Professor of Trade Regulation, Columbia University School of Law*

LL.B., 1954, B.A., 1952, Columbia

Consultant, President's Task Force on Telecommunications Policy (1968), Federal Communications Commission (1968), Ford Foundation (1967–1968); member, President's Task Force on Antitrust Policy (1967–1968), Public Service Commission of the State of New York (1970–1974). Recent publications include *Cases and Materials on Regulated Industries* (2d ed., 1976).

Kirkpatrick, Miles W., *Partner, Morgan, Lewis & Bockius*

LL.B., 1943, University of Pennsylvania; A.B., 1940, Princeton

Chairman, Federal Trade Commission (1970–1973); ABA Section for Antitrust Law (1968–1969); ABA Commission to Study the Federal Trade Commission (1969); chairman, President's Commission on White House Fellowships (since 1975).

Leontief, Wassily, *Professor of Economics, New York University*

Ph.D., 1928, University of Berlin; M.A., 1925, University of Leningrad (and many honorary degrees)

Henry Lee Professor of Political Economy, Harvard University (1953–1975). Recipient, Nobel Prize in Economics (1973); French Legion d'Honneur (1968). Has served as consultant to numerous government agencies. Recent publications include *The Future of the World Economy* (1977), *Essays in Economics* (1966), *Input-Output Economics* (1966).

Murphy, Arthur W., *Professor of Law, Columbia University School of Law*

LL.B., 1948, Columbia; A.B., 1943, Harvard

Member, Atomic Safety and Licensing Board, U.S. Atomic Energy Commission (since 1963); N.Y. State Atomic and Space Development Authority (since 1965). Trial Attorney, U.S. Department of Justice (1950–1952); private practice, New York (1953–1963). Recent publications include "Liability for Atomic Accidents and Insurance" and "Third Party Liability of Suppliers in International Nuclear Transactions" (both in *Progress in Nuclear Energy, Law and Administration*).

Noam, Eli, *Assistant Professor of Business and Lecturer in Law, Columbia University*

J.D., 1975, Ph.D., 1975, A.B., 1970, Harvard

Visiting Assistant Professor in Economics and Public Affairs, Princeton (1975–1976); consultant, Rand Corporation, FTC, and Vera Institute of Justice. Research and publications use economic analysis to investigate the legal system, particularly criminal justice, regulation, and public finance.

Pitofsky, Robert, *Commissioner, Federal Trade Commission (July 1978–), Professor of Law, Georgetown University Law Center*

LL.B., 1954, Columbia; B.A., 1951, New York University

Director, Bureau of Consumer Protection, FTC (1970–1973). Prior to July 1978: "of Counsel" to the law firm of Arnold & Porter; Chairman of Board of Directors, Institute for Public Interest Representation (since 1973); member, Senate Inter-Governmental Commission Task Force on Regulatory Reform (since 1975). Recent publications include *Cases and Materials on Trade Regulation* (with Handler, Blake, and Goldschmid, 1975).

Posner, Richard A., *Professor of Law, University of Chicago Law School*

LL.B., 1962, Harvard; A.B., 1959, Yale

Was law clerk to Justice Brennan, United States Supreme Court, and served at the FTC, as an Assistant to the Solicitor General, and as General Counsel to the President's Task Force on Communications Policy before commencing his career as a professor of law. Now editor, *The Journal of Legal Studies;* member, Senior Research Staff, National Bureau of Economic Research; consultant to government agencies and private companies. Recent publications include *Antitrust Law: An Economic Perspective* (1976), *Economic Analysis of Law* (2d ed., 1977).

Reinemer, Vic, *Staff Director, Subcommittee on Reports, Accounting and Management, Senate Government Operations Committee*

1965, George Washington University; 1949, Sorbonne; B.A., 1948, University of Montana

Mr. Reinemer had a career first as a journalist, and then as executive secretary to Senators Murray and Metcalf of Montana before joining the Subcommittee on Reports, Accounting, and Management in 1972. He is the author of numerous magazine articles. Recent publications include *Overcharge* (with Metcalf, 1967).

Scherer, Frederic M., *Professor of Economics, Northwestern University*

Ph.D., 1963, M.B.A., 1958, Harvard; A.B., 1954, Michigan

Director, Bureau of Economics, FTC (1974–1976); Senior Research Fellow, International Institute of Management (1972–1974); taught economics at Princeton and Michigan (1963–1972). While serving as Director of Bureau of Economics, "spent the better part of two years attempting to make segmental financial reporting a reality at the FTC." Has been a consultant on defense, arms control, patent policy, and antitrust matters. Recent publications include *The Economics of Multi-Plant Operation: An International Comparisons Study* (with others, 1975), *Industrial Market Structure and Economic Performance* (1970).

Scott, Bruce R., *Professor, Harvard Graduate School of Business Administration*

D.B.A., M.B.A., Harvard; B.A., Swarthmore

Consultant to European companies, French government agencies, and the Iran Center for Management Studies in Tehran. Recent publications include "The Industrial State: Old Myths and New Realities," *Harvard Business Review* (1973), *Industrial Planning in France* (1969).

Sovern, Michael I., *Dean and Professor of Law, Columbia University School of Law*

LL.B., 1955, B.A., 1953, Columbia

Permanent arbitrator for disputes between the New York City Board of Education and the United Federation of Teachers. Mediator, New York transit strike negotiations (1971); author-moderator, WNBC-TV series "Due Process for the Accused"; consultant on law to *Time* magazine. Recent publications include *Legal Restraints on Racial Discrimination in Employment* (1966), *Cases and Materials on Law and Poverty* (1969, 2d ed. 1973).

Weiss, Leonard W., *Chief Economist, Senate Government Operations Committee, Professor of Economics, University of Wisconsin*

Ph.D., 1954, Columbia; B.S., 1945, Northwestern

Professor of Economics, Wisconsin, since 1962 (on leave 1976–1977). Consultant to the Department of Justice (at present for the IBM monopolization case) and other government agencies. Recent publications include articles, monographs, and *Regulation: A Case Approach* (with Strickland, 1975).

APPENDIX 2—CONFERENCE PARTICIPANTS*

Anderson, William
Professor of Law
University of Washington

Ashley, George E.
Vice President and General Counsel
New York Telephone Company

Auerbach, Carl A.
Dean
University of Minnesota Law School

Banks, Robert S.
Vice President and General Counsel
Xerox Corporation

Biles, Elmer
Special Assistant to Associate Director
Bureau of the Census

Blake, Harlan
Professor of Law
Columbia University

Bloch, Peter B.
Executive Director
ABA Commission on Law and the Economy

Borowski, Irwin
Associate Director
Division of Enforcement
Securities and Exchange Commission

Botein, Michael H.
Professor of Law
Rutgers University

Brodley, Joseph F.
Professor of Law
Indiana University

Buhler, Warren B.
Director
Commission on Federal Paperwork

Butzner, John D., Jr.
Circuit Judge
United States Court of Appeals
Richmond, Va.

Collier, Calvin J.
Chairman
Federal Trade Commission

Costigan, John M.
Law Department
Kraftco Corporation

Dewey, Donald J.
Professor of Economics
Columbia University

Edwards, Franklin R.
Professor of Business
Columbia University

Engman, Lewis
Warner, Norcross & Judd
Washington, D.C.

* Affiliations as of the date of the Conference, November 5–6, 1976.

Feinberg, Wilfred
Circuit Judge
United States Court of Appeals
New York, N.Y.

Fox, Byron
Wiker, Gottlieb, Taylor & Howard
New York, N.Y.

Fox, Eleanor
Professor of Law
New York University

Gellhorn, Ernest
Dean
Arizona State University

Gill, David G.
Counsel
Exxon Corporation

Grad, Frank P.
Professor of Law
Columbia University

Green, Mark
Congress Watch
Washington, D.C.

Hamilton, Robert W.
Professor of Law
University of Texas

Hart, Albert G.
Professor of Economics
Columbia University

Hellawell, Robert
Professor of Law
Columbia University

Hills, Roderick
Chairman
Securities and Exchange Commission

Hulett, David T.
Chief
Economic Statistics Branch
Office of Managemenι and Budget

Klein, Gary
Office of Senator Jacob K. Javits
New York

Klitzman, Steve
Administrative Conference of the United States

Kramer, Victor H.
Professor of Law
Georgetown University

Kripke, Homer
Professor of Law
New York University

Leventhal, Harold B.
Circuit Judge
United States Court of Appeals
Washington, D.C.

Lewis, Robert J.
General Counsel
Federal Trade Commission

Liebeler, Wesley J.
Professor of Law
UCLA

Loomis, Philip
Commissioner
Securities and Exchange Commission

Lovett, William A.
Professor of Law
Tulane University

Marlin, Alice Tepper
Executive Director
Council on Economic Priorities

Marlin, John Tepper
Executive Director
Council on Municipal Performance

Marsh, David M.
Executive Director
Business Advisory Council on Federal Reports

Martin, David B. H.
Research Director
Administrative Conference of the United States

Meeks, James E.
Professor of Law
University of Virginia

Millstein, Ira M.
Weil, Gotshal & Manges
New York, N.Y.

Perkins, Roswell B.
Debevoise, Plimpton, Lyons & Gates
New York, N.Y.

Pickett, Winston H.
Counsel
General Electric Company

Pogue, Richard
Jones, Day, Reavis & Pogue
Cleveland, Ohio

Rigney, Daniel
Division of Social Sciences
Texas

Rowe, Frederick
Kirkland, Ellis & Rowe
Washington, D.C.

Scalia, Antonin
Office of Legal Counsel
Department of Justice

Schuck, Peter
Consumers Union

Schwartz, Donald
Professor of Law
Georgetown University

Schwartz, Louis B.
Professor of Law
University of Pennsylvania

Schwartz, Warren F.
Professor of Law
University of Virginia

Shapiro, Charles
Manager of Legal Information Systems and Services
McGraw-Hill Book Company

Siers, Howard
Assistant Comptroller
E. I. Dupont de Nemours & Co.

Sive, David
Winer, Neuberger & Sive
New York, N.Y.

Smith, Margery
Executive Director
Federal Trade Commission

Stevenson, Russell B.
Professor of Law
George Washington University

Strauss, Peter
Professor of Law
Columbia University

Swidler, Joseph
Leva, Hawes, Symington, Martin & Oppenheimer
Washington, D.C.

Turner, Donald
Professor of Law
Harvard University

Vargus, Phil
Director, Confidentiality-Privacy Study
Commission on Federal Paperwork

Weiss, Elliott
The Conservation Foundation
Washington, D.C.

Weston, Glen E.
Professor of Law
George Washington University

White, Lee
White, Fine & Verville
Washington, D.C.

Wyzanski, Charles E., Jr.
United States District Court
Boston, Mass.

Index